Start Here!™

Learn Microsoft®
Visual C#® 2010

John Paul Mueller

Published with the authorization of Microsoft Corporation by:
O'Reilly Media, Inc.
1005 Gravenstein Highway North
Sebastopol, California 95472

ISBN: 978-0-7356-5772-4

1 2 3 4 5 6 7 8 9 LSI 6 5 4 3 2 1

Printed and bound in the United States of America.

Microsoft Press books are available through booksellers and distributors worldwide. If you need support related to this book, email Microsoft Press Book Support at *mspinput@microsoft.com*. Please tell us what you think of this book at *http://www.microsoft.com/learning/booksurvey*.

Microsoft and the trademarks listed at *http://www.microsoft.com/about/legal/en/us/IntellectualProperty/ Trademarks/EN-US.aspx* are trademarks of the Microsoft group of companies. All other marks are property of their respective owners.

The example companies, organizations, products, domain names, email addresses, logos, people, places, and events depicted herein are fictitious. No association with any real company, organization, product, domain name, email address, logo, person, place, or event is intended or should be inferred.

This book expresses the author's views and opinions. The information contained in this book is provided without any express, statutory, or implied warranties. Neither the authors, O'Reilly Media, Inc., Microsoft Corporation, nor its resellers, or distributors will be held liable for any damages caused or alleged to be caused either directly or indirectly by this book.

Acquisitions and Developmental Editor: Russell Jones

Production Editor: Teresa Elsey

Editorial Production: S4Carlisle Publishing Services

Technical Reviewer: Russ Mullen

Indexer: WordCo Indexing Services, Inc.

Cover Design: Jake Rae

Cover Composition: Karen Montgomery

This book is dedicated to our beagle, Reese—the peanut butter dog. She's the guardian of the orchard, checker of the fire, and warmer of the lap. Her incredibly soft fur amazes and soothes at the same time.

Contents at a Glance

Contents

What do you think of this book? We want to hear from you!

Microsoft is interested in hearing your feedback so we can continually improve our
books and learning resources for you. To participate in a brief online survey, please visit:

microsoft.com/learning/booksurvey

Chapter 2   Developing a Web Project   27

Chapter 3   Basic Data Manipulation Techniques   57

Chapter 8   Working with Libraries   209

Chapter 9   Creating Utility Applications   241

What do you think of this book? We want to hear from you!

Microsoft is interested in hearing your feedback so we can continually improve our
books and learning resources for you. To participate in a brief online survey, please visit:

microsoft.com/learning/booksurvey

Introduction

C# IS AN AMAZING C-LIKE language that has almost all of the flexibility of C and C++, without any of the arcane programming rules. You can create applications quickly and easily using C#. The mixture of the Visual Studio Integrated Development Environment (IDE) aids and the natural flow of the language itself makes working with C# possible for even the complete novice. As your skills grow, you'll find that C# grows with you and makes nearly any kind of application possible, even applications that you normally don't associate with higher level languages.

Start Here! Learn Microsoft Visual C# 2010 is your doorway to discovering the joys of programming in C# without the usual exercises and rote learning environment of a college course. Instead of boring regimen, you begin programming immediately in Chapter 1, "Getting to Know C#." In fact, you'll create three completely different applications in Chapter 1 alone, which makes this book different from other novice-level books on the market. Yes, the examples are decidedly simple to begin with, but it won't take you long to begin interacting with web services, creating Silverlight applications, and working at the command line.

What's truly amazing about this book is that every tool it uses is free. You'll discover an amazing array of C# application types and it won't cost you a penny to uncover them. These aren't old school techniques either—you'll use the newest methods of creating applications such as working with Language INtegrated Query (LINQ) to ask the application to supply data to you. Of course, the techniques you learn will transfer easily to the paid versions of Microsoft's products that include a great deal more capability and provide better flexibility.

Who Should Read This Book

The focus of this book is to learn by doing. If you're a hands-on sort of a person and find other texts boring and difficult, this is the book for you. Every example is completely explained and you'll use a special tracing method to discover the inner secrets of each programming technique. You'll at least encounter most basic application types by the time you've completed this book.

Assumptions

This book was conceived and created for the complete novice—someone who has no programming experience at all. It is also appropriate for someone has been exposed to another language, but lacks significant experience in that language. This book uses a hands-on training approach, so you're not going to be doing a lot of reading—you'll be trying everything out as part of the learning process. Therefore, you need to have a system that's capable of running the tools and a desire to use that system during your learning process.

You should be able to work with Windows as an operating system. The book assumes that you know how to work with a mouse and that you've worked with other applications that have basic features such as a File menu. Even though this book is for the complete novice from an application development perspective, it doesn't do a lot of hand-holding when it comes to working with basic Windows functionality.

Who Should Not Read This Book

You're going to be disappointed if you're an advanced programmer and interested in learning C# as a second language. The examples in this book are relatively basic, and the explanations are kept simple. Developers who have a lot of experience will feel that I'm exploring the obvious—but what is obvious to experienced programmers often isn't obvious at all to someone who is just learning to write code.

Organization of This Book

Start Here! Learn Microsoft Visual C# 2010 uses a hands-on approach to learning where readers actually trace through applications and discover how they work by seeing them perform tasks. Because this book is targeted toward complete novices, it should be read sequentially; later chapters require knowledge covered in previous chapters. I strongly suggest starting at the first chapter and working forward through the book. If you do have some experience with another language, you could possibly start at Chapter 3. This book provides the following topics.

- **Chapter 1: Getting to Know C#** You'll create three desktop applications in this chapter that show the sorts of things that C# is capable of doing. Part of this process is learning how to trace through applications so that you can see how they perform the tasks that they do, so you'll learn the tracing technique used throughout the rest of the book in this chapter. This chapter also helps you download and install the tools you need to work with C#.

- **Chapter 2: Developing a Web Project**   In addition to the desktop applications introduced in Chapter 1, it's also possible to create web applications using C#. This chapter shows two completely different web applications that will help you understand the small differences involved in tracing through web applications. You'll also learn how to download and install the tools used to create web applications.

- **Chapter 3: Using Simple Data Manipulation Techniques**   The first two chapters help acquaint you with C# on the desktop and the web. This chapter exposes you to the main purpose behind most applications—data manipulation. You'll use a new technique to manipulate data that relies on LINQ. The five examples in this chapter emphasize the fact that data manipulation need not be hard.

- **Chapter 4: Using Collections to Store Data**   Although Chapter 3 focuses on simple data, this chapter begins showing you how to work with complex data. You'll discover how to create containers to store similar data together. This chapter contains three examples that emphasize three different types of data storage.

- **Chapter 5: Working with XML**   It seems as if just about everything runs on the eXtensible Markup Language (XML) today. The four examples in this chapter show you how to work with XML files so that you can do things like save application settings and work with web services.

- **Chapter 6: Accessing a Web Service**   Web services make it possible to obtain data through a remote connection. Often this connection relies on the Internet, but web services are everywhere. In fact, you'll be surprised at how many free web services exist and the impressive range of data you can access through them. The two examples in this chapter show you how to use the two techniques, REpresentational State Transfer (REST) and Simple Object Access Protocol (SOAP), that C# provides to access web services.

- **Chapter 7: Using the Windows Presentation Foundation**   Windows Presentation Foundation (WPF) is a new way to create applications with C#. It helps you create applications with impressive interfaces and new features that aren't available using older C# development methods. The four examples in this chapter emphasize techniques that you can use to create great applications using WPF.

- **Chapter 8: Working with Libraries** At some point you'll want to reuse some of the code you create. Libraries provide the means for reusing code easily and in a standardized way. The example in this chapter shows how to create and use a library as part of an application.

- **Chapter 9: Creating Utility Applications** Many people haven't used the command line, but most administrators are at least aware of it. The command line makes it possible to type a single command that performs tasks that would require multiple mouse clicks. The example in this chapter shows how to create applications that have a command-line interface so that you can work with them quickly and automate them in various ways.

- **Chapter 10: Using LINQ in Web Applications** Earlier chapters explored the use of LINQ in desktop applications. Fortunately, it's quite easy to use LINQ in web applications, too. You use LINQ for the same purpose—to ask the application to supply certain types of data. The three examples in this chapter show different ways to use LINQ in a web application.

- **Chapter 11: Working with Silverlight Applications** Silverlight applications can perform amazing tasks. You can create them to work in either a browser or at the desktop. The technology works with multiple browsers and on multiple platforms. In short, you can use Silverlight to transform your C# application into something that works everywhere. The two examples in this chapter help you understand the basics of Silverlight development using C#.

- **Chapter 12: Debugging Applications** Throughout the book you've used tracing techniques to discover how applications work. Debugging is a step further. When you debug an application, you look for errors in it and fix them. The example in this chapter extends what you already know about tracing to make it easier to begin debugging your applications.

Free eBook Reference

When you purchase this title, you also get the companion reference, *Start Here!™ Fundamentals of Microsoft® .NET Programming*, for free. To obtain your copy, please see the instruction page at the back of this book.

The *Fundamentals* book contains information that applies to any programming language, plus some specific material for beginning .NET developers.

As you read through this book, you'll find references to the *Fundamentals* book that look like this:

For more information, see <topic> in the accompanying Start Here! Fundamentals of Microsoft .NET Programming *book.*

When you see a reference like this, if you're not already familiar with the topic, you should read that section in the *Fundamentals* book. In addition, the *Fundamentals* book contains an extensive glossary of key programming terms.

Conventions and Features in This Book

This book presents information using conventions designed to make the information readable and easy to follow:

- This book relies heavily on procedures to help you create applications and then trace through them to see how they work. Each procedure is in a separate section and describes precisely what you'll accomplish by following the steps it contains.

- Boxed elements with labels such as "Note" provide additional information or alternative methods for completing a step successfully. Make sure you pay special attention to warnings because they contain helpful information for avoiding problems and errors.

- Text that you type (apart from code blocks) appears in **bold**.

- A plus sign (+) between two key names means that you must press those keys at the same time. For example, "Press Alt+Tab" means that you hold down the Alt key while you press the Tab key.

- A vertical bar between two or more menu items (such as File | Close), means that you should select the first menu or menu item, then the next, and so on.

System Requirements

You will need the following hardware and software to work through the examples in this book:

- One of following operating systems: Windows XP with Service Pack 3 (except Starter Edition), Windows Vista with Service Pack 2 (except Starter Edition), Windows 7, Windows Server 2003 with Service Pack 2, Windows Server 2003 R2, Windows Server 2008 with Service Pack 2, or Windows Server 2008 R2

- Visual C# 2010 Express edition

- Visual Web Developer 2010 Express edition

- A computer that has a 1.6 GHz or faster processor (2 GHz recommended)

- 1 GB (32 Bit) or 2 GB (64 Bit) RAM (Add 512 MB if running in a virtual machine or SQL Server Express editions, more for advanced SQL Server editions.)

- 3.5 GB of available hard disk space

- 5400 RPM hard disk drive

- DirectX 9 capable video card running at 1024 x 768 or higher-resolution display

- DVD-ROM drive (if installing Visual Studio from DVD)

- An Internet connection to download software or chapter examples

Depending on your Windows configuration, you might require Local Administrator rights to install or configure Visual C# 2010 Express edition and Visual Web Developer 2010 Express edition products.

Code Samples

Most of the chapters in this book include exercises that let you interactively try out new material learned in the main text. All sample projects, in both their pre-exercise and post-exercise formats, can be downloaded from the following page:

http://go.microsoft.com/FWLink/?Linkid=229177

Follow the instructions to download the Start_Here_CSharp_Sample_Code.zip file.

Note In addition to the code samples, your system should have Visual Studio 2010 and SQL Server 2008 installed. The instructions below use SQL Server Management Studio 2008 to set up the sample database used with the practice examples. If available, install the latest service packs for each product.

Installing the Code Samples

Follow these steps to install the code samples on your computer so that you can use them with the exercises in this book.

1. Unzip the Start_Here_CSharp_Sample_Code.zip file that you downloaded from the book's website. (Name a specific directory along with directions to create it, if necessary.)

2. If prompted, review the displayed end user license agreement. If you accept the terms, select the accept option, and then click Next.

Note If the license agreement doesn't appear, you can access it from the same webpage from which you downloaded the Start_Here_CSharp_Sample_Code.zip file.

Using the Code Samples

The folder created by the Setup.exe program creates a book folder named "Start Here! Programming in C#" that contains 12 subfolders—one for each of the chapters in the book. To find the examples associated with a particular chapter, access the appropriate chapter folder. You'll find the examples for that chapter in separate subfolders. Access the folder containing the example you want to work with. (These folders have the same names as the examples in the chapter.) For example, you'll find an example called "No-Code Windows Forms" in the "Create a New Windows Forms Application Project" section of Chapter 1 in the \Start Here! Programming in C#\Chapter 01\No Code Windows Forms folder on your hard drive. If your system is configured to display file extensions of the C# project files, use .sln as the file extension.

Acknowledgments

Thanks to my wife, Rebecca, for working with me to get this book completed. I really don't know what I would have done without her help in researching and compiling some of the information that appears here. She also did a fine job of proofreading my rough draft. Rebecca keeps the house running while I'm buried in work.

Russ Mullen deserves thanks for his technical edit of this book. He greatly added to the accuracy and depth of the material you see here. Russ is always providing me with great URLs for new products and ideas. However, it's the testing Russ does that helps most. He's the sanity check for my work. Russ also has different computer equipment from mine, so he's able to point out flaws that I might not otherwise notice.

Matt Wagner, my agent, deserves credit for helping me get the contract in the first place and taking care of all the details that most authors don't really consider. I always appreciate his assistance. It's good to know that someone wants to help.

A number of people read all or part of this book to help me refine the approach, test the coding examples, and generally provide input that all readers wish they could have. These unpaid volunteers helped in ways too numerous to mention here. I especially appreciate the efforts of Eva Beattie and Osvaldo Téllez Almirall, who provided general input, read the entire book, and selflessly devoted themselves to this project. I also appreciated Rod Stephen's input on a number of questions.

Finally, I would like to thank Russell Jones, Dan Fauxsmith, Christian Holdener, Becka McKay, Christie Rears, and the rest of the editorial and production staff at O'Reilly for their assistance in bringing this book to print. It's always nice to work with such a great group of professionals. This is my first book with this group and I hope we get to work together again in the future.

Errata & Book Support

We've made every effort to ensure the accuracy of this book and its companion content. Any errors that have been reported since this book was published are listed on our Microsoft Press site at oreilly.com:

http://go.microsoft.com/FWLink/?Linkid=229176

If you find an error that is not already listed, you can report it to us through the same page.

If you need additional support, email Microsoft Press Book Support at *mspinput@microsoft.com*.

Please note that product support for Microsoft software is not offered through the addresses above.

We Want to Hear from You

At Microsoft Press, your satisfaction is our top priority, and your feedback our most valuable asset. Please tell us what you think of this book at:

http://www.microsoft.com/learning/booksurvey

The survey is short, and we read every one of your comments and ideas. Thanks in advance for your input!

Stay in Touch

Let's keep the conversation going! We're on Twitter: *http://twitter.com/MicrosoftPress*.

Chapter 1

Getting to Know C#

After completing this chapter, you'll be able to:

- Install all of the tools required to use C# to develop applications.

- Start Visual Studio 2010 Express so that you can use it to create applications.

- Create and explore a standard desktop application without using any code.

- Create and explore a Windows Presentation Foundation (WPF) application without using any code.

C# IS AN INCREDIBLE LANGUAGE. You can use it to create just about any kind of application—desktop, web, or mobile—using less code than you're likely to need with just about any other language. However, as shown in this chapter, you may not even need to write much code; the Visual Studio Integrated Development Environment (IDE) provides a graphical interface that also writes code for you in the background. Amazing! You design how you want the program to look, then you inform the IDE about behaviors the application should have—and then the IDE writes the code for you! This chapter walks you through several no-code examples that actually do something useful. With that said, normally you'll write at least *some* code to create most applications.

Of course, before you can create a C# application, you need some sort of tool to create it with. (Technically, you could write an application using Notepad and compile it at the command line, but that's a lot of work, especially when you can obtain a tool free and use it to write useful applications the easy way.) The first section of this chapter shows how to download and install the tools you need for the rest of the examples in the book. If you already have a full version of Visual Studio installed on your system, you can skip the first section of this chapter and move right to the "Starting Visual C# 2010 Express" section.

This chapter doesn't tell you absolutely everything there is to know about the IDE; it does provide some basics to get you started. The second section of the chapter helps you launch Visual C# 2010

Express the first time; you can then look around to see what it provides. Don't worry, you'll learn a great deal more about the features of this IDE before you get through the book.

After the IDE walkthrough, the remainder of the chapter focuses on the three no-code desktop application examples. The IDE does write some code for you, and you'll examine that as part of working through the examples. The best way to learn about coding is to try things out and explore code written by someone else; this book allows you to do both.

Obtaining and Installing Visual Studio 2010 Express

Before you can do anything with C#, you need an environment in which to work. Fortunately, you can obtain a free working environment, Visual Studio 2010 Express, directly from Microsoft. After you install the required products, you'll be able to work with any of the examples in this book and be on your way to a new world of developing applications.

Downloading the Products

Microsoft produces a number of Express products that you can download from *http://www.microsoft.com/express/Downloads/,* but for the purposes of this book you need to download only the following items:

> **Important** You should download and install the packages from the download link in the order listed here.

- **Visual C# 2010 Express**   Provides a Visual Studio IDE suitable for developing C# applications.

- **Visual Web Developer 2010 Express**   Provides a Visual Studio IDE and other tools that help you develop web applications.

- **Visual Studio 2010 Service Pack 1**   Fixes bug in the two Visual Studio Express versions. You should install this last.

The download for Visual C# 2010 Express simply produces a file on your hard drive. The Visual Web Developer 2010 Express download also installs the product for you. As part of the Visual Web Developer 2010 Express installation, you also get the Microsoft Web Platform Installer; because it's part of the package you don't need to perform a separate download to obtain it. But make sure you download and install both the C# and Visual Web Developer Express versions *before* you download and install Visual Studio 2010 Service Pack 1. The next three sections provide detailed instructions for installing all three products, so you can follow along or simply follow the prompts yourself.

Note You must have an Internet connection to install the products described in this chapter. In all cases, the installer will rely on this connection to download product features as part of the installation process.

Installing Visual C# 2010 Express

To download Visual C# Express, click the bullet next to its entry on the download page, *http://www.microsoft.com/express/Downloads*. When you select a language from the drop-down list, the page starts the download automatically. The initial download is only 3.1 MB, so it won't take long. (The installer will download 104 MB more data during the installation process.) Double-click the vcs_web.exe file when the download completes. (Click Yes if you see the User Account Control dialog box.) You'll see a Setup dialog box appear for a few minutes. When you see the Welcome To Setup dialog box, you can start the installation process described in the following steps.

Note The sizes of the file downloads in this chapter are approximate and will probably change with time. The main reason for including them is to give you some idea of how large a download will be and how long it will take.

Performing the Visual C# 2010 Express Installation

1. Click Next. The License Terms dialog box appears.

2. Read the licensing terms, select I Have Read And Accept The License Terms, and click Next. The Destination Folder dialog box appears. Normally, the default destination works fine and that's the assumption this book makes when telling you about Visual C# 2010 Express-specific folders. Therefore, unless you have a good reason to change the default folder, accept the default.

3. Click Install. The installer begins downloading the required files from the Internet. The download is 45 MB, so it may take a few minutes to complete. The actual installation process begins automatically when the download is complete. So get a cup of coffee, grab your favorite magazine, and kick back for a few minutes. At some point, a dialog box appears, indicating that the installation is complete.

4. Click Exit. You're now ready to create desktop applications using Visual C# 2010 Express!

Installing Visual Web Developer 2010 Express

To download Visual Web Developer 2010 Express, click the bullet next to its entry on the download page. Click Install. You'll see a Microsoft web page where you can install the Microsoft Web Platform Installer. Click Install Now to start the download process. After a few minutes, you'll have a file named

Vwd.exe on your system. Double-click this file to open and start the installer. (Click Yes if the User Account Control dialog box appears.) The installer downloads some additional files and installs them automatically, after which you see the Web Platform Installer 3.0 dialog box shown in Figure 1-1.

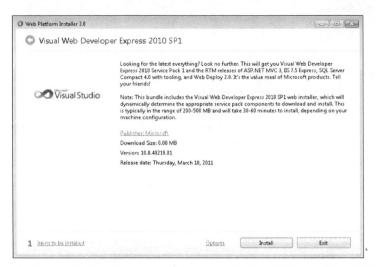

FIGURE 1-1 The Web Platform Installer starts the Visual Web Developer 2010 Express installation.

You're ready to begin installing Visual Web Developer 2010 Express. The following steps take you through the installation process:

Performing the Visual Web Developer 2010 Express Installation

1. Click Install. You'll see the Web Platform Installation dialog box shown here.

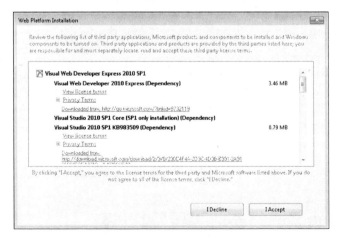

This dialog box contains a list of the applications that the installer will download and install to create a Visual Web Developer 2010 Express installation for you. Many of the items have links for privacy and licensing terms. You'll need to read the privacy and licensing terms for each product before you proceed so that you know the requirements of using that product.

> **Note** Don't change the default installation selections. For example, you won't need a copy of SQL Server to work through the examples in this book. Configuring these other items can prove difficult in some cases, so this is one situation where the default installation is best.

2. Read the privacy and licensing terms. Click I Accept. The installer will begin downloading and installing each of the products in the list for you automatically. This process will take a while, so you can gaze out the window and contemplate your weekend activities while whistling a merry tune. Eventually, you'll see the Web Platform Installer 3.0 dialog box shown here, from which you can install additional products. At this point, Visual Web Developer 2010 Express is installed and ready.

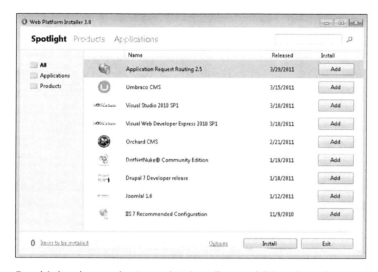

3. For this book, you don't need to install any additional products, so click Exit.

Installing Visual Studio 2010 Service Pack 1

It's possible that the newly downloaded and installed copy of Visual C# 2010 Express and Visual Web Developer 2010 Express will already have Service Pack 1 (SP1) installed. You can check for this requirement by looking at the About dialog box for each of the applications (click Help | About to see the dialog box). Of course, you might have an older copy of these Express products, or have another Visual Studio product installed on your system. The various IDEs won't start until all your Visual Studio products have SP1 installed, so check for the SP1 compliance and follow the instructions in this section only if you actually need them. In the event of a problem, a dialog box like the one shown in Figure 1-2 appears.

FIGURE 1-2 You'll see this dialog box if the Service Pack 1 installation fails.

To download Visual Studio Service Pack 1, click the bullet next to its entry on the download page. Click Install. You'll see another page load. Click Download on this page to start the download. After the download is complete, double-click the file VS10sp1-KB983509.EXE to begin the installation process. (Click Yes if the User Account Control dialog box appears.) At this point, the installation proceeds automatically. Click Finish when the installation completes.

Starting Visual C# 2010 Express

An Integrated Development Environment (IDE) provides an environment that contains tools to help you create applications. It provides editors (to write code), designers (to lay out graphical elements), a compiler (to create executable code), a debugger (to find mistakes in your code), and other tools that make the development process easier. The Visual C# 2010 Express IDE helps you create desktop applications, which is the focus of this chapter.

Note You need to register both Visual C# 2010 Express and Visual Web Developer 2010 Express. The products you download will only run for 30 days without registration. Registration is free. All you need to do is choose Help | Register Product and follow the instructions to register the applications.

Now that you have a copy of the IDE installed on your computer, it's time to start it to see what it looks like. To start Visual C# 2010 Express, choose Start | All Programs | Microsoft Visual Studio 2010 Express | Microsoft Visual C# 2010 Express. You'll see the IDE start up shown in Figure 1-3.

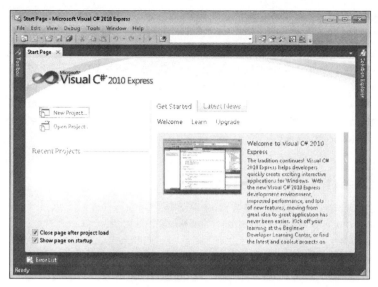

FIGURE 1-3 The Visual Studio IDE opens with the Start Page showing.

This first view of Visual C# 2010 Express is the one that you'll see every time you start the IDE. The left side of the page contains links for creating new projects or opening existing projects. After you have created some applications, you'll also see a list of applications you've recently worked with, which makes it fast and easy to open current projects. On the bottom left are options to close the Start page after you open a project (to reduce clutter) and to display the Start page every time the IDE opens. Generally, you'll leave these options set as shown in the figure to make your work environment efficient.

The right side of the Start page contains helpful information. The first tab contains information you can use to get started using C# more quickly. The second tab provides access to the latest information about C#; however, to see this information, you must click Enable RSS Feed. The page will automatically update with the latest information.

Tip Opening the latest information in the IDE can slow things down at times. A better option is to add the RSS feed to Outlook (or the RSS feed reader of your choice) by following these steps: Make sure Outlook is running. Copy the URL from the RSS Feed field and paste it into your browser's address field. Press Enter, and after a few seconds your browser will ask if you want to add the RSS feed to Outlook. Click Yes.

Creating the No-Code Web Browser

Desktop applications have been around for a long time. Initially, developers had to write all sorts of weird code to make them work, but modern IDEs make it possible to create most applications in significantly less time. This example demonstrates the Windows Forms approach, which is the approach that Windows developers have used for many years to create applications. This particular example shows how to create a fully functional Web browser. You'll actually be able to use it to surf the Internet should you desire to do so.

Understanding the Benefits of Windows Forms

Windows Forms technology has been around for many years, and it's incredibly stable. In addition, most developers have created a Windows Forms application sometime in their career. The combination of long use and familiarity make Windows Forms applications a good starting point for anyone. One of the more important reasons to create a Windows Forms application is that you have access to an astonishing array of controls and tools. If you need to support older platforms, Windows Forms is also the best choice for compatibility reasons. You don't need anything special installed on older systems to use a Windows Forms application except the version of the .NET Framework required by the application. The .NET Framework contains the code that makes C# and other .NET languages run. It is available wherever you need it. In short, even though Windows Forms applications are older technology, they're still relevant for developers today. Microsoft plans to continue supporting Windows Forms applications into the foreseeable future, so you certainly don't need to worry about the practicality of this approach for your next application.

Creating a New Windows Forms Application Project

You always begin a new project by opening the IDE and then clicking the New Project link. The IDE displays the New Project dialog box shown in Figure 1-4.

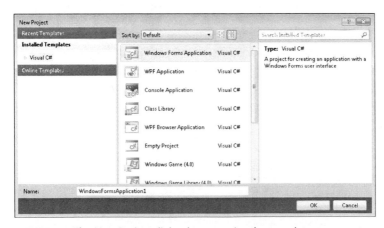

FIGURE 1-4 The New Project dialog box contains the templates you use to create new applications.

The left pane contains a list of template folders. Each folder contains a particular group of templates. In this case, you're interested in the Visual C# folder. The center pane shows the templates contained within the selected template folder. Because this project is about creating a Windows Forms application, highlight the Windows Forms Application template. The right pane contains information about the selected template.

Every project requires a name—preferably something better than the default *WindowsForms Application1*. Always give your projects a descriptive name so that you always know what they contain. In this case, type **No-Code Windows Forms** in the Name field. The name is a little long, but descriptive. Click OK and the IDE creates a new project for you like the one shown in Figure 1-5.

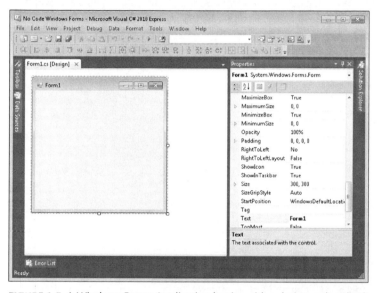

FIGURE 1-5 A Windows Forms Application begins with a designer that displays a blank form.

> **Note** It's perfectly normal to see some small differences between your display and the screenshots in this book. Visual Studio is an incredibly flexible IDE and you can configure it to meet your specific needs. However, if you see large differences (for example, the screenshot doesn't look anything at all like the one in the book), you have probably made an error in following the procedure and will need to retrace your steps. Visual Studio is also incredibly forgiving—nothing bad is going to happen if you have to start over.

Quite a few windows are visible in the figure, but don't get overwhelmed. The book discusses them as needed. For now, all you really need to know is that the form designer appears on the left side of the display and the Properties window appears on the right. You use the designer to create the user interface for your application. The Properties window lets you configure the application elements as described in the "Configuring the Windows Forms Controls" section later in this chapter. You'll get familiar with what controls are and how to use them soon. If you don't currently see the Properties window in your IDE, choose View | Other Windows | Properties Window, or press Ctrl+W,P.

Note The content of the Properties window reflects the object you select. The contents will change when you select a form instead of a specific control. Each control will also display different content in the Properties window. Later, when you use Solution Explorer, you'll find that the Properties window content will change to reflect any entries you choose in Solution Explorer. If your Properties window content doesn't match the screenshot in the book, make sure you've selected the proper form, control, or Solution Explorer entry.

You may not think you can do too much with the application yet, but you can. It's possible to configure the form. Normally, you'll perform some form configuration before you even add any controls. Start by giving your form a better name. Highlight the *(Name)* field in the Properties window, and type **BrowserTest,** as shown in Figure 1-6. (Do not put a space between the words. BrowserTest needs to be all one word for it to work.)

FIGURE 1-6 The Properties window tells you about form and controls settings in your application.

Notice that the Properties window displays a description of the property you've highlighted in a pane at the bottom of the window. If you don't see this pane, you can always display it by dragging the splitter bar that appears near the bottom of the window up to provide more space for the description. The *(Name)* property is a text property, meaning it's made up of characters (letters and/or numbers) so you simply type something to fill it. Other properties will have other ways to provide information, such as a list of acceptable values or even special dialog boxes that help you configure the property. You'll see these other kinds of properties in action as the book progresses.

Tip You can display the properties in two different ways to make them easier to find. The example in this section displays the properties in alphabetical order. You can also display the properties grouped into categories. To switch between views, click either Categorized or Alphabetical at the top of the Properties window.

It's important to give easily understood names to the controls and forms that make up your application so that they are easier to work with. A name can't start with a number, nor can it contain any spaces. Many developers use an underscore (_) as a substitute for a space. For example, you could give your form the name **Browser_Test**. If you try to give your form an invalid name, the IDE displays an error dialog box informing you that the name is invalid, and returns the name to the previous (valid) name.

Scroll down to the *Text* property. This property determines the text that appears in the form's title bar. Type **Web Browser Test** for this property's value. Notice that the title bar text changes in the Designer after you press Enter.

Saving Your Project

It's a good idea to get into the habit of saving your project regularly. Saving the project reduces the likelihood that you'll lose information. Click Save All on the Standard toolbar, choose File | Save All, or press Ctrl+Shift+S. Save All saves all the files that have been modified; Save saves only the current file. You'll see the Save Project dialog box shown in Figure 1-7.

FIGURE 1-7 Save your project often to prevent loss of changes you make to it.

The Name field contains the name of this particular project. The IDE suggests a name based on the name you provided when you created the project. The Location field tells where the project is stored. Visual Studio defaults to using the C:\Users\<User Name>\documents\visual studio 2010\ Projects folder on your hard drive, but you can store your projects anywhere. The Solution Name field contains the name of the *solution* that holds the project. A solution is a kind of container. You can store multiple projects in a single solution. For example, you might store an application as well as a program to test it in a single solution. A solution will often have a different name than the first project you create—but for now, keep the project and solution names the same.

Adding Windows Forms Controls

The IDE's border area displays some tabs, each of which corresponds to a particular window. Don't worry too much about them now, but one tab of immediate interest is the Toolbox. Clicking a tab displays its associated window. If you want the window visible without clicking it all the time, click Auto Hide (the pushpin icon in the upper-right corner of the window). Try it out now: click Auto Hide on the Properties window to hide it, and then click Auto Hide on the Toolbox to display it. Notice that the thumbtack icon changes to show whether a window will automatically hide. Your IDE will look something like the example shown in Figure 1-8.

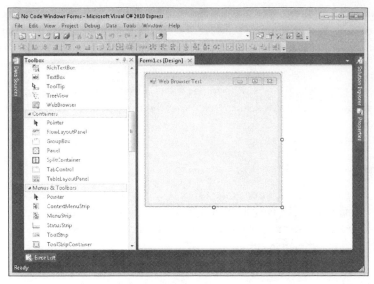

FIGURE 1-8 The Toolbox contains controls you use to create a user interface.

The Toolbox contains a wealth of *controls*. Controls are the building blocks of application development. You can snap them together in various ways to create a basic application design. Take some time to scroll through the list and explore the available controls now. As you can see, the Toolbox groups the controls into categories to make them easier to find. Otherwise, you'd spend your entire day looking for controls rather than creating incredibly useful applications. Most applications rely on the standard set of controls that you can find in the Common Controls category. One of these controls is the *WebBrowser* control used for this example.

Adding a control to your form is easy. You have three convenient ways to add the control:

- Drag the control from the Toolbox and drop it onto the form.

- Click the control within the Toolbox and then click where you want to place it on the form.

- Double-click the control within the Toolbox. This places it in a default position on the form.

Try one of these techniques now with the *WebBrowser* control. You'll see the control added to the form, as shown in Figure 1-9.

FIGURE 1-9 The *WebBrowser* control doesn't look like much when you first add it, but it contains information later.

As you can see, the control is invisible, but you can tell that the IDE added the control to the form because of the *sizing handles* (the little squares in each corner). In addition, in the upper-right corner you'll see an arrow that you can click to display a shortcut menu containing quick (and common) configuration settings. The control provides a vertical scroll bar that appears on the right side of the control in the figure. Your no-code application is ready for configuration.

Configuring the Windows Forms Controls

After you design the user interface for your application by selecting controls from the Toolbox, you'll normally hide the Toolbox window and display the Properties window again so that you can perform configuration tasks. Use the following steps to configure the *WebBrowser* control for this example.

Creating the No Code Windows Forms Application

1. Click the *WebBrowser* control in the form to select it.

2. Select the *(Name)* property and type **MyBrowser**.

3. Select the *ScriptErrrorsSuppressed* property and choose *True*. This is a *Boolean* property—it can only have one of the values *True* or *False*. Selecting *True* means that the *WebBrowser* control won't display scripting errors that occur when the control displays the URL you select.

4. Select the *Url* property and type **http://www.microsoft.com**. You could change this URL to any value you like. The *Url* property value you provide determines what resource the *WebBrowser* control displays when the application starts. At this point, the control is configured and ready for use.

Testing the Windows Forms Application

Believe it or not, you have a usable application at this point—and you haven't written a single line of code! It's true that the application doesn't do much—but it's a good place to start. To use the application, you need to tell the IDE to *compile* it. Compiling converts human-readable code into something that the computer can understand. The precise manner in which this works isn't important now, but you'll learn more about it as the book progresses. For now, simply choose Debug | Build Solution or press F6. In the lower-left corner of the IDE you'll see a message saying the build succeeded. (If you don't see the build succeeded message, it means that you made a mistake in following the previous sections and that you need to retrace your steps.) What this means is that the compiler was able to create executable code from the design you created and the executable is now ready to test.

To start the application, choose Debug | Start Debugging, or press F5, or click Start Debugging on the Standard toolbar. You'll see the application start. The browser window is going to be small at first, but you can resize it to see more of the page. Figure 1-10 shows some typical results from this application.

FIGURE 1-10 The example application displays a web page.

The application is fully functional. Click a link and you'll see the next page, just as you would in Internet Explorer. Right-click the application window and you'll see a shortcut menu containing all the usual browser controls. For example, you can move forward and backward through the history list, just as you would in Internet Explorer. Of course, it would be nice to have visible controls to perform these tasks, but you can worry about that later. For now, you've created your first usable application. To stop your application, click the Close box in the upper-right corner of the application window (the red X).

Viewing the Web Browser Code

Although you didn't write any code to make this application work, the IDE has been busy on your behalf. It generated code that matches all the design decisions you made. When you compiled the application earlier, you actually created an executable file based on the code that the IDE generated for you. Even though you won't normally edit this IDE-generated code, it's interesting to look at, because you can learn a great deal from it.

To see the Designer code, you must open a different IDE window. Hide the Properties window and display the Solution Explorer window shown in Figure 1-11.

FIGURE 1-11 Solution Explorer provides you with access to the application files.

Solution Explorer presents a view of the files in your project. In this case, the figure shows the Form1 entry opened up to display the files associated with Form1—the form that contains the *WebBrowser* control. Notice the Form1.Designer.cs file. This is the file that contains the code used to create the form. Double-click this entry and you'll see the code you've created during the design process. Hide Solution Explorer so that you can see the code a little better. If you scroll down a bit, you'll see the entries that start to look familiar, like the ones shown in Figure 1-12.

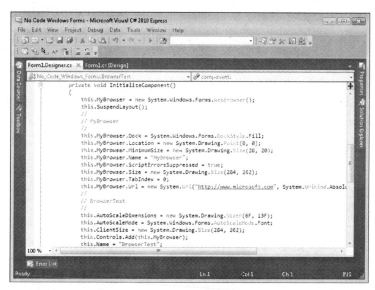

FIGURE 1-12 Even though you haven't written any code, the IDE has performed the task for you.

 Note Make sure you open the correct file—you'll only see the information shown in this screenshot if you open Form1.Designer.cs. Also, you'll need to scroll down in the file to see the *InitializeComponent()* method. You may also need to click the plus sign (+) next to Windows Forms Designer generated code to expand the code so that it looks like the code shown here.

Here you can see the results of all of the changes you made. For example, you renamed the *WebBrowser* control as *MyBrowser* and you can see a number of *MyBrowser* code entries. Look a little closer and you'll see the property changes as well. For example, the line *MyBrowser.Name = "MyBrowser"*, simply states that you changed the name of the control to *MyBrowser* using the Properties window. The line of code literally says that the *MyBrowser* control's *Name* property is *"MyBrowser"*. Try browsing through the code to see more of what the IDE has done for you, but be careful not to change any of it.

Tip One of the ways that professional programmers learn new coding techniques is the very technique you just used—trying something out using a tool and then seeing what code the tool produced. You'll use this technique several times in the book because it's so incredibly useful.

Ending Your Session

When you're finished working with an example, it's a good idea to end your session. Choose File | Exit to close the IDE. Starting the IDE fresh for each example ensures that you're working with a clean environment and that there is less of a chance that errors will occur. Make sure that you end your session after each of the examples throughout the book. The book's procedures assume that you're starting with a fresh copy of the IDE each time, so the instructions might not work if you try to use the same session for all of the examples.

Creating the No-Code WPF Web Browser

Windows Presentation Foundation (WPF) is the latest technology for creating applications. In fact, the IDE you're using to create your applications relies on WPF. The site at *http://10rem.net/blog/2010/10/28/the-present-and-future-of-wpf* provides examples of additional real-world applications that rely on WPF. You'll find that WPF has many advantages over Windows Forms applications. Of course, it's hard to compare two technologies unless you perform the same task with each of them. The example in this section does just that. It shows how to create a Web browser application with the same capabilities as the one found in the "Creating the No-Code Web Browser" section, except that in this case, you'll use WPF instead.

Understanding the Benefits of WPF

Windows Forms applications will remain a faithful standby for many years because of the infrastructure in place to support it. However, the technology is getting old and isn't well-suited to today's user needs. Microsoft created WPF to make it easy to combine multiple presentation technologies in one package. When working with WPF, you can use these types of presentations:

- Forms
- Controls
- Complex text (such as found in a PDF)
- Images

- Video

- Audio

- 2D graphics

- 3D graphics

To obtain access to this wealth of presentation technologies, you'd normally need to combine several disparate application development techniques that might not even work well together. In short, you use WPF when you want to create an application that provides all of the experiences that modern users have come to expect. However, to obtain the extra functionality, you need additional skills. For example, even with the best tools, you can't create a 3D presentation without the appropriate skill set.

Using WPF has other benefits and this book will tell you about them as it progresses. However, one benefit stands out. WPF relies on a declarative language called Extensible Application Markup Language (XAML, pronounced *zammel*) to create the user interface. This language makes it possible to create an application with less code that is less reliant on precise connections with underlying application layers. As a consequence, you can often change the user interface without changing the underlying application layers—something that causes Windows Forms developers a lot of pain today.

Starting a New WPF Application Project

The example in this section creates a browser application precisely like the one in the section "Creating the No-Code Web Browser" except that this example relies on WPF. The following steps help you create the application project:

Creating the No-Code WPF Application

1. Start the Visual C# 2010 Express IDE if you haven't started it already.

2. Click New Project. The New Project dialog box appears.

3. Select the WPF Application template from the Visual C# folder.

4. Type **No Code WPF** in the Name field.

5. Click OK. The IDE creates the new project for you, as shown here.

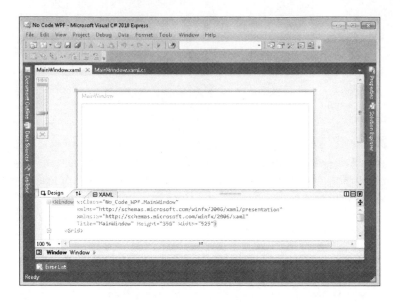

You'll notice immediately that the WPF environment is completely different from the Windows Forms environment. For one thing, it looks a lot more complex. The environment really isn't that much more complex and you'll find that it provides a lot more flexibility. The top half of the Designer window shows a graphical interface similar to the one you used to create the Windows Forms example. The bottom half shows the XAML associated with the user interface you create—similar to the Form1.Designer.cs file described in the "Viewing the Web Browser Code" section of the chapter. The only difference is that the WPF environment shows you this information from the outset so that you can create the user interface graphically or by writing XAML code to do it.

Fortunately, you don't have to look at the XAML if you don't want to. Click Collapse Pane in the Designer window and the XAML pane simply disappears, as shown in Figure 1-13.

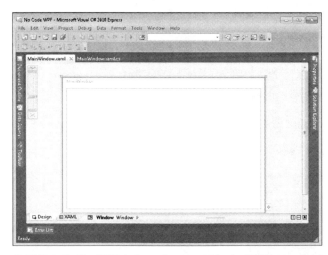

FIGURE 1-13 The WPF designer lets you hide the XAML tags from view.

If you decide later that you really do want to see the graphical environment and the XAML side-by-side, you can click Vertical Split or Horizontal Split in the Designer window. It's also possible to see the XAML by clicking the XAML tab. In this case, you see a full page of XAML instead of just seeing part of the code in a pane. So, there really isn't anything scary about this environment after all.

Before you do anything else, you'll want to give your application better title bar text so that it identifies the purpose of the application. Display the Properties window, select the *Title* property, and type **No Code WPF**. You can hide the Properties window again.

Adding WPF Controls

As with any application you develop, WPF applications rely on the Toolbox as a source of controls. To add controls to this example, you need to display the Toolbox by clicking its tab and then clicking the Auto Hide button on the Toolbox window. You can add the *WebBrowser* control (the only control used in this example) using any of the three techniques described in the "Adding Windows Forms Controls" section of the chapter.

Configuring the WPF Controls

When you add the *WebBrowser* control to your WPF application, you'll notice that it appears in the upper-right corner of the *MainWindow*. A WPF application relies on windows, not on forms as a Windows Forms application does. Because of this difference, configuring the *WebBrowser* control is a bit different from configuring it for a Windows Forms application. The following steps tell you how to perform this task:

Modifying the WPF Application Controls

1. Hide the Toolbox and display the Properties window. One thing you'll notice immediately is that the WPF properties window doesn't provide any helpful information about the property you select, as shown here.

This difference means you must know a bit more about the properties you're using when working with WPF. Fortunately, Microsoft provides detailed help for the controls and you can always refer to Help by pressing F1.

 Tip If you find that you've set a property incorrectly, you can always return it to its default value by right-clicking the property and choosing Reset Value. This feature makes it possible to experiment safely with your application settings.

2. Type **Auto** in the *Height* property. This value ensures that the control automatically adjusts to its container size in the y axis.

3. Change the *HorizontalAlignment* property value to *Stretch*. This change lets the *WebBrowser* control extend the length of the window, no matter what size the window is.

4. Type **http://www.microsoft.com** in the *Source* property. This change sets the starting URL for the *WebBrowser* control.

5. Change the *VerticalAlignment* property value to *Stretch*. This change lets the *WebBrowser* control extend the height of the window no matter what size the window is.

6. Type **Auto** in the *Width* property. This value ensures that the control automatically adjusts to its container size in the x axis. At this point, the control is configured for use.

Trying the WPF Application

It's time to try the WPF application. Like the Windows Forms application, you must compile the WPF application by choosing Debug | Build Solution or by pressing F6. You'll see a Build Succeeded message in the lower-left corner of the IDE, as before. To start the application, choose Debug | Start Debugging, press F5, or click Start Debugging on the Standard toolbar. You'll see an application that looks similar to the Windows Forms application, as shown in Figure 1-14.

FIGURE 1-14 The WPF application produces about the same output as the Windows Forms application.

The two applications aren't precisely the same in appearance, but they're very close. They do work precisely the same way. Click any link in the window and you'll go to that page. You can access all of the browser controls by right-clicking the window and choosing an option from the shortcut menu. In short, you've created a WPF version of the Windows Forms application you created earlier—all without any coding! When you're done with the application, click the Close box as usual.

Viewing the WPF Code

As with the Windows Forms example, every design decision you make when working with WPF creates code. The IDE creates this code for you in the background. You can see this code by clicking the XAML tab in the IDE. Remember that XAML is actually a form of XML, so it looks like code that you may have seen in other situations. Figure 1-15 shows what the XAML looks like for this example. (I've reformatted it for the book—the code you'll see will appear on a single line, but it's the same code.)

FIGURE 1-15 The XAML code for the example application is simpler than the Windows Forms alternative.

If anything, this code is a little clearer than the Windows Forms example code. All of the changes you made appear as part of the *<WebBrowser>* tag. Each attribute/value pair describes a single change.

You might wonder why this example didn't change the name of the form and the control as the Windows Forms example did. It turns out that these properties don't appear in the Properties window. If you want to make this particular change, you need to work with the XAML directly. For example, if you want to change the name of the *WebBrowser* control, you'd type **Name="MyBrowser"**.

Creating the No Code WPF Browser Application

Both of the applications presented so far in the chapter have one thing in common—they create a separate application that appears like any other application on your hard drive. The application starts just like any other application you've seen before. The WPF Browser Application example in this section is different. It starts up in your browser. That's right—this is a special kind of application that appears in your browser, even though you aren't accessing it from the Internet. The benefit of this kind of application is that it lets you start the user on the local hard drive and move onto the Internet or a local server without any change in appearance. The user only knows that the application appears in a browser, not where the application or its associated data resides.

Understanding the Benefits of a Mixed Application

Don't get the idea that Windows Forms and WPF are mutually exclusive—that you must choose between one technology and the other. In fact, Microsoft has purposely made it possible for each technology to host the other. It's possible to create an application that mixes the two together, so that you can get the best of each. You could potentially update an existing application with WPF elements to give users the kind of experience they demand without reworking the entire application.

The best way to use this potential is to build application programming skills a little at a time. You can start with Windows Forms applications and add WPF elements gradually until you know both technologies well. The mixed environment also makes it possible to gradually move users to the new environment so that they require less training time.

Setting Internet Explorer as the Default

Before you can use this application type successfully, you need to set Internet Explorer as your default browser. Follow these instructions to ensure that you have the correct setup:

Configuring Internet Explorer as the Default Browser

1. Choose Start | Control Panel. The Control Panel opens.

2. Click Network And Internet. The Network and Internet options appear.

3. Click Internet Options. The Internet Properties dialog box appears.

4. Click the Programs tab. This tab contains a number of options, including the default browser.

5. Click Make Default. Internet Explorer becomes the default browser (if it isn't the default already).

Starting a WPF Browser Application Project

Now that you have Internet Explorer configured, it's time to create the WPF project. The following stps show how to create a basic WPF project that won't require any coding.

Creating the WPF Browser Application

1. Start the Visual C# 2010 Express IDE if you haven't started it already.

2. Click New Project. The New Project dialog box appears.

3. Select the WPF Browser Application template from the Visual C# folder.

4. Type **WPF Browser Example** in the Name field.

5. Click OK. The IDE creates the new project for you, as shown here.

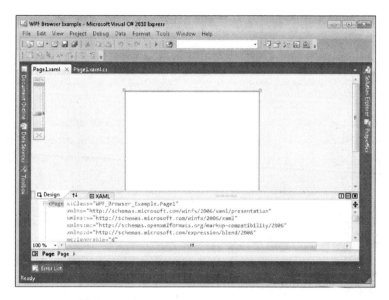

As you can see, this is another WPF application. However, notice that this application doesn't have a MainWindow—instead it has a page. That's because the application is hosted in Internet Explorer and isn't created as a-standalone application.

Adding WPF Browser Controls

This example doesn't rely on the *WebBrowser* control used for the other two examples in the chapter. If you try to use the *WebBrowser* control in your WPF Browser application, the application will likely crash. That's because you're attempting to host a copy of Internet Explorer within itself (at least, that seems to be the theory). So this example relies on a different control for demonstration purposes. Begin by displaying the Toolbox by clicking its tab and then clicking the Auto Hide button on the

Toolbox window. Add the *Image* control (the only control used in this example) using any of the three techniques described in the "Adding Windows Forms Controls" section of the chapter.

Configuring the WPF Browser Controls

When you add the *Image* control to your WPF application, you'll notice that it appears in the upper-right corner of the *Page1*. Working with an *Image* control is similar to working with the *WebBrowser*, but there are some differences. The following steps tell you how to configure the *Image* control for use:

Modifying the WPF Browser Application Controls

1. Hide the Toolbox and display the Properties window.

2. Set the *Height* property to *Auto*.

3. Change the *HorizontalAlignment* property value to *Stretch*.

4. Type **http://apod.nasa.gov/apod/image/1104/m74_baixauli_900.jpg** in the *Source* property. This change sets the picture that the *Image* control displays. If you have some other favorite picture you'd like to see, you can provide its location as a source instead.

> **Tip** If you set the *Source* property successfully, you'll see the picture appear immediately in the IDE, unlike the *WebBrowser* control where you must try the application out to see whether the *Source* property is correct. A number of controls provide instant feedback, which makes them easier to use.

5. Change the *VerticalAlignment* property value to *Stretch*.

6. Set the *Width* property to *Auto*.

Trying the WPF Browser Application

The IDE does provide certain shortcuts when working with applications. Normally, you want to compile your application first to determine whether there are any errors, and then run it. However, this time try something different. Choose Debug | Start Debugging, press F5, or click Start Debugging on the Standard toolbar to start the application without first compiling it. What you'll see is that the IDE automatically performs three tasks:

1. Saves your project to disk.

2. Compiles the application for you and displays the success message in the lower-left corner of the IDE (you need to look quickly).

3. Starts the application for you.

Even though the IDE will perform these tasks for you, it's still better to do them yourself. It's a good idea to get into the habit of saving your project often and looking for errors when you compile it. Still, it's nice to know that the IDE performs these steps for you when you forget. Figure 1-16 shows what the example application looks like.

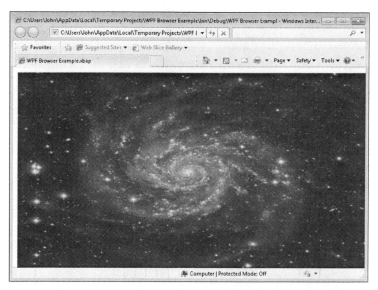

FIGURE 1-16 The WPF Browser Application displays within a browser, rather than as a desktop application.

The example shows a stunning picture of the universe (M74, a spiral galaxy). As you can see, the page exists in Internet Explorer and it could just as easily be an application that relies on both local and remote resources. Closing Internet Explorer stops the application and returns the IDE to development mode.

Viewing the WPF Browser Code

As with the previous WPF example, you click the XAML tab to see the code produced for you by the IDE. Instead of a *WebBrowser* control, you'll see the code for an *Image* control this time. Figure 1-17 shows the code you'll see (with the code reformatted for presentation in the book—your code will appear on a single line).

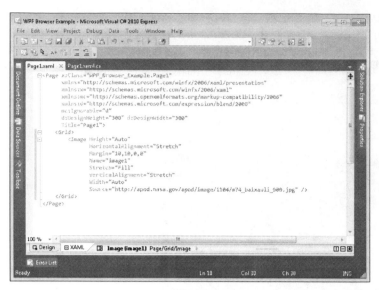

FIGURE 1-17 The XAML for this application shows the use of the Image control to display content.

Get Going with C#

This chapter gets you started with Visual C#. You install products that permit both desktop and web development. In addition, you create three desktop application examples that require no coding on your part. Of course, you now know that all three examples do have code in them and that the IDE creates this code for you. The biggest lesson you can learn from these examples is to let the IDE help you create your applications whenever possible. Using IDE features to speed development efforts means that you spend less time coding and more time enjoying some time out on the town.

You discovered some new techniques for creating an application in this chapter. Although most applications do require that you add code to make them functional, you can play around with many of the controls and develop an application that's at least partially functional. Take some time now to play around with some of the more interesting controls to see what they do. Of course, we'll cover many controls as the book progresses, but it's important to realize that working with applications can be fun and that play time (time spent seeing what happens when you do something) is a big part of application development—at least it is for the best developers.

Chapter 2, "Developing a Web Project," adds to the information you've already learned in this chapter. However, instead of working with desktop applications, you'll work with web applications. In this chapter, you opened the Visual C# 2010 Express IDE and learned some basics about it; Chapter 2 goes through the same process for Visual Web Developer 2010 Express. By the time you finish Chapter 2, you'll have created some additional no-code web examples and will understand how they differ from desktop applications.

Developing a Web Project

After completing this chapter, you'll be able to:

■ Start Visual Web Developer 2010 Express so you can build web applications with it

■ Create a standard project without writing any code

■ Create a standard website without writing any code

DESKTOP APPLICATIONS ARE STILL THE primary way that businesses interact with data—but a vast array of other options are available. One increasingly common choice relies on the Internet (or an intranet) to host various kinds of applications. This book won't show you every kind of application you can create in Visual Studio, but it does provide an overview of how to build the more popular types.

Most applications begin with the need to access some type of data from a client application. The client-server paradigm has been around for many years in a number of forms. These Internet applications are just another form.

For more information, see "client-server" in the accompanying Start Here! Fundamentals of Microsoft .NET Programming *book. To obtain your copy, see the section titled "Free Companion eBook" in the introduction to this book, or turn to the instruction page at the back of the book.*

This chapter begins by exploring the tool you use to create web applications of various types: Visual Web Developer 2010 Express. The applications you will focus on first are intended for the client. Knowing how to create a user interface for any sort of data is helpful, even data hosted by someone else. In fact, with the incredible stores of data available online, it's a wonder that people still find something new to store—but they do. Visual Web Developer 2010 Express can help you create most of the client application types that the .NET Framework supports.

After you get to know Visual Web Developer 2010 Express a little better, you'll begin working with some actual applications, creating a simple project, and using it to define a simple web application.

The second project shows you how to create a simple website and access it using a browser. These two application types go a long way toward getting you started programming the Internet, but of course, they're just the beginning. Other chapters in this book explore web applications in considerably more detail.

> **Note** This chapter assumes that you've installed Visual Web Developer 2010 Express on your system. If you haven't performed this task, look at the instructions found in the "Obtaining and Installing Visual Studio 2010 Express" section of Chapter 1. This section shows how to install both Visual C# 2010 Express and Visual Web Developer 2010 Express. It also contains instructions for updating your installation to use Service Pack 1 (SP1), which contains important fixes that affect the examples in this book.

Starting Visual Web Developer 2010 Express

After you have Visual Web Developer 2010 Express installed on your system, follow these steps to start the Integrated Development Environment (IDE) (which is different from the Visual C# 2010 Express product used in Chapter 1): choose Start | All Programs | Microsoft Visual Studio 2010 Express | Microsoft Visual Web Developer 2010 Express. You'll see the IDE start up, as shown in Figure 2-1.

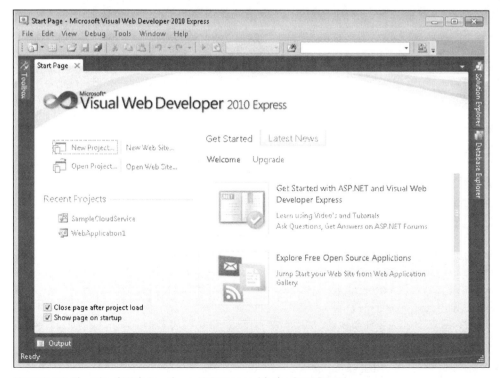

FIGURE 2-1 The Visual Web Developer IDE opens with the Start Page.

The IDE begins by displaying the Start Page. You can turn this feature off by clearing the Show Page On Startup option in the lower-left corner. If you later decide you want to see the Start Page, choose View | Start Page and select the Show Page On Startup option again. The Close Page After Project Load option works for both projects and websites. It frees up screen real estate by closing the Start Page when it's no longer needed after you create or open a project or website.

The left side of the Start Page also contains links for creating or opening a project or website. The "Understanding the Difference Between Websites and Projects" section of this chapter describes the differences between a project and website, so don't worry about it for now.

Anything you've worked on recently (both projects and websites) appears in the Recent Projects list. Click the entry for the project or website you want to open. If you're using Windows 7, remember that you also have access to the Jump Lists feature by right-clicking the Microsoft Visual Web Developer 2010 Express entry in the Start menu, and choosing the project or website you want to open.

On the right side of the display, the Get Started tab contains a number of interesting entries. These entries are all devoted to helping you become more productive with Visual Web Developer 2010 Express quickly. They're also different from the Visual C# 2010 Express offerings. Here are the four Get Started topics and why you should look at them:

- **Get Started with ASP.NET and Visual Web Developer Express**   This option doesn't display help information—you get help by pressing F1. Instead, the first link for this entry provides access to videos and tutorials you can use to learn more about Visual Web Developer. The second link provides access to the Active Server Page (ASP).NET forums where you can ask questions of other developers and various experts that roam the forums.

- **Explore Free Open Source Applications**   Click the link for this option to see open source applications at *http://www.microsoft.com/web/gallery/*. When you get to the site, you'll see a number of free applications. You can select an application and click Install to download and automatically install the application to your hard drive so that you can use it. For example, you'll find a number of interesting Content Management Systems (CMSs), such as Joomla and DotNetNuke. It pays to spend some time browsing this site even if you don't end up downloading anything, because looking at the range of available applications can provide useful ideas for your own applications.

- **Find Affordable Web Hosting**   Click this link to find a number of affordable web hosting companies at *http://www.microsoft.com/web/hosting/home*. Each company offers different features at different rates, so you're likely to find a solution that meets your needs.

 Note You don't need a web hosting company for development. You need one only when you're planning to publish your applications online—usually for public consumption.

- **Get More Software at No Cost** This section contains a number of links for free software. For example, if you click the Microsoft DreamSpark for Students link, you'll go to *http://www.microsoft.com/web/hosting/home,* where you can find out more about this product. DreamSpark is more than a single application; the site actually provides access to a number of applications, including Visual Studio 2010 Professional and Microsoft Certification exams.

The Latest News tab provides information in Really Simple Syndication (RSS) form about Visual Web Developer updates and changes. To use this feature, click the Enable RSS Feed option. However, you should know that obtaining the latest information in the IDE can slow things down at times. A better option is to add the site's RSS feed to Outlook. To do that, first make sure Outlook is running. Copy the Uniform Resource Locator (URL) from the RSS Feed field and paste it into your browser's address field. Press Enter, and after a few seconds your browser will ask if you want to add the RSS feed to Outlook.

 Note The link provided for Visual Web Developer 2010 Express is different from the one for Visual C# 2010 Express, so you'll want to add them both to Outlook.

Creating the No-Code Project

Web development is substantially different from desktop development. For one thing, when creating a web application you're always interacting with a web server, even if that server is installed on your own system. A desktop application has no such intermediary—the operating system executes the application directly on the local system. In addition, web applications normally rely on a browser to host them on the client computer. You'll encounter a number of these differences as the book progresses, but this chapter will introduce you to a few of the desktop/web application differences.

 Note Visual Web Developer 2010 Express supports multiple languages—Visual Basic .NET and Visual C#—and a wealth of project types. This book won't discuss the Visual Basic .NET features of Visual Web Developer—you can find those features discussed in *Start Here! Programming in Visual Basic .NET*—however, you'll explore all the C# project types as you progress through this book.

The example in this section is a simple project. You'll create an ASP.NET application with a basic interface. As with the desktop applications presented in Chapter 1, you'll let the IDE create the required source code for you.

Starting the New Project

This section of the chapter shows how to build a project. This process is typical for every kind of project, even if you're using a different template than the one discussed in this section. Of course, each template produces a different kind of application, so what you see after you complete the process will differ depending on which template you're using. Carefully follow these steps to get started.

Create a New Web Project

1. Choose Start | All Programs | Microsoft Visual Studio 2010 Express | Microsoft Visual Web Developer 2010 Express. You'll see the IDE start up.

2. Click New Project. You'll see the New Project dialog box shown here.

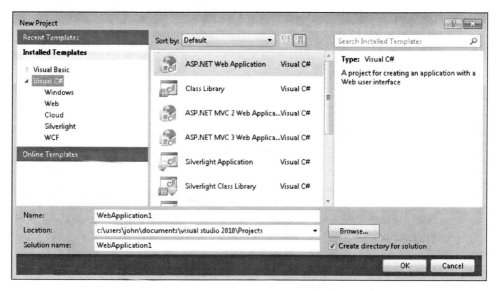

Notice that Visual Web Developer 2010 Express supports both Visual Basic .NET and Visual C#. Make sure you always select the Visual C# folder to work with the C# templates. Otherwise, you'll create a Visual Basic .NET application.

3. Highlight the Visual C# folder. You'll see a number of subfolders that help you locate application templates by type. For example, if you click the web folder, you'll see only those templates associated with web projects.

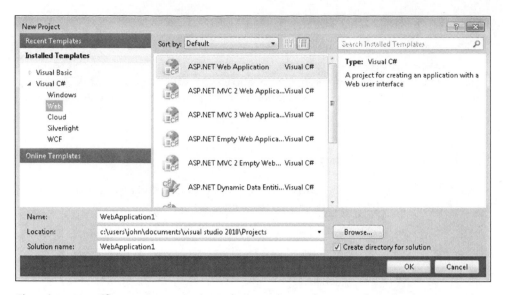

Choosing a specific type can save time when you know the type of application you want to create. The center pane of the New Project dialog box contains the list of templates within a particular folder. The right pane describes the template you select. Notice that the left pane confirms that you've selected a Visual C# template.

The New Project dialog box also contains controls to change the appearance of the center pane. You can choose small or larger icons. In addition, you can sort the templates in a specific order.

4. Select a project type. The example application uses the ASP.NET Web Application template.

5. Type the name **No Code Project** in the Name field. Notice that the Solution Name field automatically changes to reflect the name you just typed in the Name field. The Solution Name field can contain a different value. A solution is a kind of container. You can store multiple projects in a single solution. For example, you might store an application and its test program in a single solution. Thus, the Solution Name field can be different from the project name because it reflects the name for a multi-project solution.

6. Choose a location where you want to store the project files. (Click Browse to display the Project Location dialog box to choose the folder you want to use.) The default location is c:\users\<User Name>\documents\visual studio 2010\Projects; however, you can choose any location on your hard drive to store the project. Unlike the desktop applications created in Chapter 1, the simple act of creating a project stores files on disk, which is why you must choose a storage location in the New Project dialog box.

7. Select the Create Directory For Solution option if you want the solution file to appear in its own folder. This feature is useful primarily when you're creating a multiple-project solution, because each project will appear in its own subfolder. However, keeping the option selected for a single project solution doesn't cause any problems, so normally you keep this option selected.

8. Click OK. The IDE will create the new project for you based on the template you select. Some templates provide default content; others are completely blank. The template used for the example project provides the default content shown here.

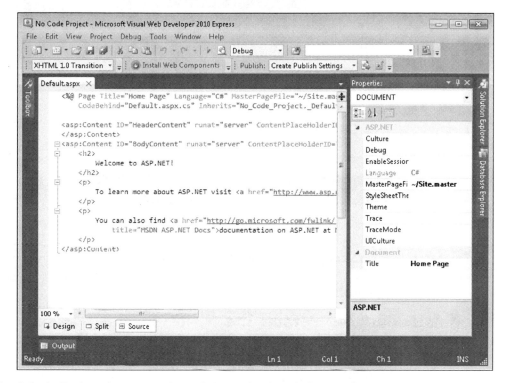

The default display takes you to the code immediately, which isn't what you want in this case. You can click Design to see the graphical interface or click Split to see a combination of the graphical interface and code. Click Design and you'll see the graphical view of the default site, as shown in Figure 2-2.

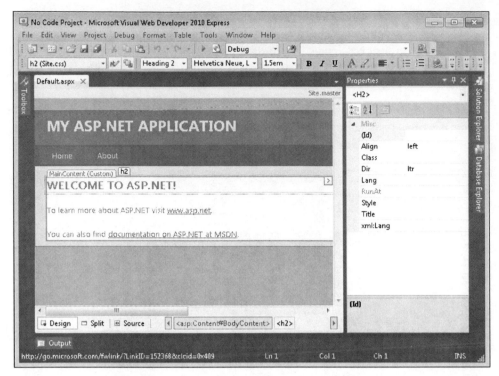

FIGURE 2-2 The sample application includes a number of interesting elements.

That's quite a bit of content. The "Understanding the Default Site" section explains all this content in a little more detail.

Understanding the Default Site

The default site that the ASP.NET Web Application template creates contains a number of individual elements. Each element contributes toward the whole site. In many cases, you'll want to keep all these elements as a starting point for your project. But because they can prove confusing, this section explains the most important elements—the ones you need to know about now to create a program without coding anything. Later, this book describes more of the template elements so you can begin coding your website.

Looking at the Elements

Before going any further, it's important to understand how these default site elements appear in the IDE. If you can see the Properties window, click the Auto Hide button in the upper-right corner. Click Solution Explorer, and then click the Auto Hide button so the window remains fixed in position. You'll see a list of the default site elements like the one shown in Figure 2-3.

FIGURE 2-3 Solution Explorer makes it possible to see all of the files for your application.

Solution Explorer provides access to all the files that make up the default site, even those you won't use for this example. The entries you need to know about for this project are:

- **Site.Master**   Provides a template that gives the entire site the same look and feel. This file is the master page—a page that controls all the other pages. Using a master page makes it possible to create complex sites with far less code. The master page contains the overall site design, so you need to make changes to the master page only when you want to change your entire site to have a different look and feel.

- **Site.css**   Describes the formatting used for the entire site. For example, if you want all headings to use a bold font, you'd place that information in this file.

- **Default.aspx**   Contains the content for the first page that anyone who visits your site sees when they enter your site using just the domain URL. (As with any other site, someone can enter a page-specific URL to access another content page directly.) This default page normally contains an overview of your site as well as links to other information on your site.

- **About.aspx**   Holds information about your site, the application, or your organization. The default site provides this simply as a placeholder page; you won't find any actual content on this page.

The default site contains a number of features that you may not require at all. For example, the master page contains a link to a login page that users can use to log on to your site. Unless you need this security feature, you probably won't keep it in place. However, for now you won't need to worry about whether these features are in place. The example in this section doesn't use them, and you don't need to worry about them.

Working with the Master Page

The master page, Site.Master, contains the overall design for your site. When you open a content page that uses the master page, you see an entry for it in the upper-right corner of the page in Design view.

> **Note** The master page file may not *always* be named Site.Master, but it is when you're working with the default site.

Begin by looking at the Def ault.aspx file that you see when Visual Web Developer 2010 Express first opens the project for you. If you place the cursor in any location controlled by the master page, you'll see a red circle with a line through it, as shown in Figure 2-4.

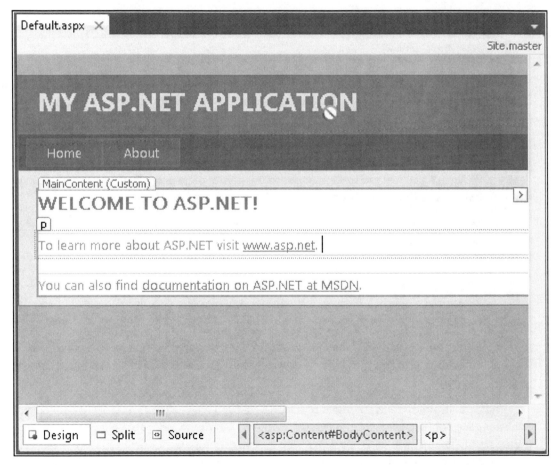

FIGURE 2-4 The master page contains all of the elements that are common to all pages on a website.

To change the site name, open the master page by clicking the Site.Master link in the upper-right corner. Figure 2-5 shows what you see when you click this link and choose the Design tab.

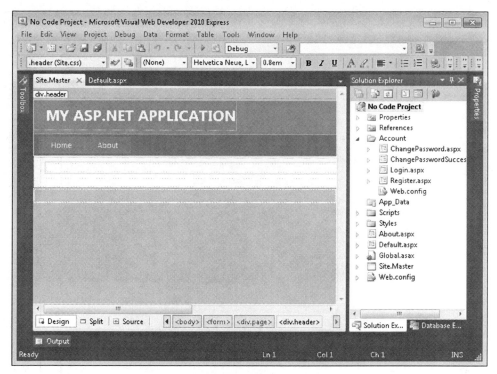

FIGURE 2-5 In order to change master page content, you must open the Site.Master file.

All the elements that were previously inaccessible are now ready to edit. Making a change here affects every page that uses this master page. Now that you can access the master page, you can make changes to it.

Edit the Master Page

1. Type **No Code Project** for the heading.

2. Press Enter to create another line.

3. Change the Block Format to Heading 2 and type **An Example of Working with an ASP.NET Application.** Notice that the color of the text is unreadable against the background.

4. Highlight the entire line, click Foreground Color, and choose Red as the new color.

5. Scroll to the right side of the page. Highlight and delete the login entries because this example doesn't use them. At this point, your Site.Master file should look like the one shown on the next page.

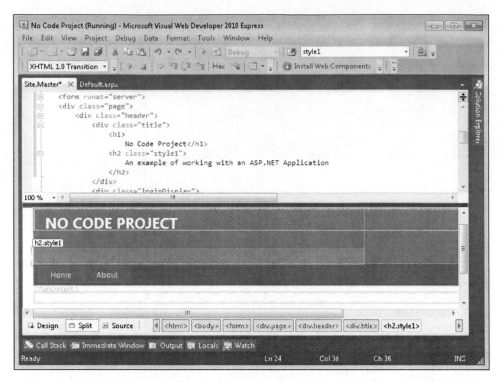

This shows the Split view of the file. As you can see at the top, the code reflects the changes made in the various steps. Notice that changing the color of the second heading creates a new style entry. This change appears only in the Site.Master file, not in the Site.css file used to control the styles for the entire site.

6. Save and close the Site.Master file.

Changing the Default.aspx Content

The Default.aspx file contains content. The master page controls the overall layout of the page and the Style.css file controls the appearance of the page. So when you work with this page, you'll typically want to focus on the actual content, using the other two resources only when you want to change the layout or appearance of all the pages on your site.

This part of the example displays a custom heading and an image as content. Use these steps to make the changes.

Add Content to Default.aspx

1. Highlight the existing heading text and type **An Image on a Web Page**. The next step is to display an actual image.

2. Highlight the existing text under the heading and delete it.

3. Click the Toolbox tab, and then click Auto Hide to keep it displayed. As with Windows Forms applications, you can use one of three techniques to add controls to a webpage:

   - Drag the control from the Toolbox and drop it onto the page.

   - Single-click a control within the Toolbox and then click the page where you want the control to appear.

   - Double-click the control within the Toolbox, placing it in a default location on the page.

4. Use one of the preceding three techniques to add an *Image* control to the webpage.

5. Close the Toolbox by clicking Auto Hide.

6. Display the Properties window by clicking its tab and then clicking Auto Hide.

7. Be sure that the *Image* control you added is selected, and then type **StellarImage** into the *(ID)* property field. The *(ID)* property serves the same purpose as the *(Name)* property for Windows Forms applications—it identifies the control so that you can access it easier later.

8. Type **400** in the *Height* property. This property sets the height of the image in pixels. If you don't set the image height, the page displays the image at the same size as the image source.

 Tip To maintain an image's *aspect ratio* (the relationship between its height and width), you can set either the *Height* or *Width* property. The image automatically resizes the image in both dimensions to maintain the aspect ratio. For example, when the source image is 800 pixels wide by 600 pixels high, setting the *Height* property to 300 automatically changes the *Width* property to 400. Use the property that matters most to your site's layout.

9. Type **http://apod.nasa.gov/apod/image/1104/m74_baixauli_900.jpg** in the *ImageUrl* property. The image will display on the page automatically.

10. Type **450** in the *Width* property. This property sets the image width in pixels. If you don't set the image width, the page will display it at the original size (839 x 746), which is too large. Your Default.aspx page should now look like this.

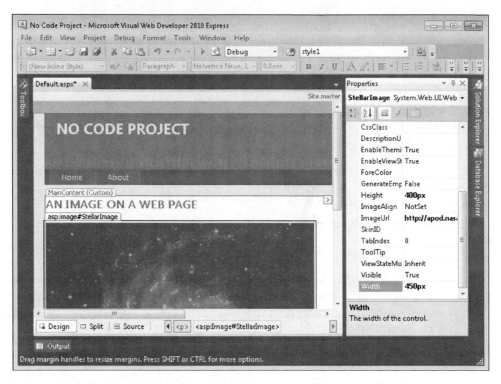

At this point, it's helpful to close the Properties window and click Source. You'll see the source code used to create Default.aspx—there isn't much, as shown in Figure 2-6.

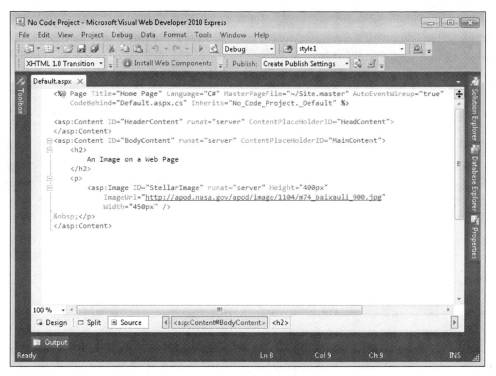

FIGURE 2-6 Even though the application output looks complex, it doesn't require much code.

The source code begins with some ASP script code. Any code you see that appears between the delimiters <% and %> is ASP script. This script defines programming-related features of Default.aspx, including the programming language (C#), the name of the master page file, and the name of the file used to hold the C# code for the page (the code behind file). Setting *AutoEventWireup* to *"true"* simply means that any events that the user generates on the page (such as clicking a button) will automatically get passed to the C# code that supports the page. The *Inherits* entry tells which class within the code behind file to use with this page. You'll discover more about ASP script later in this book; for now, all you really need to know is that entry defines some aspect of the page.

After the ASP script code, you see an *<asp:Content>* tag. This is also an ASP.NET entry that refers to a kind of control used on webpages. In this case, the control is described in the Master.Site file. The *ContentPlaceHolderID="HeadContent"* entry tells you that this is the header content from the Master.Site file. You can place header-specific information for Default.aspx here, such as *<meta>* tags that describe the page content. Meta-information is information about something else—in this case, *<meta>* tags describe the content of the page.

A second *<asp:Content>* tag appears next. This one uses the *ContentPlaceHolderID="MainContent"* entry from the Master.Site file. The content appears within this placeholder. There's a level 2 heading (the *<h2>* tag) that contains the content title you defined and a paragraph (*<p>* tag) that contains the *Image* control, which is actually an *<asp:Image>* tag. Each property you defined earlier appears as a separate attribute in the file. You'll see more examples of how this kind of content works as the book progresses.

Viewing the Master.Site File Code

The "Changing the Default.aspx Content" section earlier in this chapter explored the code used to define the default page. That code relies heavily on the master page code that resides in the Master. Site file. Reopen this file by clicking the Site.Master link in the Default.aspx file Design view. Click Source when the Master.Site opens. You'll see the code shown in Figure 2-7.

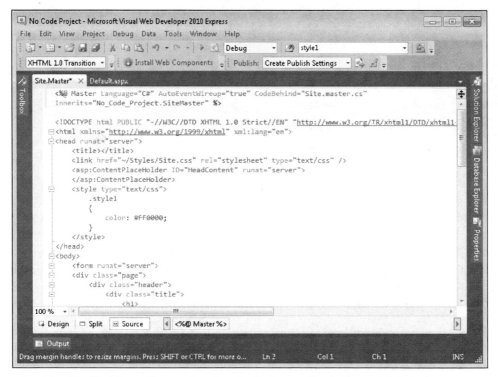

FIGURE 2-7 The Site.Master file contains a lot of code that applies to all pages that use it.

The first line is an ASP script similar to the one you saw in Default.aspx, and serves the same purpose. Of course, Master.Site doesn't contain any *MasterPageFile* entry—because it's the master page!

Immediately below the ASP script, you'll see some entries that you'd find in any webpage, such as the *<!DOCTYPE>*, *<html>*, and *<head>* tags. These are all standard for a webpage. However, look inside the *<head>* tag and you'll see some ASP.NET entries. The *<asp:ContentPlaceHolder ID="HeadContent" runat="server">* tag is a placeholder tag that defines the position of header content that will be added later by the various pages that rely on this master page. You'll remember seeing the *HeadContent* identifier from the Default.aspx file—this is where that identifier comes from. The *<head>* tag also contains a *<link>* tag that points to the Site.css file, which defines all the styles for the site.

The "Working with the Master Page" section already discussed the *<body>* tag content briefly. One of the tags you want to pay attention to in the *<body>* tag is the *<asp:ContentPlaceHolder ID="MainContent" runat="server"/>* tag. This tag describes the other content placement tag you saw in Default.aspx. Those *<asp:Content>* tags are where you'll add page-specific content in the pages that rely on this master page. The other tags in the *<body>* tag describe the layout and content features common to all pages. Don't worry about getting too deeply into this information now; just view it, start becoming familiar with the tag names, and start thinking about how the various pieces interact with each other.

Viewing the Site in a Browser

You've looked at the master page, Master.Site, and a content page that relies on the master page, Default.aspx. It's time to see the application in action. Press F5, choose Debug | Start Debugging, or click Start Debugging on the Standard toolbar. The IDE starts the ASP.NET Development Server. This server appears as an icon in the Notification Area. Right-click the icon and you'll see three options on the shortcut menu:

- **Open in Web Browser**   Opens a copy of the default page in the default browser. The server and the browser run independently. You can close the browser and reopen the page by choosing this option.

- **Stop**   Stops the ASP.NET Development Server and shuts it down. This isn't the same as shutting down a web server installed on your system. You can restart the server at any time by pressing F5 again.

- **Show Details**   Displays information about this particular ASP.NET Development server, as shown here (clicking the link opens a copy of the default page in your browser).

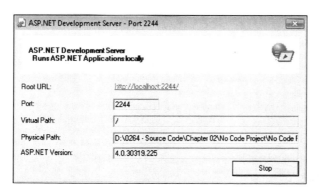

After the ASP.NET Development Server starts, it opens a copy of your default browser and displays the Default.aspx page, as shown in Figure 2-8.

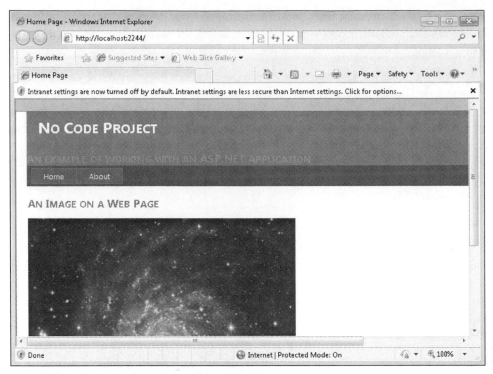

FIGURE 2-8 The example application displays a picture within a browser, and also provides access to other site features.

Notice that the URL contains a port setting (the *2244* after the *localhost* domain in the Address field). The IDE configures each of your applications to use a different, non-standard, port as a security feature. Using a non-standard port makes it less likely that someone will attempt to gain access to your system through the ASP.NET Development Server.

If you're using a default Internet Explorer setup, you'll likely see the warning note displayed at the top of the client window in this screenshot. Click the warning message and you'll see a shortcut menu. Choose the Enable Intranet Settings option. At this point, you'll see a message box warning you that intranet settings are less secure than Internet settings. Click Yes to enable the intranet settings so that you can easily debug your ASP.NET applications. The page will redisplay with all the features in a usable state.

Notice the two tabs on the page: Home and About. If you click About, you'll see the About.aspx page content. It doesn't look like the pages have changed, but the page content has. The Address field does change to show the change in pages, but the overall effect is that only the content changes, not the layout. ASP.NET provides a host of very cool effects that you'll try out as you go through the examples in the book. When you finish working with the example, right-click the ASP.NET Development Server icon in the Notification Area and choose Stop from the shortcut menu.

Creating the No Code Website

Visual Web Developer 2010 Express gives you a choice between creating a *project* and a *website*. There are situations when you will use a project instead of a website—each type has advantages and disadvantages. The purpose of this section is to explore the difference between projects and websites.

Defining a Website Location

A project always appears on your hard drive. You create the project as described in the "Starting the New Project" section of this chapter. Websites can begin on the hard drive, just like projects—but you can also create them on either a website, using the Hypertext Transfer Protocol (HTTP), or on a File Transfer Protocol (FTP) site, using FTP. The following steps help you get a new website started.

Create a New Website

1. Choose Start | All Programs | Microsoft Visual Studio 2010 Express | Microsoft Visual Web Developer 2010 Express. You'll see the IDE start up.

2. Click New Web Site. You'll see the New Web Site dialog box shown here.

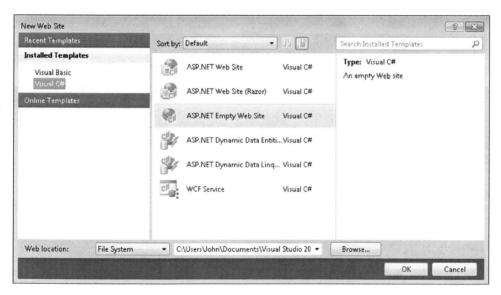

One of the first things you should notice is that fewer projects are available when working with a new website. For example, no Silverlight projects are available when using this option, nor will you find an entry for using Azure. Even though a website offers more location flexibility, you lose the option of using certain types of templates. Of course, if you need the location flexibility, using a new website project will still likely be your best choice.

3. Select a project type. For this example application, select the ASP.NET Web Site template.

4. Select an option from the Web Location drop-down list. Use File System for this example, as shown in the preceding figure.

5. Provide a location (path) and name in the location field. When working with a website, you don't have the option of using a solution to group projects together. This example uses a File System connection in the default directory, with No Code Site as its location. You need to provide one of three kinds of information in this field, depending on the option you selected from the Web Location drop-down list:

- **File System** Provide a path and website name. The default path is C:\Users\<User Name>\ Documents\Visual Studio 2010\WebSites\, but you can use any location on a local hard drive or on a network drive that you can access. As with projects, the simple act of creating a project stores files on disk, which is why you must choose a storage location in the New Project dialog box. Click Browse to display a Choose Location dialog box like the one shown here where you can choose a file system location anywhere your system can access.

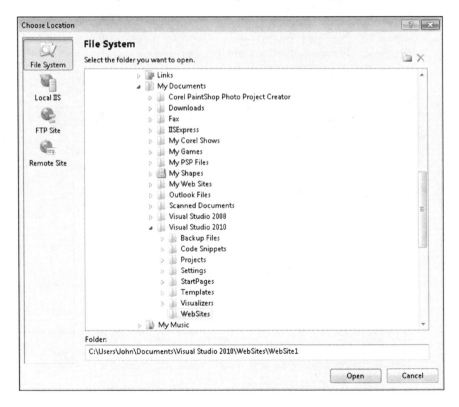

- **HTTP** Supply a fully qualified URL for the website you want to use. The URL must include the *http://* protocol. Click Browse to display the Choose Location dialog box. In this case, you can choose between Local IIS and Remote Site options. In both cases, you end up with a fully qualified URL pointing to the website. When working with a Local IIS site, you can also select the Use Secure Sockets Layer option to create a secure connection to the site (when the site supports the SSL).

- **FTP** Supply a fully qualified URL and accompanying information to access an FTP site. Unless your site allows anonymous access, you must click Browse in this case to display the FTP information. This information includes the server domain, port number, initial server directory, whether to use passive mode, and the login information (name and password).

6. Click OK. The IDE creates a new website for you. The basic site features look precisely the same as the project features described earlier.

Adding a New Page

In the project example earlier in the chapter you modified Default.aspx. You could perform precisely the same changes in this site, but you can make other changes. In this case, you'll add another page to the site using the following steps.

1. Click the Solution Explorer tab and then click Auto Hide to keep the window open. You'll see a list of folders and files contained within the site, as shown here.

2. Right-click the topmost (site) entry in the list and choose Add New Item from the shortcut menu. You'll see the Add New Item dialog box, as shown on the next page.

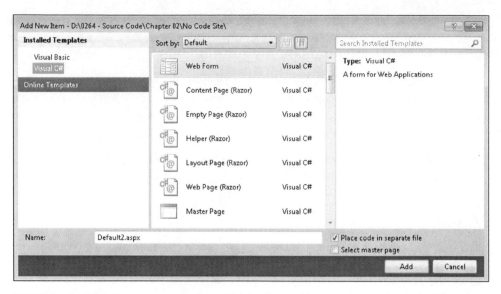

3. Highlight the Web Form entry, as shown in the figure. (As you can see from the figure, you can add quite a few items using this dialog box, some of which are discussed later in this book.)

4. Type **Image.aspx** in the Name field. This is the name of the file as it appears in Solution Explorer later.

5. Select the Select Master Page option. This selection will create a page that uses the existing master page, rather than a stand-alone page that uses its own layout and formatting.

> **Note** If you don't select this option, the resulting page won't look the same as the others on the site.

6. Click Add. You'll see the Select a Master Page dialog box shown here.

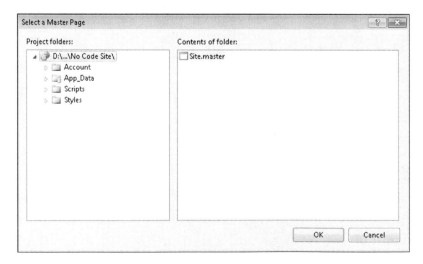

Because only one master page is associated with this site, you see only one entry in the list in the right pane. However, your site can use as many master pages as needed to fully define the characteristics of your site. If your site places the master pages in a special folder, you can navigate to that folder using the entries in the left pane.

7. Highlight Site.master and click OK. You'll see a new page added to your project as shown in Solution Explorer. The page contains only the ASP script and the two placeholder entries for the header and main content, as shown here.

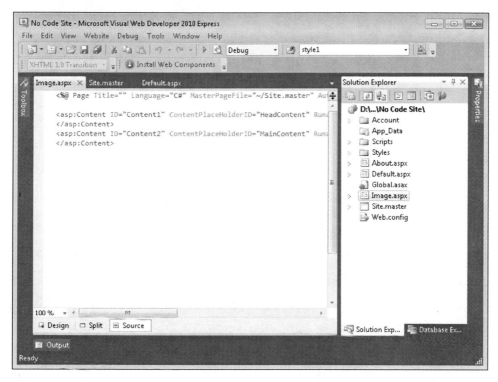

8. Click Auto Hide in Solution Explorer to hide the window. Display the Toolbox by clicking its tab and then clicking Auto Hide.

9. Drag an Image control onto the Source window so that it appears like the one shown here.

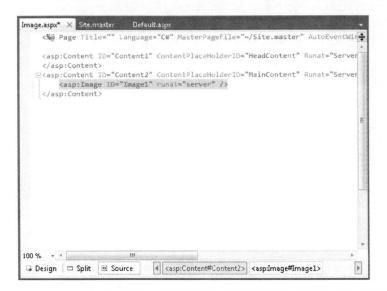

Note When working with a web project or site, you can drag and drop controls into the Design or Source windows with equal ease. You can choose whichever solution works best for you.

10. Close the Toolbox by clicking Auto Hide.

11. Display the Properties window by clicking its tab and then clicking Auto Hide.

12. Type **StellarImage** in the *(ID)* property. Notice that you can see each of the changes you're making in the Source window. This is one advantage of using the Source window over using the Design window. Of course, you can't see what's actually happening to the control—all you can see is the code that your change is generating.

13. Type **400** in the *Height* property. This example won't set the *Width* property; the page automatically maintains the aspect ratio when you set just one of the *Width* or *Height* property values.

14. Type **http://apod.nasa.gov/apod/image/1104/m74_baixauli_900.jpg** in the *ImageUrl* property. Because you're working in the Source window, you won't see the image, but the image will appear if you click Design.

15. Close the Properties window by clicking Auto Hide.

Adding the Page to the Site Menu

You have a shiny new page—but no way to access it. At this point, you need to add this new page to the master page so that you can select it in the browser.

1. Click Design on the new Image.aspx page. Click the Site.Master link in the upper-right corner. The Site.master file opens.

2. Select the square that contains the words Home and About. Notice the odd arrow that appears when you do this. Many controls provide a similar arrow. When you click the arrow, you see a Menu Tasks dialog box like the one shown here.

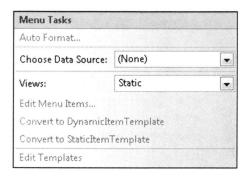

3. Click Edit Menu Items. You'll see the Menu Item Editor window shown here.

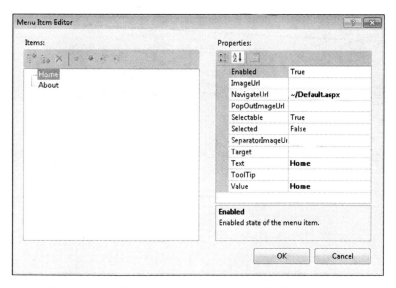

This editor lets you change the characteristics of this control without writing any code. As with many other tasks, the IDE writes the code for you in the background based on the input you provide. Writing code this way is less error prone and considerably easier, so always look for these handy control-specific editors whenever possible.

4. Click Add A Root Item. You'll see a new root item added to the list in the left pane.

5. Select the *NavigateUrl* property and then click the ellipsis button (...) that appears on the right side. You'll see the Select URL window shown here.

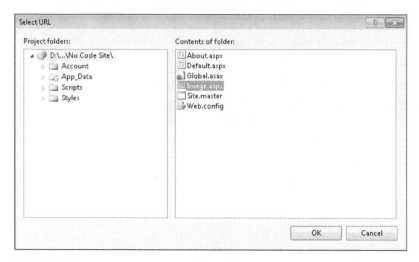

6. Highlight the Image.aspx entry in the right pane and click OK. The IDE automatically adds the correct entry to the *NavigateUrl* property for you.

7. Type **Image** in the *Text* property. Notice that the IDE automatically adds *Image* to the *Value* property for you. Click OK. The control now has a new entry, *Image*, as shown here.

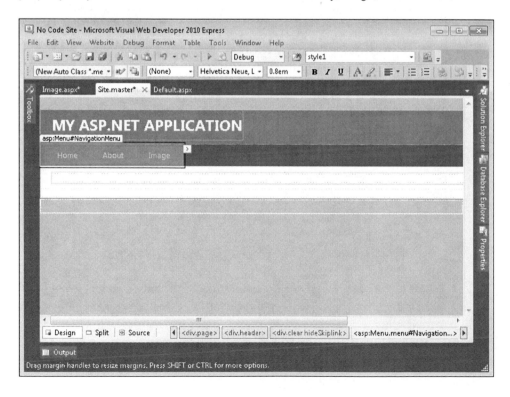

You're ready to begin using the new page. When the application runs, you'll be able to select the new page you've added simply by clicking its tab.

Trying the Site in a Browser

It's time to try out the changes you've made to the site you created. Begin by choosing File | Save All, pressing Ctrl+Shift+S, or clicking Save All on the Standard toolbar to save your application changes. Now press F5, choose Debug | Start Debugging, or click Start Debugging on the Standard toolbar to see the website in your browser. At this point you see the message shown in Figure 2-9.

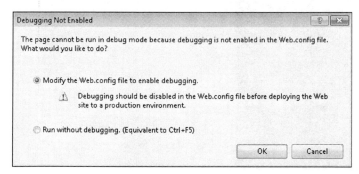

FIGURE 2-9 You must enable debugging in order to see what your website is doing.

A project is configured for a developer to work through issues from the outset and then create a production environment later. On the other hand, a site starts as a production environment, so you must specifically enable debugging. Select the Run Without Debugging option and click OK. The site opens in your browser. Click the Image tab and you'll see the new page you added, as shown in Figure 2-10.

Warning If you allow the IDE to modify the Web.config file, you'll need to compile the site code again before you can run it. Otherwise, the change won't appear when you run the site and you'll wonder why the change didn't take effect.

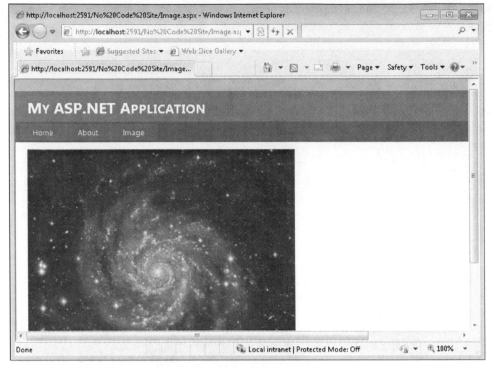

FIGURE 2-10 The new page contains an interesting image.

Feel free to explore the application. When you're finished, right-click the ASP.NET Development Server icon in the Notification Area and choose Stop. The server will stop, and you'll be able to make additional changes to your project.

Get Going with C#

This chapter introduced you to Visual Web Developer 2010 Express. As with the Visual C# 2010 Express introduction in Chapter 1, this chapter has just barely scratched the surface of creating an application, much less what you can do once you start adding code. However, it's amazing to see what the IDE can do for you without any coding on your part. Visual Web Developer helps you start the application, design the user interface, and even writes some of the code for you in the background. As you saw in this chapter, it's possible to create a small but usable application without writing any code at all. You can depend on the IDE to perform quite a lot of work for you.

You can follow many tracks just by using the information in this chapter. For example, you might want to try to create a Silverlight application using the same techniques you used in this chapter to create a project. Check out the other kinds of projects you can create as well. The right pane of the New Project dialog box describes these other project types when you select them.

Make sure you spend some time examining the Toolbox controls as well. Try playing with some of these controls in a test application to see what they do. Remember that playing with the programming environment is an extremely good way to learn. Don't be afraid to experiment. Try listing a few of the controls that you think you might be able to configure and use to create another application without writing any code. All this experimentation will build your knowledge of C# and Visual Web Developer.

> **Note** Any project you create and modify without saving is temporary. When you try to close the project, the IDE will ask if you want to save the project. Click No and the project is placed in the Recycle Bin. If you later decide that you really did want to save that project, you can drag it from the Recycle Bin to a location on your hard drive.

The next chapter introduces you to some coding techniques. However, this book takes a different approach from many other texts in that it leaps right into something truly useful, Language Integrated Query (LINQ). Using LINQ is an interesting experience because it doesn't treat programming as an obscure, abstract task that only those with vast knowledge can perform. Instead, it treats applications as a source for answering questions. That's right, the basis of LINQ is to provide you with a way to ask questions about data and obtain a result. You'll find that Chapter 3, "Basic Data Manipulation Techniques," is a real eye opener when it comes to programming.

Chapter 3

Basic Data Manipulation Techniques

After completing this chapter, you'll be able to:

- Describe how Language Integrated Query (LINQ) makes application development easy

- Create an application that uses LINQ to work with information in a List control

- Write code that relies on LINQ

- Test an application that uses LINQ

- Trace through the application to see how it works

- Extend the first application to provide additional functionality

THE PURPOSE OF MOST APPLICATIONS is to manipulate some sort of data. Manipulation can take many forms—everything from displaying the data in a certain form to changing it. Whenever you look at a user interface, it displays some type of data. Even a simple message box (one of those tiny dialog boxes that Windows seems to display for any and every reason) conveys data by displaying a particular message on screen. After you read the message, you click OK to dismiss the message box, which essentially destroys the data it contained. On the other hand, when you fill out a form, you select or enter data for each form field. When you click OK, the application stores your responses somewhere else, where the application or a person will likely evaluate and act upon it. Webpages contain data as well, and convey information in a number of ways. In short, every application you've ever used manipulates data in some fashion. So it's not too surprising to find that the first program you write in this book will manipulate data.

At one time, developers had to concern themselves with all kinds of arcane details about manipulating data. Today, technologies such as Language Integrated Query (LINQ) make it possible to concentrate more on the data and how you want to work with it, than on the actual machine operations used to perform a task. When working with these new technologies, you tell the language what you want it to accomplish and the language worries about how to do it. Things aren't quite that easy, but they're very close; in this chapter you'll find that that's precisely how you create an application.

Because the language itself does so much work for you, it's easy to forget that the task must still be performed. Consequently, this chapter helps you understand what's going on in the background, just as you discovered in Chapters 1 and 2 when you looked at how the IDE automatically writes code for your designs based on what you do in the designer. Fortunately, it's very easy to see what LINQ is doing in the background. Visual Studio comes with a special feature called the *debugger* that makes it easy to see what LINQ (or any other part of your application, for that matter) is doing.

Understanding LINQ

LINQ has an unfortunate name. It sounds complicated, when it really isn't. When you think about LINQ, think about asking the application a question, because that's what you're doing. You're telling the application that you want to obtain certain information and you're leaving it up to the application code to worry about how to perform the task.

To obtain information, you need a data source, which can be anything from a list box on a form to a special storage location you create in your application to a database found on some other computer. All you need is a data source and a question to use LINQ. This chapter uses a special control, the *ListBox*, that provides a data source. However, you can use a host of different data sources; you'll see a number of suitable data sources in this book.

Before you can use LINQ, you need to know a few things about it. First, LINQ is a *declarative* language—you declare what you want the language to do and it determines how to do it. There are many other declarative languages—you may have heard of one called Structured Query Language (SQL), which developers use to query databases such as SQL Server—Microsoft's database program. Even if you haven't heard of any other declarative languages, you'll find that they're easy to use.

For more information, see "declarative language" in the accompanying Start Here! Fundamentals of Microsoft .NET Programming *book. To obtain your copy, see the section titled "Free Companion eBook" in the introduction to this book, or turn to the instruction page at the back of the book.*

Second, you need to know a few special words. Consider them the "magic words" that LINQ requires you to say to get it to perform useful work. These words aren't anything strange, like "abracadabra"—they're words you commonly use, so they're easy to remember.

- *from*   You need to tell LINQ where to obtain the information that it provides as output. So you say, "Get it from here." Technically, the *from* keyword points to a variable—a kind of temporary storage container.

- *in*   This keyword tells LINQ that the data source is in some sort of container. A data source can be any number of things, such as a database. To make things simple, this chapter relies on a special kind of control to act as a data source, but don't worry about that now.

- **select**   It's important to tell LINQ to obtain something from the query. The *select* keyword tells LINQ what to choose (or select) based on the content of the temporary storage container. If you like, you can choose to use all the content of the temporary storage container.

You need one additional keyword to complete the picture. This one is a little odd looking, but you'll remember it quite easily because it's only three letters, *var*. The *var* keyword tells the application to create a storage container (a *variable*) to hold the results of the LINQ query. You don't care what kind of container LINQ creates, as long as it's the kind of container that the query needs. In most cases, LINQ can determine the right sort of container and create it for you, so you don't have to worry about anything.

At this point, you can put all the various pieces together to form a sort of question (a query), which you will ask LINQ to solve. This code won't actually work, but it demonstrates generally how the real LINQ queries that you create later will look.

```
var Result = from OutputContainer
             in DataSource
             select OutputContainer
```

In this case, *Result* will eventually contain everything found in *DataSource*. If *DataSource* contains One, Two, Three as three separate items, *Result* will eventually contain all of three of those items because the query says, "Store each item in *DataSource* to *OutputContainer*, then select *OutputContainer* and put it in *Result*." Don't worry too much about how this all works right now—you'll see it in greater detail later. All you need to know now is that you're asking LINQ a question based on a source of information and LINQ provides an answer.

Creating the List Project

The best way to understand how to use LINQ is to create another program. In most cases, you start a program by creating a project, adding some controls, and then configuring the controls. In fact, this part of the process is precisely the same as the steps you followed in Chapter 1, "Getting to Know C#," and Chapter 2, "Developing a Web Project." Both chapters led you through a series of steps that created a project, added controls to it, and then performed some configuration. You'll get to experiment with some new controls in this project, including:

- **Label**   Displays some text that describes what to do with other controls. Most applications contain at least one Label. This example uses one Label to identify the *ListBox* and another to identify the *TextBox*. Button controls contain text inside them, so they don't need Label controls for identification purposes.

- **Button**   A pushbutton that a user can click to make things happen. The most common Button controls are OK and Cancel—you see them used all over the place in Windows. In this case, you will use a click-on-one Button control to tell LINQ to answer a question and another to end the application.

- **TextBox**   Used to hold text of any sort. Whenever you fill out a form, the blanks used to hold the text you type are all *TextBox* controls. A *TextBox* control can also show the results of some task, which is how this application uses the *TextBox*. Later examples will show other uses for *TextBox* controls because *TextBox* controls are really quite flexible.

Starting the List Project

The steps to create the List project are similar to those for the examples in Chapter 1. You begin by starting up your copy of Visual C# 2010 Express. These steps will help you configure the project.

1.   Click New Project. You'll see the New Project dialog box shown here.

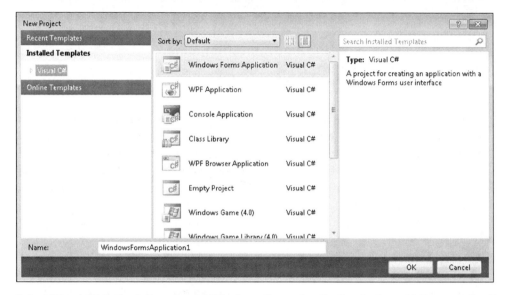

2.   Select Visual C# in the left pane and Windows Forms Application in the middle pane. You'll see a description of the template in the right pane. Do not click OK until you provide a name for the new project.

3.   Type **ListProject1** in the Name field and click OK. The IDE creates a new project for you, consisting of a single form.

Adding the Controls

The Windows Forms example in Chapter 1 contained a single control. This example includes several controls. An interesting aspect of applications is that they have a feature called *tab order*. When you start an application, the control with the lowest tab order is always selected first. When you press Tab, the focus (the control selected within the application) always shifts to the control with the next highest tab order. Well-designed applications always use a logical tab order—normally the tab order starts from the left and moves toward the right and starts from the top and moves toward the bottom—much like the text you're reading on this page. With this in mind, click the Toolbox tab and click Auto Hide to keep it displayed. Double-click the controls you need to add them to the project in the following order:

- *Button*
- *Button*

- *Label*
- *TextBox*

- *Label*
- *TextBox*

> **Note** When you double-click a control to add it to a form, the IDE places them right on top of each other in a seemingly random order. This is completely normal. You'll configure the controls later, so the ordering and position aren't important now. All you're looking for is a collection of controls on the display. The chapter will always show how the controls are supposed to appear after you configure them so that you can make sure your controls match the controls used for the example.

After you add the controls you need, close the Toolbox by clicking Auto Hide. Then you look at your form. What a mess! The controls are all over the place and some are overlapping others. At this point, you want arrange the controls so that they look like other applications you may have used in the past. To move a control, click it and drag it to a new location on-screen.

To resize a control, click the control to select it. You'll see resizing handles, as in Figure 3-1.

FIGURE 3-1 Use the resizing handles to change the size of a control.

Each one of the little squares around the outside edge of the *ListBox* control is a resizing handle. Click a resizing handle and drag it to change the control size. You can tell when you've selected a resizing handle because the mouse cursor changes to a double-ended arrow that indicates the direction the resizing handle will change the control size.

The IDE also makes it easy to give your application a professional appearance. Whenever a control is close to another control or the edge of the form, you will see little lines called *guides* appear. These lines help you place the control optimally on the form. Figure 3-2 shows an example of how one of the Label controls looks with the positioning aids displayed.

FIGURE 3-2 Rely on the guides to provide optimal placement of controls on the form.

The positioning aids appear as two light lines—one pointing up from the Label toward the top of the form and another pointing left from the Label to the left side of the form. When you see these positioning aids, you know that your control is in an optimal position on the form. You can't completely position every control on the form just yet because you have to perform some configuration first. However, you can complete most of the positioning. Work with your form until it looks like the one shown in Figure 3-3.

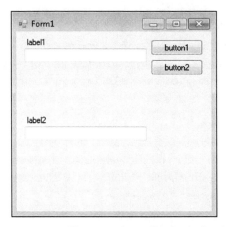

FIGURE 3-3 The example application is simple, but relies on a typical control layout.

Configuring the Controls

The examples in Chapters 1 and 2 showed you how to configure controls. Just as a reminder, you select the control you want to work with in the designer, click the Properties tab to open it, and then click Auto Hide to keep the Properties window displayed. This example has four controls for you to configure. Table 3-1 shows how to configure each of the controls.

TABLE 3-1 *ListBox1* **Control Configuration**

Control Name	Property Name	Value
button1	(Name)	btnTest
	Text	&Test
button2	(Name)	btnCancel
	Text	C&ancel
label1	Text	&Selections
txtBox1	(Name)	txtSelections
	Multiline	True
	Size.Height	95
label2	Text	&Output
txtBox1	(Name)	txtOutput

Control Name	Property Name	Value
	Multiline	True
	ReadOnly	True
	Size.Height	95

The *txtSelections* and *txtOutput* controls have an interesting new configuration requirement. Click the *Size* property and you'll notice that an arrow appears on the left side of it. Click the arrow and you'll see two sub-properties: *Width* and *Height*. You need to set the *Height* sub-property of the *Size* property to 95 for this example.

The *txtSelections* control also has a special configuration requirement. Click the *Lines* property. Notice that this property has a value of *String[ ] Array*, which simply means that it has a list of items associated with it. To set this property, you click the ellipsis (. . .) on the right side to display the String Collection Editor. Place one item on each line of the String Collection Editor, as shown in Figure 3-4.

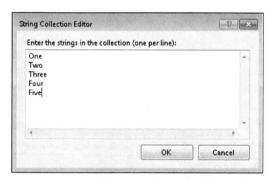

FIGURE 3-4 Use the String Collection Editor to create a list of acceptable selections.

Click OK when you're finished entering the five items. At this point the controls are all configured for use and your form should look like the one shown in Figure 3-5.

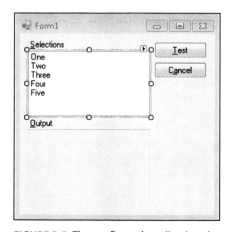

FIGURE 3-5 The configured application shows the controls as they will appear to the user.

Of course, you'll also want to provide some different text for the form's title bar so that it reflects the actual purpose of the application. Select the form. Choose the *Text* property in the Properties window, and type **List Project Version One**.

Using the Code Editor

It's finally time to add some code to your example. Don't worry—this example won't require that you become a computer science major. In fact, you may be surprised at just how much you can do with very little code using C#.

One of the essentials that you must know about is events. An event is something that happens to the control. For example, when a user clicks a *Button*, a *Click* event occurs. You can add code that the application executes every time the event occurs. For example, you can tell your application to display a message box every time the user clicks a particular *Button*. The code you assign to the Button's Click event is called an event handler because it does something about the event. The following sections describe several techniques for adding code to event handlers associated with controls in this example.

Using the Double-Click Method

Every control has a default event associated with it. When working with a *Button*, it's the *Click* event. The default event is the event that the user is likely to want handled most often. Visual Studio makes it easy to create an event handler for the default event for a control. All you need to do is double-click the control. Try it now with *btnCancel* and you'll see the Code window appear, as shown in Figure 3-6.

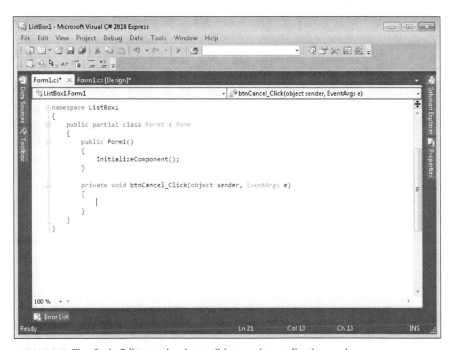

FIGURE 3-6 The Code Editor makes it possible to write application code.

Notice that Visual Studio automatically places the cursor in a position to start typing. The IDE also automatically generates the event handler code for you and gives the event handler a name. The event handler is named *btnCancel_Click()* in this case because it handles the *Click* event of the *Button* named *btnCancel*. The event handler contains some other code that you don't need to worry about now. This other code is *arguments*—data provided to the event handler. You'll rarely use it for applications of this sort.

It's time to add code to the *btnCancel_Click()* event handler. The purpose of the *btnCancel* button is to end the application. It cancels the task that you're doing so that you can do something else. There are many ways to end the application, but here you'll use the most common method for this application. Simply type **Close()**; at the cursor position. That's it: you tell the form to close, which ends the program when you're working with the last form in the application (and this is the one and only form).

You should have noticed something special when you typed the C that begins *Close()*. The editor automatically displays a list of items that begin with the letter C for you so that you don't have to remember difficult keywords, as shown in Figure 3-7.

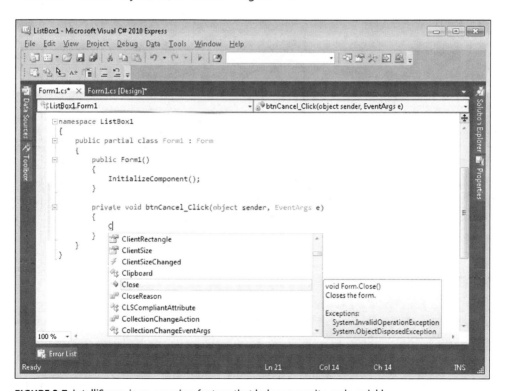

FIGURE 3-7 IntelliSense is an amazing feature that helps you write code quickly.

This feature is called IntelliSense and it's always available to you. The box that appears next to the list is also important. It tells you about the currently selected entry in the list. In this case, you discover that the *Close()* method closes the form. The Code window has a wealth of such features that you'll discover as the book progresses. For now, all you need to know is that the *btnCancel_Click()* event handler is completed.

Choosing an Event Directly

What happens if you don't want to use a default event, or you simply aren't sure what the default event is? In this case, select the control in the Designer, click the Properties tab to display the Properties window, and click Auto Hide. Click Events, and you will see a list of events associated with that control. In fact, try it right now with *btnTest*. Figure 3-8 shows the events associated with *btnTest*.

FIGURE 3-8 The Events tab contains a list of events associated with the selected object.

The Properties window even provides a brief description of each event. In this case, it tells you that the *Click* event occurs whenever a user clicks the *Button*. To create a new event handler for this event, double-click its entry. As before, you'll see the Code window appear with the cursor in the right position to begin typing.

Using the Right-Click Method

One of the things you should do as you learn to work with Visual Studio is right-click objects, which then typically display a shortcut menu. Visual Studio's shortcut menus contain all sorts of helpful items and actions. For example, if you right-click a form in Solution Explorer, you'll see menu options that let you view the Designer (where you can add controls and configure them) or the Code editor (where you can add code to event handlers), as shown in Figure 3-9.

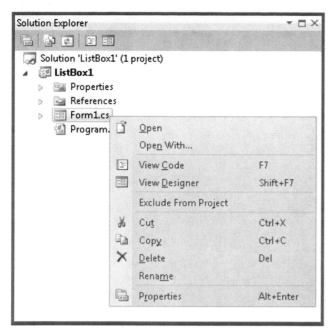

FIGURE 3-9 Most objects in the IDE have context menus associated with them.

You'll find that many objects have an entry for viewing code. For example, right-click any of the controls in the Designer and you'll find a View Code option. Choose this option and you'll see the Code Editor as you'd expect.

Understanding the Code Editor Features

You've already worked with an Code Editor feature named IntelliSense when you wrote the code for the *btnCancel_Click()* event handler. The Code Editor, like every other part of Visual Studio, has a number of other interesting features that you need to know about. This section doesn't discuss them all, but you'll learn about some features that will come in handy now.

One of the more important features is the ability use a mouseover action to quickly find information about any method you work with in your code. The resulting tooltip window shows the most common usage of the method, a description of the method, and the exceptions associated with the method. An *exception* is an event that occurs when something goes wrong. For instance, suppose you try to divide a number by zero. Because that operation is undefined, the application generates an exception that tells you that the code has attempted to do something wrong. Don't worry too much about exceptions for now—you'll discover them in later examples in the book (starting with Chapter 5).

Many developers find that keeping their hands on the keyboard is far more productive than using the mouse to select items in the editor. For example, you can select some text by pressing Shift+Right Arrow, press Ctrl+C to copy it to the clipboard, move to a new location by pressing the arrow keys, and then paste it in a new location by pressing Ctrl+V. The Visual Studio menus tell you about many of these shortcuts. You can also find a list of Visual Studio 2010 shortcuts at *http://msdn.microsoft. com/library/da5kh0wa.aspx*.

Another interesting feature is the ability to right-click everything and find a menu that contains interesting options. For example, right-click the *Close()* method and you'll see a menu with the entries shown in Figure 3-10.

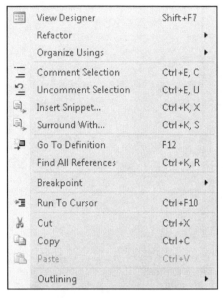

FIGURE 3-10 Even the code provides a context menu containing helpful entries.

Some of these entries will see use in other chapters, but you can use some of them immediately. For example, select View Designer to see the Designer associated with the code you're looking at.

If you think a particular piece of code is causing problems, you can choose Comment Selection. The code remains, but the IDE turns it into a comment so the compiler ignores it and you can see how the application works without that code. Try it now. You'll see that the IDE adds two slashes in front of *Close()*; to turn it into a comment. Now right-click *Close()* again and choose Uncomment Selection. The IDE removes the two slashes. You can use this feature with a whole block of code by highlighting the block, right-clicking, and choosing Comment Selection or Uncomment Selection from the menu.

For more information, see "comment" in the accompanying Start Here! Fundamentals of Microsoft .NET Programming *book. To obtain your copy, see the section titled "Free Companion eBook" in the introduction to this book, or turn to the instruction page at the back of the book.*

> **Tip** The shortcut menu also contains options for Cut, Copy, and Paste. You use these options just like you would in any editor. Many developers will copy working code and paste it into another location to save time. Even if the code isn't precisely what the developer needs, making small modifications to working code is far easier than starting from scratch.

Writing Some Simple Code

The *btnCancel_Click()* event handler already has some code in it. However, you haven't written any code for the *btnTest_Click()* event handler. In this case, the example does something simple. It examines each of the entries in *txtSelections*, changes them to uppercase, and then puts the result in *txtOutput*. At one time, a developer would have written all kinds of hard-to-decipher code to perform this task, but Listing 3-1 shows that you can use a simple LINQ statement and one additional line of code to perform this task in C#.

LISTING 3-1 Using LINQ to manipulate data

```csharp
private void btnTest_Click(object sender, EventArgs e)
{
    // Obtain the data from the Lines property of txtSelections
    // and place it in Output using TheEntry as a temporary variable.
    var Output = from TheEntry
                 in txtSelections.Lines
                 select TheEntry.ToUpper();

    // Place the contents of Output into the Lines property of
    // txtOutput.
    txtOutput.Lines = Output.ToArray<String>();
}
```

As with the *btnCancel_Click()* event handler, the example begins with the code that the IDE automatically generates for you. Don't worry about it for right now—you'll see how it works later in the book.

The *var Output* code simply creates a variable (essentially a storage container) to hold the output from the LINQ query. As you'll remember from the discussion in the "Understanding LINQ" section, *txtSelections.Lines* is the data source. This is the same property you configured earlier with One, Two, Three, Four, and Five on separate lines—each of those elements is a separate data item that's processed in the LINQ query. Each entry in *txtSelections.Lines*, such as the value One, is placed in a temporary variable named *TheEntry*. The code uses the *TheEntry.ToUpper()* method to change the content in *TheEntry* to uppercase.

When you create a LINQ query, the results appear immediately in the variable you create, but then nothing happens to that content. Output contains the preliminary results of the query and then the example uses them later in a specific way. In this case, the example outputs the information to *txtOutput.Lines* property, which is a list of items just like the *txtSelections.Lines* property. You could just as easily configure the *txtOutput.Lines* property using the String Collection Editor, but this approach lets you do something with the property when the application runs.

Remember that the *Lines* property has a value of *String[] Array*. So, you must create information of this sort to store it in the *Lines* property. You already know that Output contains the result of the LINQ query. A call to the *Output.ToArray<String>()* simply creates a *String[]* Array to put in the Lines property from the content in Output. In short, Visual Studio tells you what it wants—you need to find a way to provide it.

Testing the List Application

You've put a lot of work into this example so far and don't really have much to show for it. That's about to change. Click Start Debugging on the Standard toolbar, press F5, or choose Debug | Start Debugging (F5). The application will start and you'll see a dialog box like the one shown in Figure 3-11.

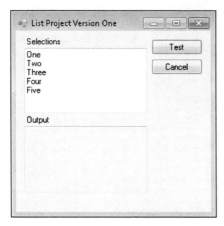

FIGURE 3-11 The example application starts with a blank Output field.

As you can see, your program looks just like any other little program you might have used in the past—except you know how this one was put together. Click Test. The Selections list stays the same, but notice that the Output list changes and that the output is in uppercase as expected, as shown in Figure 3-12.

FIGURE 3-12 Clicking Test displays the results of the code you wrote in the Output field.

You can even type new entries into Selections and see them in the output. For example, place your cursor at the last line in Selections and type **Hello**. Now click Test again and you'll see that Hello is processed and placed in Output, as shown in Figure 3-13.

FIGURE 3-13 You can add entries to the Selections field, click Test, and see the entry added to Output.

At this point, you should try the other button. Click Cancel. Notice that the program ends, just as you'd expect it to. So your first application does something interesting with very little code.

Tracing the List Application with the Debugger

When you started your application in "Testing the List Application," you probably clicked Start Debugging. Of course, it would be nice to know precisely what debugging is and why it's important to your application. Debugging is a way to look at your application in detail to see how it works. The term comes from the idea of removing bugs from your code. A bug is some sort of error that keeps the code from working right. However, you don't need to limit yourself to looking for bugs. Think of the debugger as a tool that lets you take a detailed look at your code. That's what the professionals do. Often, a professional will use the debugger simply to look at how someone else has created code and discover how it works. In fact, that's how you use the debugger in the following sections.

Discovering Application Functionality Through Tracing

When you use a debugger to explore an application, you're *tracing* it. Tracing is an extremely useful technique for learning how applications work and professional developers frequently employ the technique. It's one thing to read how something works—seeing it work is quite different. Suddenly, the light bulb goes on and you discover that you know something about the application and have learned something new about programming as well.

Note To trace through an application, you need to have its source code. You then build the application to create an executable. The source code is like a blueprint and the build process uses the blueprint to create the executable. That's what happens when you start the debugger—it automatically builds the application for you. It's also possible to perform this process separately by choosing Debug | Build Solution or pressing F6.

Creating a Breakpoint

In the "Testing the List Application" section of this chapter, you ran the example application. Even though you couldn't see it, the debugger also ran when you started the application. To see what the debugger can show you, you must place a stop sign in the application called a *breakpoint*. A breakpoint tells the debugger to stop at a certain point so that you can see what's going on beneath the hood.

There are many ways to create breakpoints, but to trace an application you only need one of them. The easiest way to create such a breakpoint is to click in the left margin area next to the line of code you want to review. Try it now with the LINQ query in the example application. Click in the left margin area (it appears light gray in the Code Editor) and you'll see a red circle appear, as shown in Figure 3-14.

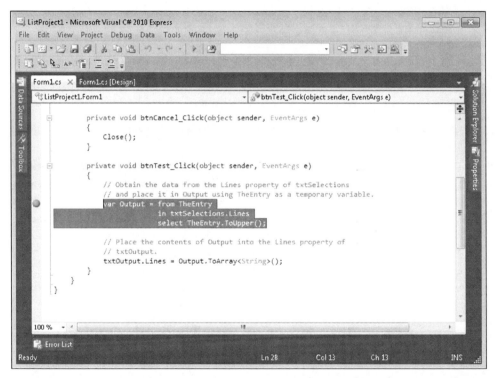

FIGURE 3-14 Breakpoints are highlighted in red so that you can't confuse them with other sorts of entries.

Notice that the breakpoint also highlights the affected code. In this case, it highlights the entire LINQ query. When debugger stops here, it treats the entire LINQ query as a single entry.

Another way to create a breakpoint is to right-click the line where you want to stop, and choose Breakpoint | Insert Breakpoint from the context menu. As before, you'll see a red circle appear in the left margin area. Try this technique with the next line of code. Again, the IDE highlights the entire line in red.

Yet another way to create a breakpoint is by placing your cursor on the line where you want to stop, then pressing F9 or choosing Debug | Toggle Breakpoint. In sum, breakpoints are important enough that Microsoft wants to be sure you can place them wherever you want.

Removing a breakpoint when you are done using it is just as easy as creating one. You can use any of these methods:

- Click in the left margin area.

- Right-click the line and choose Breakpoint | Delete Breakpoint.

- Place the cursor on the line of interest and press F9 or choose Debug | Toggle Breakpoint.

Viewing Application Data

You now have two breakpoints in place for the sample application. Normally, you'd use just one for such a small application, but using two is fine also. Start the application by clicking Start Debugging on the Standard toolbar, pressing F5, or choosing Debug | Start Debugging. The application will start and you'll see the dialog box, just as you did before. Now click Test and something new will happen—the application will stop and you'll see the debugger, as shown in Figure 3-15.

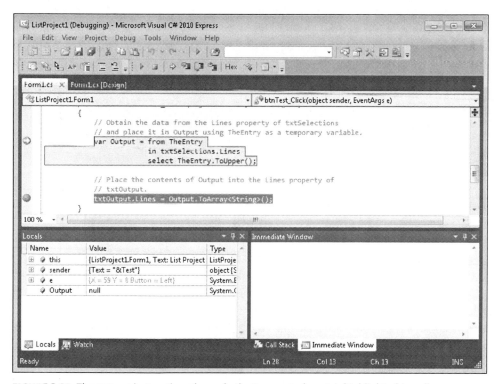

FIGURE 3-15 The current instruction, the code that's executed next, is highlighted in yellow.

The application has stopped at the first breakpoint, much as you'd expect. The LINQ query is now highlighted in yellow and you see a little yellow arrow in the red circle in the left margin. This is the instruction pointer—it tells you which instruction the debugger will execute next. So the query hasn't happened yet.

At this point, most developers look at the application data because the overriding purpose of applications is to manipulate data in some way. Variables act as the storage containers for data, so you normally look at the data by working with the variables. Visual Studio offers more than a few ways to examine your application's data. Notice the Locals window in the lower-left corner of the figure. This window contains a list of the variables in use by the *btnTest_Click()* event handler. *Output* is the last variable in the list. Notice that the current value of *Output* is *null*, which means it contains nothing.

> **Note** You've been introduced to a number of different Visual Studio windows at this point, so it's worth mentioning that you can reach *any* of these windows through the View menu. Select View | Other Windows for a full list. This feature is particularly useful when you have closed a window for space or convenience reasons and then want to reopen it.

You can't see *txtSelections* or *txtOutput* in the Locals window because they aren't local to the *btnTest_Click()* event handler. These two controls appear outside of the event handler. In the lower-right corner you see the Immediate window. You can type questions there and get a response from the debugger. For example, try typing **? txtSelections.Lines**. Notice that IntelliSense is also available in the Immediate window. As soon as you type *txtSelections*, IntelliSense displays a list of items you can choose from. Press Enter, and you'll see what *txtSelections.Lines* contains, as shown in Figure 3-16.

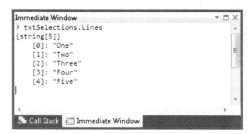

```
Immediate Window                          ▼ □ ×
? txtSelections.Lines
{string[5]}
    [0]: "One"
    [1]: "Two"
    [2]: "Three"
    [3]: "Four"
    [4]: "Five"
|

◄                                            ►
📚 Call Stack  🔲 Immediate Window
```

FIGURE 3-16 The Immediate window lets you ask questions about your code.

The output tells you that *txtSelections.Lines* contains a list of five items as a *String[]* array. You can also see each of the values and the position each value has in the list. You can use this technique with local variables too. Type **? Output** and press Enter. The Immediate window will also report that *Output* contains a *null* value. You should perform one final check before moving on. Type **? txtOutput.Lines** and press Enter. You might expect that this value is also going to be *null*, but you see *{string[0]}* instead. This output tells you that the property isn't empty, but that the list it contains is empty—it contains zero items.

Part of tracing an application is to see how things change. So it's time to go to the next step. Click Continue on the Standard toolbar (the green, right-pointing arrow), press F5, or choose Debug | Continue. The yellow highlight and its associated arrow will move to the second breakpoint. Try typing the three commands in the Immediate window that you tried before. You'll notice that *Output* is no longer *null*—it contains some odd-looking data, but it does contain data now. So the previous step filled *Output* with data. However, *txtOutput.Lines* is still an empty list.

At this point, you no longer have any breakpoints set. It would be nice to see *txtOutput.Lines* change, but there doesn't seem to be any way to do it. Click Step Over on the Debug toolbar, press F10, or choose Debug | Step Over. The Step Over command moves the instruction pointer to the next line. Anything required to do that happens in the background. Notice that the instruction pointer does, in fact, move to the next line, which is a closing curly bracket. The curly bracket is also highlighted. Check on the value of *txtOutput.Lines* again and you'll see that it has changed. It contains precisely the information that you'd expect—the content of *txtSelections.Lines* in uppercase.

Testing a Theory

Another part of discovering how applications work is to play with them. To think about how something might work, develop a theory and then test it. You need to answer the question of what could happen if something occurs. Interestingly enough, you already have the knowledge to do just that. It's possible for you to change something and see what happens when you do. The following sections examine two simple theories and help you test them.

Changing the TextBox Data

In the "Viewing Application Data" section, you ended the debugging session with the instruction pointer at the curly brace at the end of the *btnTest_Click()* event handler. If you're still there, you're ready to go. If not, use the information in that section to get the instruction pointer to that location in the code. It's at this point that the *txtOutput.Lines* property contains the output you expect from the application. However, what would happen if you changed the *txtOutput.Text* property and gave it another value? Type **txtOutput.Text = "Hello World"** in the Immediate window and press Enter. You'll see Hello World appear immediately after the command. Unfortunately, that doesn't tell you anything about the application. Click Continue to tell the application to finish the *btnTest_Click()* event handler code. The Output text box will contain something other than the text you expected as shown in Figure 3-17.

FIGURE 3-17 Changing data in the Immediate window also changes the application output.

This little test has shown you something interesting. It's possible to affect the content of the text box using various properties (both *Lines* and *Text* in this case). In addition, if something in your code works other than it should, it could produce unexpected results in the output. Many novice developers end up spending hours trying to figure out this little principle, but you've discovered it with your first application. Amazing!

Selecting Other Elements

Graphical environments can sometimes prove confusing until you play with them for a while. For example, you know that when you click a button, the application automatically highlights it. The act of highlighting the button is called giving it the focus. Any control can receive the focus. Generally, only one control has the focus at any given time. You know that when you're testing the sample application, anytime you click Test, it receives the focus and the application highlights it.

You might wonder whether some other control could receive the focus, even if you've already selected something else. Give it a try. Click Test. The debugger will stop at the first breakpoint you created. (Get rid of the second breakpoint by clicking the red circle in the left margin—you don't need it any longer.) Try giving the Cancel button the focus. Type *btnCancel.Focus()* in the Immediate window and press Enter. You'll see *true* appear under the command you typed. Click Continue. The Cancel button does indeed have the focus, as shown in Figure 3-18.

FIGURE 3-18 The Immediate window also makes it possible to execute commands that change control appearance.

This same technique works with any other control in the application. Give it a try—it's fun. For example, if you type *txtSelections.Focus()* and press Enter, you'll see that all of the text within the Selections text box is selected when you click Continue. Understanding how focus works is another important lesson in creating great applications. At this point, you can click Cancel to end the application. If you're in the debugger, you can click Stop Debugging, press Shift+F5, or choose Debug | Stop Debugging instead.

Creating the List 2 Project

The second list project is going to build on the first one. You'll use essentially the same interface, but you'll extend the code to perform some additional tasks. The following sections tell you how to build this extended version, describe how to test it, and then help you discover some new programming principles using it.

Starting the Second List Project

This second list project uses the same approach as the first list project. Simply follow instructions found in the "Starting the List Project" section of this chapter. Instead of naming your project ListProject1, name it ListProject2.

Copying the Controls

In the "Adding the Controls" section of this chapter, you add a number of controls to List Project 1. Of course, you'll always have to go through this process for new projects where you don't already have a template. However, what happens (as in this case) when you want to create another project with essentially the same controls? It's possible to copy the controls from one form to another. Simply open List Project 1 and select the controls in the form you created earlier, as shown in Figure 3-19.

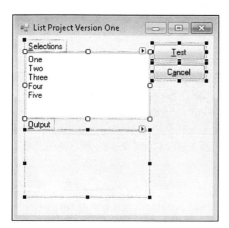

FIGURE 3-19 You can save time by copying and pasting controls as needed between applications.

Notice that every one of the controls is selected. You can use the Ctrl+click approach to do this or simply lasso the entire group of controls by dragging the mouse cursor to encompass all of them. At this point, you can copy the controls to the clipboard by clicking Copy or by pressing Ctrl+C. Now, choose List Project 2 and click the form to select it. Paste the controls you copied into place by choosing Paste or by pressing Ctrl+V. You'll see the fully configured controls appear on the form. All you need to do is nudge the controls into place by selecting the entire group and dragging them so that the first *Label* control is in the right spot in the upper-left corner of the form.

Finessing the Controls

At this point, you have a project with fully configured controls to use. However, you should have noticed something when you worked with List Project 1. The *TextBox* controls do a wonderful job of displaying the lines of text. However, once you get so many lines displayed in the *TextBox*, you can't see the remaining lines and there isn't any indicator to tell you there are more lines. Try it yourself. Start List Project 1, type **Six** and **Seven** on separate lines in Selections, and then click Test. You'll get the result shown in Figure 3-20.

FIGURE 3-20 The first version of the example application has user interface problems.

You can't see Seven in the Output text box. If you select Output and scroll down you can see it, but there isn't any indicator that the text box contains additional information. Even though the application works, it doesn't provide all of the information the user requires. Programmers call this a *fit and finish problem*—you need to finesse the controls to get the desired view. In this case, select *txtSelections* in List Project 2. Open the Properties window, select the *Scrollbars* property, and set it to *Vertical*. Perform the same task with the *txtOutput* control. You've now fixed a problem that would normally confuse the user in your second application.

> **Tip** Often you won't even see fit and finish problems as you work with the application because you'll automatically compensate for any shortcomings the application might have. It's human nature to do so. That's just one reason why companies like Microsoft invest so heavily in beta testers. Someone else can often see the warts in your application that you've failed to notice because you work with the application constantly.

This is also the second version of the list project. So, you'll need to change the title bar text. Select the form. Choose the *Text* property and type **List Project Version Two.**

Adding the Extended Code

There are many ways to modify the simple query shown in Listing 3-1. In this case, the example shows how to work with a variable. Remember that a variable is simply a container used to temporarily store data in memory. The variable doesn't contain the query this time. Instead, it contains a count of the number of items that the query processes. The example outputs this count as part of the information you see in the Output textbox. Listing 3-2 shows the extended code for this example.

LISTING 3-2 Defining a More Advanced Query

```
private void btnTest_Click(object sender, EventArgs e)
{
    // Create a variable to hold a count of the number of
    // entries in txtSelections.
    var Count = 0;

    // Obtain the data from the Lines property of txtSelections
    // and place it in Output using TheEntry as a temporary variable.
    var Output = from TheEntry
                 in txtSelections.Lines
                 select (Count = Count + 1) + " " + TheEntry.ToUpper();

    // Place the contents of Output into the Lines property of
    // txtOutput.
    txtOutput.Lines = Output.ToArray<String>();
}
```

The code begins by creating a new variable. Later you'll discover that you can create a specific kind of container to hold specific kinds of data. For now, the example uses the *var* keyword to create a variable of unknown type named *Count*. It also places data in *Count*—a value of 0.

The query comes next. The basic query is the same as before. However, notice that the *select* clause contains some additional information. You can make the select clause as complicated as you want. In this case, the code adds 1 to Count and then outputs *Count*, a space, and *TheEntry* as uppercase. Creating a complex output like this using the plus sign (+) is called *concatenation*. Every time LINQ processes one of the entries in *txtSelections.Lines*, it also adds 1 to *Count*, so *Count* will always display the current line number of the *txtSelections.Lines* entry. If the first line in *txtSelections.Lines* is One, the output would be 1 ONE (the value of *Count*, a space, and the word One in uppercase).

The output code is the same as the first example. It outputs the content of *Output* as an array to *txtOutput.Lines*. As a result, you see whatever the LINQ query created as output. Figure 3-21 shows a typical example of output from this version of the application.

FIGURE 3-21 The second version of the example application makes it possible to see more entries.

Tracing Through the Extended Example

As you might expect, this example works similarly to the first example, but it also has a few differences. This section traces through the example and points out some of the differences you should notice. In some cases, you'll find that code you locate online or as part of your daily work is like this too. You can find a simple version of the source code to check first, and then a more complex example that builds on the first example. Begin this part of the example by creating a breakpoint at the *var Count = 0;* line.

Begin the tracing process by starting the application and clicking Test. Look at the Locals window. You'll see an entry for *Count,* as shown in Figure 3-22.

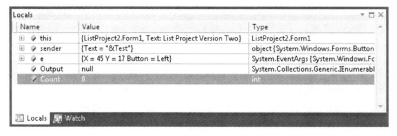

FIGURE 3-22 Use tracing as a means of comparing two applications.

Click Step Over twice. As before, *Output* will now have a value other than *null*. This time you want to see how the LINQ query works because it has suddenly become a little more complex. Click Step Into, press F11, or choose Debug | Step Into. You'll actually move into the LINQ query because the display code must call it to determine what to display on-screen. This is a nice feature of LINQ queries because you can gain a better understanding of why something is or isn't working. Notice that the Locals window changes to show just *TheEntry* and Count, as shown in Figure 3-23. (Remember that *ThisEntry* is type *string* and *Count* is type *int*—this information will come in handy in the "Understanding Data Types" section of this chapter.)

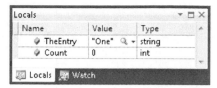

FIGURE 3-23 The Locals window shows only the variables associated with the current scope.

It may be a mystery as to why *Count* is 0. Isn't it supposed to be 1? Remember that the actual output of *Count* is *Count + 1* (or 1 in this case). The code stores this value (*Count + 1*) into *Count* for the next query. Click Step Into again. You'll see that the values have changed to Two and 1. Click Step Into four more times. After each click you'll see the values in the Locals window update just as you'd expect them to. In short, you're seeing how a LINQ query actually creates the output.

At this point, you should be back to the *txtOutput.Lines = Output.ToArray<String>();* line of the code. Click Continue and you'll see the output displayed. You can try tracing through the example as many times as needed to start understanding how precisely the code does its work.

Understanding Data Types

So far, the chapter has discussed variables in a non-specific manner. The two tracing sections in the chapter show that variables have a particular type, even though you've looked at them as simple containers. It's true that variables are containers for data, but they contain a specific kind of data. The *var* keyword creates a variable of unknown type. Although using *var* makes it easier to write code, the *var* keyword also makes it harder to read the code. No one knows what kind of data appears in the variable—it's as if you've created a mystery box.

In addition, the *var* keyword keeps the compiler from performing part of its work. When you tell the compiler what sort of information should appear within a variable, it can verify that the variable does indeed contain that sort of data and that you don't accidently try to put the wrong kind of data in the variable.

The "Tracing Through the Extended Example" section of the chapter shows two kinds of variables: *string* and *int*. You'll find that you use these two types of data quite often when you create programs. However, there are many other kinds of data. Table 3-2 provides a brief description of each of these data types. Don't worry about committing them to memory now—you'll begin to memorize the data types as you create additional applications throughout the book. In addition, future examples will highlight special features of each data type.

TABLE 3-2 Common (Built-in) Data Types Found in C#

C# Data Type Name	.NET Framework Name	Range	Description
bool	System.Boolean	true or false	Contains a yes or no answer. It's a logical value you can use to test the truth of something.
byte	System.Byte	0 to 255	A numeric value that requires eight bits of storage space and stores only positive values.
sbyte	System.SByte	-128 to 127	A numeric value that requires eight bits of storage space and can store both positive and negative values.
ushort	System.UInt16	0 to 65,535	A numeric value that requires 16 bits of storage space and stores only positive values.
short	System.Int16	-32,768 to 32,767	A numeric value that requires 16 bits of storage space and can store both positive and negative values.
uint	System.UInt32	0 to 4,294,967,295	A numeric value that requires 32 bits of storage space and stores only positive values.
int	System.Int32	-2,147,483,648 to 2,147,483,647	A numeric value that requires 32 bits of storage space and can store both positive and negative values.
ulong	System.UInt64	0 to 18,446,744,073,709,551,615	A numeric value that requires 64 bits of storage space and stores only positive values.
long	System.Int64	−9,223,372,036,854,775,808 to 9,223,372,036,854,775,807	A numeric value that requires 64 bits of storage space and can store both positive and negative values.
float	System.Single	$\pm 1.5 \times 10^{-45}$ to $\pm 3.4 \times 10^{38}$	C# supports whole numbers (integer types) and real numbers (floating point numbers with a decimal point). This 32-bit floating-point data type provides a container for smaller numbers. It provides seven significant digits of precision.
double	System.Double	$\pm 5.0 \times 10^{-324}$ to $\pm 1.7 \times 10^{308}$	This 64-bit floating-point data type provides a container for large numbers. It provides 15 to 16 significant digits of precision.
decimal	System.Decimal	$\pm 1.0 \times 10^{-28}$ to $\pm 7.9 \times 10^{28}$	Computers use base 2 numbers, which don't always represent decimal (base 10) numbers very well. This 128-bit data type helps you perform financial calculations with greater accuracy. It provides 28 to 29 significant digits of precision.
char	System.Char	U+0000 to U+ffff	A single 16-bit Unicode character. Characters are tricky because to the computer, they're simply a number. The application environment gives the number significance as a character. For now, you really don't need to worry about character sets or their use in applications. You can read more about character sets and see a list of character sets at *http://www.i18nguy.com/unicode/codepages.html*.

C# Data Type Name	.NET Framework Name	Range	Description
string	System.String	N/A	A string is simply a list of characters. You can use it to store words, sentences, entire paragraphs, or any other sequence of characters that you want. Think of a string as simply text, like the text you're reading right now.
object	System.Object	N/A	C# needs a way to model the real world and complex data. Later you'll discover that you can create a container to hold any kind of data you can imagine and many types of data you haven't ever seen. All of these special data types rely on the object data type as a starting point.

Tip The C# data type name is used only in C#. These types correspond to specific .NET Framework type names. Any language that the .NET Framework supports can use these names. Savvy developers often use the .NET Framework type name to ensure that anyone reading the code can understand it, even if C# isn't the viewer's native language.

This is just an overview of data types. You'll discover that data types are extremely flexible as the book progresses. It's possible to model any sort of data in C#, even data that you've simply made up for the fun of it! You'll also discover some important considerations for using data types as the book progresses. For now, you have everything you need to work with simple applications. Your knowledge will increase as the complexity of the examples found in the book increases.

Changing the Code to Match the Data Type

It's time to put your newfound knowledge of data types to work. The code in Listing 3-2 is ambiguous because it doesn't provide specific data types for at last two of the variables. You now know that *Count* is of type *int* and *TheEntry* is of type *string*. To make your code easier to read and to take full advantage of all of the features of the compiler, you could change the code in Listing 3-2 to look like Listing 3-3.

LISTING 3-3 Adding Specific Data Types

```
private void btnTest_Click(object sender, EventArgs e)
{
    // Create a variable to hold a count of the number of
    // entries in txtSelections.
    int Count = 0;

    // Obtain the data from the Lines property of txtSelections
    // and place it in Output using TheEntry as a temporary variable.
    var Output = from string TheEntry
                 in txtSelections.Lines
```

```
                        select (Count = Count + 1) + " " + TheEntry.ToUpper();
        // Place the contents of Output into the Lines property of
        // txtOutput.
        txtOutput.Lines = Output.ToArray<String>();
}
```

This code doesn't work any differently from the code you viewed earlier. The only difference is that now it's easier to read and debug because the data types are specific.

Mixing Data Types in the Text Box

Now that you know more about data types, you might wonder what happens when you type odd data types within a text box. It's time to experiment a little. Change the LINQ query so it looks like this:

```
var Output = from TheEntry
             in txtSelections.Lines
             select (Count = Count + 1) + " " + TheEntry.ToUpper()
                + " " + TheEntry.GetType();
```

The *GetType()* method tells you what sort of type of information *TheEntry* contains. This is a very handy way to discover more about data types. Notice also that if a line gets too long (as it is with the *select* statement) that you can simply continue it on the next line. A good practice is to indent the continuation line so that you know it's a continuation line. Now, start your application and type true (*bool*), 1 (*int*), and 2.3 (*float*) on three separate lines. Click Text. You'll see the output shown in Figure 3-24.

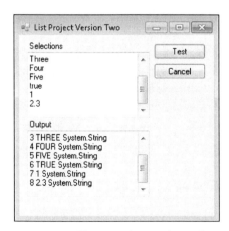

FIGURE 3-24 The example now shows the entry number, value, and data type.

As you can see, the text box treats all data it contains as the string data type (which is the .NET Framework *System.String* data type), even if you'd normally look at the entry as some other type. The "Selecting Specific *TextBox* Elements" section of the chapter discusses this topic in more detail, but you'll find that you can detect other types of data in text boxes and also convert that data into a specific data type.

Testing Selection Theories

The LINQ queries you create can include a *where* clause. You use the *where* clause to choose specific entries based on some criterion. For example, you could select entries of a specific length or of a particular data type. That's what the examples in the following sections show you how to do, but you'll see a number of additional selection examples in the book.

Skipping *TextBox* Elements

A simple way to test the *where* clause is to look for items of a particular length. Of course, you can use this technique to test for all kinds of other things as well. For example, you could use it to test for specific strings or character sequences. In fact, you can use this technique to test for just about anything you want as long as C# provides a means to test it. Listing 3-4 shows how you can check for items of a specific length.

LISTING 3-4 Selecting Specific Entries by Length

```
private void btnTest_Click(object sender, EventArgs e)
{
    // Create a variable to hold a count of the number of
    // entries in txtSelections.
    int Count = 0;

    // Obtain the data from the Lines property of txtSelections
    // and place it in Output using TheEntry as a temporary variable.
    var Output = from string TheEntry
                 in txtSelections.Lines
                 where TheEntry.Length <= 3
                 select (Count = Count + 1) + " " + TheEntry.ToUpper();

    // Place the contents of Output into the Lines property of
    // txtOutput.
    txtOutput.Lines = Output.ToArray<String>();
}
```

This code behaves much as the other examples have. However, the *where* clause tells LINQ not to include any strings that are over three characters in length in the output. The *Length* property always contains the length of a particular item. In this case, *TheEntry* contains a single line from *txtSelections*, so *Length* contains the length of the text in that line.

Try tracing through this example using the debugger so that you can see how the selection criterion works. You'll see that the debugger goes to the *where* clause first. When the *where* clause is true (the *Length* is less than or equal to 3) the debugger next goes to the *select* clause. However, when the *where* clause is false, the debugger skips the select clause. Try adding a few more lines to your example. Figure 3-25 shows some typical output. (Notice that only One, Two, and Six are selected.)

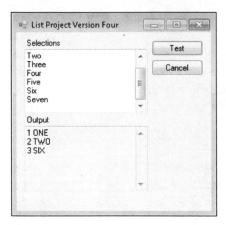

FIGURE 3-25 Tracing shows how the LINQ statement works in the background.

Selecting Specific *TextBox* Elements

It's possible to detect various kinds of text box elements, even though the text box doesn't work with anything but strings. In this case, you must try to convert the data to a different type. If the conversion works, then the data is the type you want. Listing 3-5 shows how to perform this task.

LISTING 3-5 SelectingT Specific Entries by Type

```
private void btnTest_Click(object sender, EventArgs e)
{
    // Create a variable to hold a count of the number of
    // entries in txtSelections.
    int Count = 0;

    // Create a variable to hold the converted data.
    int OutputNumber = 0;

    // Obtain the data from the Lines property of txtSelections
    // and place it in Output using TheEntry as a temporary variable.
    var Output = from string TheEntry
                 in txtSelections.Lines
                 where Int32.TryParse(TheEntry, out OutputNumber)
                 select (Count = Count + 1) + " " + OutputNumber.ToString() +
                    " " + OutputNumber.GetType();

    // Place the contents of Output into the Lines property of
    // txtOutput.
    txtOutput.Lines = Output.ToArray<String>();
}
```

Notice that the code begins by creating the counter variable, *Count*, and a variable to hold the converted data, *OutputNumber*. The method used to place data in *txtOutput.Lines* is the same as before, which leaves the LINQ query.

The *where* clause contains something new. The .NET Framework data types often have special features. Look at Table 3-2 and you'll see the *System.Int32* data type is the same as the *int* data type. The *Int32.TryParse()* method will try to convert the string found in *TheEntry* into an *int*. it places this converted data in *OutputNumber*. Because *OutputNumber* is an output, you include the special *out* keyword next to it. C# tells you when to use this special keyword, so don't worry too much about it. The result of the *Int32.TryParse()* method is a Boolean value—*true* or *false*. When *TheEntry* contains a value that the *Int32.TryParse()* method can convert, the result is *true*, so the LINQ query calls the *select* clause to output data. Otherwise, LINQ checks the next entry. You can see this for yourself using the tracing technique in the debugger. (Try it now, I'll wait.)

The select clause is also different. In this case, it sends OutputNumber to *txtOutput.Lines*. However, remember that *Lines* only accepts strings. So, you must convert *OutputNumber* to a string using the *ToString()* method. This example shows how to convert from a string to a number and back again. Just so you can be sure it really is a number, the example also outputs *OutputNumber.GetType()*. To make this example work better, the *txtSelections* control contains some different entries: text, numbers, and a Boolean value, as shown in Figure 3-26.

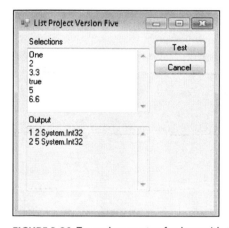

FIGURE 3-26 Try various sorts of values with the example until you truly understand how the LINQ statement works.

Here's a brief discussion of these six entries. The first line isn't output because it's a string. The second line is output because it's an *int*. Now, look at the third line: it looks like it could be an *int*, but it's really a *float*, so it doesn't convert without data loss. The fourth line is a Boolean value. The fifth line is an *int* and the sixth is a *float*, so the output is perfectly predictable.

Get Going with C#

This chapter has helped you understand how to use the *ListBox* control as a source of information for a LINQ query. You've created an application that takes the information from the *ListBox*, asks a question about it, and then displays a result on screen. Believe it or not, you've learned an essential fact about all applications—they manipulate data of some sort. As long as you keep that in mind, you'll find that creating applications is significantly easier.

Playing is an important part of learning how to work with code. You've just created a simple but interesting example application—much better than the Hello World application that most people start with. Take some time to work through the application using the debugger. Keep tracing through the things that the application does until you understand how it operates. Any good developer uses precisely the same approach to discover new coding techniques, so you're already using professional techniques with your first application! Try playing with the LINQ query a little to see what happens when you do. For example, trying changing the *select* criterion to see what happens to the output. The big thing is not to worry about messing up anything—this application is straightforward and simple—nothing bad will happen even if it stops working while you try different things out. You can always get a fresh copy of the application online and start over if you like.

When you go to the library and see a shelf stacked with books, the librarian calls it a collection. Likewise, you go to a friend's house and see a carefully arranged display of like items and your friend calls it a collection. In fact, collections are part of your daily life—everyone collects something. It turns out that computers also collect like items and store them in collections. That's what Chapter 4, "Using Collections to Store Data," is all about. You'll take the information you've learned in this chapter and use it to work with groups of like information placed in a special container called a collection.

Chapter 4

Using Collections to Store Data

After completing this chapter, you'll be able to:

- Describe how arrays store data

- Use an array within an application

- Describe how dictionaries store data and differ from arrays

- Use a dictionary within an application

- Describe how structures store data and differ from other collection types

- Create and use a structure within an application

MANY TEXTS MAKE A BIG deal out of telling readers that collections are complex. In fact, collections are easy. Most people have a collection of some sort. In fact, most people have multiple collections. For example, I have a wonderful fictional book collection and another collection of technical texts. A collection is simply a group of like items. It doesn't matter whether you're organizing your personal library or writing an application—the meaning of the word *collection* is the same.

Note As with every rule, there are exceptions when it comes to collections. Generally, collections do organize like items. However, you can create a collection of objects and objects can be anything at all. In this one instance, you can create a collection of unlike items.

The term *collection* refers to the items. A group of books is a collection. Where you store the books is another matter entirely. Most people would use a bookshelf to store books because a bookshelf provides an easy method to store and retrieve items from the book collection. Of course, you could store your books in a box, but a box is a far less convenient storage method. The same can be said of collections used in programs. The collection refers to the group of like items. However, you also need something to store the collection—a kind of bookcase or box. One storage method works well for some types of collections; another storage method works well for other types of collections. It's almost always possible to force the wrong sort of storage container to work for any kind of collection, but using the right storage container makes things easier.

C# can use a variety of storage containers to hold data. In fact, if you find that C# doesn't support a storage container you like, you can always create one of your own. However, some storage containers are definitely more popular than others. The world abounds with bookshelves and boxes—applications abound with arrays, dictionaries, and structures. This chapter explores all three of these popular storage techniques, but you need to remember that C# does offer access to a wide variety of other storage methods. After you get a feeling for how the storage containers described in this chapter work, you'll want to choose the container that works best for a particular situation.

Understanding Arrays

Arrays are the simplest form of storage container for collections offered by C#. An array is simply a series of boxes (called *elements*)—one for each of the data items that you want to store. When you envision an array, think about the pigeon holes used to store bits of information at a hotel. You could also compare an array to a mailbox setup at an apartment complex where all the mailboxes appear in one place, but each apartment has its own box. The main advantage of an array is that it's simple. You can place a data item in a particular element and take it back out of that element later.

Every element in an array has a number. In fact, the elements are numbered from 0 to one less than the largest number of elements in the array. For example, if an array has 100 elements, the elements are numbered from 0 to 99. You can access any particular element by providing its number in your code. Don't worry too much about how this access occurs; for right now it's enough to know that providing the number does allow you to interact with the data.

To create an array, you simply tell the compiler how many elements it should contain and what sort of data you want to put into it. For example, you can easily create an array to hold individual numbers or strings. Arrays can hold any number of like items, each of which has its own value. The next section shows how to create and access an array. You'll use the debugger to trace through the example and better understand how this simple storage technique works.

Creating the Array Project

The best way to discover more about arrays is to create a project containing one and then trace through it. This section does just that. You'll create a new array project that relies on a Language Integrated Query (LINQ) query as a starting point for interacting with the array. After you see how a LINQ query works, the section helps you discover how to perform other sorts of looping.

Starting the Array Project

This section shows how to create yet another form of project. In this case, you'll create an example that shows three techniques for working with the same array. That said, it does build on your knowledge gained from the example in Chapter 1, "Getting to Know C#." These steps will help you configure the project.

Create the Array Project

1. Click New Project. The New Project dialog box appears.

2. Select Visual C# in the left pane and select Windows Forms Application in the middle pane. You'll see a description of the template in the right pane.

3. Type **ArrayUsage** in the Name field and click OK. The IDE creates a new project consisting of a single form.

Adding the Array Project Controls

Because this project shows how to use an array three different ways, you need three test buttons to activate each test separately (to see the results separately). In addition, you need to provide a means to end the program when it's complete. However, the array provides the data storage, so you don't need a separate control for this task as you did in the examples in Chapter 3, "Basic Data Manipulation Techniques." With this in mind, you can create an application consisting of four Button controls, as shown in Figure 4-1.

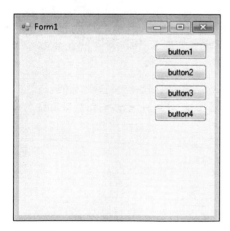

FIGURE 4-1 Create an example form that has four buttons on it.

Configuring the Array Project Controls

It's time to configure the controls for this example. Just as a reminder, you select the control you want to work with, click the Properties tab to open it, and then click Auto Hide to keep the Properties window displayed. This example has four controls for you to configure. Table 4-1 shows how to configure each of the controls.

TABLE 4-1 *ArrayUsage* Control Configuration

Control Name	Property Name	Value
button1	(Name)	btnLINQ
	Text	LIN&Q
button2	(Name)	btnLoop
	Text	&Loop
button3	(Name)	btnConditional
	Text	&Conditional
button4	(Name)	btnQuit
	Text	&Quit
Form1	Text	Using an Array
	AcceptButton	btnLINQ
	CancelButton	btnQuit
	FormBorderStyle	FixedDialog

This example does a few new interesting configuration tasks with the form. First, notice that it has an *AcceptButton* property. This is the button that the form selects automatically when the application begins. If a user starts the application and then presses Enter, the form automatically selects *btnLINQ* and causes its *Click()* event handler code to execute.

Second, notice that the form also has a *CancelButton* property. The Cancel button automatically activates when the user presses Esc. In this case, the *btnQuit Click()* event handler will execute, closing the form as shown here.

```
private void btnQuit_Click(object sender, EventArgs e)
{
    // End the application.
Close();
}
```

The use of the *AcceptButton* and *CancelButton* properties makes the form significantly easier for keyboardists to use. In addition, adding these features makes it possible for users with special needs to use your application with greater ease. Always include entries for both properties when you can.

> **Note** All of the examples in the book will ask you to create event handlers for buttons and other controls. After you create the event handler shell, you type the code shown between the curly braces ({}) in the listing into your code. As an alternative, downloading the code from the book's website will make it easier to obtain the code and ensure that it doesn't contain any typos.

Third, this form uses the *FixedDialog* option for the *FormBorderStyle* property. Many users find it annoying when a form is able to resize when there's no reason for it to resize. This example doesn't have any reason to offer resizing, so changing the *FormBorderStyle* property is an important fit and finish change.

Adding the Array Code

This example shows you a number of new coding techniques you can use with any application. You use the first of these to create a *global variable*. A global variable is a variable that every part of your application can use. This example uses a global variable to hold the array so that all three of the techniques can rely on the same array for input. Normally you only use global variables in places like this, where more than one method must have access to the data. Listing 4-1 shows the code used to create the global variable, which is an array.

LISTING 4-1 Creating a Global Variable

```
// Create an array.
String[] TestArray;

public Form1()
{
    InitializeComponent();

    // Initialize the array.
    TestArray = new String[] {"One", "Two", "Three", "Four", "Five"};
}
```

The code begins by creating an array. You define an array by adding the brackets next to the variable type declaration as shown. The use of *String[]* defines an array of unknown size that's used to store data of the *String* type. This array is named *TestArray*. At this point, it's only defined and not useful for holding anything.

To make the array useful, you need to *initialize* it as part of the form's *constructor*. A constructor is simply a blueprint that tells the compiler how to create the form. The constructor always has the same name as the form's class, which is *Form1* in this case. The *Form1()* method is the constructor. The first method call in *Form1()* always appears there, called *InitializeComponent*, and it simply tells the compiler to add the components to the form and configure them properly. You don't need to worry about calling *InitializeComponent()* yourself because the IDE always creates and maintains it for you.

The next line of code tells the compiler to create the array. The example code also places values in the array. It looks complicated, but it really isn't.

In this case, the *new* keyword tells the compiler to create a new *String[]* array of unknown size and assign it to *TestArray*. As part of the same call, the code initializes the values—the strings *"One"*, *"Two"*, *"Three"*, *"Four"*, and *"Five"* and stores them in the array. When you see values within curly braces, as shown in the preceding code example, you know that those values will appear in the array.

Now it's time to create code that does something with the array. You'll need to create an event handler for the *Click()* event of *btnLINQ*. In this case, the code uses a LINQ query to interact with the array, and then it outputs the data from a single result entry. Listing 4-2 shows the code you need to perform this task.

LISTING 4-2 Accessing the global variable using a LINQ query

```
private void btnLINQ_Click(object sender, EventArgs e)
{
    // Create the query.
    var Output = from String TheEntry
                 in TestArray
                 select TheEntry.Substring(0, 3);

    // Display one of the results.
    MessageBox.Show(Output.ToArray<String>()[2]);
}
```

The query follows the same pattern as those shown in Chapter 3. However, in this case the query relies on the *Substring()* method to return a particular part of the source string. Remember from previous discussions that *TheEntry* contains a single entry from the source, which is a *String* in this case. The *Substring()* method accepts two arguments as input. The first argument describes where to start accepting output from the string. The second argument describes how long to make the string. For example, if you start out with the word *"Three"*, tell the *Substring()* method to start at position 0, and return three characters, you'll see *Thr* as output. However, let's say that you decide to start at position 1, and return four characters. In this case, the result is *hree* instead.

Look at the next line. *Output* now contains the modified versions of each of the array entries. That means that *One* and *Two* appear as they did before because they each contain three letters, but *Three*, *Four*, and *Five* have been modified as *Thr*, *Fou*, and *Fiv*. String manipulation is an often used feature of programming languages, so the more you learn about this feature, the better. The *ToArray<String>()* method converts the content of *Output* to a standard *String* array—a handy method of changing the storage container that LINQ provides to something that's easier to understand. The addition of *[2]* selects the third element of the resulting array, so the result is a single string. The *MessageBox.Show()* method can accept a single argument, which must be a string. The result of this line of code is a dialog box that shows the modified third element of the original array, as shown in Figure 4-2.

FIGURE 4-2 The example output shows the combination of the LINQ statement and *ToArray()* method.

Using Alternative Coding Methods

When writing applications you have many ways to perform the same task. In some cases, performing the task in a particular way has a benefit. For example, if you use a specific approach, the code might run faster, be more reliable, or provide additional security. However, developers often use an approach to coding that's simply comfortable or familiar.

The *btnLINQ_Click()* event handler could use several different methods to obtain the same results—none of which is superior to any other. For example, instead of converting the output to an array before displaying the message box, you could create the array directly as part of the LINQ statement like this:

```
private void btnLINQ_Click(object sender, EventArgs e)
{
    // Create the query.
    var Output = (from String TheEntry
                in TestArray
                select TheEntry.Substring(0, 3)).ToArray<String>();

    // Display one of the results.
    MessageBox.Show(Output[2]);
}
```

This approach would work best if you need the array form of *Output* in several different places. In fact, you don't have to convert *Output* to an array at all. You can use the *ElementAt()* method instead like this:

```
private void btnLINQ_Click(object sender, EventArgs e)
{
    // Create the query.
    var Output = from String TheEntry
                in TestArray
                select TheEntry.Substring(0, 3);

    // Display one of the results.
    MessageBox.Show(Output.ElementAt<String>(2));
}
```

This approach might be a little less readable than the approach used in the previous example, but the results are precisely the same. The point is that all three methods work and it's up to you to choose which method works best for you.

Tracing Through the Array Example

It's essential that you get used to tracing through all the examples in this book to explore how they actually work. Tracing might not seem all that important when working through a simple example, but it's an essential skill to build.

Tracing the Array Project

1. Start the example application and place a breakpoint on the line that reads: *MessageBox. Show(Output.ToArray<String>()[2]);*.

> **Note** If you haven't tried tracing through an application before, try the example described in the "Tracing the List Application with the Debugger" section of Chapter 3.

2. At this point, you can click LINQ on the example application. The debugger will stop at the line where you set the breakpoint. Of course, the question is whether LINQ reacts differently to an array than it does to the *Lines* property of the *Textbox* control in the previous chapter's example.

3. Click Step Into or press F11 to see the first part of the query. Unfortunately, the Locals window doesn't really show you what you need to know. It shows the *original* value of *TheEntry*, not the selected value.

4. Fortunately, you can fix this problem. Click the Watch tab. Highlight the entire selection criteria, *TheEntry.Substring(0, 3)* and drag it to the Watch window. You'll now see the actual selection output.

5. Click Step Into twice more and you'll notice that the Watch window now has an odd-looking green circle with a double arrow in it. Click the green circle to refresh the contents of the Watch window and you'll see how this method works, as shown here.

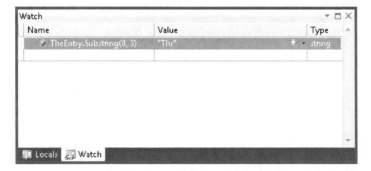

Using the Watch window is another way to improve your ability to trace through an application and discover its secrets. It's possible to drag and drop just about any method from your code to the Watch window. You can view properties or variables as well. If a variable, property, or method you choose doesn't actually work in the current context, you'll see a red circle with an exclamation mark inside it (called a *bang*). It doesn't mean that you can't *ever* look at the entry's content—you simply can't look at it now.

6. Click Step Into twice more, and you'll end up back at the initial stopping point. At this point, you can select the Locals tab to see the *Output* variable. Expand *Output* to see the Results View shown here.

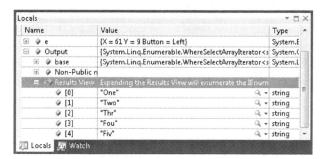

The results are precisely as you expect. Each original array entry has been truncated to just three letters. You can also view these results in the Immediate window.

7. Highlight the *Output.ToArray<String>()[2]* part of the output, click Copy, type a *?* (question mark) in the Immediate window followed by a space, and then paste the text.

Using the Immediate window lets you play with the code a little to see other results. For example, try changing the array index from 2 to some other number. Figure 4-3 shows some typical results that you might see. (Notice that typing a value of **5** results in an error message because the last element is actually numbered 4 even though the array contains five elements.)

FIGURE 4-3 Use the Immediate window to play with the code to obtain different results.

Testing Looping Theories

So far you've used LINQ queries to process the data sources in the book. This isn't the traditional approach that most programmers have learned from the outset—it's actually a new approach that Microsoft developed to make things fast and easy. However, you're going to encounter more than a little code that uses the older approach, so it's important to know both ways of doing things.

Now that you have an understanding of the underlying approach used to work with data sources, it's time to explore the time-honored approach to working with a data source—using a loop.

The term *loop* is precise in this case. It simply marks a section of code that an application should continue doing something until it runs out of material to process. C# provides a number of loop structures; this example will use only one of them, the *for* loop. A *for* loop processes data source entries until it reaches a certain count, and then it stops. It doesn't matter if the data source has additional entries to process—all that matters is the count.

Of course, using a count to track the number of times to perform a task means that you have to create a variable to hold the current count. If you say that you want the *for* loop to process 10 entries, you need a counter variable to tell the *for* loop when it has achieved its goal. The comparison of the current counter variable content against the eventual goal is called a *condition*. All traditional loops require some sort of condition.

Let's look at an example of a traditional *for* loop. Double-click the Loop button on the test application to create a *btnLoop_Click()* event handler. Listing 4-3 shows the code used to perform array processing using a loop.

LISTING 4-3 Accessing the global variable using a loop

```
private void btnLoop_Click(object sender, EventArgs e)
{
    // Create a variable to hold the result.
    String Output = "";

    // Perform the array processing.
    for (Int32 Counter = 0; Counter < TestArray.Length; Counter++)
    {
        Output = Output+TestArray[Counter]+"\r\n";
    }

    // Display the result on screen.
    MessageBox.Show(Output);
}
```

This code begins by creating *Output*. Notice that unlike the LINQ query, you actually give *Output* a specific type. It's also important to give *Output* an initial value, which is a blank string in this case.

The start of the *for* loop has three sections. The first section creates the counter variable, *Counter*, and assigns it an initial value of 0. You can give *Counter* any starting value desired (in fact, this makes for interesting tracing to see precisely how the *for* loop works). The second section provides the condition. In this case, the code specifies that the *for* loop should continue to process information while the value of *Counter* is less than the length of *TestArray*. A condition is always a comparison of some sort; you'll see a number of them in the book. The third section tells the *for* loop to update the value of *Counter* by adding 1 to it each loop. That's what the ++ (increment) operator does—it adds 1 to the value of the variable. If you don't provide some means of updating the counter variable, its value remains the same and the loop will never meet the ending condition (resulting in an error condition called an endless loop). Taken together, this *for* loop does the following things:

1. Creates a variable named *Counter*.

2. Sets the initial value of *Counter* to *0*.

3. Compares *Counter* to *TestArray.Length*.

4. What happens next depends on the result of the comparison in step 3. If *Counter* is less than the value of *TestArray.Length,* the loop continues at step 5. When *Counter* is equal to or greater than *TestArray.Length,* the loop exits.

5. Performs all the tasks found within the curly braces.

6. Adds *1* to the value of *Counter*.

7. Goes to step 3.

Of course, a loop has to have work to perform to be useful. In this case, the code accesses each of the array entries one at a time and adds it to *Output* to create one large string. The addition of "\r\n" creates a carriage return and a linefeed—that's exactly what happens when you press Enter in a word processor, and the effect is the same here: it effectively places each value on a separate line. The *TestArray[Counter]* entry accesses a single array entry—the one pointed to by *Counter*. For example, when *Counter* is equal to 0 it retrieves the first entry in *TestArray*. You could replace this statement with *TestArray[0]*, which accesses the first array element in *TestArray* (but then the loop wouldn't work properly, because it would access the same value each time).

The final bit of code displays the content of *Output* in a message box. Notice that you don't need to perform any conversion of *Output* in this case because *Output* is already a string and the first argument for *MessageBox.Show()* is always a string. Figure 4-4 shows the output of this example:

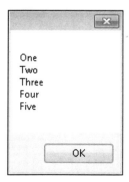

FIGURE 4-4 The output shows the content of *TestArray*.

Try placing a breakpoint on the *for* loop. Notice that the entire statement isn't highlighted. The IDE places the highlight on *Int32 Counter = 0;* instead. Start the example and click Loop. The code will stop execution at the highlighted code. Click Step Into or press F11. You'll notice that the instruction pointer moves to the conditional statement next. Continue clicking Step Into and watch how the loop works. You'll notice that the code performs precisely as described earlier in this section. Watching the loop work is educational because many application errors occur from faulty loops. Often, the error is subtle—a loop executes once too often or not often enough to perform the desired task.

Testing Conditional Theories

It's important to realize that you have a vast array of methods at your disposal to accomplish a given task. Some developers spend considerable time and effort looking for the most efficient or speediest method of performing a task. In fact, some books on the market are devoted solely to the topic of which method works best in a particular situation. Don't get mired in these details until you've spent a lot more time writing code. Sometimes there isn't a right answer—there's just the answer you prefer.

The example in the "Testing Looping Theories" section shows how to use a loop to access all the entries in an array and output the result on screen. This section introduces yet another wrinkle in loops—a condition. A condition specifies that the code should only perform a task when one or more variables meet specific criteria. The following example uses an *if* statement to perform the task. The *if* statement uses the logic that when a condition is *true*, the code should perform a specific task. Listing 4-4 shows the code used to perform the task. Compare this code to the code shown in Listing 4-3 and you'll see that it adds an *if* statement to perform conditional processing.

LISTING 4-4 Accessing the global variable using a loop and a condition

```
private void btnConditional_Click(object sender, EventArgs e)
{
    // Create a variable to hold the result.
    String Output = "";

    // Perform the array processing.
    for (Int32 Counter = 0; Counter < TestArray.Length; Counter++)
    {
        // Place a condition on the task. Perform the task only for the
        // third array element.
        if (Counter == 2)
        {
            Output = Output + TestArray[Counter].Substring(0, 3) + "\r\n";
        }
    }

    // Display the result on screen.
    MessageBox.Show(Output);
}
```

The loop portion of this example works precisely the same as the example in the "Testing Looping Theories" section. However, this example only adds information to *Output* when *Counter* equals 2. The rest of the time the loop simply moves onto the next value. This example also adds the *Substring*() method to truncate any values added to *Output*. As a result, the output from this example is precisely the same as the output of the example in the "Adding the Array Code" section. (See Listing 4-2.) The execution is different because the LINQ version works on all the values, while this example works only on the third value. As you can see, the LINQ query code is shorter and easier to understand, but both examples produce precisely the same result. Make sure that you trace through this example with the debugger to see how it works.

Understanding Dictionaries

The *Dictionary* is another sort of storage container for like data. However, this storage container is more complex than an array and it can make retrieval easier in many cases. One of the problems with an array is that you have to use the element number to access the individual elements. If you don't know the number of the element that holds a particular data value, you must use a loop or LINQ query to search the array until you find it. If the array is large, the search time can become significant enough to slow your application considerably. In addition, searches of this sort can be hard to read in code and tend to produce errors. The *Dictionary* is a special storage container that combines a *key* with each data element (called a *value*). The *Dictionary* is akin to being able to look for a particular word in a dictionary, and then reading its meaning as part of the dictionary entry.

Using a *Dictionary* requires more storage space because you're saving both a key and its associated data. Configuring a *Dictionary* is more complicated because you have to add code to manage the keys. The *Dictionary* can also require more processing time, so it isn't as efficient as an array. However, the *Dictionary* offers considerable flexibility. For example, you can sort the entries using the keys. This means you don't have to enter the data in any order—you can rely on the *Dictionary* to order the data for you. The key can be a different data type from the data, so you can use a *Dictionary* to associate entries containing unlike types. There are many other reasons to use a *Dictionary* that are well beyond this initial discussion; the only issue you need to consider now is that a *Dictionary* trades some complexity and efficiency for flexibility and ease of access.

Creating the Dictionary Project

Anything that you can define with a key and associated data is a good candidate for a *Dictionary*. Of course, an actual dictionary entry is probably the candidate most people think about, but many other sorts of data fit within this pattern. For example, anything that has a name that uniquely describes it is a good candidate. A list of services and a description of each service would work with a *Dictionary*. The example in this chapter uses the names of herbs and a short description of their uses. You can find these descriptions at *http://www.gardensablaze.com/Herbs.htm*. As with the other examples, the following sections describe how to build the application, test it, and then explore how it works using debugger tracing techniques.

Starting the Dictionary Project

This project begins like many others in the book, by creating a new project.

1. Click New Project. The New Project dialog box appears.

2. Select Visual C# in the left pane and select Windows Forms Application in the middle pane. You'll see a description of the template in the right pane.

3. Type **DictionaryUsage** in the Name field and click OK. The IDE creates a new project for you consisting of a single form.

Adding the Dictionary Project Controls

This example uses a completely different control arrangement from the other examples you've seen so far in this book. Applications sometimes use something other than a *Button* control to make something happen. For example, sometimes when you select an item in a list, the user interface automatically does something with that selection. In fact, that's precisely what this example does. When you click the name of an herb in the *ListBox* control, the description for that herb appears in the *TextBox* control. Two *Label* controls provide a description for the *ListBox* and *TextBox*.

Of course, the example requires a *Button* to end the application. Two additional *Button* controls provide extensions to the example that are discussed later in this section. The first *Button* will show how to sort a *Dictionary*, a feature that's incredibly useful. The second *Button* describes how to obtain some statistical information from the *Dictionary*. Statistics are also incredibly useful, even if you don't use them every day. Your form should look like the one in Figure 4-4 after you add the controls.

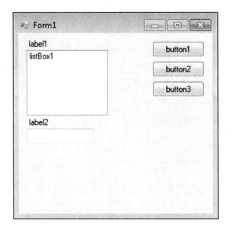

FIGURE 4-4 Create a form that contains the controls shown here.

Configuring the Dictionary Project Controls

This example requires a bit more configuration than previous examples because it uses a different approach to the user interface. Of course, you'll begin by configuring the *ListBox* control because that's the first control the user accesses. Just as a reminder, you select the control you want to work with, click the Properties tab to open it, and then click Auto Hide to keep the Properties window displayed. This example has seven controls for you to configure. Table 4-2 shows how to configure each of the controls.

TABLE 4-2 *DictionaryUsage* Control Configuration

Control Name	Property Name	Value
label1	Text	&Choose Herb
listBox1	(Name)	lstHerbs
	Size.Width	179
	Size.Height	95
label2	Text	&Description
textBox1	(Name)	txtDescription
	Multiline	True
	ReadOnly	True
	ScrollBars	Both
	Size.Width	179
	Size.Height	111
button1	(Name)	btnSort
	Text	&Sort
button2	(Name)	btnStats
	Text	S&tats
button3	(Name)	btnQuit
	Text	&Quit
Form1	Text	Using a Dictionary
	CancelButton	btnQuit
	FormBorderStyle	FixedDialog

Because of the extensive configuration for this example, you'll want to double-check everything before you move to the next section. Figure 4-5 shows how your application should look at this point.

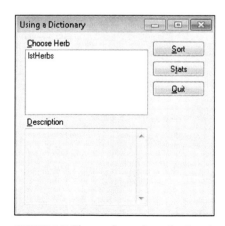

FIGURE 4-5 The configured application shows what the user will see.

You may wonder why this example doesn't have an *AcceptButton* setting. That's because the default action is choosing an option from *lstHerbs*. The *AcceptButton* is a default action—and there isn't a default action in this case.

Adding the Dictionary Code

As previously mentioned, a *Dictionary* contains a key and an associated value for each entry. The key makes it easy to locate a particular value using a human-readable term. The key and the value can be any data type. However, this example uses the *String* type for both the key and the value, as shown in Listing 4-5.

LISTING 4-5 Creating a global dictionary and filling it with data

```
// Create a global storage location.
Dictionary<String, String> Herbs;

public Form1()
{
    InitializeComponent();

    // Instantiate the dictionary.
    Herbs = new Dictionary<string, string>();

    // Add entries to the dictionary.
    Herbs.Add("Basil",
        "A somewhat minty herb used mainly with meat dishes.");
    Herbs.Add("Caraway",
        "A licorice-tasting herb commonly used in German cooking.");
    Herbs.Add("Chives",
        "An onion-tasting herb used in soups and salads.");
    Herbs.Add("Bay",
        "A minty-tasting herb used in leaf form in soups and sauces.");
    Herbs.Add("Garlic",
        "A pungent herb that comes in many varieties from mild to spicy.");
    Herbs.Add("Anise",
        "An herb with a strong licorice taste and smell.");
    Herbs.Add("Mint",
        "An invasive leafy herb that comes in a vast array of flavors.");
    Herbs.Add("Savory",
        "A piney/peppery herb used mainly to season meat dishes.");

    // Show the keys in lstHerbs.
    lstHerbs.Items.AddRange(Herbs.Keys.ToArray<String>());
}
```

The code begins by creating a *Dictionary* named *Herbs*. The *<String, String>* part of the variable declaration tells what short of data type is used for the key and the value. If you had wanted to use a number for the key, you might have declared *Herbs* using *Dictionary<Int32, String>* Herbs; instead. The first entry is always the key and the second entry is always the value.

Before you can use the data source, you must define it. Because *Dictionary* is a kind of object, programmers use a fancy term, *instantiate*, to say that the program is able to use *Herb*. In this case, the code says that *Herb* is equal to a new *Dictionary* object that relies on a *String* for the key and a *String* for the value. At this point, *Herb* is empty, so the code adds some entries to it using the *Add()* method. In each case, the code adds a key (Basil for the first entry) and an associated value ("A somewhat minty herb used mainly with meat dishes.") for the first entry.

For more information, see "instantiation" in the accompanying Start Here! Fundamentals of Microsoft .NET Programming *book. To obtain your copy, see the section titled "Free Companion eBook" in the introduction to this book, or turn to the instruction page at the back of the book.*

Creating the *Dictionary* doesn't display it anywhere on-screen. The application uses *lstHerbs* to display all the keys (the herb names) to the user. To get the herb names in a form that *lstHerbs* understands, the code first accesses the *Keys* property, which returns all the key values, and turns those key values into an array of strings using the *ToArray<String>()* method. *lstHerbs* stores all these entries in the Items property. The *AddRange()* method adds all the keys found in *Herbs* to *lstHerbs* using a single line of code.

All the examples to this point in the book have relied on the *Click* event to perform a task. The *Click* event is the most common event to handle for a control. However, this example relies on a *ListBox* control and the default action in this case is *SelectedIndexChanged* rather than *Click*. Whenever a user clicks an entry in the list, the example calls the *SelectedIndexChanged* event handler shown in Listing 4-6. In Design mode, simply double-click *lstHerbs* to create this event handler (just as you double-click a *Button* control to create the *Click* event handler). When the *SelectedIndexChanged* event fires, you can discover which item is selected using the *SelectedItem* property.

LISTING 4-6 Accessing the global dictionary and displaying an item

```
private void lstHerbs_SelectedIndexChanged(object sender, EventArgs e)
{
    // Display the current selection in the description.
    txtDescription.Text = Herbs[lstHerbs.SelectedItem.ToString()];
}
```

Note This code is less direct than the code you've seen so far. You'll explore it using the debugger in a minute, but briefly: the code *Herbs[lstHerbs.SelectedItem.ToString()]* first calls the *lstHerbs.SelectedItem* property to obtain the currently selected item in the list. Because that method returns a *ListItem* object, the code then calls *ToString()*. For a *ListItem*, calling *ToString()* returns a textual representation of the object it contains—in this case, a string that holds the herb name. That string gets passed to the Herbs dictionary, which then returns the value associated with that key—the herb description. As you'll recall, the herb names are the keys to the *Dictionary* values. Finally, that herb description gets assigned to the *txtDescription.Text* property, which causes the *TextBox* to display the description.

A *Dictionary* works like an array in some respects—you can access a specific element by providing an index. Unlike arrays, a *Dictionary* relies on the key you define as an index. If you supply the word *Basil* as an index, the *Dictionary* will return the associated value. This feature makes the *Dictionary* significantly easier to use. You'll better see how it works in the "Tracing Through the Dictionary Example" section of the chapter.

You still need some method of ending the application. The *Quit* button performs this task. Double-click the *Quit* button to create a *Click* event handler. Here's the simple code used to end the application in this case.

```
private void btnQuit_Click(object sender, EventArgs e)
{
    // End the program.
    Close();
}
```

Tracing Through the Dictionary Example

A large part of this example's code is in the setup, so that's where the tracing begins this time. Set a breakpoint at the *Herbs = new Dictionary<string, string>();* line of code shown in Listing 4-5. Of course, you also want to see how the selection occurs, so set a second breakpoint at the *txtDescription.Text = Herbs[lstHerbs.SelectedItem.ToString()];* line of code shown in Listing 4-6. In many situations you'll need to set multiple breakpoints to properly trace through an example.

Click Start Debugging to start the application. The application automatically stops at the first breakpoint you set. This example introduces a new way to work with data while you debug it. Hover the mouse over *Herbs* and you'll see a tooltip pop-up like the one shown in Figure 4-6.

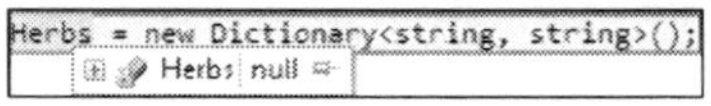

FIGURE 4-6 Tooltips tell you about the code that the mouse is pointing at.

Notice the little thumbtack icon on the right side of the pop-up. Click this thumbtack and the IDE will pin the information about *Herbs* to the display. If you later want to remove the *Herbs* information from the display, hover the mouse over it again and click the thumbtack icon again to unpin the information from the display. The thumbtack icon will appear on a separate graphic, as shown in Figure 4-7.

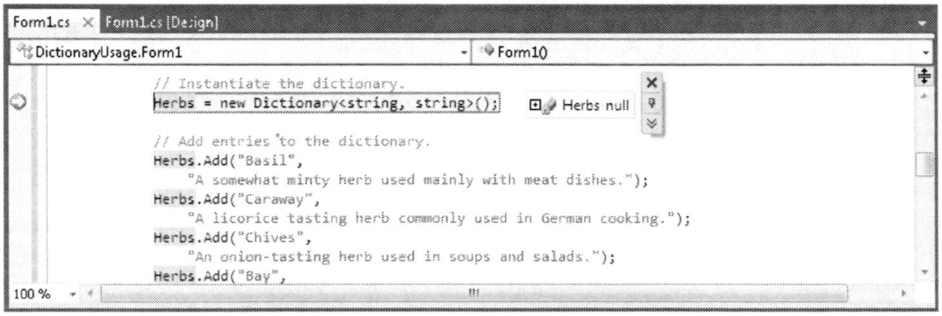

FIGURE 4-7 The thumbtack icon lets you pin information to the Code window.

Tip You can drag the Herbs entry anywhere you desire on screen. The initial position places it at the end of the line of code for convenience.

Click Step Over. The display shows that *Herbs* no longer equals *null*—it now has a count of 0, as shown in Figure 4-8.

```
Form1.cs × Form1.cs [Design]

DictionaryUsage.Form1                                  Form1()

        // Instantiate the dictionary.
        Herbs = new Dictionary<string, string>();   ⊞ Herbs Count = 0

        // Add entries to the dictionary.
        Herbs.Add("Basil",
            "A somewhat minty herb used mainly with meat dishes.");
        Herbs.Add("Caraway",
            "A licorice tasting herb commonly used in German cooking.");
        Herbs.Add("Chives",
            "An onion-tasting herb used in soups and salads.");
        Herbs.Add("Bay",
100 %
```

FIGURE 4-8 The pinned information shows any changes to the content of the variable.

Click Step Over. The count will change to 1. If you expand the variable now by clicking the plus signs (+), you'll see details about the *Dictionary*. The first entry will appear as a key/value pair as shown in Figure 4-9.

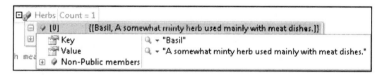

FIGURE 4-9 Once the *Dictionary* contains data, you can see how it works.

Continue clicking Step Over and you'll see the entries added one at a time. Eventually, you get to the last line of code. When you examine the *lstHerbs.Items* property, you see that it doesn't contain anything—the count is 0. However, look at *Herbs.Keys* and you'll see that it contains eight entries formatted as an array.

Click Step Over one more time. The instruction pointer should now be at the curly brace. When you examine *lstHerbs.Items* now, it contains eight entries. Unfortunately, you can't directly examine the eight entries, but they're the same as those contained in *Herbs.Keys*.

Click Continue. The form displays complete with the eight herb entries as shown in Figure 4-10. Notice that the Description doesn't contain anything yet because no one has selected an herb.

FIGURE 4-10 The user must select an herb before the Description field will contain anything.

Click Caraway. The debugger stops in the *lstHerbs_SelectedIndexChanged()* event handler. At this point, you can examine three important entries. First, hover your mouse over *txtDescription.Text*. You'll see that it doesn't contain anything, as shown in Figure 4-11.

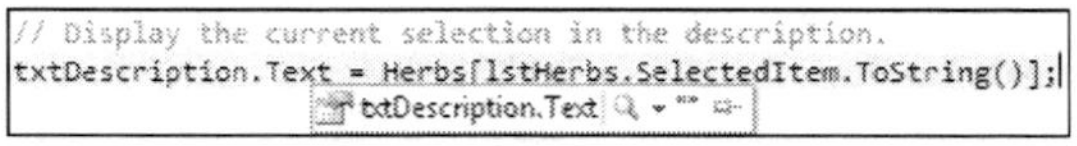

```
// Display the current selection in the description.
txtDescription.Text = Herbs[lstHerbs.SelectedItem.ToString()];
              txtDescription.Text  ▼  ""
```

FIGURE 4-11 Use the debugger to verify that *txtDescription.Text* doesn't contain anything.

Second, hover the mouse over *Herbs*. You'll find it contains eight entries, just as you'd expect, and that you can drill down into these entries if you wish.

Third, hover the mouse over *lstHerbs.SelectedItem*. You'll see that it contains the item you selected, Caraway, as shown in Figure 4-12.

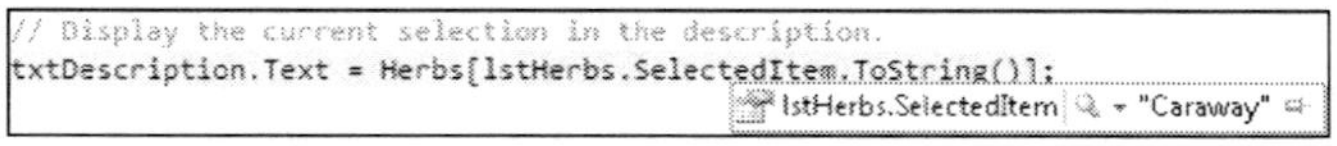

```
// Display the current selection in the description.
txtDescription.Text = Herbs[lstHerbs.SelectedItem.ToString()];
              lstHerbs.SelectedItem  ▼  "Caraway"
```

FIGURE 4-12 The *SelectedItem* property contains the user selection from the Choose Herb field.

Click Step Over. Hover the mouse over *txtDescription.Text* again. You'll find that it now contains the value associated with the key, *Caraway*. Clicking Continue brings you back to the form. Not surprisingly, the form now contains the descriptive text, as shown in Figure 4-13.

FIGURE 4-13 The debugging process finally results in the application output you anticipated.

Finish the process by clicking Quit. The application will end so that you can add some additional features to it.

Testing Sorting Theories

A data source seldom receives information in any particular order. However, humans often require some sort of order to make good use of information. The example has only a few entries, yet it could prove difficult to use because the entries aren't sorted. If you were asked to find Anise, it would require a few seconds, because the entry doesn't appear at the top of the list as you'd expect. Fortunately, the *ListBox* makes it easy to show information in sorted order. Listing 4-7 shows how to perform this task.

LISTING 4-7 Sorting the entries to make them easier to find

```
private void btnSort_Click(object sender, EventArgs e)
{
    // Tell the ListBox to display the information
    // in sorted order.
    lstHerbs.Sorted = true;
}
```

The simple act of setting *lstHerbs.Sorted* to *true* will place the entries in sorted order. Now consider that if you were using an array, changing the order of the *ListBox* items could cause a problem, because the numeric order of the entries is important. You'd use that numeric order to determine which item a user had clicked, and then use that number as the index to access the information in the array. A *Dictionary* overcomes this problem because it uses a text-based index. Try tracing through the application again to see how this works. Click Sort to sort the entries, and then click any of the entries in the Choose Herb list. You'll find that the use of the text-based index ensures that the application always selects the correct value to go with the key.

Testing Statistical Theories

Statistics are used to quantify all sorts of information. Of course, one of the simplest statistical forms is simple counting. Knowing how much of something exists is one of the few universal statistics that appears to affect everyone. LINQ can help you perform this task using very little code. Listing 4-8 shows how to perform this task.

LISTING 4-8 Counting entries that begin with C

```
private void btnStats_Click(object sender, EventArgs e)
{
    // Obtain a list of keys that begin with C.
    var Count = from String TheEntry
                in Herbs.Keys.ToArray<String>()
                where TheEntry.Substring(0,1) == "C"
                select TheEntry;
```

```
// Count the number of entries and display a message box
// showing the count.
MessageBox.Show("The number of entries that begin with C: " +
    Count.Count<String>().ToString());
}
```

The code begins by creating the variable *Count*, which contains a list of keys that begin with the letter C. In this case, the *from* clause contains a *String*, *TheEntry*, that's found in the array of *Herbs.Keys*. It's interesting to trace through this example because the *where* clause uses just the first letter of each key, which you obtain by calling the *Substring()* method. Remember that strings begin at position 0 and that the second argument to *Substring()* contains the number of letters you want to obtain from the string (1 in this case). When the *Substring* method returns a "C" LINQ performs the *select* clause. The result is that *Count* contains only the keys beginning with C.

To display the output from *Count*, the example relies on the *MessageBox.Show()* method. This method accepts a string as the first input. The example creates an explanatory string and adds the count to it. The *Count.Count()* method returns the number of entries in *Count* as a number. The *ToString()* method converts that number into a string that's compatible with the *MessageBox.Show()* method. (Remember that the string "2" and the number 2 are not the same thing; one is a string, and the other is a number.) Figure 4-14 shows what you'll see when you click Stats on the example application. (Click OK to clear the dialog box when you're finished.)

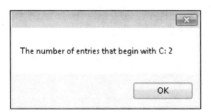

The number of entries that begin with C: 2

OK

FIGURE 4-14 Clicking Stats shows the number of entries that begin with the letter C.

Understanding Structures

You're going to encounter situations where Microsoft can't provide the precise form of storage that your application needs. For example, you might need to create an address list that includes a name, address, city, state, and ZIP code (imagine this address is complete for the sake of simplicity—real addresses are much more complex). None of the forms of storage that C# provides will accommodate an address, so you need to define your own storage, or rather, you need to tell C# what you want to store so that it can create appropriate storage for you. One way (of many) of performing this task is to create a *structure*. A structure is a kind of blueprint that tells C# how to organize information in a way that makes sense for your application. Structures are extremely flexible storage bins.

Many sources make structures sound complex, but they're really quite simple. Think of a structure as a bundle of items that go together. You already create similar bundles all the time in real life.

For example, packing a lunch into a container so you can go on a picnic is a real-life example of working with a structure. You're bundling things that go together into a single package. Creating a structure in an application is the same thing, except you're describing data items, rather than elements of a picnic.

Structures normally exist as separate entities from the code used for your application. To define a structure, you begin with the keyword *struct*—an abbreviation that C# understands. You need to know one other keyword, *public*. C# treats everything you tell it as secret unless you tell it otherwise. The *public* keyword tells C# that it's OK to share something. Don't worry too much about the need to make things public or keep them secret for now—that's a topic for a later discussion.

Creating the Structure Project

The example in this section shows an extremely simple list of addresses and how you might store them using a structure. It's important to know that structures fulfill many purposes in applications, but that they aren't the only way to store complex data. However, structures are the simplest way to store complex data, which is the reason you use a structure in this example. The following sections will help you create and examine structures in more detail.

Starting the Structure Project

Follow the instructions found in the "Starting the Dictionary Project" section of the chapter. However, give your application the name **StructureUsage** in place of *DictionaryUsage*.

Adding the Structure Project Controls

Applications that work with individual pieces of data require a larger number of controls than the examples you've seen so far. First, you need controls that let you perform a number of tasks with the data:

- Display
- Add
- Delete
- Modify

This example application keeps things simple by focusing on displaying the data. To perform this task, you need two *Button* controls—one that causes the next address to display, and one to display the previous address. A third *Button* control will close the application. A typical address book application would also include buttons to move to the first address and to the last address, along with a *TextBox* control to go to a specific address. This example won't include these controls to reduce complexity, but you need to know that they'd normally exist.

A structure provides the means to work with several pieces of data. Each data element requires a separate control set if you want to change it separately. The control set will include a *Label* (for identification) and a *TextBox* (for display/editing) in this example. The following data elements are supported by this application:

- Name

- Address

- City

- State

- ZIP Code

> **Note** In an actual address application, you'd include more than a simple Name field. The application would include separate fields for the person's title, first name, middle initial, last name, and possibly a suffix (a total of 10 fields because each entry would require a *Label* control for identification and a *TextBox* for the data). In many cases, real-world applications use special controls to make it easier for users to interact with the data. This example simplifies the control structure so you don't get bogged down in details that don't matter too much at this point.

Figure 4-15 shows how the controls should look on the form.

FIGURE 4-15 Create a form that contains the controls shown here.

Configuring the Structure Project Controls

Address applications normally appear as part of a resizable window rather than as a fixed-size dialog box. Fortunately, C# provides control settings that make it possible to allow a form to resize and retain the proper control appearance. However, that means making some additional control settings changes. Table 4-3 shows the control configuration for this example.

TABLE 4-3 *StructureUsage* Control Configuration

Control Name	Property Name	Value
button1	(Name)	btnNext
	Anchor	Top, Right
	Text	&Next
button2	(Name)	btnPrevious
	Anchor	Top, Right
	Text	&Previous
button3	(Name)	btnQuit
	Anchor	Top, Right
	Text	&Quit
label1	Text	Na&me
textBox1	(Name)	txtName
	Anchor	Top, Left, Right
	ReadOnly	True
	Size.Width	179
	Size.Height	20
label2	Text	&Address
textBox2	(Name)	txtAddress
	Anchor	Top, Left, Right
	ReadOnly	True
	Size.Width	179
	Size.Height	20
label3	Text	&City
textBox3	(Name)	txtCity
	Anchor	Top, Left, Right
	ReadOnly	True
	Size.Width	179
	Size.Height	20
label4	Text	&State
textBox4	(Name)	txtState
	Anchor	Top, Left, Right

Control Name	Property Name	Value
	ReadOnly	True
	Size.Width	179
	Size.Height	20
label5	Text	&ZIP Code
textBox5	(Name)	txtZIPCode
	Anchor	Top, Left, Right
	ReadOnly	True
	Size.Width	179
	Size.Height	20
Form1	Text	Using a Structure
	CancelButton	btnQuit

The *Anchor* setting requires a little additional explanation because it uses a special technique. Anchoring is the process of attaching the control a certain distance from the side(s) of the form. When users resize the form, the control remains at that fixed distance from the sides of the form to which it is anchored—even if that means making the control larger or smaller. Consequently, when you attach a *Button* to the top and right side of the form, it means that the control will move with the right side of the form when you resize it. In contrast, the *TextBox* control is anchored to the top, left, and right sides of the form, meaning that the control will grow horizontally when you resize the form. When you click the down arrow in the *Anchor* property, you'll see a special dialog box appear like the one shown in Figure 4-16.

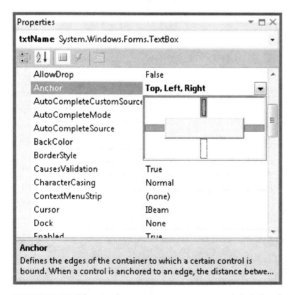

FIGURE 4-16 The *Anchor* property uses a special dialog box to help describe how to anchor a control to its form.

The control you're anchoring is represented by the box in the center. The anchors appear as bars emanating from the control. Click a bar to create or remove an anchor to that side. A gray bar tells you that the anchor is enabled. In this figure, the control is anchored to the *Top*, *Left*, and *Right* sides of the form, but not anchored to the *Bottom*.

Creating a Structure

It's time to begin defining the structure you'll use to hold the address data for this example. Right-click *Form1* in Solution Explorer and choose Show Code from the context menu. You'll see the code editor. As previously mentioned, a structure normally appears separately from the form code. The example uses a structure named Addresses. Create and place this structure as shown in the bold code in Listing 4-9.

LISTING 4-9 Adding a structure to the application

```
namespace StructureUsage
{
    public struct Addresses
    {
    }

    public partial class Form1 : Form
    {
        public Form1()
        {
            InitializeComponent();
        }
    }
}
```

The *Addresses* structure isn't complete; it's simply a framework. However, the listing does show how to start the structure. Notice that you include three words: *public* (to make the structure accessible to anyone), *struct* (to define the structure), and *Addresses* (the name of the structure). This is the way you normally add a structure to an application.

Now that you have a structure framework, you can fill out the structure with the data items that it will store. Listing 4-10 shows the completed structure.

LISTING 4-10 Defining the structure content

```
// Defines a single address.
public struct Addresses
{
    public String Name;     // Person's name.
    public String Address;  // Person's street address.
    public String City;     // City in which the person lives.
```

```
    public String State;    // State in which the person lives.
    public String ZIPCode;  // Location's ZIP code.
}
```

Each of the entries is declared as *public* so that you can access it. The element's data type comes next, followed by the element's name. Make sure you document each of the elements so that no one (including you) has to guess the element's use. Use an easily remembered and logical name for each element.

At this point, the structure is complete from a data perspective. You have one variable for each of the elements you want to store. However, structures commonly need an easy way to add new entries. A structure can have a special constructor that accepts all the data values when the code creates a new object based on the structure. This example adds the special constructor, shown in Listing 4-11, to the structure as a whole.

LISTING 4-11 Adding a special constructor

```
// Defines a single address.
public struct Addresses
{
    // Make it easy to add new names by providing a special
    // constructor.
    public Addresses(
        String NewName, String NewAddress, String NewCity,
        String NewState, String NewZIP)
    {
        // Add each input value to the value inside the structure.
        Name = NewName;
        Address = NewAddress;
        City = NewCity;
        State = NewState;
        ZIPCode = NewZIP;
    }

    public String Name;     // Person's name.
    public String Address;  // Person's street address.
    public String City;     // City in which the person lives.
    public String State;    // State in which the person lives.
    public String ZIPCode;  // Location's ZIP code.
}
```

This is the first time you've added a constructor to anything in the book. A constructor is simply a set of instructions that the application uses in this case to construct (create) the structure. This constructor simply accepts a data value for each of the structure's entries and then makes the appropriate assignments.

Adding the Structure Example Code

From working through the other examples in this chapter, you know that one of the first things you'll need to do is create a public variable used to hold a number of the Addresses structures. No one has just one address. You could use an array for this task, but another object works better—a *List*. If you create your structure carefully, using a *List* to interact with it is easy, and you won't have to write a lot of code. Listing 4-12 shows the code used to create a *List* of *Addresses* and fill it with data.

LISTING 4-12 Creating a List of Addresses

```
// Declare a List of addresses.
List<Addresses> MyAddresses;

// Keep track of the current entry.
Int32 CurrentEntry;

public Form1()
{
    InitializeComponent();

    // Initialize the array.
    MyAddresses = new List<Addresses>();

    // Add entries to the array.
    MyAddresses.Add(
        new Addresses(
            "Mark Hanson", "123 Anywhere Street", "Somewhere", "UT", "99999"));
    MyAddresses.Add(
        new Addresses(
            "Kim Abercrombie", "456 5th Avenue", "Outback", "AK", "99998"));
    MyAddresses.Add(
        new Addresses(
            "Armando Pinto", "9925 Galaxy Drive", "Nowhere", "IN", "99997"));

    // Set the initial entry.
    CurrentEntry = 0;

    // Display the first element on screen.
    ShowEntry();
}
```

The code begins by defining *MyAddresses*, which is a *List* of type *Addresses*. Because this example works with a list of addresses, you also need some means of tracking the current entry, so the code also creates *CurrentEntry*. You'll see how this variable is used in the "Tracing Through the Structure Example" section of the chapter. For now, all you need to know is that it's important to track the current entry number.

The next step is to initialize *MyAddresses* and fill it with data. One of the reasons to use a *List* is that an array doesn't provide you with the *Add()* method shown here. In fact, if you try to use an array, you'll write tons of code simply to manage the act of adding new entries. Using a *List* is far simpler. You can also see the reason now for the special constructor in the *Addresses* structure. The code adds a new address entry by creating a new *Addresses* object and supplying the values that should appear in that entry. It's a neat and simple way to accomplish the task.

The code also initializes *CurrentElement* to zero. It then calls the *ShowEntry()* method. The *ShowEntry()* method is special. Sometimes you perform a sequence of steps so often and from so many places, that you don't want to repeat the code. After all, who wants to do all that typing? In addition, placing the code in one place means that you only have to change the code once when a change is required. Creating special methods when needed also makes the code easier to understand. For all these reasons and more, this example creates a special method called *ShowEntry()*, as shown in Listing 4-13.

LISTING 4-13 Defining the *ShowEntry()* method

```
public void ShowEntry()
{
    // Display each of the address elements.
    txtName.Text = MyAddresses[CurrentEntry].Name;
    txtAddress.Text = MyAddresses[CurrentEntry].Address;
    txtCity.Text = MyAddresses[CurrentEntry].City;
    txtState.Text = MyAddresses[CurrentEntry].State;
    txtZIPCode.Text = MyAddresses[CurrentEntry].ZIPCode;
}
```

As you can see, this method simply copies the content of the current entry—the one pointed to by *CurrentEntry*—to the *TextBox* controls on the form. The use of a variable as an index makes this method useful anytime you need to display the data. It doesn't matter which record is current; this code will always work as long as *CurrentEntry* is kept up to date.

If you ran the example right now, you'd see the first address entry (also called a *record* by database programmers) for Mark Hanson displayed when the form appears on-screen. However, you couldn't see any of the other entries because the Next and Previous buttons don't work yet. Double-click each of these controls in turn to create the required event handlers. Listing 4-14 shows the code used to update the display to show each of the elements in turn.

LISTING 4-14 Displaying different address entries

```
private void btnNext_Click(object sender, EventArgs e)
{
    // Determine if this is the last entry.
    if (CurrentEntry+1 == MyAddresses.Count)
    {
```

```csharp
        // If so, disable the Next button.
        btnNext.Enabled = false;

        // Tell the user that this is the last entry.
        MessageBox.Show("Last Entry!");
    }

    else

        // Update the current entry.
        CurrentEntry++;

    // Determine if it's acceptable to enable the Previous button.
    if (MyAddresses.Count > 1)

        btnPrevious.Enabled = true;

    // Display the current entry.
    ShowEntry();
}

private void btnPrevious_Click(object sender, EventArgs e)
{
    // Determine if this is the first entry.
    if (CurrentEntry == 0)
    {

        // If so, disable the Previous button.
        btnPrevious.Enabled = false;

        // Tell the user that this is the last entry.
        MessageBox.Show("First Entry!");
    }

    else

        // Update the current entry.
        CurrentEntry--;

    // Determine if it's acceptable to enable the Next button.
    if (CurrentEntry+1 < MyAddresses.Count)

        btnNext.Enabled = true;

    // Display the current entry.
    ShowEntry();
}
```

These two event handlers work in a similar way, which is why you're seeing them together. It's a good idea to look at these two event handlers carefully to see how they're the same and how they differ. The code begins by looking at the value of *CurrentEntry*. When *CurrentEntry* is either at the last entry or the first entry, the code disables the appropriate button (so that you see that there aren't any more entries to see) and also displays a message box. Otherwise, the code updates the value of *CurrentEntry*. Clicking Next adds 1 to *CurrentEntry* (so that the display moves to the next entry in the list), whereas clicking Previous subtracts 1 from *CurrentEntry* (so that the display moves to the previous entry in the list).

The next step is to determine the status of the other button. If the code doesn't provide a way to enable buttons after disabling them, both buttons will become disabled and you'll never be able to see any other records. When working with the Previous button, the *List* must contain more than one entry (otherwise, there will never be a previous entry). When working with the Next button, *CurrentEntry* can't point to the end of the *List* (otherwise, there isn't a next entry). At this point, the code calls *ShowEntry()* to display the entry based on the value of *CurrentEntry*. Now you can understand a little better why there's a common way to display information on screen.

By now, you know how to create the *btnQuit_Click()* event handler. The "Adding the Dictionary Code" section shows how to add the code for that example—you can use the same code in this case.

Tracing Through the Structure Example

This is the most complex example so far in the book. However, it demonstrates some important ideas that you'll find in many applications. Being able to update a form is incredibly important.

A First Run Through the Structure Application

1. Begin by clicking Start Debugging, without setting any breakpoint. You'll see the initial form shown here.

2. Click Next, and you'll see the next entry in *MyAddresses* (Kim Abercrombie).

3. Click Next again and you'll see the third entry (Armando Pinto).

   If you click Next again, you'll see a message box saying that this is the last entry. In addition, the code disables the Next button, making it impossible to try to move to the next entry again.

4. Click through the entries in reverse, using the Previous button, and you'll see that that feature also works as you would expect. Playing with an application often tells you something about how it works.

5. Click Quit to end the program.

This application does quite a bit, but you can see it all by setting breakpoints at the following lines of code:

- *MyAddresses = new List<Addresses>(); (in Form1())*

- *if (CurrentEntry+1 == MyAddresses.Count) (in btnNext_Click())*

- *if (CurrentEntry == 0) (in btnPrevious_Click())*

A More Detailed Debugging Session

1. Click Start Debugging. The application will stop at the first breakpoint. You can use the technique described in the "Tracing Through the Dictionary Example" section to pin the *MyAddresses* variable to the display area so that you can watch it easily. At this point, *MyAddresses* is *null* because it hasn't been initialized.

2. Click Step Over and you'll see that *MyAddresses* is now initialized but has 0 entries.

3. Click Step Into. Suddenly you'll find yourself in that special constructor you created for the *Addresses* structure.

4. Click Step Over. You can now hover the mouse over the *Name = NewName;* line of code. *Name* is currently equal to *null*, but *NewName* contains the value you expect.

5. Click Step Over again, and *Name* will now have the value you expect. You could follow each line of code in the constructor at this point, but because the application creates several addresses, doing so is simply repetitive.

6. To get back to your original location, click Step Out, press Shift+F11, or choose Debug | Step Out. Doing so takes you back to that first entry.

   The count is still 0 at this point. If you click either Step Into or Step Over, you'll end up at the next line of code and the *MyAddresses* count will increase to 1. In this case, it doesn't matter which of the two buttons you click because you've already stepped into the code. However, now you need to look at *MyAddresses*. When you look at entry 0, you'll see that it does indeed contain the expected data as shown here.

```
// Initialize the array.
MyAddresses = new List<Addresses>();          ⊟ ⚷ MyAddresses  Count = 1

// Add entries to the array.                    ⊟  ✓ [0]        {StructureUsage.Addresses}
MyAddresses.Add(                                ⊞  ⚷ Address  🔍 ▾ "123 Anywhere Street"
    new Addresses(                                 ⚷ City     🔍 ▾ "Somewhere"
        "Mark Hanson", "123 Anywhere Street"       ⚷ Name     🔍 ▾ "Mark Hanson"
MyAddresses.Add(                                   ⚷ State    🔍 ▾ "UT"
    new Addresses(                                 ⚷ ZIPCode  🔍 ▾ "99999"
        "Kim Abercrombie", "456 5th Avenue", "Outback", "AK", "99998"));
```

7. Click Step Over three more times until you get to the *ShowEntry();* line of code.

8. Click Step Into. Now you'll find yourself in the *ShowEntry()* method.

9. Click Step Over. Hover the mouse over *txtName.Text*, and you'll find that it's currently empty. However, if you hover the mouse over the *Name* portion of *MyAddresses[CurrentEntry]. Name*, you'll find that it contains the correct name to put in the *txtName.Text* property. The debugger shows that it knows which entry to use based on the value of *CurrentEntry*, which is *0* in this case. If you hover the mouse over *MyAddresses*, you'll see that it contains three entries and that you can drill down into any of the entries.

10. Click Continue and you'll see the form appear.

    By now, you have a pretty good idea of what's going on with at least part of the Next and Previous buttons, but it's important to actually trace through them to see how things work.

11. Click Next. The debugger stops at the second breakpoint (the one in *btnNext_Click()*). Look at that first line of code. If you hover the mouse over *CurrentEntry*, you'll see that it has a value of *0* (unless you've played around with the application, in which case it will contain the value of whatever entry you last worked with). Hover the mouse over the *1* and you'll see a value *1* more than the value of *CurrentEntry*, just as you'd expect. When you hover the mouse over the *Count* portion of *MyAddresses.Count*, you'll see a value of *3*. Finally, hover the mouse over the *==* and you'll see that the debugger tells you that the statement is false, which means that the first part of this statement shouldn't execute.

12. Click Step Over. The instruction pointer goes right to the *CurrentEntry++;* line of code as expected. Click Step Over again, and you'll see that the value of *CurrentEntry* increments to *1* so that the application will display the next *MyAddresses* entry.

    It's time to look at the truth value of *MyAddresses.Count > 1*. When you hover the mouse over the > sign, you see that this statement is *true*.

13. Click Step Over twice more, and you'll see that the code does indeed enable the Previous button. At this point, click Continue and you'll see the form with the next entry displayed.

Try tracing through the Previous button code at this point to see how it differs from the Next button code.

Get Going with C#

This chapter explored a new method for storing data—collections. C# has access to many collection types and you can even create your own collection types when necessary. The most commonly used collections are arrays, dictionaries, and structures. Arrays are the easiest of the collection types to use, but they have access limitations in access and the things you can do to the data members using just a little code. A general rule to remember is that code constructs that are simpler to use typically limit flexibility in some way—in other words, you gain simplicity at the cost of flexibility.

You've worked through several examples in this chapter. Make sure you trace through each of the examples to ensure that you know how they work. The chapter sections traced through only some of the code, so you have plenty of opportunity to explore. Try changing the code slightly to see what happens when you do. For example, when working with the LINQ query version of the array example, try changing the array element that the code accesses.

Another popular method for storing data is XML. Unlike the methods shown in the book so far, XML provides a straightforward way to store data permanently on the hard drive. In other words, you can make changes to the data and then see those changes again when you restart the application. XML is used in many technologies today, so learning about it is extremely important if you want to be able to work with as many different code techniques as possible. Chapter 5, "Working with XML," provides a good start for working with XML, but you'll see XML in other chapters of the book as well.

Chapter 5

Working with XML

After completing this chapter, you'll be able to:

- Describe the basics of XML

- Using XML and LINQ to create a query

- Save XML data to disk

- Read XML data from disk

- Create an application that stores user settings using XML

FROM YOUR APPLICATION'S PERSPECTIVE, *data* is the information created or used by your application, including things such as settings that the user relies on to configure or customize the application, or an external source of information that your application uses. So far, all the applications in this book have relied on short-term data that "evaporates" when the application closes. Most applications also provide long-term data storage, saving users' information so that the next time they open the application, their data will be present, too. To provide meaningful data storage, an application must not only store the data, but also define how that data is used. For example, storing just the user's name won't tell you how the data is used. However, storing the user's name with context information saying that this information is used to associate other data with that particular user is helpful.

There are many ways to store data together with its context. One of the most popular ways is to use the eXtensible Markup Language (XML) to provide the context information, along with a storage container. You can find XML everywhere. It appears online, within Windows, and on other platforms as well. XML is a sort of universal storage methodology, which is why you really need to know how it works. The following sections describe XML, tell you why XML is such an important technology, show you how XML is constructed, and demonstrate how to use XML in your applications.

Understanding XML

A single chapter can't describe XML in detail—entire books are devoted to the topic of XML. Fortunately, the basic idea behind XML is easy to understand—and you don't need much more than a basic idea to work through the examples in this book. This section provides enough information about XML to allow you to work through the examples and understand what you're seeing, but it won't turn you into an XML expert.

One of the most important things to remember is that XML is *pure text*. You can create and view an XML file using any text editor, such as Notepad. Because XML is pure text, you can use it on literally any platform without worrying about compatibility. In the past, data storage used odd, customized formats that you often couldn't read in Notepad and that didn't transfer very well to other platforms. The use of these other formats caused developers significant grief. Just to demonstrate how this all works, here's how to use Notepad to create an XML file.

Create an XML File in Notepad

1. Begin by opening Notepad. Every XML file begins with a simple declaration that says, "I'm an XML file!" The declaration also tells the XML version number. The declaration doesn't change much from file to file. There are a few permutations that you don't have to worry about. An XML declaration normally looks like this:

    ```
    <?xml version="1.0"?>
    ```

2. Type the preceding XML declaration into Notepad. Of course, a declaration without any data isn't useful.

    XML files use what is called a *tree structure*. Don't worry too much about what this means just yet. All you really need to think about for the moment is that XML files look sort of like trees with branches and leaves. The first part of any tree is a root, and it's the same for XML. An XML file contains just one root.

3. Press Enter to get to a new line, and then type the following root into your XML file:

    ```
    <sample>
    </sample>
    ```

    These two entries are called *tags*. A tag begins with an opening angle bracket (<), and contains an identifier without spaces and then a closing angle bracket (>). Taken together, these entries are a *node*—specifically, a root node. Notice that the second tag contains a slash (/). The slash tells you that this tag closes the node. So the first tag opens a node and the second tag, which starts with </, closes it.

    You can place any number of nodes you want within the root nodes. These nodes are called *children* of the root node and from their perspective the root node is their *parent*.

4. Add two *data* nodes like this between the opening and closing root node:

```
<data>
</data>
<data>
</data>
```

 Note To make it easy to see the levels of an XML file, most developers indent child nodes, but XML doesn't require any indentation.

At this point, you have lots of nodes, but no data. The nodes define the context of the data.

5. Add some data between each of the *<data>* nodes. Add **Hello** between the first opening and closing *<data>* tag and **Goodbye** between the second opening and closing *<data>* tag. Your XML file will look similar to this:

6. It's time to save the file. Choose File | Save. In the Save As Type field, select the All Files (*.*) entry. This option lets you save files with something other than a .txt extension. Choose Desktop as the destination for the file. Type **Sample.XML** and then click Save. Notepad will save your XML file to the Desktop where you can access it easily.

You can open this file for viewing in a number of ways. For example, if you double-click the file, it will normally open in Internet Explorer, as shown in Figure 5-1 (if it doesn't open in Internet Explorer, it means that the default Windows file extension association for XML files has somehow gotten changed on your system):

FIGURE 5-1 The XML file should appear in Internet Explorer when using the default file association.

The nice part about viewing XML files using Internet Explorer is that it formats and color codes the contents. In this case, the XML declaration appears in blue type, the nodes in brown, and the data in black. Internet Explorer automatically reformats the entries for easy viewing, no matter how you created them in the first place. At this point, you can close both Notepad and Internet Explorer.

Combining XML and LINQ

You might have noticed in previous examples that the form code is always placed within a namespace that has the same name as the example. For example, the form code for the *StructureUsage* example in Chapter 4, "Using Collections to Store Data," is placed within the *StructureUsage* namespace. Look again at Listing 4-9 and you'll see how the namespace acts as a container. As you can see, a namespace is always defined by the *namespace* keyword, followed by the namespace name.

The .NET Framework provides a host of namespaces. Up until now you haven't had to worry about them because the programs have been simple. However, when you start creating applications that mix XML and Language Integrated Query (LINQ), you must become aware of namespaces because this combination requires use of a special namespace, *System.Xml.Linq*. This namespace contains special features that make it easy to create XML documents within your application. The project in this section demonstrates how to use the *System.Xml.Linq* namespace to create an XML document that you can then display within your application.

Defining the XML_LINQ Project

Follow the instructions found in the "Starting the Array Project" section of Chapter 4. However, give your application the name **XML_LINQ** instead of *ArrayUsage*.

Adding and Configuring the XML_LINQ Controls

This example uses a simple interface. It includes two *Button* controls. The Test button lets you test the application. The Quit button provides a way to end the application. A *Label* and *TextBox* combination provide the means for displaying the application's output. You'll place the controls much as you have for the other examples in the book. Table 5-1 shows how to configure these controls.

TABLE 5-1 XML_LINQ Control Configuration

Control Name	Property Name	Value
button1	(Name)	btnTest
	Anchor	Top, Right
	Text	&Test
button2	(Name)	btnStats
	Anchor	Top, Right
	Text	S&tats
label1	Text	&XML Output

textBox1	(Name)	txtOutput
	Anchor	Top, Left, Right
	Multiline	True
	ReadOnly	True
	ScrollBars	Both
	Size.Width	179
	Size.Height	225
Form1	Text	Defining XML Using LINQ
	AcceptButton	btnTest
	CancelButton	btnQuit

Notice that this example uses the window style (rather than a dialog box style) and it has a default Accept button. After you configure the controls, your form should look like the one shown in Figure 5-2.

FIGURE 5-2 The configured application should include a Test button and XML Output field.

Using the *System.Xml.Linq* Namespace

As previously mentioned, this example is different from previous examples because now you need to think about the namespaces the application requires to work. This example provides only part of the namespace picture—you'll get more of it in later examples. In this case, you add a *using* statement to the beginning of the code. The *using* statement simply tells the compiler to use a particular namespace. To see the other *using* statements at the beginning of the example, right-click Form1.cs in Solution Explorer and choose View Code. You'll see the Code Editor, as shown in Figure 5-3.

FIGURE 5-3 The Code window automatically appears when you choose the View Code option on the context menu.

All these *using* statements appear at the top, before the application's namespace declaration. This is where you should place any additional *using* statements. In this case, add the following *using* statement for the example:

```
usingSystem.Xml.Linq;
```

Adding the XML_LINQ Code

Double-click *btnClose* and add the usual event handler code for ending the application. This is the same code you used in the "Configuring the Array Project Controls" section of Chapter 4.

Double-click *btnTest* and you'll see a new event handler. This event handler creates the XML document (much as you did using Notepad earlier) and then displays the result in *txtOutput*. Listing 5-1 shows the code you need to perform this task.

LISTING 5-1 Creating an XML document using code

```csharp
private void btnTest_Click(object sender, EventArgs e)
{
    // Build the XML document.
    XDocumentNewDoc = new XDocument(
        new XDeclaration("1.0", "UTF-8", "yes"),
        new XElement("sample",
            new XElement("data", "Hello"),
            new XElement("data", "Goodbye")));
    // Display the result on screen.
    txtOutput.Text = NewDoc.Declaration + "\r\n" + NewDoc.ToString();
}
```

The code begins by creating an XML document, *NewDoc*, using an *XDocument* object. As with the Notepad example, you begin by creating an XML declaration. This declaration contains a little more information than the original. The first argument is the XML version number, *"1.0"*. The second argument tells what kind of text formatting to use. This example uses 8-bit Unicode Transformation Format (UTF) characters. There are other forms of UTF and you can read about them at *http://unicode. org/faq/utf_bom.html*, but it's a complex subject, and all you really need to know is that UTF-8 is the standard format for XML documents. The third argument, *"yes"*, simply states that this is a stand-alone document.

The next step is to add the root node, *<sample>*. The example does this by creating a new *XElement* object. The first argument is always the name of the element, which is *sample* in this case. The second argument is the content of the element. This example creates two *<data>* nodes within the *<sample>* node. It can be easy to get lost in the layers if you're not careful, so make sure you format your code carefully, as shown in Listing 5-1, to keep things straight. The *<data>* nodes contain specific values.

There isn't any way to display everything *NewDoc* contains directly. The example sets *txtOutput. Text* equal to a combination of *NewDoc.Declaration*, which contains the XML declaration, and *NewDoc.ToString()*, which provides the rest of the XML as formatted output (much as Internet Explorer does it, but without the color coding). When you run this application, you'll see the output shown in Figure 5-4.

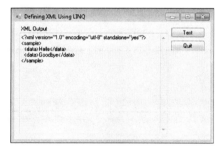

FIGURE 5-4 The example output is the XML file that you created earlier.

Developing the XMLSave Application

The example shown in the "Combining XML and LINQ" section of this chapter creates a new XML document in memory. However, the document isn't permanent. To make the document permanent, you must save it to the hard drive. The example described in the following sections demonstrates how to save an XML document to the hard drive (to the Desktop in this case).

Creating the XMLSave Project

Follow the instructions found in the "Starting the Array Project" section of Chapter 4. However, give your application the name **XMLSave** instead of *ArrayUsage*.

Adding and Configuring the XMLSave Controls

All you need for this example are two buttons. The first button, Save, creates the XML document and saves it to disk. The second button, Quit, ends the application. Table 5-2 shows the configuration for these controls.

TABLE 5-2 XMLSave Control Configuration

Control Name	Property Name	Value
button1	(Name)	btnSave
	Text	&Save
button2	(Name)	btnQuit
	Text	&Quit
Form1	Text	Saving XML to Disk
	AcceptButton	btnTest
	CancelButton	btnQuit
	FormBorderStyle	FixedDialog

Adding XMLSave Application Code

It's time to add some code to this application. Add the usual code to *btnQuit* so that you can exit the application. Double-click *btnSave* to create the required event handler. Listing 5-2 shows the coded you need for this example.

> **Note** Just about every example in this book is going to contain *btnQuit*. From this point on, unless you read something to the contrary, assume that the *btnQuit* code will remain consistent.

LISTING 5-2 Saving an XML document to disk

```
private void btnSave_Click(object sender, EventArgs e)
{
    // Build the XML document.
    XDocumentNewDoc = new XDocument(
        new XDeclaration("1.0", "utf-8", "yes"),
        new XElement("sample",
            new XElement("data", "Hello"),
            new XElement("data", "Goodbye")));

    // Save the document to the hard drive.
    NewDoc.Save(
    Environment.GetFolderPath(
```

```
    Environment.SpecialFolder.DesktopDirectory) +
        "\\XMLSave.XML");

    // Display a success message.
    MessageBox.Show("File saved!");
}
```

This example starts with the save XML document shown in Listing 5-1 and it works the same as before. The statements create the same XML document as before in an *XDocument* object named *NewDoc*.

After you create the XML document, you can perform a number of tasks with it. One of those tasks is saving it to disk. To do that, you have to tell the application where to store the information. This example uses a special method named *Environment.GetFolderPath()* to obtain the location of the user's Desktop. No matter where the Desktop is stored, this method will find it for you. All you need to supply is *Environment.SpecialFolder.DesktopDirectory* to tell the method that you want this specific location. (It can find many other locations for you as well.) The name of the file comes last—XMLSave. XML. You have to add a double backslash (\\) to separate the filename from the folder path.

Before you can compile this application, you need to add the required *using* statement. Make sure you add this code to the beginning of the application with the other *using* statements:

```
usingSystem.Xml.Linq;
```

Testing the XMLSave Application

At this point, the example is ready to try. Begin the process by setting a breakpoint at the line that begins *XDocument NewDoc*. Click Start Debugging. You'll see the example form appear on-screen. Click Save and the debugger will stop at the breakpoint. Click Step Into. One of the limitations of the debugger and the tracing technique used in this book is that the instruction pointer moves to the next line. If you want to see how this code works, you'll have to break it up into smaller pieces.

For now, pin *NewDoc* to the editor. You'll find that you can drill down into the XML document, as shown in Figure 5-5, and see how it's put together.

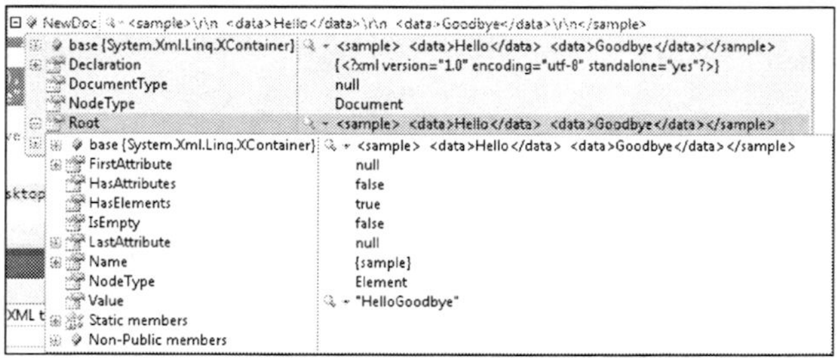

FIGURE 5-5 Use the IDE features to drill down into variables and see how they're constructed.

Notice that the *Declaration* and *Root* properties are treated separately, which is why you must work with them separately in code. The IDE also supports a special way of viewing XML called a visualizer. Click the down arrow next to the magnifying glass entry in the *Root* entry and you'll see three options:

- Text Visualizer

- XML Visualizer

- HTML Visualizer

Choose the XML Visualizer option. The IDE displays a dialog box containing the content of the *Root* property in XML form, as shown in Figure 5-6.

FIGURE 5-6 The XML Visualizer makes it easy to see the XML data in your application.

The purpose of visualizers is to make it easier to see how the data will actually appear outside of the application. Some data is simply too complex to interpret without the use of a visualizer. The example uses simple XML so that it's easy to work with, but using a visualizer might be the only way to properly interpret more complex XML used by a real-world application. After you are done looking at the XML, click Close.

The next line of code presents a challenge as well. If you hover the mouse over this code, you'll find that the IDE doesn't provide a means to view it. However, you can view the code output using a number of techniques. For example, you could drag each of the individual lines to the Watch window to produce a single line of code like this:

```
Environment.GetFolderPath(Environment.SpecialFolder.DesktopDirectory) + "\\XMLSave.XML"
```

The code must appear in a single watch statement or the IDE won't be able to interpret it. However, this value won't change for the entirety of the application. So the best way to view it is to copy the individual lines to the Immediate window. This option provides instant feedback, as shown in Figure 5-7 (your output will look different than mine because your output will reflect the setup of your system):

FIGURE 5-7 Sometimes you must use the Immediate window to view the content of a variable.

The result shows you precisely where the file will appear on your system. Click Continue. You'll see a dialog box telling you that the file has been saved. In addition, you'll see the XMLSave.XML file appear on your Desktop. Click OK to clear the dialog box. Click Quit to exit the application.

Viewing the XMLSave Output

The proof that this application works is in how the output appears. Many applications work with XML on your computer, but the easiest way to view the file is to use a browser. Double-click XMLSave. XML on your desktop, and you should see the Internet Explorer display shown in Figure 5-8 (or in the program associated with XML files on your system).

FIGURE 5-8 Internet Explorer shows the content of the XMLSave.XML file.

The result is what you hoped to obtain. The file contains everything that you originally created in the Sample.XML file, but in this case, the output is created programmatically. To get a better understanding of how all this works, try adding or removing nodes from the original example code. Check the output to see what you get from the example. XML is extremely flexible and one of the best ways to discover how it works is to play with the code. For example, what do you see if you substitute this code for the original document creation code?

```
// Build the XML document.
XDocumentNewDoc = new XDocument(
    new XDeclaration("1.0", "utf-8", "yes"),
    new XElement("sample",
        new XElement("data", "Hello"),
        new XElement("data", "Goodbye"),
        new XElement("colors",
            new XElement("data", "Yellow"),
            new XElement("data", "Blue"))));
```

Developing the XMLRead Application

At this point, you can create an application that can output XML to a file and open that file for viewing. It may not sound like much, but being able to perform this basic step gives you incredible flexibility in storing data for later use. Storing the data is only half the process, though. If you can't read the data stored on disk into your application, it doesn't make much sense to store it. After all, data stored but never used doesn't serve much of a purpose. The example in this section shows how to read the data in the XMLSave.XML file into an application, and display it on-screen.

Creating the XMLRead Project

Follow the instructions found in the "Starting the Array Project" section of Chapter 4. However, give your application the name **XMLRead** instead of *ArrayUsage*.

Adding and Configuring the XMLRead Controls

The purpose of this example is to read XML data from disk, place it into a local variable document, and then display that document on-screen. This example begins with two buttons. The Test button reads the XML document, places the content into a local variable, and displays the data on-screen. The Quit button ends the application. You also need a *Label* to identify the output and a *TextBox* to hold the output. The setup is similar to the XML_LINQ example described earlier. Table 5-3 shows the configuration for these controls.

TABLE 5-3 XMLRead Control Configuration

Control Name	Property Name	Value
button1	(Name)	btnTest
	Anchor	Top, Right
	Text	&Test
button2	(Name)	btnStats
	Anchor	Top, Right
	Text	S&tats
label1	Text	&XML Output
textBox1	(Name)	txtOutput
	Anchor	Top, Left, Right
	Multiline	True
	ReadOnly	True
	ScrollBars	Both
	Size.Width	179

	Size.Height	225
Form1	Text	Reading XML from Disk
	AcceptButton	btnTest
	CancelButton	btnQuit

Adding the XMLRead Application Code

At this point, you'll want to add code to read the information from disk. Double-click *btnTest* to create the required event handler. Listing 5-3 shows the code used for this part of the example.

Listing 5-3 Reading an XML document from disk

```
private void btnTest_Click(object sender, EventArgs e)
{
    // Read the document from disk.
    XDocumentNewDoc = XDocument.Load(
    Environment.GetFolderPath(
    Environment.SpecialFolder.DesktopDirectory) +
        "\\XMLSave.XML");

    // Display the result on screen.
    txtOutput.Text = NewDoc.Declaration + "\r\n" + NewDoc.ToString();
}
```

This part of the example relies on a new technique for creating an XML document. In this case, you declare a variable, *NewDoc*, of the *XDocument* type and then use something called a static method, *XDocument.Load()*, to load the information from disk. A static method is a special kind of method that you can call even if you haven't created a variable of the required type. The idea is that you should be able to load an XML file from disk without creating the variable first because the variable is based on the content of that XML file.

Notice that this example uses precisely the same method to discover the location of XMLSave.XML as the *XMLSave* example did. If this setting were somehow stored in the registry or another location, you could use it for any application that required it. A simple change would make it possible to use a new location or file, yet keep all applications that rely on the setting in sync. The "Using XML to Store Application Settings" section of the chapter discusses how to work with settings in more detail, but keep in mind that applications often need to store all kinds of information that doesn't affect the user directly, such as the location of files.

After the application retrieves the XML data from disk, it stores it in the local variable, *NewDoc*. The next step is to display the information on-screen. This example uses precisely the same technique as the XML_LINQ example to perform this task. At this point, a light should go off in your head. This example combines portions of other examples in new ways to perform a unique task. You'll find that you often combine elements from different applications in different ways to achieve a new result. That's another reason why it's so important to document your code fully—to save time later.

As with previous examples in this chapter, you also need to add the appropriate *using* statement to the beginning of the file:

```
usingSystem.Xml.Linq;
```

Testing the XMLRead Application

Start this example up and then click Test. You'll see the output showing the contents of the XMLSave. XML file, as shown in Figure 5-9. (End the example by clicking Quit when you get done viewing the output—you did remember to add the Quit button code, right?)

FIGURE 5-9 The example shows the data it read from the XMLSave.XML file.

Tracing the XMLRead Application with the Debugger

Tracing examples, even if you have a good idea of how they work, is still the best way to discover the particulars. For this example, start by placing a breakpoint at the line that begins with *XDocumentNewDoc*. Start the application and click the Text button. The debugger opens at the breakpoint so you can trace through the *btnTest* code.

Of course, the big question of this example is how to check the results of the *XDocument.Load()* method. This is a static method, so the method is directly accessible in the Immediate window. All you need to do is type a **?** and then copy the individual lines into a single line, as shown in Figure 5-10.

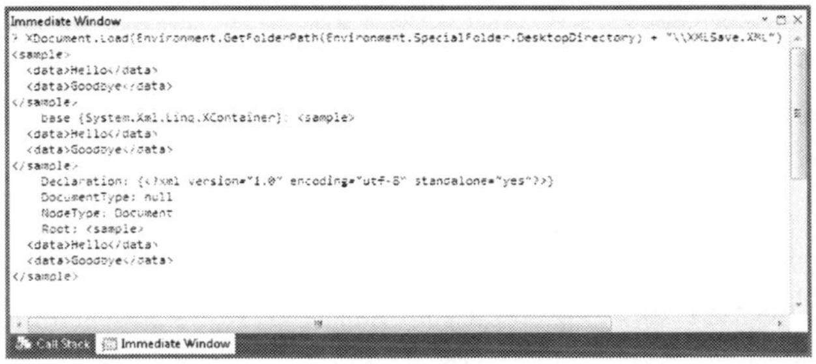

FIGURE 5-10 Use the Immediate window to see the results of the *XDocument.Load()* method.

The loading process displays the XML (without the declaration), and then it displays something called a *base class* (the class on which *XDocument* is based), which is *System.Xml.Linq.XContainer*. Don't worry too much about base classes now. However, you'll notice that the *Declaration* and *Root* properties are actually defined as part of the base class and that they appear as output in this case. In short, it's possible for you to view the output of a static method in the debugger.

Accessibility to static methods in the Immediate window means that you can try some "what if" scenarios with the code. For example, if you still have Sample.XML on your Desktop (and I hope you do), you can replace XMLSave.XML with Sample.XML in the Immediate window to see what happens. To do this, press the up arrow. You'll see the previous command reappear. Now use the standard editing keys to change the filename. Figure 5-11 shows what you'll see as output.

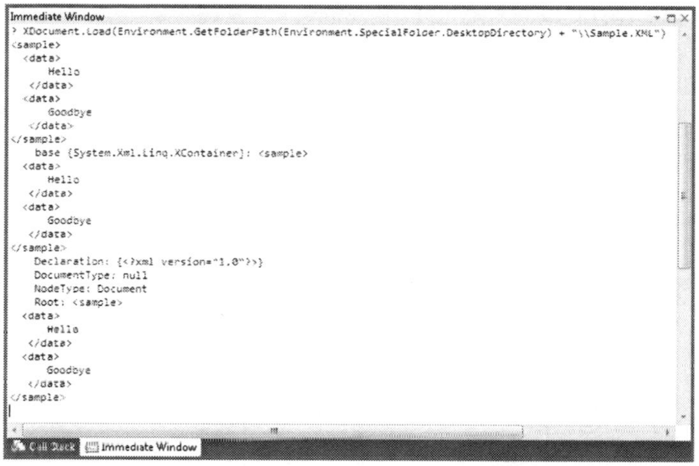

FIGURE 5-11 Use the Immediate window to play "what if" scenarios with static methods.

The Immediate window displays the results you expect. Use the Immediate window to experiment and discover how code works by modifying the parameters a little. Even if the code doesn't work, the worst you'll see is an error message. You won't ever lose data or cause the system to crash—this is a harmless sort of experimentation that can yield huge gains in knowledge about how your application works.

Click Continue. You'll notice that fiddling with the code in the Immediate window hasn't changed the application output. Click Quit to end the example.

Handling XML Exceptions

Sometimes your application won't work as expected. In some cases, the problem is in your code and it's called a bug. In other cases, the problem lies outside your code. When taken together, these two scenarios are described as an *exception*—essentially, the application is working differently from the rules that you set forth for it—an exception to the rule.

This section discusses a very important exception. You can write the best code in the world, but in some situations the user can sabotage your efforts. For example, what would happen if the user deleted the XMLSave.XML file? Well, let's give it a try. Highlight the XMLSave.XML file and press

Delete to remove it from your Desktop (placing it in the Recycle Bin) and then run the XMLRead application. Click Test. Suddenly you'll see the *FileNotFoundException* dialog box, shown in Figure 5-12.

FIGURE 5-12 Exception dialog boxes tell you when something goes wrong with your code.

No matter what you do, the application will refuse to do anything more with *NewDoc* at this point. The user will see the same dialog box and then the application will stop working. Well, this is definitely not the way your application is supposed to work. Click Stop Debugging, press Shift+F5, or choose Debug | Stop Debugging to stop the debugger. It's time to update your code to handle the problem. Alter your code so it matches the code in Listing 5-4.

LISTING 5-4 Handling an XML exception

```csharp
private void btnTest_Click(object sender, EventArgs e)
{
    // Define the document outside the try block.
    XDocument NewDoc = new XDocument();

    // Tell the application to try the operation.
    try
    {
        // Read the document from disk.
        NewDoc = XDocument.Load(
        Environment.GetFolderPath(
        Environment.SpecialFolder.DesktopDirectory) +
        "\\XMLSave.XML");
    }
    catch (FileNotFoundException exception)
    {
        MessageBox.Show("The " + exception.FileName + "is missing.\r\n" +
        "Did you accidentally delete it?");
    }

    // Display the result on screen.
    txtOutput.Text = NewDoc.Declaration + "\r\n" + NewDoc.ToString();
}
```

In addition to these code changes, you need to add another *using* statement to the top of the application like this one because the *FileNotFoundException* class is found in this namespace:

```
using System.IO;
```

The code in Listing 5-4 is a little more complicated than Listing 5-3, but it essentially works the same way. The big difference is that this code offers protection against changes a user makes to the environment. This protective code appears in the form of a *try...catch* block. What the *try* and *catch* structures mean is that the application should first try an action. If that action generates an exception, the application should catch the exception (rather than display it to the user), and do something to handle the problem. Of course, it helps if you can tell the application what exception to catch. In this case, the code tells the application to catch the *FileNotFoundException* error.

Using a *try...catch* block comes with a little catch: Anything you declare inside the *try...catch* block is invisible outside it. As a result, this form of the application must also declare *NewDoc* outside the *try...catch* block so that the information it contains is accessible later.

Tip It's good practice to make the *try...catch* block as small as possible so that you can work with specific pieces of problem code. Otherwise, the *try...catch* block becomes less effective. In addition, make the *catch* part of the *try...catch* block as specific as possible to improve the chances that you'll be able to handle the exception that the application has generated.

Unfortunately, if the user deletes the file, you can't do much about it except present a friendly message telling the user what's wrong. That's what the *catch* clause does. It displays a message box containing the name of the file and suggesting that the user might have deleted it, as shown in Figure 5-13.

FIGURE 5-13 Good exception handling means providing the user with an understandable message that includes a course of action.

It's important to trace through this example to see how it works.

Trace Through the *try/catch* Example

1. Begin by setting a breakpoint at the *XDocumentNewDoc = new XDocument();* line of code.

2. Start the application and click Test. The debugger will stop at the breakpoint.

3. Click Step Over. Look at *NewDoc* in the Locals window. You'll see that even though it has been created and initialized, it doesn't contain anything as shown here.

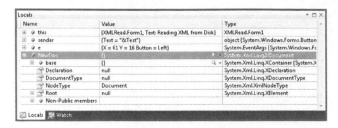

4. Click Step Over twice. The application will attempt to load an XML document that you know doesn't exist. As expected, this action takes you to the *catch* clause of the *try...catch* block.

5. Click Step Over again. The *FileNotFoundException* variable, *exception*, now contains information about the problem. Because you're using a specific kind of exception class, you obtain extra information, such as the *Filename* property shown here.

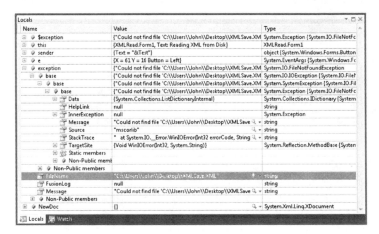

Exceptions provide a lot of information about what went wrong. If you drill down into exception, you'll find all kinds of useful nuggets of information. You don't need to worry too much about this additional information for now, but it's important to realize that it exists. Chapter 10, "Using LINQ in Web Applications," will discuss exceptions in more detail.

6. Click Continue. Click OK to close the dialog box.

The question you should ask now is whether the application still works if the file is present.

7. Open the Recycle Bin, right-click the XMLSave.XML you deleted earlier, and choose Restore. The file will reappear on the Desktop.

8. Click Test. Trace through the application again to see what happens this time.

Using XML to Store Application Settings

The previous examples in this chapter showed how to work with XML at a basic level. At this point, you possess enough information to do something more interesting with XML. This section shows you how to save and restore application settings using a simple technique. The technique won't work in every circumstance, but it offers enough flexibility to perform simple tasks, and you'll find that it works well as a starting point for more complicated scenarios for saving settings.

Creating the XMLSetting Project

Follow the instructions found in the "Starting the Array Project" section of Chapter 4. However, give your application the name **XMLSetting** instead of *ArrayUsage*.

Adding and Configuring the *XMLSetting* Controls

You could add as many controls as needed to exercise this example fully. However, in the interest of simplicity, the example relies on a *Label* and *TextBox* combination for a text setting and a *CheckBox* control for a true/false setting. A single *Button* control, *Quit*, provides the means to exit the application. Table 5-4 shows how to configure the controls for this example.

TABLE 5-4 XMLSetting Control Configuration

Control Name	Property Name	Value
button1	*(Name)*	*btnQuit*
	Text	*&Quit*
label1	*Text*	*&Type Something*
textBox1	*(Name)*	*txtMessage*
checkBox1	*(Name)*	*chkChecked*
	Text	*&Check Me*
Form1	*Text*	*Saving and Restoring Values*
	CancelButton	*btnQuit*
	FormBorderStyle	*FixedDialog*

Adding the XMLSetting Application Code

This application must perform two tasks. First, it must automatically save the application settings to disk. In this case, the application will save the *txtMessage* and *txtChecked* values so that the application can restore them later. Second, the application must restore the settings automatically when it starts so that that user immediately sees the settings that were available at the end of the last session.

Saving the Settings

Saving the settings comes first. Because you can't assume that users will remember to save the settings, the application must save them automatically. Fortunately, it's possible to create an event handler that will always occur when the form closes. Select the form and then open the Properties window. Click Events so that you can see the event listing. Double-click the *FormClosing* event to create the event handler. Listing 5-5 shows the code used to save the application settings.

LISTING 5-5 Saving the settings

```
private void Form1_FormClosing(object sender, FormClosingEventArgs e)
{
    // Create a document to hold the settings.
    XDocumentSettingData = new XDocument(
        new XDeclaration("1.0", "utf-8", "yes"),
        new XElement("Settings",
            new XElement("txtMessage", txtMessage.Text),
            new XElement("chkChecked", chkChecked.Checked)));

    // Save the settings to disk.
    SettingData.Save(SettingsFile);
}
```

This code should look familiar. It's a variation on the XMLSave application you created earlier. In this case, the code begins by creating an XML declaration (which is always the first entry). It then creates a *<Settings>* root node, followed by *<txtMessage>* and *<chkChecked>* child nodes. The values associated with these two nodes are the current application settings. Whatever the user has done with the application will appear in the settings file.

The event handler ends by using the *SettingData.Save()* method to save the data to disk. The string variable *SettingsFile* is a global variable, as discussed in the "Restoring the Settings" section. All you need to know now is that this variable contains the physical location of the settings file on disk.

Restoring the Settings

You must resolve one problem before you can restore the settings. The settings file might not exist—it certainly won't exist the first time you run the application. The code shown in Listing 5-6 demonstrates how to resolve this problem. It also shows another way to avoid the issue described in the "Handling XML Exceptions" section of the chapter.

LISTING 5-6 Restoring the settings

```
// Create a global variable containing the name and
// location of the settings file.
String SettingsFile;

public Form1()
```

```
{
    InitializeComponent();

    // Store the location of the settings file.
    SettingsFile = Application.LocalUserAppDataPath + "\\Settings.XML";

    // Check for a settings file.
    if (File.Exists(SettingsFile))
    {
        // Load the file containing the settings.
        XDocumentSettingData = XDocument.Load(SettingsFile);

        // Change the control settings to match the file settings.
        txtMessage.Text = SettingData.Root.Element("txtMessage").Value;
        chkChecked.Checked = Boolean.Parse(SettingData.Root.Element("chkChecked").
Value);
    }
}
```

This code begins by creating a *String* variable named *SettingsFile*. It contains a pointer to the Windows storage location for user application data. The *Application* object contains all sorts of interesting information about your application. This example uses the *LocalUserAppDataPath* property, which is a special folder used to hold settings for your specific application and for the user currently working with the application (you, in this case). In short, this folder is unique—it won't interfere with any other application, nor will multiple users working with your application on the same computer interfere with each other. All you need to do is supply the name of a file, as shown in the code. In this case, the code uses the filename Settings.XML to store the settings information.

The next step is to avoid the problem of a missing settings file. The *File.Exists()* method looks on the hard drive for the file you specify. If the file exists, the *FileExists()* method returns *true*; otherwise, it returns *false*. The *if* structure performs the tasks shown when *File.Exists()* returns *true*.

This code should also look a little familiar. It's somewhat similar to the *XMLRead* example discussed earlier, but with a few changes. The code begins by creating a new *XDocument*, *SettingData*, and loading the file pointed to by *SettingsFile* into it using the *XDocument.Load()* method. Now *SettingData* is filled with information about the application.

Setting *txtMessage* is relatively easy. All you need to do is extract the *Value* of the *<txtMessage>* node by accessing *SettingData.Root*. In fact, you can use this approach to drill down into the XML data structure as far as needed by adding additional *Element()* method levels.

You need to massage the data a little. Remember, XML documents are plain text, so *SettingData. Root.Element("chkChecked").Value* returns a string. However, the *chkChecked.Checked* property accepts and returns a Boolean value, so the two aren't compatible. The data types have to match, so you need to turn the string stored in the XML file into a Boolean value. The *Boolean.Parse()* method does that for you; it accepts a properly formatted string (either *"true"* or *"false"*) as input and outputs the corresponding Boolean value.

Defining the *Using* Statements

This example requires that you add a couple of *using* statements to the beginning of the file. Otherwise, it won't compile.

```
usingSystem.Xml.Linq;
using System.IO;
```

Testing the XMLSetting Application

You have a shiny new application to try—one that's probably more practical than any application you've encountered so far in the book. It's time to test how the application works. To actually see this application in action, set two breakpoints at the following lines of code:

- SettingsFile = Application.LocalUserAppDataPath + "\\Settings.XML";

- XDocumentSettingData = new XDocument(

These breakpoints will make it possible to see how the application works. The following sections trace application functionality and give you a better idea of what the application does.

Creating Some Settings

1. Click Start Debugging. The application will automatically stop at the first breakpoint.

2. Click Step Over. The application creates *SettingsFile*. Hover your mouse over the variable and you'll see that it points to a folder on your local hard drive, such as C:\Users\John\AppData\ Local\Microsoft\XMLSetting\1.0.0.0 (your folder will differ from mine). This folder includes the user's name, the locality of the data, the company name (which you can change), the name of the application, and the application version number (which you can also change). As you can see, the location is unique.

3. Click Step Over. The code skips the contents of the *if* statement because the file doesn't exist yet. You can check this yourself. Type **?File.Exists(SettingsFile)** in the Immediate window and you'll see that the output value is *false*. The code is behaving precisely as expected by skipping the *if* statement content.

4. Now you need to set some values in the controls. Click Continue, and you'll see the form. Notice that the checkbox is currently clear and that the textbox is blank.

5. Type **Hello** in the textbox and select the checkbox, as shown.

6. To save the settings, click Quit. The debugger automatically stops in the *Form1_FormClosing()* event handler.

7. Click Step Over. The code creates *SettingData* for you.

8. Click the down arrow next to *SettingData* in the Locals window and choose XML Visualizer from the list. You'll see the XML Visualizer containing the settings, as shown here.

9. Click Close to close the visualizer and then click Continue to end the application.

At this point, your settings folder should contain a new Settings.XML file in it. Use Windows Explorer to find this folder and file. Double-click the file and you'll see that it does indeed contain the settings, as shown in Figure 5-14.

FIGURE 5-14 Use Internet Explorer to verify that the settings file does indeed contain the settings you created in the application.

Tip Creating a settings file this way makes it possible to move a user anywhere. It also makes it quite easy to save application settings without resorting to any weird sort of backup routine. Of all of the methods you have at your disposal to save application settings, using the technique shown in this chapter is the simplest and least error prone. Even better, the XML file is plain text, so you can repair it easily if it becomes damaged. Using this technique, you get flexibility and reliability all in one package.

Restarting the Application

It's great that the settings file appeared on disk as expected and it contains the data you wanted. Of course, none of this is any good if the application doesn't restart with the settings you selected in place.

1. To test whether the application restores the settings, click Start Debugging. The debugger will stop at the first breakpoint again.

2. You already know that the application will create the *SettingsFile* variable, so click Step Over three times. You end up at the *XDocumentSettingData = XDocument.Load(SettingsFile);* line of code within the *if* statement. As you can see, the *File.Exists()* method detected the file as it was supposed to. (Test it in the Immediate window again if you like and you'll see that the result is now *true*, rather than *false* as it was before.)

3. Click Step Over. The *SettingData* variable will now contain an *XDocument* with the settings that were saved earlier to disk. In fact, test this out using the XML Visualizer.

4. Just to verify that nothing odd is going on, hover your mouse over *txtMessage.Text*. You'll see that it contains a blank value. Likewise, *chkChecked.Checked* contains *false*, which means it isn't checked.

5. Click Step Over twice, and you'll find that these two properties have changed to match the settings that were saved earlier.

6. Click Continue and you'll see that the form appears—this time with the previously saved settings in place.

You can try this application out with any set of values and it'll always save and restore them as expected.

Get Going with C#

This chapter provided basic information about XML and walked you through several sample projects that made use of XML. It's important to remember that the methods discussed in this chapter illustrate just one way to accomplish the tasks. XML is an extremely flexible technology and offers you many ways to accomplish the same goal. However, the techniques shown in this chapter are the ones that you'll use most often in C#. If you take away one concept from this chapter, it should be that using XML to store application settings is preferable to using other techniques, such as writing settings to the Windows Registry (a database that Windows maintains for storing various settings), or designing your own custom settings storage and retrieval scheme. Using XML makes it easier to move application settings to other locations and to create setting backups as a hedge against a system failure.

So you've seen some XML basics, but one chapter can't tell you everything there is to know about the topic. Fortunately, some outstanding, free XML tutorials are available online. One of the best tutorials is at *http://www.w3schools.com/xml/default.asp*. Try this tutorial as a starting point for increasing your knowledge about XML. Anything you learn is going to be useful because XML appears in all sorts of places. If the first site doesn't work well for you, the tutorial at *http://www.xmlfiles.com/xml/* is also an excellent source of information.

Spend some time looking for other XML files on your system. If possible, view the files in the browser of your choice. Of course, the important thing is to understand what you're seeing. The information in this chapter will certainly help you decipher the file content. Make sure you check out the tutorials to build on this knowledge, so that you can understand each of the files you're seeing. What's amazing is that you'll likely find that you can understand a majority of the XML content you find without really knowing too much about the application that created it. XML truly is a universal format.

One of the most prominent uses of XML today is for *web services*. A web service is a sort of online data source that's made available for public or private use. The web service provides access to all sorts of information. For example, there are web services exposed by Google, eBay, Amazon, and Twitter—all of which provide access to the data generated by these organizations. Every web service transfers information using XML. Therefore, the information you've obtained in this chapter is a starting point for gaining access to external sources of information provided by web services. Chapter 6, "Accessing a Web Service," provides more detail on accessing web services. When you finish Chapter 6, you'll be able to access information from any public web service that provides good documentation about the format of the requests you can make and the responses you'll receive.

Accessing a Web Service

After completing this chapter, you'll be able to:

- Describe the basics of web services
- Define and use the SOAP method of accessing web services
- Define and use the REST method of accessing web services

MANY PEOPLE ARE USED TO working with websites in an interactive fashion. For example, when you want to buy a book from Amazon, you go to the Amazon site, choose the book, and then follow a series of prompts to purchase it. Likewise, when you want to interact with eBay, Google, Twitter, or hundreds of other sites, you manually perform the tasks required for the interaction. However, most of these sites recognized long ago that businesses often require some sort of automated way to interact with a website efficiently. Many automated website features are offered in the form of *web services* that a company or individual can access purely through code. This is just one form of web service—there are many others.

Note Web services come in numerous forms. For example, many companies now create private web services to handle information transfers between sites and with other entities such as partners. Specialty web services provide semi-private access to information for a fee or other consideration. This book doesn't discuss private or specialty web services because they're unique. In any case, discussion would prove pointless because you couldn't easily try the examples. However, whether a web service is public, private, or special, it operates essentially the same way. By knowing how the public web services used for the examples in this chapter work, you also know how private or specialty web services work.

The interesting feature about web services is that they rely on eXtensible Markup Language (XML). In addition, web services provide a documented interface so that anyone with the right credentials can access them—no matter what platform the requestor is using. Access to web services is consistent and uses one of several standardized technologies to ensure unimpeded admission. In short, web services let any client with the correct information in the right format make a request and receive a response based on that request.

This chapter provides an overview of web services from the C# perspective. Even though the client access is consistent from the web service, the actual mechanics of gaining access varies by programming language and platform to some extent. As part of this discussion, you'll explore the Simple Object Access Protocol (SOAP) and Representational State Transfer (REST) techniques for accessing a web service. Before you start this chapter, however, make sure you understand the XML basics provided in Chapter 5, "Working with XML," because nearly all forms of web services rely on XML to do their work.

Note The topic of web services is huge. Authors have written entire books on using a single web service. Many other books and articles discuss web services in various forms. A single chapter (or even several volumes) can't discuss such an immense topic. Consider this chapter the barest introduction to the topic. If you're interested in additional information about web services, you'll want to spend some time researching the topic using a search service such as Google. You'll also want to spend some time with online tutorials, such as the one at the W3Schools site at *http://www.w3schools.com/webservices/default.asp*. It's also a good idea to examine Microsoft's vision of the topic at *http://msdn.microsoft.com/library/w9fdtx28.aspx*.

Defining Web Services

The mystique about web services is both ill-deserved and unhelpful. The image is perpetuated by drawings such as a huge cloud (with or without lightning bolts) with lines going into the cloud, but apparently never coming out. A web service is actually an easy concept to understand once you throw the cloud metaphors away and come up with a better picture of what's happening. What you're looking at is a *service*. When you go to the restaurant, a server comes with a menu, and then returns later and asks what you'd like to eat. You tell the server what you'd like and at some point you receive what you requested (at least in most cases). A web service performs essentially the same task. Your application makes a request for a menu of items that the web service can provide. Later, the application tells the service which item it would like and the service delivers that item. Web services truly aren't any more difficult to understand than that—yet some people make them sound like the most complicated bits of software in the entire world.

As mentioned previously, web services generally rely on XML to make requests and receive responses. The XML can be more complex than the examples shown in Chapter 5, but the concepts are the same, and you'll find that the Visual Studio IDE does help you make the requests to a certain extent. You still have to decide what to request, but the IDE can help you create the information in the right form, which makes it a lot easier to deal with the XML. The following sections provide additional background on how web services and XML work together to help you obtain information from online sources.

Note Not every web service relies on XML, but the vast majority do. Most public web services rely on XML because it's the only method of exchange guaranteed to work with any programming language and on multiple platforms. Some public web services also provide output in JavaScript Object Notation (JSON) or atom syndication format—neither of which appear in this chapter. In addition, you may find a private web service that relies on some other method of data exchange—usually binary. This chapter doesn't consider these binary web services because there simply aren't many of them and you're unlikely to need access to them immediately. If you do require access to such a web service, the web service owner will provide the documentation you require.

Web Services and XML

Chapter 5 demonstrated some basic techniques for working with XML. You used it to store data in various ways. Web services can use XML in the same way—to store data in a structured manner. However, when working with a web service, the data flows in two directions: from the client to the server, and from the server to the client. This two-way communication creates a conversation between the client and the server.

The communication generally begins with the client making a request of some type. The examples in this chapter show two kinds of requests:

- **Specially formatted URL**   The REST technique can use a specially formatted URL to send a request to the server. This is actually an advantage when you want to learn about web services because you can use a browser to explore the web service and see the response the server sends. However, using a specially formatted URL can prove a little more difficult when writing applications in C# because the IDE doesn't provide as much automation. In addition, using a specially formatted URL isn't as flexible as using an XML document.

- **XML document**   The SOAP technique always relies on an XML document to send a request. In some cases, you also send a request using an XML document when working with REST. Using an XML document makes it nearly impossible to see how the web service works using a browser. However, the automation that the IDE provides makes this the fastest method for working with web services. The IDE will create a special class to create the XML document for you. All you do is provide the required information in properties that the special class will then use to create the XML document.

Assuming that the client has sent the correct information in the proper format, the server will obtain the requested information and send it back to the client. The output will always be in XML for the purposes of this chapter. In the real world, web services often dish up information in a number of formats. Part of the client request describes the form of output that the client prefers. Because of the support that the IDE provides, you'll normally want to obtain the response in XML format to simplify the coding process. However, it's possible to process JSON and other formats using C# as well—you simply need to be willing to perform a little more coding to do it.

Note Many web services require that you provide some sort of authentication information. The web service may not cost anything or convey anything secret, yet you're asked to provide a credential of some sort. The most common reason for this requirement is that the web service provides free access for a certain number of requests in a given timeframe. The credential ensures that you don't exceed the limit. Web services such as eBay also require that your application pass certain tests before it's allowed on the live site. (They provide a test site, called a *sandbox*, that you can use to build your application.) The purpose of the credential is to prove that your application can access the web service without causing damage to the data it provides or a potential crash of the servers. This chapter relies on web services that don't require a credential in the interest of simplicity, but web services that do require a credential usually provide interesting features.

It's important to note that the original request usually contains more than a simple definition of the data that the client wants. One of the additional inputs is the form the response should take. Another occurs when a server requires authentication information or other data required to service the request that have nothing to do with the actual output data. This chapter doesn't dive into these details because they vary by web service. You need to check the web service documentation to discover any special needs for using the web service. These special needs are more often than not the culprit of failed requests. For example, failure to provide authentication information when it's needed will always result in a failed request. The server sends failure information in the response instead of the requested data.

Working with REST Web Services

There's a good reason to start your exploration of web services using REST instead of SOAP—REST services let you play with the web service without writing any code whatsoever. All you need is a specially formatted URL and a browser. The web service still sends data back in XML (or whatever format you choose), but the request itself is an easily understood URL. The example in this section uses the web service found at *http://api.wunderground.com*. The Weather Underground site provides weather information using a graphical interface or through a web service, making it the perfect site for experimentation. You can verify your results by manually checking the information using the graphical interface.

 Tip The Weather Underground actually provides a number of interesting web services— this chapter uses only one of them. You can discover more about these web services at *http://wiki.wunderground.com/index.php/API_-_XML*. The documentation is pretty clear and you'll likely have all of the knowledge you need to use them by the time this chapter is complete. For example, this web service provides access to geographical information and the locations of webcams that you can use to see the current weather.

The example in this section actually uses the fifth web service listed for the Weather Underground site—ForecastXML. To use this service, you provide the URL and a location. For example, if you want to determine the weather in Milwaukee, Wisconsin, you'd use *http://api.wunderground.com/auto/wui/*

geo/ForecastXML/index.xml?query=Milwaukee,WI as the query URL. Most of this URL is precisely the same for every request. The only part that varies is the location. In addition to an actual city name and state, you can provide a ZIP code (such as 53215) or a three- or four-letter airport abbreviation (such as MKE). Theoretically, providing latitude and longitude will work, too, but could prove tricky if you don't have a good source for this kind of information. Give the example URL a try now and you'll receive results similar to the results shown in Figure 6-1. (Naturally, the weather varies, so your precise results will vary, too.)

The root node for the response is *<forecast>*. If you want to see the terms of service for using this web service, you look at the *<termsofservice>* node. This node uses something you haven't seen yet—an *attribute*. An attribute is data contained within the node itself, rather than as a separate value. A single node can have just one value, but it can contain any number of attributes. The *<termsofservice>* node contains a single attribute, *link*, with a single value consisting of the location of the terms of service online.

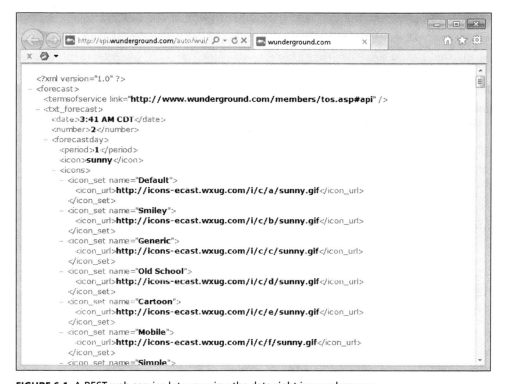

FIGURE 6-1 A REST web service lets you view the data right in your browser.

```
<termsofservice link="http://www.wunderground.com/members/tos.asp#api" />
```

Most people are going to be interested in the *<txt_forecast>* node, which contains a series of *<forecastday>* nodes. Each of these child nodes contains the forecast for a single day. You'll see how they work in the sample application. For now, peruse the results of the query to see if you can determine what the various data mean. You may be surprised to find that you can figure out most of the response without doing anything special. Good web services are designed to make working with the data as simple as possible.

While you're at it, try other locations and use different techniques to query the data. For example, you can discover the current weather at Seattle-Tacoma International using a URL of *http://api.wunderground.com/auto/wui/geo/ForecastXML/index.xml?query=SEA*. In this case, you're using a three-letter airport abbreviation. If you're more of an East Coast person, try finding the weather at Deer Isle, Maine, using an URL of *http://api.wunderground.com/auto/wui/geo/ForecastXML/index.xml?query=04627*. In this case, you're using a ZIP code to find the information. You can also locate weather for places like Adana, Turkey, using a three-letter airport abbreviation: *http://api.wunderground.com/auto/wui/geo/ForecastXML/index.xml?query=ADA*.

Working with SOAP Web Services

SOAP web services require that you create an XML document and send it to the server, rather than use a specially formatted URL. Creating such a document could be time-consuming and difficult without help. Fortunately, SOAP provides the help you need in the form of the Web Services Description Language (WSDL). Like many other aspects of web services, WSDL relies on XML to perform its task. For example, if you want to obtain information directly from the government, you can use SOAP to do it. The WSDL document at *http://www.weather.gov/forecasts/xml/DWMLgen/wsdl/ndfdXML.wsdl* contains the information you need. Try opening the document now and you'll see the confusing-looking XML document shown in Figure 6-2.

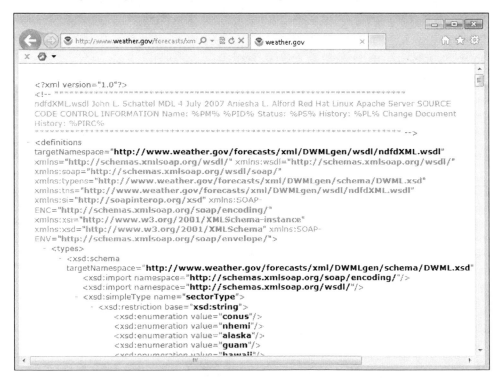

FIGURE 6-2 SOAP web services rely on a WSDL document to describe the web service connection.

Don't worry, you won't have to read this document—the IDE does it for you—but it's educational to look at. You can see a new type of entry near the top of this XML document. The node that starts with *<!--*and ends with *-->* is a *comment*. Comments can appear anywhere in an XML document. They serve to help humans understand the document, but applications ignore the comments.

The root node for this document is *<definitions>*. It contains a wealth of special attributes called namespaces. Namespaces provide information about specific entries in the document. The URL points to a source of additional information about specific node types so that the application reading the document knows what to do with the data it finds. You won't have to worry about namespaces for the sorts of applications created in this book, but you should know that they're important additions to the XML document because they make it possible to use the document to perform specific tasks (such as setting up a web service in an IDE).

Developing the REST Web Service Application

This example helps you obtain the current weather information from Weather Underground and display it on-screen. You'll actually build on a number of examples that you created in past chapters as you work through this example. For example, one of the tasks is to display the proper icon to show the kind of weather to expect. The example in Chapter 1, "Getting to Know C#," is a good starting point, but this chapter takes you much further. The following sections will get you started.

Creating the RESTService Project

Follow the instructions found in the "Starting the Array Project" section of Chapter 4, "Using Collections to Store Data." However, give your application the name **RESTService** in place of *ArrayUsage*.

Adding and Configuring the RESTService Controls

This example uses a number of controls you haven't worked with in the past. It also uses at least one control in an unusual way—a way that many developers wouldn't use. When you request weather information from Weather Underground, you actually get several different forecasts, so the application needs Next and Previous buttons so you can navigate through the results. It also requires the usual Quit button. To let users select a different location, you also need to include a *Label* and *TextBox* pair the user can rely on to enter a location.

The application requires controls for output as well. You can use several methods to display the weather-related icon. However, this example uses a *WebBrowser* control in a unique way to perform the task. Because each forecast can use several different versions of the same icon to display the weather, you also need a *NumericUpDown* control and its associated label to select the icon you prefer. The weather has a title represented by a *Label* and *TextBox* pair. Another *Label* and *TextBox* pair displays the text version of the weather report. You could extract a lot more information from this web service, but this is enough information for the example. Table 6-1 shows how to configure the various controls.

TABLE 6-1 RESTService Control Configuration

Control Name	Property Name	Value
button1	(Name)	btnNext
	Text	&Next
button2	(Name)	btnPrevious
	Text	&Previous
button3	(Name)	btnQuit
	Text	&Quit
label1	(Name)	lblLocation
	Text	&Location
textBox1	(Name)	txtLocation
	AcceptsReturn	True
	Size.Width	179
	Size.Height	20
webBrowser1	(Name)	wblcon
	ScrollBarsEnabled	False
	Size.Width	80
	Size.Height	80
label2	(Name)	lblIconSelect
	Text	&Icon Selection
numericUpDown1	(Name)	IconSelect
	Size.Width	44
	Size.Height	20
label3	(Name)	lblTitle
	Text	&Title
textBox2	(Name)	txtTitle
	ReadOnly	True
	Size.Width	260
	Size.Height	20
label4	(Name)	lblForecast
	Text	&Forecast
textBox3	(Name)	txtForecast
	Multiline	True
	ReadOnly	True
	Scrollbars	Both

Control Name	Property Name	Value
	Size.Width	260
	Size.Height	61
Form1	Text	Weather Forecaster
	CancelButton	btnQuit
	FormBorderStyle	FixedDialog

Wow! That's a lot of configuration, but you'll find that you perform a lot more configuration as your applications do more for the user. Notice that *txtLocation* has the *AcceptsReturn* property set to *True*. If you don't change this property, the user won't see any result when pressing Enter in the text box. Otherwise, this configuration isn't very different from the other applications in the book—you're simply using more controls. Figure 6-3 shows how your dialog box should look when you're done.

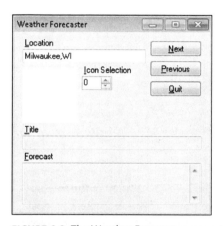

FIGURE 6-3 The Weather Forecaster uses a somewhat complex configuration.

Adding the RESTService Application Code

This application is quite a bit more complex than previous examples in the book. When you start working on applications with added complexity, it's a good idea to work with one task at a time. Consequently, the following sections break up the application into smaller pieces so that you can better see how it works. However, before you do anything else, make sure you add the following required *using* statements to the beginning of the application code:

```
using System.Xml.Linq;
using System.Net;
```

Creating the Global Variables

Like many applications in this book, this one requires a number of global variables. These variables hold data used by a number of the application methods. Listing 6-1 shows the variables you need to define for this application.

LISTING 6-1 Defining the required global variables

```
// Holds all of the weather data.
XDocument GetData;

// Contains just the forecast.
IEnumerable<XElement> Forecast;

// Specifies which forecast to use.
Int32 ForecastNumber;

// Defines the maximum number of forecasts.
Int32 MaxForecasts;

// Contains a list of icons associated with the forecast.
IEnumerable<XElement> Icons;

// Specifies which icon to use.
Int32 IconNumber;
```

You worked with *XDocument* in Chapter 5. In this case, *GetData* contains all of the forecast information retrieved from Weather Underground. For the purpose of this example, the most important information is the individual forecasts. The forecast information includes a number of forecasts (contained within *<forecastday>* nodes), as shown in Figure 6-4.

FIGURE 6-4 Use your browser to determine how data from the web service is formatted.

Tip You can collapse various levels of an XML document in Internet Explorer by clicking the minus sign (-) next to the entry. Collapsing entries lets you get an overview of the data. To expand a collapsed entry, simply click the plus sign (+) next to its entry.

The next variable is a little puzzling. When you see a variable type that begins with an *I*, that's normally an indication that it's an interface—a description of how the type should work, rather than the actual type. An interface describes a specific set of methods and properties that a class will use, but the interface itself contains no implementation. So, *IEnumerable* is the enumerable (countable) interface. The angle brackets (< >) contain a type name. In this case, it's *XElement*. What this type description says is to create an enumerable collection of *XElement* entries by using the definition provided by the *IEnumerable* interface. The *Forecast* variable simply contains an enumerated collection of forecasts obtained from *GetData*. The next variable, *ForecastNumber*, contains the number of the current forecast in the *Forecast* collection. The application uses *MaxForecasts* to detect when it has hit the last forecast in the *Forecast* collection.

Each forecast contains a number of icons used to pictorially describe the forecast data. These entries appear within the *<icons>* node that appears as a child of the *<forecastday>* node. Theoretically, each forecast could use a different set of icons, but the icons are standard across the forecasts. The individual *<icon_set>* nodes have names such as Default and Smiley, as shown in Figure 6-5.

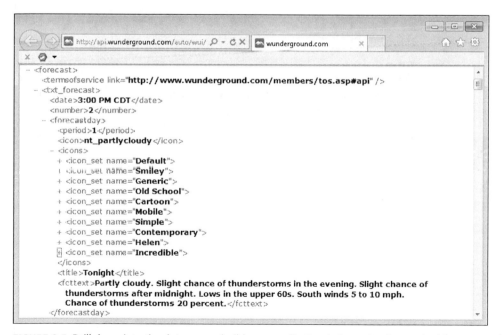

FIGURE 6-5 Drill down into the data as you build your application to learn details required for your code.

Again, you need an enumerated collection to store this information. In this case, *Icons* contains a collection of icon descriptions for the current forecast. The *WebBrowser* control, *wblcon*, can display only one icon at a time, so *IconNumber* tells the application which icon to use.

Getting a Forecast

The primary task of this application is to obtain a set of forecasts. Of course, it's the first task that the application performs when you start it, so that users don't face a blank screen. In addition, if a user requests another location, the application will have to obtain a new forecast for that location. Because the application can request a forecast for a number of reasons, it makes sense to place this code in a separate method called *GetForecast(),* as shown in Listing 6-2.

LISTING 6-2 Obtaining the forecast

```
public void GetForecast()
{
    // Contains the result of a retry request.
    DialogResult TryAgain = DialogResult.Yes;

    // Keep trying to get the weather data until the user
    // gives up or the call is successful.
    while (TryAgain == DialogResult.Yes)
    {
        try
        {
            // Get the weather data.
            GetData =
                XDocument.Load(
                    "http://api.wunderground.com/auto/wui/geo"
                    + "/ForecastXML/index.xml?query="
                    + txtLocation.Text);

            // End the loop.
            TryAgain = DialogResult.No;
        }
        catch (WebException WE)
        {
            TryAgain = MessageBox.Show(
                "Couldn't obtain the weather data!\r\nTry Again?",
                "Data Download Error",
                MessageBoxButtons.YesNo,
                MessageBoxIcon.Error);
        }
    }

    // Obtain all the forecasts.
    Forecast =
```

```
    GetData.Element("forecast").Element("txt_forecast").Elements("forecastday");

    // Define the maximum number of forecasts.
    MaxForecasts = Forecast.Count() - 1;

    // Specify which forecast to use.
    ForecastNumber = 0;

    // Specify which icon to use.
    IconNumber = 0;

    // Reset the buttons.
    btnNext.Enabled = true;
    btnPrevious.Enabled = false;
}
```

This code is an extension of the code used in Chapter 5 to load XML from the disk. In fact, it uses the *XDocument.Load()* method to perform the task. The code used to load the document is the same—only the location is different. However, unlike your hard drive, the Internet is not always available. Consequently, *GetForecast()* contains some additional code to allow the user to try retrieving the forecasts again when the application fails to perform the task the first time. Whenever the *XDocument.Load()* method fails to load a document from Weather Underground, the code executes the *catch* clause of the *try...catch* block and the user sees the dialog box shown in Figure 6-6.

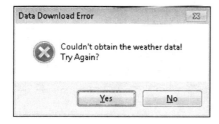

FIGURE 6-6 Because web services can't provide a constant connection, your application requires robust error handling.

The output from a dialog box is a *DialogResult*. So, the first variable in Listing 6-2, *TryAgain*, contains the result of a user click in a dialog box. This example begins with a *while* loop that executes as long as *TryAgain* contains *DialogResult.Yes* (the user clicked Yes). The variable starts out with *DialogResult.Yes* so that the *while* loop will execute at least once.

Inside the *while* loop, the code tries to call *XDocument.Load()* with the web service's URL. If it's successful, the application sets *TryAgain* to *DialogResult.No* and the *while* loop ends. Otherwise, the code calls the *catch* clause of the *try...catch* block. Notice that this application uses an expanded version of the *MessageBox.Show()* call to display a dialog box with more features, including:

- A message to the user
- A title for the message box

- Specialized button selections (Yes and No in this case)

- An icon symbolizing the type of dialog box (with associated sound effect if the user has selected one)

Getting Additional Information from Help

IntelliSense provides enough information to use the language features provided by C# in most cases. However, at times you simply don't get enough information from IntelliSense to understand how to use a particular feature. Fortunately, the IDE comes with more detailed help. For example, if you want to learn more about *MessageBox*, highlight *MessageBox* in your code and press F1. The Help Library Agent will start and then you'll see a Microsoft Help Viewer window that contains more information about the *MessageBox* class.

The Help files may not always provide everything you need. In this case, a human answer may be helpful. Choose Help | MSDN Forums and a new window will open in the IDE where you can access human help online. Start by typing a simple question in the Search field and then pressing Enter. You'll see a list of topics that contain the keywords you typed. Look for your answer in the list of returns. If you don't see your answer, sign into the forums by clicking Sign In. After you've signed in, ask your question using the site features. Begin by clicking Forums. You'll see a list of topics for using the forums on the left side of the window—click the links that direct you to the information you need (such as the Using Forums topic).

Don't forget that you can also rely on help outside of Microsoft by using searches on services such as Google. For example, if you search for C# MessageBox Buttons, you'll see links for the *MessageBoxButtons* enumeration, but you'll also see answers for questions such as obtaining the user's click from a *MessageBox.Show()* call. Using short, concise, but targeted search terms will produce the best results. Don't be afraid to try out third-party sites—they often provide significant information that you won't find elsewhere.

After a successful call, *GetForecast()* has to do something with the data in *GetData*. This is where knowledge of how the web service returns data becomes important. You have to work through the list of nodes starting from the root node. Look again at the output presented earlier from Weather Underground. The nodes follow this sequence:

- *<forecast>* (the root node)

- *<txt_forecast>*

- *<forecastday>*

Now, look at the code used to create *Forecast*. It begins with the root node and works its way down to the series of *<forecastday>* nodes. In the first two cases, you need a single *Element*. The last case, *<forecastday>*, is an enumerated series of *Elements*. After this call, *Forecast* contains all the *<forecastday>* nodes.

It's important to remember that all enumerations begin with 0 in C#. Consequently, if an enumeration contains eight members, they're numbered 0 through 7. A call to *Forecast.Count()* will return the full number of *<forecastday>* nodes in *Forecast*. To account for the 0 starting point, the code subtracts one from this value when setting *MaxForecasts*. The code also sets *ForecastNumber* and *IconNumber* to 0, so that the application uses the first forecast and the first icon within the first forecast for the display.

The final bit of code for this part of the example resets the Next and Previous buttons. Because the code sets the *ForecastNumber* variable to 0, there's never going to be a previous forecast to select after getting a new forecast. In addition, the forecast is always set to show the first forecast in the series (normally, the service returns six forecasts—a day and evening forecast for three days). To ensure that the Next and Previous buttons are set correctly, the code sets the *btnNext.Enabled* to *true* and the *btnPrevious.Enabled* property to *false*.

Displaying the Data

As well as getting the forecasts, the application needs to display the forecast information in a number of situations. For example, whenever the user clicks Next or Previous, the application should update the forecast information on-screen. Therefore, the application uses the *DisplayData()* method to display the information on-screen, as shown in Listing 6-3.

LISTING 6-3 Showing a forecast on-screen

```
public void DisplayData(Int32 FNumber)
{
    // Display the title of the current forecast.
    txtTitle.Text = Forecast.ElementAt(FNumber).Element("title").Value;

    // Display detailed forecast information.
    txtForecast.Text = Forecast.ElementAt(FNumber).Element("fcttext").Value;

    // Obtain a list of icons associated with the forecast.
    Icons = Forecast.ElementAt(FNumber).Element("icons").Elements("icon_set");

    // Define the maximum number of available icons.
    IconSelect.Maximum = Icons.Count() - 1;

    // Display the icon on screen.
    wbIcon.Url = new Uri(Icons.ElementAt(IconNumber).Element("icon_url").Value);
}
```

The *DisplayData()* method accepts an *Int32* value, *FNumber*, as input. This variable tells *DisplayData()* which forecast to display. You could also rely on the global variable, *ForecastNumber*, but using this approach does improve flexibility somewhat. Using input arguments makes the information that the method receives specific to that particular call. Later, you'll discover that using global variables can be problematic in many situations because multiple parties can change the global value—making it easy to obtain corrupted information.

Look again at the output of the web service. You'll notice the *<title>* and *<fcttext>* nodes near the end of each *<forecastday>* node. The values of these nodes contain the text information describing each forecast, so the application places this information directly in *txtTitle.Text* and *txtForecast.Text*, as shown in the listing.

Each forecast contains a number of icons. The icon names won't vary for the forecasts on a particular day, but the URL that points to a specific icon will vary by forecast depending on the weather that day. Consequently, the code creates *Icons* for each forecast and places the set of icons associated with that forecast in *Icons*.

Users select a particular icon by changing the value in the *NumericUpDown* control, *IconSelect*. Of course, you don't want the user to select an icon that doesn't exist, so the code sets the *IconSelect.Maximum* property so users can only select valid numbers.

The last task is to display an icon in the *WebBrowser* control, *wbIcon*. The code must create a *Uri* that the *wbIcon.Url* property will understand, using the text URL found in the *<icon_url>* node as shown in Figure 6-7.

FIGURE 6-7 Weather Underground supplies the URL used to access an icon associated with the predicted weather.

As with other data access for this web service, you drill down into the XML document using the *Element* and *Value* properties. By now, you should have discovered that when you work with REST, you must know how the XML document is put together to write your application. Otherwise, you'll spend a lot of time guessing about how things work.

Initializing the Application

The user is going to expect to see a forecast immediately after starting the application. Just about every application you ever create will have this requirement. Users don't really want to think too much about your application—they simply want to use it. As with other applications in the book, you place the initialization code in the *Form1()* constructor, as shown in Listing 6-4.

LISTING 6-4 Creating the initial display

```
public Form1()
{
    InitializeComponent();

    // Obtain the forecast.
    GetForecast();

    // Display the forecast data.
    DisplayData(ForecastNumber);
}
```

This code obtains a forecast using *GetForecast()*, and then displays it using *DisplayData (ForecastNumber)*. Both the *ForecastNumber* and *IconNumber* are set to 0 for the initial update. When you run the example, you see a sample forecast for Milwaukee, WI, as shown in Figure 6-8, but you can set the forecast for any location you want. (Try several, in fact.)

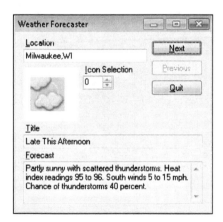

FIGURE 6-8 Try the application out with several locations to better understand how it works.

Selecting the Next and Previous Forecasts

You don't have any method of knowing how many results a web service will return. In addition, web service developers often change the conditions under which results are returned, so even if the web service returns a certain number of results today, the number could change tomorrow. With this in mind, you need to create Next and Previous button code that doesn't assume anything about the number of results that the web service will return, as shown in Listing 6-5.

LISTING 6-5 Choosing between the next and previous forecasts

```csharp
private void btnNext_Click(object sender, EventArgs e)
{
    // Enable the Previous button.
    btnPrevious.Enabled = true;

    // Determine whether there is a next forecast.
    if (ForecastNumber < MaxForecasts)

        // Increase the forecast number.
        ForecastNumber++;

    // Otherwise, disable the Next button.
    else
        btnNext.Enabled = false;

    // Display the information.
    DisplayData(ForecastNumber);
}

private void btnPrevious_Click(object sender, EventArgs e)
{
    // Enable the Next button.
    btnNext.Enabled = true;

    // Determine whether there is a previous forecast.
    if (ForecastNumber > 0)

        // Decrease the forecast number.
        ForecastNumber--;

    // Otherwise, disable the Previous button.
    else
        btnPrevious.Enabled = false;

    // Display the information.
    DisplayData(ForecastNumber);
}
```

Both event handlers work in the same way. The code begins by enabling the opposite button. This makes sense because clicking Next will necessarily create a previous entry to select. Likewise, clicking Previous will create a next entry to select. The code then checks the boundary for the clicked button. When *ForecastNumber* is at the end of the next or previous list, it disables the appropriate button. Otherwise, it selects the next or previous entry. The final step is to call *DisplayData()* with the updated *ForecastNumber* value.

Entering a New Location

This application wouldn't be much good if you couldn't enter a new location. The three location types that are tested for this web service are:

1. City and state

2. Three- or four-letter airport abbreviation

3. ZIP code

The web service could eventually make other sorts of location types available, but for now, you can enter any of these types in the Location field of the application. From an application perspective, users will expect the application to change the location based on two events:

- The user selects another field or control.

- The user presses Enter.

Consequently, the application code has to handle both of these events using different event handlers. Select the *txtLocation* control and then open the Properties window. Click Events. You'll see a list of events that *txtLocation* can provide. Double-click the *Leave* event to create an event handler to change the display when the user selects another field or control. The IDE will create the required event handler for you. Double-click the *KeyDown* event to create an event handler that fires when the user presses a key. You'll see how to test which key the user pressed (you're interested in the Enter key here). Listing 6-6 shows the code for these two event handlers.

LISTING 6-6 Selecting a new location

```
private void txtLocation_Leave(object sender, EventArgs e)
{
    // Obtain the forecast.
    GetForecast();

    // Verify that there are forecasts to process.
    if (Forecast.Count() == 0)

        // If not, display an error message.
        MessageBox.Show(
            "No weather data available for location!",
            "Data Download Error",
            MessageBoxButtons.OK,
            MessageBoxIcon.Error);


    // Otherwise, display the forecast data.
    else
        DisplayData(ForecastNumber);
}
```

```csharp
private void txtLocation_KeyDown(object sender, KeyEventArgs e)
{
    // Detect pressing of the Enter key.
    if (e.KeyCode == Keys.Enter)
    {
        // Obtain the forecast.
        GetForecast();

        // Verify that there are forecasts to process.
        if (Forecast.Count() == 0)

            // If not, display an error message.
            MessageBox.Show(
                "No weather data available for location!",
                "Data Download Error",
                MessageBoxButtons.OK,
                MessageBoxIcon.Error);


        // Otherwise, display the forecast data.
        else
            DisplayData(ForecastNumber);
    }
}
```

The action of leaving the Location field is the easiest event to handle. It begins by getting a new forecast by calling *GetForecast()*. The user could easily enter some invalid information such as, "My Place" instead of a valid entry. If this happens, the number of entries returned by *Forecast. Count()* is 0 and the code displays an error message (otherwise, the user will never realize that there's a mistake in the entry). When the user enters a valid location, the code displays the first forecast by calling *DisplayData(ForecastNumber)*.

One task you might have to perform with an application is to detect special keys that the user presses. When you create a *KeyDown* event handler, the application passes a special type, *KeyEventArgs*, to your application in the *e* parameter. The *txtLocation_KeyDown()* event handler is called for every key that the user presses, but you're only interested in the Enter key. So, the first thing that the event handler does is check *e.KeyCode* for *Keys.Enter*, which indicates that the user has pressed Enter.

When the user presses Enter, the code obtains a new forecast by calling *GetForecast()*. It verifies that the user has supplied valid information by checking *Forecast.Count()* for a value of 0. When *Forecast.Count()* is greater than 0, the code displays the forecast by calling *DisplayData(ForecastNumber)*; otherwise, it displays an error message.

Choosing a Different Icon

Each of the forecasts comes with a number of icons that graphically depict the upcoming weather. In fact, the web service typically provides 10 different icons that present the weather in different ways. Which icon you choose is a matter of personal preference—some people will prefer one icon while others prefer another. Changing icons is relatively easy using the *NumericUpDown* control. All you need to look for is a change of value as shown in Listing 6-7.

LISTING 6-7 Choosing between icons

```
private void IconSelect_ValueChanged(object sender, EventArgs e)
{
    // Set the icon value to the value of the up/down control.
    IconNumber = (Int32)IconSelect.Value;

    // Display the information.
    DisplayData(ForecastNumber);
}
```

The *IconSelect.Value* property is somewhat special because it's a *Decimal* value. A *Decimal* value is a high-precision number often used for working with financial information; you usually don't need decimal precision for situations such as this one. Unfortunately, *Decimal* values aren't compatible with the *Int32* value used for *IconNumber*, so the code must perform a conversion. In this case, the *(Int32)* part of the code coerces the *Decimal* value to an *Int32* value, which results in minimal information loss. In fact, you'll use data coercion quite often when you write applications. The code ends by calling *DisplayData(ForecastNumber)* to display the updated icon.

Testing the RESTService Application

This application does more than previous examples did and you'll understand just how much more during testing. You'll need to place breakpoints in each of the event handlers to see how they work. It's also a good idea to place a breakpoint in the *Form1()* constructor to see how the initial presentation is created. Use the same tracing technique described in previous chapters to see how the application actually works.

One concept you should begin to grasp by completing this example is that it's very hard to test every possible contingency in a production application of any complexity. This application is considerably more complex than those you created earlier, but it's not nearly complex as many applications that you see on your desktop. Even with scores of testers, checking every possible permutation in a production application is normally impossible, which is one of the reasons that bugs go undetected in applications. Careful programming and testing later help remove most of these bugs, but as the book progresses, you'll begin to see that finding every potential source of error really is impossible.

Part of your testing process for this application should involve typing incorrect or invalid information. Try all kinds of wild entries to see how the application reacts. Does the application break at some point? If it does, then you've found another place where you need to add some error trapping code. This example should probably handle most errors with aplomb, but intense testing is always a good idea. In fact, most companies have special groups set aside that do nothing but try to break applications created by developers like you.

Developing the SOAP Web Service Application

The example in this section relies on SOAP rather than REST to communicate with the web service. Each form of communication has certain benefits and restrictions. In this case, you'll be working with a simple SOAP service that accepts a city name as input and provides a single-word weather forecast as output. You can see the base page for this web service at *http://www.deeptraining.com/ webservices/weather.asmx*. The WSDL for this service (shown in Figure 6-9) looks similar to the one for the government site described in the "Working with SOAP Web Services" section of the chapter.

As you work through this example, you'll find that it requires some special setup and a little more work at the outset. The payoff is that you perform less work later—the IDE automates certain parts of the communication process and makes it considerably easier to make requests. With this in mind, try following the steps in the following sections through to their completion before you make any comparisons between the two techniques. When you're done, you'll probably have a preference that you can exercise later when calling web services that offer both SOAP and REST.

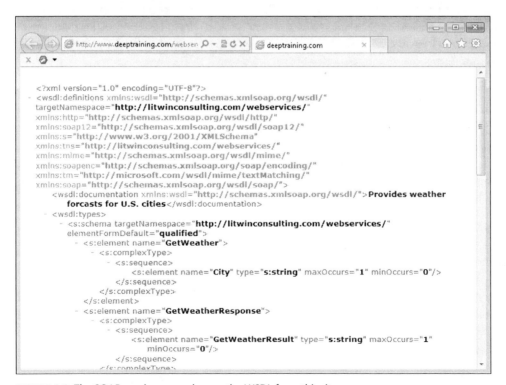

FIGURE 6-9 The SOAP service example uses the WSDL from this site.

Creating the SOAPService Project

It takes more time and effort to create a project that relies on SOAP. The initial steps are the same, but you end up doing more work to get the project going. The following steps show how to create the SOAPService project; these same steps are standard for most SOAP-based web services.

Create the SOAPService Project

1. Click New Project. The New Project dialog box appears.

2. Select Visual C# in the left pane and Windows Forms Application in the middle pane. You'll see a description of the template in the right pane.

3. Type **SOAPService** in the Name field and click OK. The IDE creates a new project for you consisting of a single form.

4. Open the Solution Explorer window.

5. Right-click References and choose Add Service Reference. An Add Service Reference dialog box appears.

6. Type **http://www.deeptraining.com/webservices/weather.asmx?WSDL** in the Address field and click Go. The IDE will find the weather service and display information about it, as shown here.

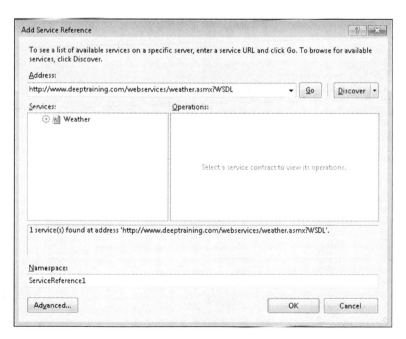

7. Type **NationalWeather** in the Namespace field and click OK. The IDE will automatically add a Service References folder that contains a NationalWeather entry like the one shown here. (Your folder might not automatically expand like the one shown here.)

At this point, the web service is completely accessible from within your application. Unlike a REST web service, you'll spend less time figuring out the data format and more time making requests.

Adding and Configuring the SOAPService Controls

The SOAPService example is relatively simple from a control perspective. You need one button to test the application and another to end the application. A label and text box combination will receive the name of the city to look up using the web service, and another label and text box combination will provide the results. Table 6-2 shows the configuration for this example.

TABLE 6-2 SOAPService Control Configuration

Control Name	Property Name	Value
button1	(Name)	btnWeather
	Text	&Weather
button2	(Name)	btnQuit
	Text	&Quit
label1	(Name)	lblCity
	Text	&City
textBox1	(Name)	txtCity
	Size.Width	179
	Size.Height	20
	Text	Milwaukee, WI
label2	(Name)	lblResults
	Text	&Results
textBox2	(Name)	txtResults

Control Name	Property Name	Value
	ReadOnly	True
	Size.Width	179
	Size.Height	20
Form1	Text	SOAP Weather Service
	AcceptButton	btnWeather
	CancelButton	btnQuit
	FormBorderStyle	FixedDialog

Adding the SOAPService Application Code

The SOAPService example is simpler than the RESTService example. All it does is obtain a one-word description of the weather for the city of interest. Even so, the code in Listing 6-8 is representative. No matter how complex the data, the query shown will place the information in *WeatherResults*.

LISTING 6-8 Requesting a weather summary

```
private void btnWeather_Click(object sender, EventArgs e)
{
    // Create an instance of the Weather service.
    NationalWeather.WeatherSoapClient Client =
        new NationalWeather.WeatherSoapClient();

    // Make a query to the Weather service.
    var WeatherResults = from Forecast
                         in Client.GetWeather(txtCity.Text)
                         select Forecast;

    // Combine the individual characters of the forecast into
    // a single string.
    txtResults.Text = "";
    foreach (Char Letter in WeatherResults)
        txtResults.Text = txtResults.Text + Letter;
}
```

The example begins by creating an instance of the *NationalWeather* SOAP client. When you create a Service Reference, the IDE defines a class for that reference in the background. This class provides all of the mechanisms needed to converse with the web service and you don't need to do anything special to create it in most cases. The WSDL describes how to create this class for the IDE, so all you need to do is tell the IDE where to find the WSDL.

Note You're likely to encounter a lot of older, SOAP-specific code for C# on the Internet that won't look anything like the code in this example. This older code is likely based on a Web Reference and procedural language combination, rather than a Service Reference. Visual Studio relied on Web References in earlier versions of the product and that feature is still available in Visual C# 2010 Express. The examples in this book use the newest technique that Microsoft has to offer, which relies on a combination of a Service Reference and LINQ. Using a Service Reference is considerably more flexible than using a Web Reference in many situations. In addition, LINQ is more reliable and less prone to coding errors than procedural code. However, depending on the web service you select, you may actually need to use the older Web Reference technique demonstrated in those online examples.

The *Client* is an object just like any other object you work with in your code. When you type the object's name, the IDE will display the usual helpful information about the class used to create Client. This example uses a LINQ query to obtain the weather information provided by the *Client.GetWeather()* method. As part of this call, you must supply a city name, which the code obtains from *txtCity.Text*. The output is supposed to be a *String*, but what you get instead is a *Char* array. There's no documented reason for this conversion to occur—it simply does with some web services (which is why you want to work with the web service a bit at a time as you construct your application).

To convert the data back to a string, the code uses a *foreach* loop. It extracts each letter out of *WeatherResults* and places it in *txtResults.Text*. Figure 6-10 shows some typical results of this application in action.

FIGURE 6-10 The SOAP Weather Service application outputs a weather forecast.

Have you noticed that you didn't work with any XML in this example? That's right, you can use SOAP without having to worry too much about XML in most cases. In some situations you still have to worry about XML, even when using this approach, but you'll find that SOAP generally requires less XML knowledge than REST does.

Testing the SOAPService Application

The LINQ used for this example works much like the other LINQ examples in the book, but it's interesting to see it in action anyway by tracing through it. Unfortunately, you can't trace through the code used to make the SOAP call in this case. It's there in the background, but you don't see it. The best place to put a breakpoint in this example is on the *foreach* line of the *btnWeather_Click()* event handler. Remember to click Step Into so that you can actually see the LINQ in action.

This application has another interesting feature. Try typing an incorrect value into the application, such as **Hello**. Click Weather and trace through the application. You'll find that it doesn't fail. The web service simply provides bogus results for the query. Some web services behave this way. Rather than error out, they'll simply provide something useless as output. The advantage of this approach is that the application is more reliable—it continues running even when the user fiddles with it. The disadvantage is that you don't have an easy method to determine when the user has provided incorrect input. The only way to overcome this problem is to validate the information manually before you pass it along to the web service.

Get Going with C#

This chapter has provided you with an overview of web services. If you take away one important piece of information from this chapter, it should be that web services offer a means of exchanging information that normally relies on XML. Web services can provide either one-way or two-way communication, depending on how they're designed. In some cases, a web service will provide one-way communication for some features and two-way communication for other features. The two main methods of creating a request and response when working with a web service are REST and SOAP. REST is the easier of the two to test, while SOAP offers the best automation in C#.

This chapter has provided information about a few carefully chosen web services. However, many web services are available online. These web services provide access to all sorts of information that you might not even know exists on a web service. For example, check out some of the interesting offerings on this site: *http://flash-db.com/services/.* Another good place to look is *http://free-web-services.com/,* which provides information about a host of web services that you can use without any sort of payment (you may have to sign up to use these web services). The point is that you can probably find a web service to meet a significant number of coding needs.

Try out some of these web services to see what you can do with them. For example, even a home user will likely find the UPC Lookup web service interesting. Use the WSDL URL of *http://www.flash-db.com/services/ws/upcLookup.wsdl* to create a SOAP connection to it. This service offers a description, manufacturer, and size/weight as output. You call the *getProductInfo()* method to make the call with *Anything* as the first argument, *Anything* as the second argument, and the UPC code as the third argument.

Note The fact that the UPC Lookup web service was originally created for Flash developers is unimportant. The age of the web service is also a non-issue as long as the web service continues to provide outside access. Any web service is accessible from any language that provides the required support—this is a useful fact to take away from this chapter because some developers are under the misconception that web services are somehow platform-specific. It doesn't matter how the originator originally planned the web service. If the web service follows the standards and relies on either REST or SOAP for communication, you can access it from C#.

Chapter 7, "Using the Windows Presentation Foundation," discusses the Windows Presentation Foundation (WPF) in detail. You'll use WPF to create three applications that all rely on a data source of some type: local XML file, SOAP web service, and an in-memory object. As you create these three examples, you'll discover a number of details about how WPF works. In addition, you'll explore some of the strengths and weaknesses of WPF for creating applications.

Chapter 7

Using the Windows Presentation Foundation

After completing this chapter, you'll be able to:

- Describe the differences between WPF and Windows Forms applications

- Explain the XML basis for XAML

- Create a basic XML data storage application with WPF

- Access a SOAP web service using WPF

- Develop and use a data source with WPF

THE WINDOWS FORMS APPLICATIONS THAT you're already familiar with represent the traditional Windows approach to creating applications. Most application development today still revolves around the Windows Forms approach. However, there's a newer approach that relies on a newer technology called the Windows Presentation Foundation (WPF). The key reason that Microsoft provides WPF is to help developers create attractive and effective user interfaces, which means being able to use graphics to good effect without a degree in art. (You can read about the many other reasons for using WPF at *http://msdn.microsoft.com/en-us/library/ms748948.aspx* and *http://en.wikipedia.org/wiki/Windows_Presentation_Foundation*.) This chapter explores the reasons that you'd use WPF for an application and helps you to understand situations where the Windows Forms might still be better.

The basis for the WPF interface code is the eXtensible Application Markup Language (XAML), which is pronounced *zammel*. XAML is yet another form of XML, so many of the techniques you are already familiar with from your work with XML will also work with XAML. Of course, XAML is a specific form of XML, so it requires its own special rules. This chapter will explain those rules. As with a Windows Forms application, you don't necessarily need to know anything about XAML to create an application—you can simply drag and drop the controls you want to use onto the form and then configure them.

This chapter provides three examples that help you explore and understand WPF. These examples are similar to the Windows Forms applications you've seen in previous chapters. You'll work with a basic XML data storage application, a web service application that relies on SOAP, and a data source application that relies on an object for storage. When you complete this chapter, you'll have a good idea of just how WPF compares to Windows Forms and be able to choose the appropriate technology for your particular application.

Considering the WPF Differences with Windows Forms Applications

A developer may wax philosophical about tightly written code or a particularly elegant solution to a problem, but users are most concerned with the interface that an application provides—and first impressions are important. When a user starts your application, the impression that the application makes determines whether the user gets excited about using it or slogs along to meet some requirement. In short, writing applications has a whole psychological element that you might not have considered.

WPF and Windows Forms are two different tools you can use to create an application interface. Both tools should have a place in your programmer toolbox. WPF makes it easy to add great graphics to an application. Don't equate graphics to eye candy—many applications today use graphics to good effect in presenting information in a form that the user will find easier to understand, more accessible, or simply more appealing. However, WPF is more than simply graphics—it lets you incorporate all sorts of media types into a single application. For example, you can create an application that provides graphics, video, and audio in one package using considerably less code than is necessary for a similar Windows Forms application.

Tip WPF also makes it possible to create applications faster in specific situations. Developers usually don't have a lot of media skills and companies rely on designers to provide this service. Because of the way WPF works, it's possible for you to focus on the application code while a professional designer creates the interface. However, for the purposes of this book, you'll be the designer so that you can understand the entire WPF process.

Windows Forms applications are more suited toward business applications that present quantities of data in either a form-based or tabular format. Many applications fall into this category. Any data entry application will work well with Windows Forms and you'll find that you spend a lot less time creating the application using this approach. It's important to understand that the Windows Forms designers are older and more refined than those employed by WPF. You spend less time fiddling with the interface when working with Windows Forms. It's a no-nonsense approach to development that many developers appreciate.

Fortunately, you don't have to choose one technique over the other. It's possible to combine WPF and Windows Forms into a single application. The technique is a little more complex than this book allows, but once you gain some skills using WPF and Windows Forms alone, you'll want to spend some time discovering techniques for combining the two technologies. You may find that a business application requires some fancy graphics to display the tabular data that users normally see in a friendlier way—using a combination of WPF and Windows Forms would answer this need.

Currently, Windows Forms developers also have a significant advantage over WPF developers in the way of third-party support. More controls and libraries are available to Windows Forms developers. If your application requires one of the existing Windows Forms controls or libraries, and no equivalent WPF-specific version is available, you might need to add Windows Forms support to a WPF application. As you work more with WPF and Windows Forms, keep these differences in mind. You have the freedom to choose the right tool for the job, or to combine both tools to create a mixture that will work just right.

Understanding XAML

The user interface of a WPF application is created from a special XML file written in XAML. A XAML file isn't a complete XML file—it lacks the declaration usually found in an XML file. However, it contains just one root node, as do all XML files, and it uses the same basic functionality as any XML file, so for all intents and purposes a XAML file is an XML file. To better understand how XAML works, consider the window shown in Figure 7-1.

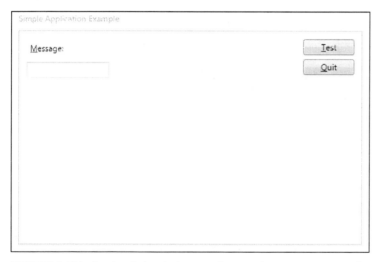

FIGURE 7-1 This simple window helps contain controls you can use to understand XAML better.

The window contains two buttons, a label, and an associated text box. As you might imagine, clicking Test displays a message box showing the content of the Message field, while clicking Quit ends the application. The details aren't important in this case. Adding controls to the window, changing entries in the Properties window, and modifying a few items in the XAML editor create the XAML code shown in Listing 7-1.

LISTING 7-1 Viewing a simple XAML example

```xml
<Window x:Class="SimpleWPF.MainWindow"
        xmlns="http://schemas.microsoft.com/winfx/2006/xaml/presentation"
        xmlns:x="http://schemas.microsoft.com/winfx/2006/xaml"
        Title="Simple Application Example" Height="350" Width="525">
    <Grid>
        <Button Content="_Test" Height="23" HorizontalAlignment="Left"
            Margin="416,12,0,0" Name="btnTest" VerticalAlignment="Top" Width="75"
            Click="btnTest_Click" TabIndex="0" />
        <Button Content="_Quit" Height="23" HorizontalAlignment="Left"
            Margin="416,41,0,0" Name="btnQuit" VerticalAlignment="Top" Width="75"
            Click="btnQuit_Click" TabIndex="1" />
        <Label Content="_Message:" Height="28" HorizontalAlignment="Left"
            Margin="12,12,0,0" Name="lblMessage" VerticalAlignment="Top"
            TabIndex="2" />
        <TextBox Height="23" HorizontalAlignment="Left" Margin="12,46,0,0"
            Name="txtMessage" VerticalAlignment="Top" Width="120" TabIndex="3" />
    </Grid>
</Window>
```

WPF applications rely on windows, not on forms, so the root entry for the window shown in the figure is *<Window>*. The *<Window>* element always contains an attribute that defines the class used to hold code associated with the window. In addition, you see attributes that define the namespaces used to create the child elements of the window. A window can optionally (and normally does) contain attributes that define the window *Title*, *Height*, and *Width*. Removing these attributes won't cause the application to fail, but you also won't have control over these window features.

Tip Many developers complain that WPF lacks an alternative to the *FormBorderStyle* property provided by a Windows Forms application; however, carefully setting XAML properties can create windows with similar effects. For example, to obtain a window that acts much like a Windows Forms application that uses the *FixedDialog* style, use the *ResizeMode="CanMinimize"* attribute in XAML. The result isn't precisely the same, but it works well enough for most purposes. Another alternative is to set the minimum and maximize window sizes the same as the *Height* and *Width* attributes, so that the result for this example is: *Height="350" Width="525" MaxHeight="350" MaxWidth="525" MinHeight="350" MinWidth="525"*.

The default XAML window configuration relies on a *Grid* control (specified by the *<Grid>* element) to organize content into rows and columns. Even though you can set properties for the *Grid* control, the default configuration doesn't use any—and you typically don't need to set any to create an application. However, it's important to explore this control at some point because it can do more for you than simply organize controls displayed in a window.

Each control you add to a WPF application is represented by a distinct XAML element. In this case, you can see *<Button>*, *<Label>*, and *<TextBox>* elements. Other examples in this chapter and those that follow will use additional elements. The attributes for each of these elements change the appearance of the control. Here's a description of the common attributes used for this example:

- **Content**   Contains the information that appears to the user on the control. For example, the *content* attribute describes the caption on a button or label, or the information inside a text box. It replaces and unifies the *Text* property and other properties used with Windows Forms controls, such as *Caption*.

- **Height**   Controls the height of the control as a whole. This property replaces the *Size.Height* property used with Windows Forms controls.

- **HorizontalAlignment**   Determines how the control is aligned horizontally within the host container. The default setting aligns controls from the left side of the window. However, you can also choose *Right*, *Center*, or *Stretch* as values. This property works with the *Margin* property to determine a control's horizontal placement within a host container (normally a *Grid* control).

- **Margin**   Specifies the distance between the left, top, right, and bottom sides of a control and its host container. This property works with the *HorizontalAlignment* and *VerticalAlignment* properties to place the control within the host container. For example, if the *HorizontalAlignment* is set to *Left* and the first *Margin* property value is *40*, the control's left edge is placed 40 pixels from the left side of the host container. In many respects, this combination replaces the *Location X* and *Location.Y* property values used with Windows Forms controls, but XAML is considerably more flexible.

- **Name**   Defines the name of the control. This property is a replacement for the (*Name*) property found in Windows Forms applications.

- **VerticalAlignment**   Determines how the control is aligned vertically within the host container. The default setting aligns controls from the top of the window. However, you can also choose *Bottom*, *Center*, or *Stretch* as values. This property works with the *Margin* property to determine a control's vertical placement within the host container (normally a *Grid* control).

- **Width**   Controls the width of the control as a whole. This property replaces the *Size.Width* property used with Windows Forms controls.

- **Click**   Creates a connection between the *Click* event and an event handler.

- **TabIndex**   Determines the selection order when a user moves between controls by pressing Tab. The application automatically sets the focus to whatever control has a *TabIndex* of *0* when the application first starts.

As you progress through the WPF examples in the book, you'll find that they all start with a window and include some sort of container control that in turn holds one or more controls. You configure each control using a combination of properties that define appearance, functionality, or event handlers.

Developing the WPF Data Store Application

The best way to become more familiar with WPF is to create an application with it. In this case, the example is an extremely simple XML data store. You'll find a similar example in the "Using XML to Store Application Settings" section of Chapter 5, "Working with XML." The former example relied on Windows Forms, whereas this example relies on WPF. Comparing the two examples will give you further insights into how WPF differs from Windows Forms.

Creating the WPF_XML Project

WPF is all about presentation. However, the process of creating the project used to store the application is similar to Windows Forms, so you won't find many differences between the two. The following steps describe how to create a WPF project used to store and read XML data from disk.

Create the WPF_XML Project

1. Click New Project. The New Project dialog box appears.

2. Select Visual C# in the left pane and WPF Application in the middle pane. You'll see a description of the template in the right pane, as shown here.

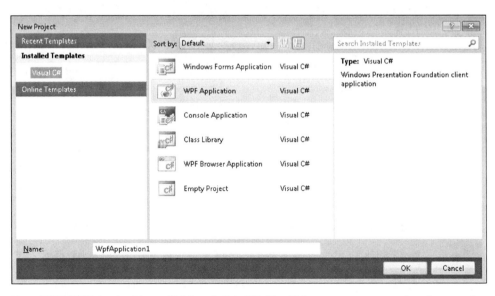

3. Type **WPF_XML** in the Name field and click OK. The IDE creates a new project for you that consists of a single window.

Adding and Configuring the WPF_XML Controls

As with the Windows Forms version of this example, the focus of this example is to see how the basic code works rather than to create a fully fledged application. With this in mind, the example relies on a *Label* and *TextBox* combination for a text setting and a *CheckBox* control for a true/false setting. A single *Button* control, *Quit*, provides a way to exit the application. You'll find that you need to perform a few extra configuration tasks to make WPF work the same as a Windows Forms counterpart. Table 7-1 shows how to configure the controls for this example—the text that follows explains how to perform some of the newer configuration tasks (such as selecting a *Target* property value).

TABLE 7-1 WPF_XML Control Configuration

Control Name	Property Name	Value
button1	*Name*	*btnQuit*
	Content	*_Quit*
	IsCancel	*True (checked)*
	TabIndex	*0*
label1	*Name*	*lblMessage*
	Content	*_Type Something*
	TabIndex	*1*
	Target	*txtMessage*
textBox1	*Name*	*txtMessage*
	TabIndex	*2*
checkBox1	*Name*	*chkChecked*
	Content	*_Check Me*
	TabIndex	*3*
Window	*Title*	*Saving and Restoring Values*
	ResizeMode	*CanMinimize*

Setting the *Name* property for a control is different when working with a WPF project than it is when working with a Windows Forms project. The *Name* property doesn't actually appear in the list of properties in the Properties window; instead, it appears at the top of the window next to the control type. You click next to the control type to reveal a text box where you type the control name, as shown in Figure 7-2.

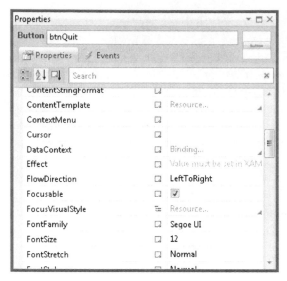

FIGURE 7-2 Use the text box next to the control type to change the control name.

Note Windows in WPF are missing some of the properties found in forms. For example, a window doesn't have a *CancelButton* property. Instead, you set the *IsCancel* property for the control you want to use to cancel an operation to *true* instead. Similarly, there's no *DefaultButton* property. Instead, you set the control's *IsDefault* property to *true*. When multiple controls in a window have the *IsCancel* property set *true*, the first control in the tab order takes precedence—the same holds true for the *IsDefault* property.

When working with a Windows Form application, a label that appears immediately before a text box in the tab order of the controls is automatically associated with that text box. This means that the hotkey (T in this example) for the label automatically selects the text box instead. When working with WPF, you must specifically assign the label to the text box, so that when the user presses Alt+T, the application selects the text box. To perform this task, you must set the *Target* property so that the label binds with the text box. Click the *Binding* value in the *Target* property to display the Source dialog box shown in Figure 7-3.

Select the *ElementName* entry in the left pane, the *txtMessage* entry in the middle pane, and then press Enter. This action associates *lblMessage* with *txtMessage*, so that pressing Alt+T will select the text box as expected.

FIGURE 7-3 Create a connection between the label and its associated text box.

Adding the WPF_XML Application Code

Even though the WPF version of this example has a number of changes when compared to the Windows Forms version, both applications must perform the same tasks. In both cases the application saves the settings on exit and restores the settings on startup (when such settings are available). As you'll see in the following sections, the basic logic of the code behind the application is the same, although there are some differences due to the differences in the user interface and associated controls.

Defining the Using Statements

Windows Forms and WPF applications both rely on the .NET Framework. There isn't a special version of the .NET Framework for WPF. With this in mind, you'll find that you rely on the same *using* statements for business logic when working with WPF as you do when working with a Windows Forms application.

However, this WPF application must also access some information within the assembly itself, so it requires a special reference to *System.Reflection*. This particular assembly is akin to a mirror—the assembly "looks into the mirror" to discover information about itself. With this in mind, you need to add the following *using* statements to the beginning of the code found in *MainWindow.xaml.cs*:

```
using System.Xml.Linq;
using System.IO;
using System.Reflection;
```

Ending the Application

The purpose of *btnQuit* is the same for both WPF and Windows Forms applications—it ends the application. The code is similar as well. Whether you close a window or close a form, you call the *Close()* method, as shown here:

```
private void btnQuit_Click(object sender, RoutedEventArgs e)
{
    // End the application.
    Close();
}
```

All of the WPF examples in this book will use a similar *btnQuit* event handler, unless specifically noted otherwise. Consequently, you won't see this particular code repeated, even though you need to add it to every example that includes a *btnQuit* control.

Saving the Settings

WPF window support many of the same events as the forms used in a Windows Forms application. One of those is the *Closing* event, which WPF calls right before the window closes. The result is the same. When a user chooses to close the window, the application calls this event before it actually begins the closing process. Your code can contain a *Closing* event handler to perform cleanup, cancel the close operation, or do whatever else you might need to do before your application closes. Use the following steps to create an event handler for the *Closing* event.

Define the Closing Event Handler

1. Select the window (not the Grid control) by clicking the border area.

2. Open the Properties window and click Events. Locate the *Closing* event, as shown. (Notice that the word *Window* appears in the upper-left corner of the dialog box.)

3. Double-click *Closing* to create the event handler.

Now that you have an event handler to work with, it's time to add some code to it. Listing 7-1 shows the code you need for this part of the example.

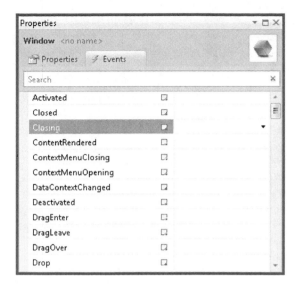

LISTING 7-1 Saving the settings.

```
private void Window_Closing(object sender, System.ComponentModel.CancelEventArgs e)
{
    // Create a document to hold the settings.
    XDocument SettingData = new XDocument(
        new XDeclaration("1.0", "utf-8", "yes"),
        new XElement("Settings",
            new XElement("txtMessage", txtMessage.Text),
            new XElement("chkChecked", chkChecked.IsChecked)));

    // Create the folder used to store the data if necessary.
    if (!Directory.Exists(SettingsDirectory))
        Directory.CreateDirectory(SettingsDirectory);

    // Save the settings to disk.
    SettingData.Save(SettingsFile);
}
```

The example code looks similar to the code in Listing 5-5. However, the subtle differences, even in this simple example, could take the unwary programmer by surprise. Of course, the most obvious change is that the event handler is named *Window_Closing()* and that it has a different argument than a Windows Forms application. (Windows relies on the *System.ComponentModel.CancelEventArgs* type, whereas forms rely on the *FormClosingEventArgs* type.)

A more important difference is that the *chkChecked.Checked* property value has changed to *chkChecked.IsChecked*. If you're moving your code from a Windows Forms environment to WPF, you need to be aware of these control differences or you may find that you have to perform a lot of debugging to get your application code to work.

Unlike the Windows Forms version, you must verify that the settings directory exists. Otherwise, when the code calls *SettingData.Save()* to save the data, the application could raise an error. The *Directory.Exists()* method returns true when the directory exists—the special *!* (not) symbol tells the code that when the directory doesn't exist, it should create it using the *Directory.CreateDirectory()* method.

It's also important to note what *hasn't* changed. This example still creates the *XDocument*, *SettingData*, the same as the Windows Forms application. It also saves that data using precisely the same technique as before. The bottom line is that you can use much the same business logic when working with WPF as you do with a Windows Forms application.

Restoring the Settings

Saving the settings isn't much good unless your application can also restore them. Listing 7-2 shows the WPF version of the code used to check for a file containing settings information, and if the file exists, to restore the settings contained in the file.

LISTING 7-2 Restoring the settings

```
// Create a global variable containing the name and
// location of the settings file.
String SettingsFile;

// Create a global variable used to hold the directory
// for the settings file.
String SettingsDirectory;

public MainWindow()
{
    // Perform the default configuration.
    InitializeComponent();

    // Obtain the configuration information for this application.
    Object[] Configuration = Assembly.GetEntryAssembly().GetCustomAttributes(false);

    // Obtain the company name.
    String CompanyName = "Company";
    foreach (var Value in Configuration)
        if (Value.GetType() == typeof(AssemblyCompanyAttribute))
        {
            CompanyName = ((AssemblyCompanyAttribute)Value).Company;
            break;
        }
```

Jandy Aquapure 1400 parts

4.75 x (2)   R0412700   2" Black O-ring
$9.20 x (2) R0412500   Union Nut 2" inch

Poolcenter.com

7.50
1840

$27.90

$9.98   R487000   Knob, valve

$16.81   1301   03A - Handle, Value

$26.79

www.poolpartsonline.com

```
    // Obtain the executable name.
    String Title = "Title";
    foreach (var Value in Configuration)
        if (Value.GetType() == typeof(AssemblyTitleAttribute))
        {
            Title = ((AssemblyTitleAttribute)Value).Title;
            break;
        }

    // Obtain the version number.
    String Version = "0.0.0.0";
    foreach (var Value in Configuration)
        if (Value.GetType() == typeof(AssemblyFileVersionAttribute))
        {
            Version = ((AssemblyFileVersionAttribute)Value).Version;
            break;
        }

    // Store the location of the settings directory.
    SettingsDirectory =
        Environment.GetFolderPath(Environment.SpecialFolder.LocalApplicationData) +
        "\\" + CompanyName + "\\" + Title + "\\" + Version;

    // Store the location of the settings file.
    SettingsFile = SettingsDirectory + "\\Settings.XML";

    // Check for a settings file.
    if (File.Exists(SettingsFile))
    {
        // Load the file containing the settings.
        XDocument SettingData = XDocument.Load(SettingsFile);

        // Change the control settings to match the file settings.
        txtMessage.Text = SettingData.Root.Element("txtMessage").Value;
        chkChecked.IsChecked =
            Boolean.Parse(SettingData.Root.Element("chkChecked").Value);
    }
}
```

In this case, one important difference between WPF and Windows Forms is that the WPF *Application* object doesn't include a *LocalUserAppDataPath* property. Consequently, you must create a standard storage path for the settings file using some other method. Obtaining this information requires a little extra work in WPF, but it's a good discussion.

The storage path for the Windows Forms example in Chapter 5 is *C:\Users\John\AppData\Local\ Microsoft\XMLSetting\1.0.0.0\Settings.XML* on my system. The location on your system will be somewhat different. The *C:\Users\John\AppData\Local* portion of the path is a standard folder called

LocalApplicationData. To obtain the other pieces of information, you have to look at the *AssemblyInfo. cs* file that's automatically generated when you create your application. Open this file now and you'll see something like the window shown in Figure 7-4.

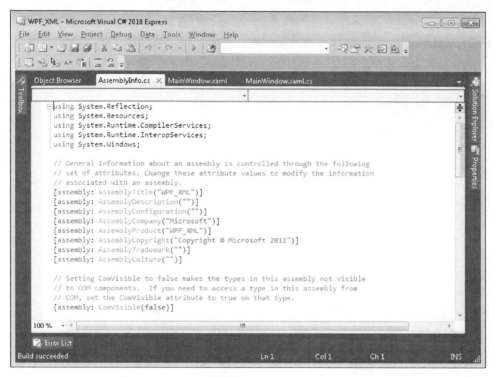

FIGURE 7-4 The *AssemblyInfo.cs* file contains information about your assembly such as the copyright.

Each of the *assembly* entries is an attribute. An attribute describes the assembly in some way, just as attributes such as brown hair and green eyes could describe you. Look down the list of attributes and you see a company name, application title, and a version number—just the information you need to create a path for the storage data.

The code looks into the mirror provided by the *System.Reflection* assembly to obtain the information in these attributes when the application is running. The *Assembly.GetEntryAssembly()* method obtains a copy of the current assembly to look at. It then uses the *GetCustomAttributes()* method to obtain a list of the attributes for the assembly. What you end up with is an *Object[]* array named *Configuration* that contains all the assembly attributes.

Now it's time to obtain a specific attribute. The example begins with the company name and places it in the *CompanyName* variable. It's entirely possible that the assembly won't have a company name defined if someone has modified the *AssemblyInfo.cs* file, so you always give *CompanyName* a default value so the rest of your code won't fail. The *foreach* loop places the attributes found in *Configuration* into *Value*, one at a time. It then compares the type of Value using *Value.GetType()* to the type of *AssemblyCompanyAttribute*, which happens to be the kind of attribute that holds a company name. When the types match, the code converts Value into a *AssemblyCompanyAttribute* and places the

Company property value into *CompanyName*. After the code has found the correct attribute, it's pointless to look at the remaining attributes, so the code uses a *break* statement to end the *foreach* loop. The same process occurs for *Title* (the name of the application) and *Version*.

Obtaining these values makes it possible to create a *SettingsDirectory* variable that contains the same location information as its Windows Forms counterpart. Of course, this path will be unique to the WPF_XML application. When the code adds the filename to the path, it obtains the same *SettingsFile* information as in the Windows Forms example. The remaining code works just like the Windows Forms version, except that you have to store the current state of *chkChecked* in *IsChecked* instead of *Checked*.

Testing the WPF_XML Application

The WPF_XML example works much like the XMLSetting example from Chapter 5. When you start the application, you'll see a dialog box like the one shown in Figure 7-5.

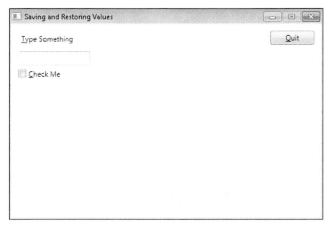

FIGURE 7-5 The WPF_XML example looks much like its counterpart in Chapter 5.

Type **Hello** into the Type Something field and select the Check Me check box. Click Quit. This act creates an XML file in the appropriate directory (*C:\Users\John\AppData\Local\Microsoft\ WPF_XML\1.0.0.0* on my system) containing the settings data. When you open *Settings.XML* in this directory, you see the settings information, as shown in Figure 7-6.

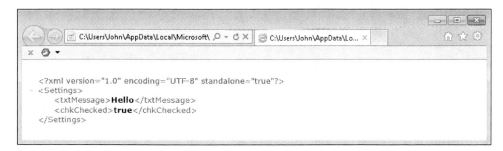

FIGURE 7-6 The *Settings.XML* file contains any settings changes you make to the application.

Tracing the WPF_XML Application with the Debugger

This example has several interesting bits of code that you should trace through using the debugger technique found in the rest of the book. Of course, you can easily trace through the entire application if desired. The first breakpoint you should set is in the *MainWindow()* constructor at the line that begins with *Object[] Configuration*. When the application first starts, it calls the constructor and stops at this line. At this point, *Configuration* should have a value of *null* in the Locals window. Click Step Over. Now *Configuration* will display a list of available attributes, as shown in Figure 7-7, when you click the plus sign next to its entry. (You should probably see 14 entries, but you may see more or less than that number on your computer depending on the number of entries in *AssemblyInfo.cs*.)

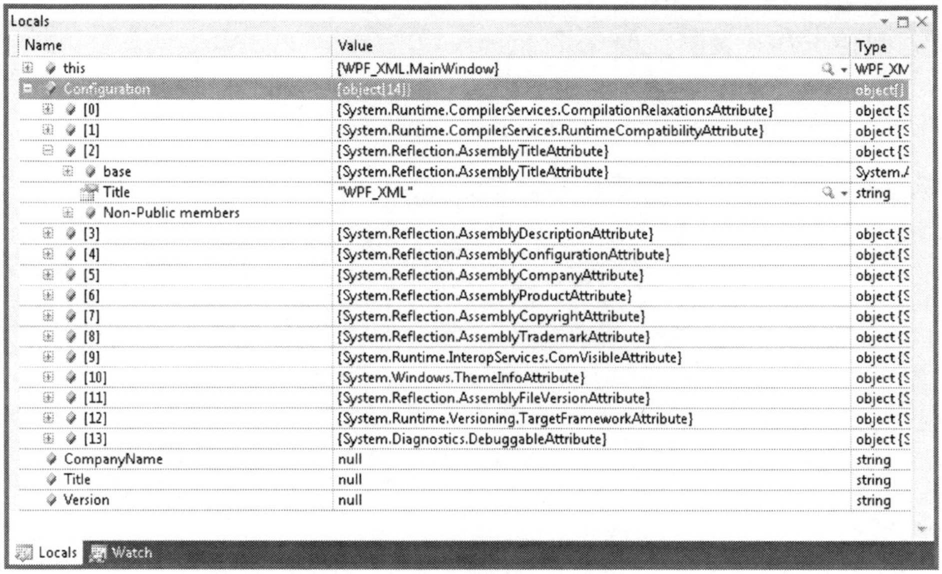

FIGURE 7-7 Configuration contains the entries from the *AssemblyInfo.cs* file.

Each of these attributes contains additional data that you can peruse. The figure shows the *AssemblyTitleAttribute* entry opened so that you can see the information in the *Title* property. This array is interesting because it contains a selection of like items—attributes in this case—but each of these items is of a different type. In many situations you need to store data of different types together in a single array like the one shown here. It's not uncommon to use an *Object[]* array in this case. When you do use an *Object[]* array, you must convert the individual *Object* entries into a type that reflects the original content. You'll see how this works later during the tracing process.

Click Step Over again and you'll reach the first *foreach* statement. When you click Step Over again, you'll see that that instruction pointer moves to *Configuration*. The next steps move it to *in*, then to *var Value*. These are common steps for any *foreach* loop.

At this point, the instruction pointer moves to the *if* statement. This is where it's handy to create entries in the Watch window. To perform this task, highlight *Value.GetType()* and drag it to the Watch window. You'll see that the IDE automatically creates the entry for you. Perform the same task with

typeof (AssemblyCompanyAttribute). Create a third watch statement with *Value.GetType() ==*
typeof (AssemblyCompanyAttribute). Your Watch window should now look like the one shown
in Figure 7-8.

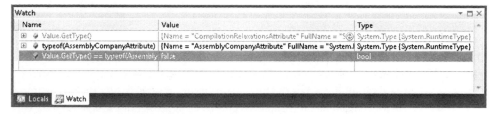

FIGURE 7-8 Create some watch statements so that you can see how the application works.

Using this setup lets you trace through the code and see precisely what happens at each stage
of the process. Continue clicking Step Over and watch the values in the Watch window. Eventually,
the *Value.GetType() == typeof(AssemblyCompanyAttribute)* statement will become *true*. At that
point, you'll see the instruction pointer move to the curly brace, instead of back up to the *foreach*
statement after the comparison. Click Step Over twice and you'll see a company name assigned to
CompanyName. Click Step Over again and the break will execute, placing the instruction pointer on
the *Title* declaration, even if additional elements remain to process in *Configuration*. Now you see the
value of using *break*—it lets the loop end early and saves time. *CompanyName*, *Title*, and *Version* all
work the same way.

The second breakpoint you'll definitely want to set is at the *if (!Directory.Exists(SettingsDirectory))*
statement in the *Window_Closing()* event handler. After you set the breakpoint, click Continue so that
the application completes the initialization process and you can see the form. Type a value in Type
Something and select the Check Me check box. Click Quit. At this point, you'll see the application stop
at this second breakpoint.

The *SettingsDirectory String* will have the value assigned to it during initialization. If this directory
exists, the application will bypass the content of the *if* statement when you click Step Over. Otherwise,
the application creates the directory before it attempts to save the file to disk. This step may not seem
all that important, but it's amazing how often you need to verify the presence of a directory or file.
In fact, this is one bit of code you should commit to memory. Every time you use a directory or folder,
you should verify that it exists first, to avoid potential error messages. Otherwise, you have no way of
knowing whether the user has decided to delete the folder or file you need for the application.

Developing the WPF SOAP Web Service Application

The "Developing the SOAP Web Service Application" section of Chapter 6 shows how to create
a Windows Forms version of an application that relies on a SOAP service to access weather
information. The example in this section performs the same task using a WPF application.

Creating the WPFSOAPService Project

Before you can do anything, you need to create the WPFSOAPService project. Use the same technique as described in the "Creating the WPF_XML Project" section of this chapter. The only change is that you need to use **WPFSOAPService** as the project name instead of WPF_XML.

Adding a New Service Data Source

As with any SOAP application, you need to add a reference to the web service to use as a data source. Even though the data source is external to your application (unlike the previous example where it appears on the local machine), the application will act as if the data source is local. That's the advantage of using SOAP over REST. Of course, WPF provides support for both service types, just like Windows Forms applications. The following steps show how to add the web service reference.

Define the Weather Service Reference

1. Open the Solution Explorer window.

2. Right-click References and choose Add Service Reference. An Add Service Reference dialog box appears.

3. Type **http://www.deeptraining.com/webservices/weather.asmx?WSDL** in the Address field and click Go. The IDE will find the weather service and display information about it, as shown here.

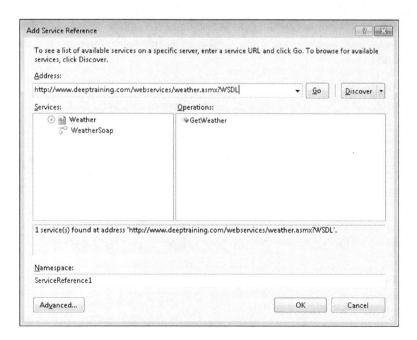

4. Type **NationalWeather** in the Namespace field and click OK. The IDE will automatically add a Service References folder that contains a NationalWeather entry like the one shown here. (Your folder might not automatically expand like the one shown here.)

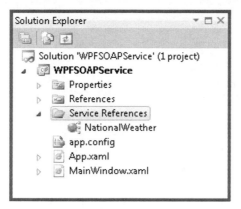

Adding and Configuring the WPFSOAPService Controls

This example uses the same basic interface as the SOAPService example in Chapter 6. However, this example uses WPF, rather than Windows Forms as the basis for the user interface, resulting in some differences. Table 7-2 shows the configuration information required for the two buttons and two label and text box sets required for the application.

TABLE 7-2 WPFSOAPService Control Configuration

Control Name	Property Name	Value
button1	Name	btnWeather
	Content	_Weather
	IsDefault	true
	TabIndex	0
button2	Name	btnQuit
	Content	_Quit
	IsCancel	true
	TabIndex	1
label1	Name	lblCity
	Content	_City
	TabIndex	2
	Target	txtCity
textBox1	Name	txtCity
	Text	Milwaukee, WI
	TabIndex	3
	Width	398

Control Name	Property Name	Value
label2	Name	lblResults
	Content	_Results
	TabIndex	4
	Target	txtResults
textBox2	Name	txtResults
	IsReadOnly	True
	TabIndex	5
	Width	398
Window	Title	SOAP Weather Service
	ResizeMode	CanMinimize

All of the same notes for the first example in this chapter hold true for this example. Some of the property names, such as *Content*, are replacements for Windows Forms properties, such as *Text*, but they function the same way. The *TabIndex* value isn't automatically assigned, so you must create one. In addition, default and cancel button status is set on the control, rather than the window. Finally, you must associate labels with text boxes directly by using the *Target* property.

Adding the WPFSOAPService Application Code

Because of the way in which web services are handled and the use of *TextBox* controls in this example, there really isn't much difference between the WPF version of the code and the Windows Forms version. It isn't often that you can move code from one environment to another with nary a change. Listing 7-3 shows the code used for this example. (Compare it with Listing 6-8.)

LISTING 7-3 Requesting a weather summary

```csharp
private void btnWeather_Click(object sender, RoutedEventArgs e)
{
    // Create an instance of the Weather service.
    NationalWeather.WeatherSoapClient Client =
        new NationalWeather.WeatherSoapClient();

    // Make a query to the Weather service.
    var WeatherResults = from Forecast
                         in Client.GetWeather(txtCity.Text)
                         select Forecast;

    // Combine the individual characters of the forecast into
    // a single string.
    txtResults.Text = "";
    foreach (Char Letter in WeatherResults)
        txtResults.Text = txtResults.Text + Letter;
}
```

Except for changes in the event handler definition, you won't see any differences between the two listings. The description of how this code works is also the same. Don't count on this sort of compatibility very often, but also be aware that it can (and does) happen, especially when working with web services.

Testing the WPFSOAPService Application

The two versions of this application work the same. You type the name of a city, provide a three-letter acronym for an airport, or supply a ZIP code as input in the City field. Click Weather and you'll see a single-word description of the weather in that city, as shown in Figure 7-9.

FIGURE 7-9 Create a WPF version of the SOAP Weather Service application.

Developing the EmbeddedSource Application

It's time to look at a unique WPF application. The other examples in this chapter compare WPF to Windows Forms applications. This example is going to look at another sort of data source—data embedded within the application. It's useful to know how to embed and then access resources in your application. Embedding the resource makes it impossible for the user to delete it. In addition, you gain some reliability and security using this approach. The downside of using embedded resources is that you must recompile the application to change those resources, so you don't want to use this technique with something that will change very often.

This example relies on an XML file as the embedded data source. The same technique works for any other resource you want to embed, such as icons, videos, pictures, and sounds. It's quite useful to embed certain XML files into your application. For example, it's unlikely that a list of state abbreviations will change anytime soon, so embedding a list of abbreviations into your application is a good idea to ensure constant access. Using an XML file makes it possible to store the data in structured form for easier editing.

Starting the EmbeddedSource Project

Begin this example by creating the EmbeddedSource project. Use the same technique as described in the "Creating the WPF_XML Project" section of this chapter. The only change is that you need to use **EmbeddedSource** as the project name instead of WPF_XML.

Creating an Embedded Resource

The Visual Studio IDE can help you create a number of different resources. It does a great job with some resources, such as XML files. You can't use Visual Studio to create other resources, such as icons, pictures, videos, and audio files. However, you can import existing resources and embed them into the application. The following steps describe how to create and embed an XML file.

Creating and Embedding the XML File

1. Right-click the project entry in Solution Explorer and choose Add | New Item. The Add New Item dialog box appears.

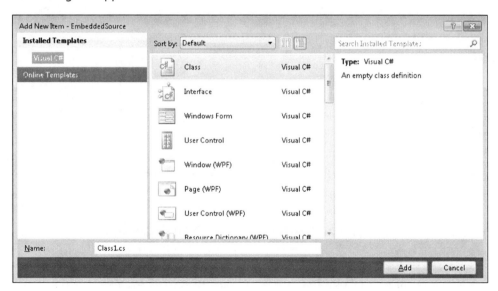

 Tip When you want to add a resource created using another application, choose Add | Existing Item. You'll see an Add Existing Item dialog box where you can locate the file you want to add to the application as a resource. The remaining configuration steps (starting with step 3) are the same as for the XML file shown in this example.

2. Scroll down to the XML File entry and highlight it. Type **TestData.XML** in the Name field and click Add. Visual Studio adds a new XML file to your application. The XML file will already have the proper declaration in place.

3. Highlight the TestData.XML entry in Solution Explorer.

4. Open the Properties window and you'll see the properties for TestData.XML, as shown here.

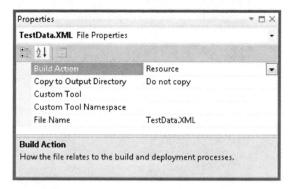

5. Select Resource in the Build Action property to add the file to the application as a resource.

6. Select Do Not Copy in the Copy To Output Directory property. You don't need to copy this file to the output directory when you've added it as a resource.

Now that you have an XML file and the compiler will add it to the application as a resource, you need some data for it. Listing 7-4 shows the complete source code for the XML file used in this example.

LISTING 7-4 XML data added as a resource

```xml
<?xml version="1.0" encoding="utf-8" ?>
<Data>
  <Item>One</Item>
  <Item>Two</Item>
  <Item>Three</Item>
  <Item>Four</Item>
</Data>
```

Adding and Configuring the EmbeddedSource Controls

This example begins by displaying the first data entry in the XML file. Of course, you'll want to move between entries, so you'll need a Next button and a Previous button. In addition, it's always a good idea to include a Quit button. The data for this example are simple. All you need is a label and text box pair to display each data item in turn. Table 7-3 shows the list of controls needed for this example and their configuration.

TABLE 7-3 EmbeddedSource Control Configuration

Control Name	Property Name	Value
button1	Name	btnNext
	Content	_Next
	TabIndex	0
button2	Name	btnPrevious

Control Name	Property Name	Value
	Content	_Previous
	TabIndex	1
button3	Name	btnQuit
	Content	_Quit
	IsCancel	true
	TabIndex	2
label1	Name	lblValue
	Content	_Setting Value
	TabIndex	3
	Target	txtValue
textBox1	Name	txtValue
	IsReadOnly	true
	TabIndex	4
Window	Title	Using an Embedded Resource
	ResizeMode	CanMinimize

The example doesn't include a default button because the user could need either the Next or Previous button. Consequently, none of the buttons has *IsDefault* set to *true*. Otherwise, the controls have the standard changes made to them.

Adding the EmbeddedSource Application Code

This example requires the usual addition of some *using* statements to allow easy access to part of the .NET Framework. The user will want to see the first item when the application starts, so you must also modify the application's constructor to display the first item after the initial configuration is finished. Finally, this application requires code for the Next and Previous buttons. The following sections describe the code required to perform all three tasks.

Adding the Required *using* Statements

The code used in this example requires access to .NET Framework XML and resource functionality. You've already worked with a number of XML examples. The resource functionality appears in the *System.Windows.Resources* namespace. Add these two *using* statements at the beginning of the code file with the existing *using* statements:

```
using System.Xml.Linq;
using System.Windows.Resources;
```

Performing the Application Setup

The application constructor needs to display the first item in the embedded XML file. To perform this task, it must also create a data storage variable to hold the XML file and provide the means of tracking the current item number. Listing 7-5 shows the code used to perform this task.

LISTING 7-5 Displaying the first item

```
// Create a global storage variable.
XDocument MyData;

// Track the current item number.
Int32 CurrentItem;

// Record the maximum number of items.
Int32 MaxItems;

public MainWindow()
{
    InitializeComponent();

    // Create a URI that points to the data embedded in the
    // application.
    Uri FileUri = new Uri("/TestData.XML", UriKind.Relative);

    // Open a connection to this data.
    StreamResourceInfo Info = Application.GetResourceStream(FileUri);

    // Use the connection as a means of loading information into
    // the global storage variable.
    MyData = XDocument.Load(Info.Stream);

    // Place the first data item into txtValue.
    txtValue.Text = MyData.Root.Element("Item").Value;

    // Configure the buttons for use.
    btnNext.IsEnabled = true;
    btnPrevious.IsEnabled = false;

    // Set the current item number.
    CurrentItem = 0;

    // Obtain the maximum number of items.
    MaxItems = MyData.Root.Elements().Count();
}
```

The code begins by creating a special sort of *Uri* object, *FileUri*. This Uniform Resource Identifier (URI) is a superset of a URL. In this case, it points to a resource inside the application called *TestData.XML* using a relative path (the best way to locate the resource). After you have a URI, you can use it as input to the *Application.GetResourceStream()* method to obtain a *StreamResourceInfo* object, *Info*. Think about *FileUri* as saying what to get and *Info* as saying where to get it.

Other examples in the book have used *XDocument.Load()* to load an XML document from various sources, such as on disk or from a web service. In all cases, the example code relied on a *String* to define where to locate the information. This example uses a *Stream* to tell where to obtain the information. A *Stream* is simply a kind of connection. When you stream audio from an online radio, you're relying on a *Stream* (a kind of connection) to do it. That's precisely what's happening here. The *XDocument.Load()* method uses the *Stream* object to connect to the application and stream the file from the application into the local variable, *MyData*.

> **Note** You may have noticed that this example doesn't use error-trapping code like the web service code shown in Listing 6-2. Because *TestData.XML* resides within the application, it's safer to assume that it will always exist unless a programmer working on the project makes a mistake. So, although the code in Listing 6-2 has to have error-trapping code to handle an unreliable network connection, this code doesn't have the same requirement.

At this point, *MyData* looks and acts like any other *XDocument* object you've created in the past. The code uses the *MyData.Root* property to access the root element, and then relies on the *Element()* method to access the *<Item>* child elements. The *Value* property provides the information required by *txtValue.Text*.

The remainder of the constructor code performs setups. It's important to ensure that the right buttons are enabled on the window so that the user doesn't try to perform a task that's impossible. The application also needs to know the current item number and the maximum number of items in *TestData.XML* (as described by *MyData*).

Moving Between Items

When the application starts, the user sees the first item in the XML file displayed. The Next button is enabled because the first item is displayed and there are several more in the list. The Previous button is disabled because there aren't any previous items to display. So, the user can see the first item in the list and click either Next or Quit (to exit the application). When the user clicks Next, the application displays the second item, so now both the Next and Previous buttons are enabled because at least one next item and one previous item are available to work with. Moving between items is an essential part of many business applications. Listing 7-6 shows the code used to move between items in this example.

LISTING 7-6 Displaying a different item

```
private void btnNext_Click(object sender, RoutedEventArgs e)
{
    // Determine if there are more items to display.
```

```csharp
    if (CurrentItem + 1 < MaxItems)
    {
        // Increment the item number.
        CurrentItem++;

        // Change the output.
        txtValue.Text = MyData.Root.Elements().ElementAt(CurrentItem).Value;

        // Make sure the Previous button is enabled.
        btnPrevious.IsEnabled = true;
    }
    // Otherwise, there aren't any more items to display.
    else
    {
        // Disable the Next button.
        btnNext.IsEnabled = false;

        // Display a message to the user.
        MessageBox.Show("End of the items!");
    }
}


private void btnPrevious_Click(object sender, RoutedEventArgs e)
{
    // Determine if there are more items to display.
    if (CurrentItem > 0)
    {
        // Decrement the item number.
        CurrentItem--;

        // Change the output.
        txtValue.Text = MyData.Root.Elements().ElementAt(CurrentItem).Value;

        // Make sure the Next button is enabled.
        btnNext.IsEnabled = true;
    }
    // Otherwise, there aren't any more items to display.
    else
    {
        // Disable the Previous button.
        btnPrevious.IsEnabled = false;

        // Display a message to the user.
        MessageBox.Show("Beginning of the items!");
    }
}
```

Even though the code used to load the XML file into memory is different in this example, the code used to move between items looks much like the code shown in Listing 6-5. That's because both applications rely on an *XDocument* object to hold the data. (See Listing 6-1.) This example does use a slightly different technique because the data is simpler and also to show that there are multiple ways to perform any task.

The basic ideas are the same. The code determines whether there's a next or previous item (as necessary). When there's a next or previous item, the code increments (adds 1 to) or decrements (subtracts 1 from) *CurrentItem* so that *CurrentItem* correctly reflects the new item number. The code then retrieves the current item value and places it in *txtValue.Text*. The code also ensures that all of the correct buttons are enabled.

When there isn't a previous or next item, the code disables the associated button and displays a message to the user. At this point, the user sees that the list of items is at one end or the other.

Testing the EmbeddedSource Application

The data provided by this example is relatively simple. The point is to show how to access an embedded resource. You can move this application anywhere without also moving *TestData.XML* because the file resides within the application. However, for now, try starting the application and you'll see the initial dialog box shown in Figure 7-10.

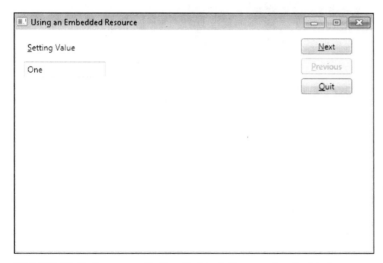

FIGURE 7-10 Design an application that tests the use of embedded resources.

As you can see, the first item's value appears in the Setting Value. Click Next and you'll see that the value changes to Two. In addition, the Previous button is enabled. Work all the way to the end and you'll see the expected message. The Next button also becomes disabled. In short, play with the buttons for a bit to see how the application works. It's simple, but it gets the point across.

Tracing the EmbeddedSource Application with the Debugger

It's educational to compare the functioning of this application to the REST web service example in Chapter 6. In fact, many developers use comparison to discover new coding principles. Tracing is the first technique; comparison is the second. Begin by tracing through the constructor in Listing 6-4. Now, do the same thing with the constructor shown in Listing 7-5 by placing a breakpoint at the *Uri FileUri = new Uri ("/TestData.XML", UriKind.Relative);* line. It's important to answer the question of how the flow of these two constructors differ—what principles change when working with a direct contact specified by a string versus a stream.

As stated in the "Moving Between Items" section of the chapter, the methods for moving between records are remarkably similar in these two examples. However, this example purposely uses some different techniques from the REST example in Chapter 6. The question is whether either technique is better in some way—faster, more reliable, more secure, or easier to understand. Asking yourself these sorts of questions will greatly improve your ability to write great code.

Get Going with C#

This chapter explored WPF application development using three different applications: XML storage, SOAP web service, and object data store. The most important thing you should take away from this chapter is that you can create an application using either WPF or Windows Forms. The difference is in the user interface. Windows Forms applications have a more business-like appearance, whereas WPF applications are far more customizable, and rely heavily on graphics. This difference changes the user's perspective of the application. The way users view an application makes a big difference in how they interact with the application and whether the application is a success.

The previous chapters presented a number of Windows Forms examples that you've explored. For example, in addition to a SOAP web service, you saw a REpresentational State Transfer (REST) application in Chapter 6. Just as you created a SOAP web service application in this chapter using WPF, you can also use REST with WPF. Try converting the example in Chapter 6 to WPF using the SOAP example in this chapter as a guide. You'll find that the task is actually a lot easier than it looks because the code behind the task remains the same—only the interface differs. The point of this exercise is to demonstrate that you can convert many business applications to use WPF when the need arises.

Chapter 8, "Working with Libraries," begins an interesting new addition to your coding skills. Up until now, all of the applications you've created have resided in a single file. Sometimes you write code that you can reuse in multiple applications. In this case, you place the reusable code into a library. Just like a physical library, it can be used by any application desiring to check out the code and use it. Libraries make it easier to write complex applications because you only need to create reusable code once and then any application and use it.

Chapter 8

Working with Libraries

After completing this chapter, you'll be able to:

- Define and describe reusable code

- Define and describe classes

- Create an application that relies on a library

- Add a test application to the library solution

- Test a solution that uses multiple projects

A LIBRARY PROVIDES A MEANS of storing code in such a way that many applications can use it. Just as you borrow a book from a physical library to read and use its content, an application can borrow code from a code library to read and utilize it. Libraries offer many benefits to the developer—the most basic of which is the ability to write code once and use it many times. As you've seen, some of the examples in this book so far have reused code principles to accomplish seemingly different tasks. As applications become more complex, the opportunities for code reuse increase.

> **Note** The term *library* is appropriate and perhaps the most common designation, but you'll hear other developers use other terms for libraries. Some of these terms express how the library interacts with the application, such as a Dynamic Link Library (DLL). In other cases, the term is language specific, such as the term *module* used with languages such as FORTRAN or the package used with Java.

Libraries can store any sort of resource. For example, you could create a library of icons, pictures, video clips, or anything else required to create your application. However, the basic library stores code in an easily used form. Because the .NET Framework is based on namespaces and classes, you'll find that assemblies used as libraries with C# store code in classes. These namespaces can also hold enumerations and other sorts of code, such as application features. The point is that you should create separate libraries as you recognize opportunities to place commonly used resources in a central storage location. Don't worry too much about the content for now—the kinds of resources you should store will become apparent as the need arises.

A good way to understand libraries is to build a simple library and then use it from a test application. In fact, most libraries are created in just this way. Some developers create the library first, and then write an application, called a *test harness*, to test every aspect of the library. A test harness is useful for ensuring that every addition to the library is fully tested. Just as no one individual will borrow every book from a physical library, no one application will use every resource found in a code library. To ensure that the library performs as expected, someone must create and maintain a test harness to verify the library's content.

Understanding Reusable Code

The concept of reusable code existed long before Windows even arrived on the scene. The idea of writing code in such a way that many applications can use it even when the developer doesn't understand what's happening within the library code is appealing. As an illustration, you've relied on reusable code for every example in the book so far, even the examples where you didn't write any code. The entire .NET Framework—the underlying part of the C# language—is reusable code that itself relies on even lower-level reusable code. So you've already used code without having to understand how it works internally. For example, you don't need to understand the code used to create a button control to use it in an application. In short, the most common and understandable reason to create reusable code is that it makes things simpler.

Placing reusable code inside libraries is the next step. Yes, you can create reusable code for your application by adding methods to the existing application classes. In fact, you used this approach for the REST example in Chapter 6, "Accessing a Web Service." However, the code shown in Listings 6-2 and 6-3 is accessible only to that application. Placing this code inside a library would make it accessible to any .NET Framework application that needs it. So libraries make it possible to share reusable code in a way that's easy to understand.

There are a number of other good reasons to create and use libraries containing reusable code. The following list provides just a few of the most common reasons for writing libraries:

- **Debugged code** Library code can be fully tested to work in a specific way using a test harness. Consequently, when you work with a library—for example, when troubleshooting a problem—you can focus on the unique code required to perform a task, rather than the common code used to perform any number of tasks.

- **Speed** After a library is completed, developers tune it to provide maximum speed. All the optimizations are in place for this code, so you should actually see a speed gain for your application even as you develop it.

- **Reliability** Because library code is typically tested extensively, it's usually quite reliable. In addition, fixed bugs are fixed for every application using the library after a new version of the library is issued. Having a lot of eyes looking at the code makes it possible to find errors more readily.

- **Faster development** Anytime you don't have to write code because someone else has already written it for you, you save time.

- **Simplicity** Using libraries places some application functionality into a black box—you don't have to care how it works, just as long as it does. Simplifying application development using libraries makes it less likely that developers will make mistakes.

Not all code is reusable. However, when some developers get a taste for reusable code, they try to force all code to become reusable, usually resulting in ill-conceived libraries that don't work well—or worse, actually cause significant application problems. You'll find that certain rules apply to working with reusable code. The following list provides guidelines that help you understand when code is reusable and when it isn't:

- **Generic** Good library code is generic enough to fulfill a variety of needs. For example, many application interfaces require buttons, so such code definitely belongs in a library. Likewise, a method that can calculate compound interest for a loan is a good library candidate. In contrast, code that creates output for a specific loan isn't generic enough, so it isn't a good library candidate.

- **Multiuse** If you can't figure out multiple ways in which to use the code, it probably isn't a good candidate for a library. The code required to access a web service is an example of something that you could use in multiple ways. On the other hand, the code required to display the output from a web service in a particular user interface isn't a good candidate because it works only for that application and in that situation.

- **Well-defined** Sometimes a developer will have a good idea, but it isn't well-defined. Library code should perform a specific task, such as display a control, configure the operating system, or access the network. Code that can detect strange events isn't a good candidate because the strange events aren't well defined.

- **Time saving** Code segments can be short or long, complex or simple. When code becomes too short and simple, the time required to use the library is actually longer than the time saved by the developer. Anytime a developer could more easily type the code in by hand, the code isn't a good candidate for inclusion in a library.

Considering How Classes Work

Throughout the book you've worked with classes without really understanding what classes are. A class is a kind of container—it provides the means for storing code and data in one place so that they're easy to access. You'll discover all sorts of heavy primers about classes that veil the entire topic in deep mystery, but the bottom line is that a class is a kind of storage device for code and data that are associated with each other. It's true that all kinds of deep discussions about classes are possible, but you won't need them to work with the examples in this book. What you do need at this point is a basic understanding of how classes work so that you can understand what's happening with the library example in this chapter.

The following sections break classes down into easily understood pieces. Each piece provides a classification of a kind of code or data element within a class. For example, you've been working quite a bit with a special kind of method called an *event handler*. The event handlers you've created contain code that answers a request from the user. For example, when the user clicks a button, the event handler performs the requisite task.

Defining Methods

Classes contain methods that define a way of doing something. For example, if you want to display something on the user interface, you must define the way to do that or the application won't know how. A method answers the question of what procedure or process you want the application to use when performing a task.

You use methods to perform all sorts of tasks. Every time the application needs to display something on the user interface, interact with the network, manipulate data, or make a request of the operating system, you use a method to do it. In fact, all your code will appear in a method of some sort. For the purposes of this book, you work with three sorts of methods:

- **General method**   A general method is used to provide a central location for code used by multiple other methods in a class. The code shown in Listings 6-2 and 6-3 contains good examples of general methods. In this case, multiple event handlers call this code to help them perform specific tasks.

- **Event handler**   Anytime something interacts with the application, such as a user clicking a button or the operating system signaling that something has changed, that interaction generates an event. Your application can simply choose to ignore the vast majority of events that the user, operating system, network, or some other entity generate. When your application does decide to respond to an event, it'll do so using an event handler. Listing 6-5 shows a good example of an event handler that responds to a user click.

- **Constructor**   Part of the purpose of a class is to describe how to build something. In this regard, the class becomes a sort of blueprint. Each class has a *constructor*, which is a special method that tells the application to perform certain tasks when building an object based on the class. These instructions initialize the display, set up variables, and perform other essential tasks.

Defining Properties

You use properties to define how an object based on a class works or appears. A property defines the object in certain ways. Think about an apple for a moment. An apple has a color property—it can be red, green, or yellow. It also has a taste property—it can be sweet or sour. When you view the apples in a basket, you use the apple's properties to differentiate one apple from another. The size, shape, smell, color, taste, and other properties of the apple make it unique. Likewise, when you create a class, you use properties to describe the objects created from that class and to differentiate one object from another.

Most of the examples in this book use properties. A property can accept information (*get*), provide information (*set*), or do both (*get/set*). In addition, you've seen properties that accept a specific data type such as a *String* or require a value in the form of an enumeration. (See the "Using Enumerations" section of this chapter for details.) It's important to provide properties with the type of value they expect, or your application will generate an error. Properties generally have a default value, but in some cases you must define a property value before using the methods in the associated class or the class will generate an error. You'll discover more about working with properties in the examples in this chapter.

Understanding Fields versus Properties

Many of the examples in this book use global variables that are accessible by every method in the class. When variables of this sort are accessible from outside a class that's meant to be used by multiple applications, they're called *fields*. Each field is simply an exposed variable. Using fields in your class is a bad idea because anyone can change a field in an uncontrolled way. In contrast, a property provides a controlled method of accessing variables. This control helps you maintain the purity of the data, enhances security, and improves reliability. The example later in this chapter demonstrates how to avoid using fields in your application.

Defining Events

A class can define events—things that can happen given the right stimulus. When a *Button* class detects a mouse click within the area that it has drawn for the button on-screen, it generates a *Click* event. If the application wants to detect this event, it creates a *Click* event handler to interact with it. Events are extremely useful because they provide a way to create responses to various kinds of activity. The kind of events that a class defines depends on the class purpose. For example, only GUI controls require a *Click* event—users can't click a Timer control because it isn't visible.

Using Enumerations

An *enumeration* is a list of items. For example, a list of state abbreviations is an enumeration. You can use enumerations to create any sort of list desired with any sort of data type. The purpose of an enumeration is to limit choices. If you have a property named *StateAbbreviation*, you obviously don't want a full state name or a ZIP code provided as input. By creating the property in a particular way, you can tell anyone using the class that you want only one or more values from a specific list of items as an input.

Enumerations may sound very limiting. However, they have some significant benefits; using enumerations whenever you can is actually a good idea. The following list describes some of the ways in which using enumerations can improve your class:

- **Security** If you create a property that accepts a *String* as input, the developer interacting with your class can provide any sort of *String*. The *String* could contain an incorrect value or it could contain characters that your code isn't designed to handle. In some cases, the *String* could also contain a virus or a script designed to gain access to your application in ways that you never intended. The same issue can occur with data of any type (although the *String* type seems to provide greater opportunities for abuse than any other type). Using an enumeration makes it impossible for someone to send data you don't want. Although it's limiting, an enumeration makes it possible to safely handle *String* data all of the time.

- **Reliability**   Anytime something breaks with your application—when it behaves in an unexpected way—your application becomes unreliable. One common form of breakage is unexpected data. If you leave the properties of your class wide open and don't check the information they receive, someone is going to find a way to break your application. Using enumerations—and thereby by making it tough to break by using incorrect data—is the surest way to improve the reliability of your application.

- **Understandability**   Many programming errors occur because the developer using a class doesn't understand the requirements for interacting with its properties. A developer might think that a *State* property will accept the full state name when you really intended it to accept only an abbreviation. Misunderstandings of this sort are perfectly understandable, common, and extremely frustrating. Using an enumeration makes the choices for a property clear and precise, which saves the developer using the class considerable time and effort.

- **Development speed**   Anytime you can make a class more secure, reliable, and understandable, you obtain a significant improvement in development speed. A developer working with your class will spend less time trying to figure it out, writing the code, debugging errors, and optimizing the result. In short, well-designed classes use enumerations to improve development speed.

Enumerations have a lot to offer to the developer of a class and the developer using the class. You'll see an example of how to work with enumerations in the example in this chapter.

Understanding Structures

For the purposes of this book, a structure is a special method of packaging data together. For example, you might want to collect address information for your class. The address information consists of a number of *String* values that contain name, address, telephone number, and so on. You could provide access to these values using individual properties, which would make it hard for the developer using your class to determine where the address information ends and general class data begins. Using a structure makes it possible for someone to use your class in an organized manner. All the data required to address a specific need resides within this single entity. You'll see how structures work in the example in this chapter.

Creating the UseLibrary Solution

For the first time in the book, you need to be able to differentiate between a project and a solution. A *solution* is a container that can hold one or more projects. Each *project* is a stand-alone code environment. In this case, the example will use the UseLibrary solution to hold the TestLibrary and TestApplication projects. The TestLibrary project is a library containing reusable code in the form of a class. The TestApplication project is an application that uses the library and tests its various features. The following sections begin by creating the UseLibrary solution and TestLibrary projects. After you create these entities, you'll define a class that contains the reusable code for the example.

Starting the TestLibrary Project

Creating a project within a solution isn't much different than creating a standalone project as you've done throughout the book. There are a few small differences though, and often, these little important details are missed. The following procedure helps you create the TestLibrary project and then save that project within the UseLibrary solution.

Creating a Library Project and Placing it in a Solution

1. Click New Project. The New Project dialog box appears.

2. Select Visual C# in the left pane and Class Library in the middle pane. You'll see a description of the template in the right pane.

3. Type **TestLibrary** in the Name field and click OK. The IDE creates a new project for you consisting of a single C# file without any graphical interface, as shown here.

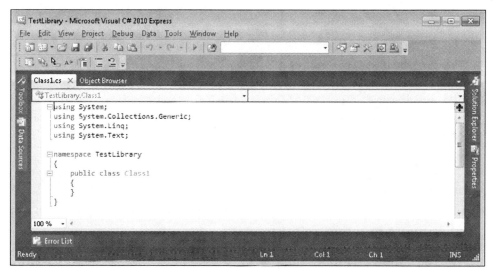

4. Right-click Class1.cs in Solution Explorer and choose Rename. The IDE will make it possible to rename the file.

5. Type **TestClass.cs** and press Enter. You'll see a dialog box asking you whether you want to rename all instances of *Class1* in the file to TestClass.

6. Click Yes. The *Class1* references are all changed to *TestClass* now.

7. Click Save All, press Ctrl+Shift+S, or choose File | Save All. A Save Project dialog box appears. Notice the Create Directory For Solution check box in this dialog box.

8. Select Create Directory For Solution and type **UseLibrary** in the Solution Name field. Your dialog box should look similar to the one on the next page. (Your Location field entry will differ from mine.)

9. Click Save. Visual Studio creates a solution named UseLibrary and a project named TestLibrary in the location you specified.

Adding the TestLibrary Code

At this point, you've created a namespace—a container for holding classes—named *TestLibrary* and a class named *TestClass*. The class doesn't have any content. It contains no properties, methods, events, structures, or enumerations. Even though it will compile, this class is useless right now. The following sections help you create a class with a number of elements in it. This isn't the sort of class you'd create for real-world use—it's designed as an instructional aid so that you can see all of the elements at work.

The example class keeps track of a list of colored balls. Each of the balls has a specific list of properties associated with it, such as color, size, and name. The balls are kept in a list that you can use to add and remove balls by name. The example relies on enumerations for as many of the properties as possible and a structure to hold the various ball descriptive elements. The application will also generate events when specific actions occur, such as the addition or deletion of balls from the list. Even though this example seems simple, it does exercise the most common features of classes.

Creating a Constructor

As previously mentioned, a constructor describes what to do when an application creates an object based on the elements described in the class. The class is a blueprint of sorts that an application uses to create an instance of the class, or an object. The act of creating an instance of the class is called instantiation. All these fancy terms simply mean that you're building an object based on a particular class definition—nothing more.

Every class requires a constructor, which has precisely the same name as the class and no return type. If you don't specifically create a constructor, the compiler uses a default constructor—a constructor that doesn't require any input arguments or perform any useful work. The default constructor is empty. The example class will use the constructor to assign values to the variables that the class requires to work and perform other essential startup tasks. Listing 8-1 shows the constructor for this example. The global variables appear alongside their matching properties in the "Creating the Private Variables and Public Properties" section of the chapter. You won't understand everything in the constructor just yet, but you will by the time you reach the end of this part of the example.

LISTING 8-1 Defining the class constructor

```
// Define the class constructor to initialize variables
// and perform other useful tasks.
public TestClass()
{
    // Allow additions and deletions.
    _AllowAdditions = true;
    _AllowDeletions = true;

    // Create an empty ball list.
    _BallList = new List<BallData>();
}
```

The _AllowAdditions_ and _AllowDeletions_ variables determine whether the caller can add or remove balls from the list. The constructor sets these variables to *true* because most developers will want to add and remove balls at the outset.

> **Note** It's a common convention to start private variable names, such as _AllowAdditions_ and _AllowDeletions_, with an underscore character (_) to show that they're private variables. A public property that works with a private variable, such as *AllowAdditions* and *AllowDeletions*, would have no underscore. However, both variable and property have the same name to show they're meant to work together.

The actual ball list is a *List* of type *BallData*. You'll learn more about the *BallData* type in the "Defining a Structure" section of the chapter. The example could have used a simple array to hold the list of balls, but using a *List* provides access to additional methods that make managing the list easier. All that the constructor does is initialize _BallList_—it doesn't add any balls to the list because the developer wouldn't expect that.

Defining an Enumeration

Two of the ball properties will work fine with an enumeration—size and color. Someone could probably argue that balls come in a large number of sizes, but the fact is that the number of sizes is finite and therefore adaptable to an enumeration. You use the *enum* keyword to define an enumeration. Then, you create a list of comma-separated entries to go into the enumeration, as shown in Listing 8-2.

LISTING 8-2 Enumerating the ball colors and sizes

```
// Create an enumeration that contains a list of acceptable ball colors.
public enum BallColor
{
    Red,
    Yellow,
```

```
    Green,
    Blue,
    Purple
}

// Create an enumeration that defines the possible ball sizes.
public enum BallSize
{
    Small,
    Medium,
    Large
}
```

If you plan to use the enumeration outside the class, you must define it as *public*. It's rare that you'd define an enumeration as *private* (which means that no one else can see it). Each enumeration must also have a unique name, which is *BallColor* and *BallSize* in this case.

Enumerations also usually reside outside the class structure, but within the namespace. This makes the enumeration easier for the developer using your class to access. Consequently, your code should look something like the window in Figure 8-1 after you add the enumerations to it.

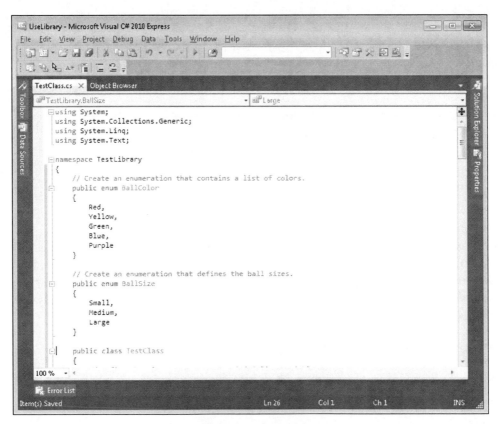

FIGURE 8-1 Create the required enumerations for this example.

Creating the Private Variables and Public Properties

Your class will use global variables to hold data, but you don't want just anyone looking at this information in an uncontrolled manner. Instead, you want to control access to the data through properties. Using properties makes it possible check incoming data in a number of ways to ensure that it's safe for your class. In addition, you can filter and format outgoing data if desired. As a consequence, variables should always be private in a class, but properties will normally be public so that everyone can access them. Listing 8-3 shows the private variables and their associated public properties for this example.

LISTING 8-3 Defining the variables and properties

```
// Make it possible to control additions and deletions.
private Boolean _AllowAdditions;
public Boolean AllowAdditions
{
    get { return _AllowAdditions; }
    set { _AllowAdditions = value; }
}
private Boolean _AllowDeletions;
public Boolean AllowDeletions
{
    get { return _AllowDeletions; }
    set { _AllowDeletions = value; }
}

// Define the list of balls for this application.
private List<BallData> _BallList;
public List<BallData> BallList
{
    get { return _BallList; }
}

// The person using the class may want to know how
// many balls are in the list.
public Int32 BallCount
{
    get { return _BallList.Count; }
}
```

Properties can take a number of forms. The most common form is shown with *_AllowAdditions* and *AllowAdditions*. The *AllowAdditions* property shows how you declare a standard property—one that doesn't do anything special and allows both *get* (read) and *set* (write) access. You can use this sort of setup as long as you're certain that the class user won't do anything with the property that will cause damage to the object. In this case, *Boolean* values are safe. The *_AllowDeletions* and *AllowDeletions* pair works the same way.

Tip Another way to create standard properties is to rewrite *AllowAdditions* as *public Boolean AllowAdditions2 { get; set; }*. This shorthand method creates a standard property that has an internal private variable and uses the same code shown in the example. You can't access the private variable and using this setup can make debugging a bit harder at times. Still, this shorthand method is a great way to reduce the amount of typing you do for properties that will never have anything but the default code associated with them.

The *_BallList* variable is a *List* of type *BallData*. Each element contains the information for one ball in the list. The *BallList* property only allows *get* access as a security feature. You don't want anyone to supply their own list of balls; instead, you want to manage the list with your class. It's essential to control the data in such a way as to make your class reliable and secure. This way, the developer using your class can access the list of balls, but can't force the object holding the list to do anything other than supply the data as output.

Sometimes a property won't have a variable associated with it. In fact, you'll find many such properties in real-world classes. The *BallCount* property doesn't directly manipulate *_BallList*. Instead, it returns the number of elements in *_BallList* so that the caller knows whether there are any balls to process. Theoretically, the caller could obtain the same information quite easily, but there's a chance that the callers list of balls is outdated. Providing this property ensures that the count the caller gets is the right one.

These aren't the only ways to work with properties. You'll see another property example in the "Defining a Structure" section of the chapter.

Defining a Structure

Structures serve a number of essential purposes. However, the most important reason to use them is to create structured data elements in your application. Unlike a class, structures only contain data elements for the most part. You define a structure using the *struct* keyword. Like enumerations, structures usually reside outside the class (within the namespace) to make them easier to access. Listing 8-4 shows an example of a structure.

LISTING 8-4 Creating a structure to hold ball data

```
// Define a structure to hold the ball information.
public struct BallData
{
    // It's possible to define Color and Size as fields
    // because their content is strictly controlled by the
    // enumeration.
    public BallColor Color;
    public BallSize Size;

    // Use a private field and a public property for the Name.
```

```
private String _Name;
public String Name
{
    get
    {
        return _Name;
    }
    set
    {
        // Check the name length for potential problems.
        if (value.Length <= 10)

            // When the name is the right length, use it.
            _Name = value;
        else

            // Otherwise, tell the developer using the class
            // that there is an exception.
            throw new
                ArgumentOutOfRangeException(
                    "Provide a string that is ten characters long.");
    }
}
}
```

This structure contains three data entries: *Color, Size,* and *Name. Color* and *Size* are relatively safe entries because the information they contain is strictly controlled by the associated enumerations. Someone using the class won't be able to provide unwanted information in either of these two entries.

However, *Name* is simply a *String.* Someone could provide the wrong kind of information when working with it. The name could be too long, filled with spaces, or damaging in some other way. A developer with nefarious intent could even send a script instead of a name, just to see what would happen. In this case, the code simply verifies that *Name* isn't too long. However, in a production application you'd include additional checks to ensure that the data is correct.

Important This class is also the first use you've seen of an *exception.* A class has no outside access. You can't easily capture incorrect input and ask the user to fix it. Even overcoming errors through retries and other means is fraught with potential problems because you don't know how the caller is using the class. In most cases, the safe course is to throw an exception. Always use the most specific and pertinent exception that you can. In this case, the code relies on the *ArgumentOutOfRangeException* exception because the *Name* is too long. Some classes rely on custom exception handling to provide even more specific information. For the purposes of this example, you'll see standard .NET exceptions used.

Describing Events

Many classes provide events to alert the caller to specific conditions. When you think about events, think about actions because that's what events are all about. Events typically have five elements:

- **Delegate** A delegate is a description of a method used to raise and handle events. It's a signature that consists of the return type, delegate name, and calling arguments—just like any other method you've used. However, a delegate is just a signature. It describes the information for the event and its handler, but it contains no working code. You declare a delegate using the *delegate* keyword.

- **Event declaration** The event declaration associates a delegate with an event name. When someone wants to raise an event, they use the event name, but the arguments for the event are determined by the delegate. As with a delegate, an event declaration contains no working code. You declare an event using the *event* keyword.

- **Event raising** You signify when an event occurs by raising that event. Essentially, raising an event looks much like calling a method. If the event requires arguments, you must supply them as part of the call. The "Developing Methods" section of the chapter shows how to raise the events defined in this section.

- **Associating an event with a method** The IDE automatically performs this task for you in many cases. For example, when you go to the Events tab of the Properties window and double-click the *Click* event to create an event handler, the IDE automatically creates the code required to associate the *Button* class Click event with the method in the application. The "Handling Class Events" section of this chapter shows how to perform this task manually with the example class.

- **Event handling** When an event occurs, an application can choose to handle it by declaring a method that has the same signature as the event's delegate. All of the examples in the book so far have event handlers. For example, all of the examples have methods that handle user clicks. You'll see a typical event handler for this class in the "Handling Class Events" section of the chapter.

This section discusses how to create the delegate and the event declaration for three events: *OnBallAdded*, *OnBallDeleted*, and *OnEndOfBalls*. These events signal changes in *_BallList* that a developer may need to know about. Listing 8-5 shows the code required to perform this task.

LISTING 8-5 Raising events as needed to indicate activity

```
// Tell the user when balls are added.
public delegate void BallAdded(BallData Ball);
public event BallAdded OnBallAdded;

// Tell the user when balls are deleted.
public delegate void BallDeleted(BallData Ball);
public event BallDeleted OnBallDeleted;

// Indicate there are no more balls in the list.
public delegate void EndOfBalls();
public event EndOfBalls OnEndOfBalls;
```

This doesn't look like much code, but a lot is going on behind the scenes. As you can see, the first line declares a delegate in each case. The delegate could return a value, but normally it doesn't. Many delegates do require input arguments, such as the *BallData* type uses for two of the delegates.

The second line contains the event declaration. Each declaration is *public* so developers working with the class can access the events. The *event* keyword comes next. The third element is the name of a delegate to associate with the event that controls the event signature. Finally, the code provides an event name. Most event names start with the word *On*, followed by the name of their associated delegate. However, nothing says that you absolutely must follow this policy.

Developing Methods

When creating a class, most developers create the groundwork, as this example has done. All of the elements are in place now for creating methods that finalize the class interaction with the application. Listing 8-6 shows the classes provided with this example.

LISTING 8-6 Adding methods that manage the *BallList*

```
// Create methods for adding and removing balls.
public List<BallData> AddBall(BallData NewBall)
{
    // Verify that we can add the ball.
    if (_AllowAdditions)
    {

        // Add the new ball.
        _BallList.Add(NewBall);

        // Raise an event to indicate the addition.
        if (OnBallAdded != null)
            OnBallAdded(NewBall);

        // Return the updated list.
        return _BallList;
    }
    else
    {
        // Tell the developer there is a problem.
        throw new InvalidOperationException("Additions not allowed.");
    }
}

public List<BallData> DeleteBall(BallData OldBall)
{
    // Verify that there is a ball to delete.
    if (_BallList.Count == 0)
        throw new InvalidOperationException("There are no balls to delete!");
```

```csharp
        // Verify that deletions are allowed.
        if (_AllowDeletions)
        {
            // Remove the existing ball.
            _BallList.Remove(OldBall);

            // Raise an event to indicate the deletion.
            if (OnBallDeleted != null)
                OnBallDeleted(OldBall);

            // Raise an event if this is the last ball.
            if (_BallList.Count == 0)
                if (OnEndOfBalls != null)
                    OnEndOfBalls();

            // Return the updated list.
            return _BallList;
        }
        else
        {
            // Tell the developer there is a problem.
            throw new InvalidOperationException("Deletions not allowed.");
        }
    }

    // Define a method for obtaining a list of ball names.
    public List<String> GetNames()
    {
        // Create an empty list to hold the name.
        List<String> Names = new List<String>();

        // Obtain a list of names from the internal list.
        foreach (BallData Item in _BallList)
            Names.Add(Item.Name);

        // Return the resulting list.
        return Names;
    }

    // Define a method for returning a specific ball.
    public BallData GetBall(String Name)
    {
        // Check each item in the list for the name.
        foreach (BallData Item in _BallList)

            // If the name matches, return the item to the
            // caller and exit the loop.
```

```
        if (Item.Name == Name)
        {
            return Item;
        }

    // Otherwise, throw an exception to indicate that the
    // ball wasn't found.
    throw new KeyNotFoundException("The ball name doesn't exist.");
}
```

Because of the way the class is constructed, it must have the following two methods: *AddBall()* and *DeleteBall()*. Otherwise, the class user could never interact sufficiently with *_BallList* to make the class usable. Many classes have methods such as these that must be in place to make the class useful. You should make a list of them as part of defining the class. In both cases, the method determines whether an addition or deletion is allowed. If it's allowed, the code adds or deletes a ball as required, and then raises an appropriate event—either *OnBallAdded()* or *OnBallDeleted()*. The method then returns the current *_BallList* to the caller for further processing if necessary. When additions or deletions aren't allowed, the method throws an exception.

> **Warning** Many developers forget to check whether an event actually has a handler. If you try to raise an event without an associated handler, the code will generate an exception. Because some events are buried and not called often, this sort of bug can remain hidden for a long time and be very hard to find. Always check event handlers against a null value (such as *if (OnBallAdded != null)*), to ensure that the event actually has an event handler assigned to it.

Deleting a ball is a special operation. You can keep adding balls to the list until the system runs out of memory (a very long time for modern systems). However, you can't delete balls that don't exist. The *DeleteBall()* method looks for this problem and throws an exception if that condition occurs. To help prevent someone from trying to delete a ball when the list is empty, the method also raises the *OnEndOfBalls()* event when the list is exhausted after a previous deletion. The caller can handle this event and disable deletions in the application by using it.

The *GetNames()* method has a number of uses. The most obvious use is to populate a list box in the calling application with the names of balls currently in the list. A second use is to obtain a list of possible names to delete. An application may decide to delete all balls that begin with the letter *S*, which would require obtaining a list of the ball names first. The *GetNames()* method returns a *List* of type *String* to the caller that's obtained by accessing each ball in *_BallList* using the *foreach* loop and adding its name to the list. If there are no names in the list because there are no balls in the list, the method returns an empty list, which is what the caller will expect.

The *GetBall()* has just one use for the most part. When you want to delete a ball from the list, you must supply a *BallData* object to the *DeleteBall()* method. It's possible to obtain this information directly using a local *_BallList* object, but it's better to call the class for the information so that you can ensure that the data is both current and correct. In this case, the code uses a *foreach* loop to locate a ball with the required name. It then returns the *BallData* object to the caller when found. If the object isn't found, the method raises an exception that the application should handle.

Adding the TestApplication Project

You have a shiny new class to use with an application, but no application to test it. The purpose of this section is to create an application that tests the class you just created. The following sections show how to add an application project to an existing solution, add the test library to it, and then build an interface you can use to test the class.

Starting the TestApplication Project

Generally, you start by creating a new project in a new solution. However, this time you'll add a project to an existing solution. The following procedure is a little different from what you've done in the past, but real-world applications often use this approach.

Adding an Application Project to an Existing Solution

1. Right-click the solution entry (Solution 'UseLibrary') in Solution Explore and choose Add | New Project. The Add New Project dialog box appears. However, in this case, the Location information is already filled out.

2. Select Visual C# in the left pane and Windows Forms Application in the middle pane. You'll see a description of the template in the right pane.

3. Type **TestApplication** in the Name field and click OK. The IDE creates a new project for you consisting of a single form. Notice that Solution Explorer now shows two projects instead of the usual one, as shown here.

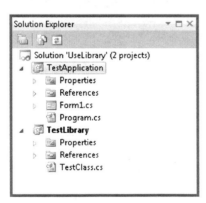

Setting TestApplication as the Startup Project

It's incredibly important to perform this next task or you won't be able to test the class later. When a solution has multiple projects in it, only one of those projects is the startup project—the one that starts when you start the debugger. A class can't execute on its own—only applications can do that. Right now, the class is set as the startup project, so clicking Start Debugging will display the error dialog box shown in Figure 8-2.

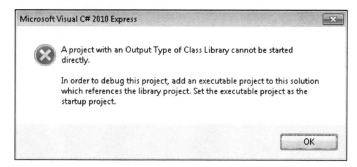

FIGURE 8-2 Change the starting project to point to the executable, rather than the class.

Of course, you've just added an executable to the solution, so something is available to execute. The answer to this problem is to set TestApplication as the startup project. Right-click TestApplication in Solution Explorer and choose Set As Startup Project to set this application as the startup project. Solution Explorer should now have TestApplication in bold print, as shown in Figure 8-3.

FIGURE 8-3 The bold project entry in Solution Explorer is the startup project.

Defining the TestLibrary Reference

Even though TestLibrary and TestApplication reside in the same solution, TestApplication can't use TestLibrary right now. You must create a reference to TestLibrary before TestApplication can use it. The following steps help you create a TestLibrary reference.

1. Right-click References in the TestApplication project and choose Add Reference. Click the Projects tab. You'll see a list of projects (other than the current project) associated with the solution, as shown here.

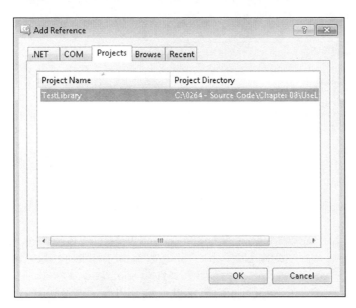

2. Highlight TestLibrary and click OK. Visual Studio adds the required TestLibrary reference to the TestApplication project.

Adding and Configuring the TestApplication Controls

This application manages to use a single form for adding, deleting, and displaying the various balls. It does use a message box to display a list of all of the balls, but the message box is a standard one and doesn't require the addition of a form. A production application might rely on several forms to perform the same task for the sake of clarity—to ensure that the user understands each of the tasks separately from the others. However, a single form does work just fine in this case.

In this case, you need a total of six buttons to perform the various tasks. The Next and Previous buttons let you move between balls to display the information individually. The Add and Delete buttons add and remove balls from the list. The Show Names buttons displays a list of all of the balls in the list using a message box. Finally, the Quit button exits the application.

Each ball has three data elements: Name, Color, and Size. The application uses a text box for the name because you can choose any name that fulfills the criterion for a name—any text fewer than 10 characters. The Color and Size values are provided by comboboxes. You don't want the user to choose just any color or size—the user must choose just one specific entry. Table 8-1 shows how to configure the controls for this example.

TABLE 8-1 TestApplication Control Configuration

Control Name	Property Name	Value
button1	(Name)	btnNext
	Text	&Next
	Enabled	False
button2	(Name)	btnPrevious
	Text	&Previous
	Enabled	False
button3	(Name)	btnAdd
	Text	&Add
button4	(Name)	btnDelete
	Text	&Delete
button5	(Name)	btnShow
	Text	&Show Names
button6	(Name)	btnQuit
	Text	&Quit
label1	(Name)	lblBallName
	Text	&Ball Name
textBox1	(Name)	txtBallName
label2	(Name)	lblColor
	Text	&Color
comboBox1	(Name)	cbColor
	DropDownStyle	DropDownList
label3	(Name)	lblSize
	Text	Si&ze
comboBox2	(Name)	cbSize
	DropDownStyle	DropDownList
Form1	Text	Testing TestClass
	CancelButton	btnQuit
	FormBorderStyle	FixedDialog

Organize this form carefully. It's one of the more complex forms in the book so far. Your form should look like the one shown in Figure 8-4.

FIGURE 8-4 Use this form to test the class you've created.

Adding the TestApplication Application Code

At this point, you're ready to start adding code to the application. This application actually has two phases. The first phase is to add code to the *Click* event handlers for each of the buttons. You've performed this task in every other application in the book so far. The second phase is to add event handlers and associated code for each of the *TestClass* event handlers. This phase requires the creation of some specialized code, but the IDE makes things quite simple, so don't worry. The following sections lead you through each of the code additions.

Adding the Required Using Statements

As in most cases, you need to add a *using* statement to your code to make certain classes available. In this case, the only class you need to make available is *TestClass*. Consequently, you add the following *using* statement:

```
using TestLibrary;
```

Configuring the Application

The application needs to perform a few tasks when it starts. For example, it must instantiate a copy of the *TestClass* for use with the application. Of course, you'll create a number of global variables used with the application methods. Listing 8-7 shows the code needed for this purpose.

LISTING 8-7 Adding code to the constructor

```
// Create an instance of TestClass.
TestClass TheClass;
```

```
// The current ball.
List<BallData> CurrentBalls;

// The selected ball within the list.
Int32 SelectedBall;

public Form1()
{
    InitializeComponent();

    // Initialize the TestClass.
    TheClass = new TestClass();

    // Set the source of information for the comboboxes.
    cbColor.Items.AddRange(Enum.GetNames(typeof(BallColor)));
    cbSize.Items.AddRange(Enum.GetNames(typeof(BallSize)));

    // Create an empty ball list.
    CurrentBalls = new List<BallData>();

    // Set the selected ball number.
    SelectedBall = 0;
}
```

The first global variable is *TheClass*, which is the instance of *TestClass* used for this application. The constructor instantiates *TheClass* without any balls added to it.

You'll use *CurrentBalls* to store a list of the balls currently in *TheClass*. This information is especially useful when debugging the application, but it also comes in handy for display purposes. Because there aren't any balls in *TheClass* at the outset, *CurrentBalls* is initialized to a blank list in the constructor.

Because it's important to keep track of the current ball in the list, the application creates *SelectedBall*. This value is updated every time the user adds or deletes balls, and also when the user moves from one ball to another using the Next and Previous buttons. In short, *SelectedBall* always points to the ball displayed on screen.

The constructor also has some odd-looking code that initializes the list of items in *cbColor* and *cbSize*. The *Enum.GetNames()* method obtains a list of names based on the strings inside of *BallColor* and *BallSize*. These names are presented to *cbColor* and *cbSize* as an array of strings, which you add using the *AddRange()* method. The result is a list of strings like the one shown in Figure 8-5 for *cbColor*.

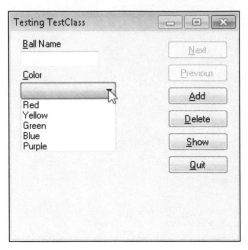

FIGURE 8-5 In some cases, it's best to dynamically fill a combobox with entries, rather than use a static list.

Displaying the Ball Data

It helps to have a centralized means of displaying the ball data. You have to think about two situations. In the first situation there aren't any balls in the list. When the application starts, there aren't any balls in the list, so all of the fields should be blank. There won't be any balls in the list when the user deletes the last ball either, so the fields should again be empty. The second situation is when there are balls in this list. In this case, the code should display the data pointed at by *SelectedBall*. Listing 8-8 shows the code used to display information in these two scenarios.

LISTING 8-8 Interacting with the user interface

```
private void DisplayCurrentBall()
{
    if (TheClass.BallCount == 0)
    {
        // Clear the form.
        txtBallName.Text = "";
        cbColor.SelectedIndex = -1;
        cbSize.SelectedIndex = -1;

        // Disable the Next and Previous buttons.
        btnNext.Enabled = false;
        btnPrevious.Enabled = false;
    }
    else
    {

        // Enable or disable the Next and Previous buttons as needed.
        btnNext.Enabled = true;
        btnPrevious.Enabled = true;
```

```
            if (SelectedBall == TheClass.BallCount - 1)
                btnNext.Enabled = false;
            if (SelectedBall == 0)
                btnPrevious.Enabled = false;

            // Obtain the information for the selected element.
            BallData ThisBall = CurrentBalls.ElementAt(SelectedBall);

            // Place the information in the form.
            txtBallName.Text = ThisBall.Name;
            cbSize.SelectedItem = ThisBall.Size.ToString();
            cbColor.SelectedItem = ThisBall.Color.ToString();
        }
    }
```

One of the questions that people ask relatively often online is how to clear the content of a combo box once you set it. The answer is to set the *SelectedIndex* property value to -1. For some reason, setting the *Text* or *SelectedText* property won't work. Clearing a text box is much easier. You simply set its *Text* property to a blank string, as shown.

Part of the process for working with the balls is to ensure that the Next and Previous buttons are set properly. The code begins by enabling both of them. When specific conditions are *true*, such as *SelectedBall* pointing to the beginning of the list, the associated button is disabled. When there's zero or one ball, neither of the buttons is enabled because there aren't any other balls to see. Otherwise, you'll see the correct buttons enabled.

When displaying ball information, you need specifics about a particular ball. The code uses the *ElementAt()* method to obtain this information from *CurrentBalls* using *SelectedBall* as the selector. When the code obtains this information, it can transfer the information directly to the user interface as shown.

Adding and Removing Balls

A central part of the application is adding and removing balls from the list. Otherwise, the application can't exercise any of its other functions. Listing 8-9 shows the code used to add and remove balls.

LISTING 8-9 Changing the ball list

```
private void btnAdd_Click(object sender, EventArgs e)
{
    // Don't allow blank values.
    if ((txtBallName.Text == "") | (cbColor.Text == "") | (cbSize.Text == ""))
    {
        MessageBox.Show("You must provide values for all three fields.");
        return;
    }

    // Crate a new BallData structure.
    BallData NewBall = new BallData();
```

```csharp
    // Fill it with data.
    try
    {
        // The name may not meet the criterion.
        NewBall.Name = txtBallName.Text;
    }
    catch (ArgumentOutOfRangeException AOORE)
    {
        // If not, display an error message, display the
        // previous data, and exit.
        MessageBox.Show(AOORE.Message);
        DisplayCurrentBall();
        return;
    }
    NewBall.Color = (BallColor)cbColor.SelectedIndex;
    NewBall.Size = (BallSize)cbSize.SelectedIndex;

    // Create the new ball.
    CurrentBalls = TheClass.AddBall(NewBall);

    // Change the ball selection.
    SelectedBall = CurrentBalls.Count - 1;

    // Display the ball information.
    DisplayCurrentBall();
}

private void btnDelete_Click(object sender, EventArgs e)
{
    // Create a blank BallData object.
    BallData DeleteBall = new BallData();

    // Obtain the correct ball to delete based on the entry
    // in the text box.
    try
    {
        DeleteBall = TheClass.GetBall(txtBallName.Text);
    }
    catch (KeyNotFoundException KNFE)
    {
        // Display an error message if the ball isn't found and
        // exit the event handler.
        MessageBox.Show(KNFE.Message);
        return;
    }
```

```
    // Use the information to delete the ball.
    try
    {
        CurrentBalls = TheClass.DeleteBall(DeleteBall);
    }
    catch (InvalidOperationException IOE)
    {
        // Display an error message if necessary.
        MessageBox.Show(IOE.Message);
    }

    // Check the number of remaining balls.
    if (TheClass.BallCount > 0)
    {
        // Reset the selected ball and redisplay if possible.
        SelectedBall = 0;
        DisplayCurrentBall();
    }
    else
        DisplayCurrentBall();
}
```

The first task to perform when adding a ball is to ensure that the entry is at least complete. The initial *if* statement checks for values in each of the fields. When any of the fields are blank, the application tells the user to provide additional information. More advanced applications would actually highlight the field missing the data. The point is that you must perform checks like this when adding information to any sort of data source. Even the most conscientious user will occasionally forget to provide required information.

The next step is to create a new *BallData* object, *NewBall*, to fill with data. Remember that the *Name* entry is actually a property that checks for invalid input, so you must place this part of the code within a *try ... catch* block, as shown. Make sure you catch the correct exception, which is *ArgumentOutOfRangeException* in this case. Because you don't want the incorrect information displayed on-screen, the code calls *DisplayCurrentBall()* to reset the display to show correct information. If the *Name* property check succeeds, the code finishes adding the information to *NewBall*. It then calls *AddBall()* to create the ball, updates *SelectedBall*, and calls *DisplayCurrentBall()* to show the ball information on-screen.

Deleting a ball follows a different process than adding one. The application doesn't force the user to try to remember the specifics about a ball—just the ball name. It then uses the *GetBall()* method to obtain a *BallData* object from the class that contains the full ball information. If two balls in the list have precisely the same name, the application deletes the first one. In a production application you can add code that displays a list of all of the balls that have the correct name and tell the user to choose one. The example takes this route in the interest of simplicity and because many real-world applications work precisely this way. When the name the user has requested doesn't exist, the class throws a *KeyNotFoundException* and the application must be ready to handle it.

After the application obtains a *BallData* object, it uses it to call *DeleteBall()*. Again, a potential exception is associated with this call, so you must provide code to handle it. Handling each potential exception separately makes it possible to create a more reliable application and one that provides better information to the user about the source of problems.

It's possible that deleting the requested ball will empty the list. Consequently, the code relies on the *BallCount* property to check for additional balls. If there's an additional ball, the code sets *SelectedBall* to 0 and displays the first ball in the list by calling *DisplayCurrentBall()*. When there aren't any balls to display, the code simply calls *DisplayCurrentBall()* to clear the fields and disable the Next and Previous buttons.

Moving Between Balls

Most of the hard work has been done for this application. All you really need now is a way to move between the ball entries. Listing 8-10 shows how to perform this task.

LISTING 8-10 Displaying the balls one at a time

```
private void btnNext_Click(object sender, EventArgs e)
{
    // If we're not at the end of the list, increment the
    // selected ball count and display the new information.
    if (SelectedBall != TheClass.BallCount - 1)
    {
        SelectedBall++;
        DisplayCurrentBall();
    }
}

private void btnPrevious_Click(object sender, EventArgs e)
{
    // If we're not at the beginning of the list, decrement the
    // selected ball count and display the new information.
    if (SelectedBall != 0)
    {
        SelectedBall--;
        DisplayCurrentBall();
    }
}
```

In both cases, the code determines whether there's actually a next or previous ball in the list. If there is, the code changes the value of *SelectedBall* and calls *DisplayCurrentBall()* to display it.

Displaying a List of Balls

Users may want to see a list of all of the balls. The form that the application uses is a detail form, but many users will want some form of grid. Because the example is so simple, you can get by using a message box for the task. However, in a real-world application with complex data requirements, you'd use multiple forms to perform the task. Listing 8-11 shows how to display a list of ball names for this example.

LISTING 8-11 Displaying a list of ball names

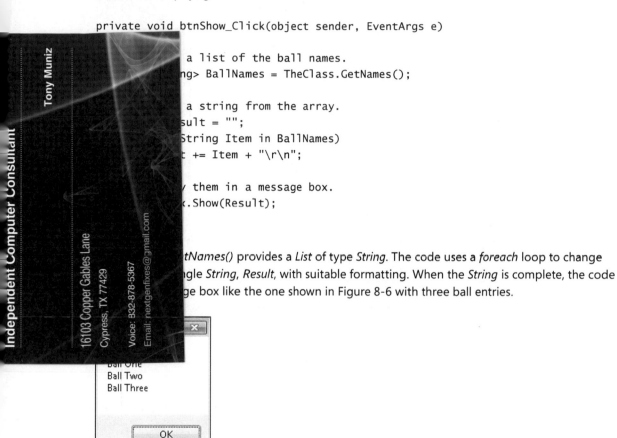

```
private void btnShow_Click(object sender, EventArgs e)

            a list of the ball names.
         ng> BallNames = TheClass.GetNames();

            a string from the array.
         sult = "";
         String Item in BallNames)
         t += Item + "\r\n";

          them in a message box.
         .Show(Result);
```

tNames() provides a List of type String. The code uses a foreach loop to change
gle String, Result, with suitable formatting. When the String is complete, the code
ge box like the one shown in Figure 8-6 with three ball entries.

Ball One
Ball Two
Ball Three

OK

FIGURE 8-6 The application output shows the list of balls stored in TheClass.

Handling Class Events

TestClass has three events that the application should handle. This is not because the application is incomplete as it is right now, but simply because this is your test harness application and must test every aspect of the application. Plus, you'll want to know how to work with events found within classes at some point. To perform this task, you must add some code to the constructor. The IDE helps add this code, but you'll need to get it started. The following procedure shows how to add the event handlers.

Creating Class-Based Event Handlers

1. Add a line to the end of the constructor. Type **TheClass.O** and you'll see a list of events like the one shown here.

2. Double-click OnBallAdded in the list. You see the entry added to your code.

3. Type +=. The IDE will suggest the code needed to create the event handler connection, as shown here.

```
// Add event handlers for the class.
TheClass.OnBallAdded +=
                    new TestClass.BallAdded(TheClass_OnBallAdded);   (Press TAB to insert)
```

4. Press Tab. The IDE will create the required code for you. The IDE will then suggest the next part of the task, which is to generate the event handler as shown here.

```
// Add event handlers for the class.
TheClass.OnBallAdded +=new TestClass.BallAdded(TheClass_OnBallAdded);
                    Press TAB to generate handler 'TheClass_OnBallAdded' in this class
```

5. Press Tab. The IDE creates the event handler for you.

6. Perform steps 1 through 6 for *OnBallDeleted* and *OnEndOfBalls*. In each case, the IDE will help you create the required event handler linkage with the event in the class.

At this point, you have three event handlers that won't do very much except to say they aren't implemented. You need to add some code to them. The application doesn't require the events for the tasks that it's performing, so a simple message box will work just fine. Listing 8-12 shows the code you need for this part of the application.

LISTING 8-12 Adding code for class events

```
void TheClass_OnEndOfBalls()
{
    MessageBox.Show("End of the list!");
}
```

```
void TheClass_OnBallDeleted(BallData Ball)
{
    MessageBox.Show("The ball was deleted.");
}

void TheClass_OnBallAdded(BallData Ball)
{
    MessageBox.Show("The ball was added.");
}
```

As you can see, each event handler reports on a status change. The user will get feedback now saying that the task completed successfully.

Testing the UseLibrary Application

This test harness lets you test the application thoroughly. Every feature that the class provides appears somewhere in the application so that you can see it work. Before you can do anything, you need to add some balls to the list. Start your application by clicking Start Debugging. You'll see a blank application form appear. Try adding a new ball with Ball One as the name, Red as the color, and Small as the size. When you click Add, you'll see a confirmation dialog box and the new entry, as shown in Figure 8-7.

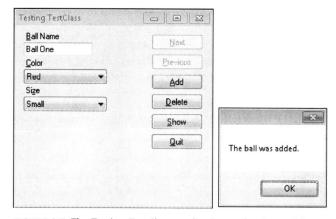

FIGURE 8-7 The Testing TestClass application makes it possible to see how the class functions work.

Click OK to remove the message box. Now try clicking Delete. The application displays a confirmation message. Click OK in the message box. Because this is the last record in the list, you'll see an end of the list message box next. Click OK again and you'll see that the form goes back to a blank display.

Spend some time adding a few balls to the list. Each time you'll see confirmation messages. After you add the second ball, the Previous button will become enabled. You'll be able to check the functionality of the Next and Previous buttons at this point.

Try adding a ball that has a name that's too large and you'll see that the application displays the appropriate error message. You can also try adding an entry with a blank field (the Name field will work at this point). Again, the application will display an appropriate error message.

Once you're sure that the application works as expected, you can start setting some breakpoints to trace through it. Because you have the source code for the class, you can actually trace into the class and see how it works when the application calls a method. Set a breakpoint in each of the application event handlers to check out their operation.

Get Going with C#

This chapter has helped you understand, create, and test a library. You've been using libraries from the start, but now you have a better understanding of precisely what a library is and how you can create one of your own. Libraries are an essential part of the modern coding experience. If developers had to rewrite every line of code required to create every application, some applications would never be written because they would take far too long to complete. Of course, it's easy to abuse libraries. Remember that libraries should contain only reusable resources—those that many applications can use or a single application relies upon in multiple modules.

A large part of writing a library is creating a black box that's easy for someone to understand without understanding the content of the library. Someone shouldn't have to know how you wrote the code for a library to use it. If you were to write a library to hold the code used to move between the next and previous items in the "Developing the EmbeddedSource Application" application in Chapter 7, "Using the Windows Presentation Foundation," how would you do it? Would it be possible to write this library in such a way that it would also work with the REST application in Chapter 6? Even if you don't actually write the code for such a library, spend some time thinking about how you'd accomplish this task. Explore other applications in the book and determine whether there's a potential for library code in them.

You may or may not work much at the command line. At one time, the command line was the only environment supplied with a computer—you typed a command and the computer complied by performing the requested task. The command line still exists—access it by choosing Start | All Programs | Accessories | Command Prompt. When you display the command prompt, you can execute commands such as Dir (to obtain a listing of the contents of the current folder). GUI applications such as Notepad also provide a command line interface so that you can perform tasks with them using automation such as batch files. Chapter 9, "Creating Utility Applications," shows how to build applications that work at the command prompt. Whether your application relies on a GUI or a text interface doesn't matter—any application can provide a command-line interface that helps administrators automate the tasks that the application performs.

Creating Utility Applications

After completing this chapter, you'll be able to:

- Define what's meant by a utility application and how utility applications are used

- Develop a console application

- Create useful command-line handling characteristics

- Test a utility application

- Trace through the functionality provided by a utility application

THE COMMAND LINE WAS THE first interactive environment for applications, and it's still the environment of choice for some purposes. For example, many administrators like to work at the command line because a single command often accomplishes more than multiple clicks in a GUI. The command line is also essential when working with utilities such as Telnet that access other systems remotely. In some cases, users also rely on the command line. One of the most popular command-line utilities is the Dir utility because it helps you find a particular file on a drive with accuracy and speed. Power users and developers often employ the FindStr utility to locate data inside files. In short, there are many reasons to use command-line utility applications. The first part of this chapter provides a bit more of an introduction to the command line and helps you understand how to use it better.

Note Telnet is a special program you can use to access the command prompt on another system. Administrators commonly use it on routers and other systems stored in closets, but you can use it with any system. You can read more about Telnet at *http://www.telnet.org/* and *http://blog.johnmuellerbooks.com/categories/Windows Command-Line Administration Instant Reference.aspx.*

Console applications provide the text-based user interface required at the command line. You can use a console application to create your own utilities. These utilities can do just about anything that doesn't require a GUI; you may find that a console application meets many of your development needs at a lower development cost. The lack of a GUI means that you can focus on business logic and the inner workings of the application—outputting text only as needed to help the user understand what's going on. This chapter also helps you create a console application, test it, and then trace through it so you can see how this kind of application differs from the GUI applications you've written in previous chapters.

Working at the Command Line

Most users have gotten away from the command line because the command line has received bad press over the years, and users often perceive the command line as difficult to use. It's true that the GUI environment does make things easier to use because it provides constant reminders of what you're supposed to do next. However, this ease of use comes at a cost of lower user efficiency. In addition, sometimes the GUI isn't all that helpful—a developer can still hide necessary commands beneath layers of menus or in toolbars. In fact, some GUIs, such as the ribbon interface used by Office and other products, are actually designed to hide complex commands, making it necessary to hunt for what you need every time you need it. The command line hides nothing—every element of the utility is accessible at all times. The following sections describe how to open the command line and configure it and also describe how the command line is commonly used today.

Note That the command line is alive and well is evident in many ways. For example, you might have noticed that some installation programs flash the command line on-screen when performing tasks that use the command-line interface. Some applications actually display the command line briefly when you perform a task; the command-line window usually appears somewhere in the background.

Opening and Using the Command Line

Microsoft hides access to the command line beneath several layers of menus. To open the command line, choose Start | All Programs | Accessories | Command Prompt. (If you plan to use the Command Prompt relatively often, you can pin it to the Start Menu or the Taskbar by right-clicking the Command Prompt entry and choosing either Pin to Start Menu or Pin to Taskbar.) You'll see a special window like the one shown in Figure 9-1. (Your window will have a black background with silver letters—the book uses a white background with black letters to make things easier to see.)

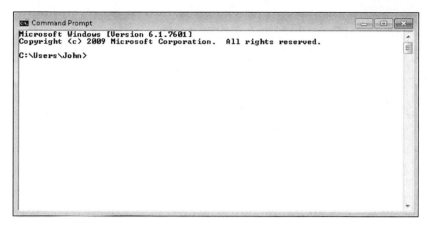

FIGURE 9-1 The Command Prompt is a place where you can type commands instead of using the mouse.

This screenshot demonstrates the daunting nature of the command line—it doesn't tell you anything. The text you see is the current directory, which is your user folder—the blinking little square after the text is the cursor. The combination of the text and the cursor is called the *prompt* and you type commands at the prompt. All of the commands are accessible as long as they're part of your environment, but the command line tells you nothing about them—you must know that they exist. Fortunately, you can get a list of at least some of the commands. Type **Help** and press Enter, and you'll see a list of these commands like the one shown in Figure 9-2. (The screenshot shows the start of the list.)

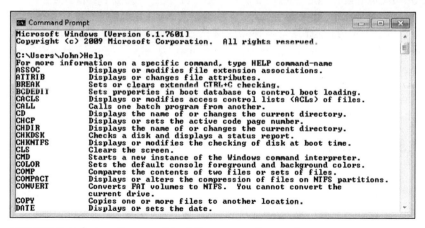

FIGURE 9-2 Help is easily accessible at the command prompt.

At least the Help command provides you with a list of candidates and a short description of them, but this list is far from complete. It does provide enough information to get started, though. Two interesting entries in the list are CLS (clear screen) and Dir (directory). Try them now. Type **CLS** and press Enter. You'll see that all of the previous information goes away. To learn how to use Dir, type **Dir /?** and press Enter. You'll see helpful information about the Dir utility, as shown in Figure 9-3.

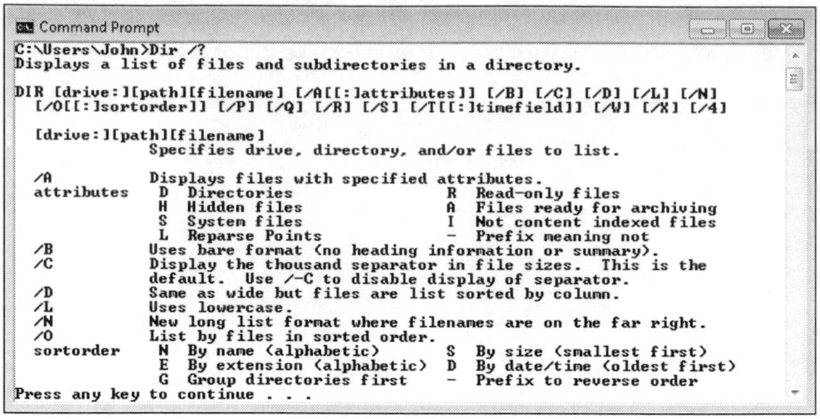

FIGURE 9-3 Use the /? command-line switch to obtain help from individual utilities.

Most command-line utilities support the /? command-line switch. Every command-line switch begins with either / (slash) or – (dash), followed by some characters that define the command-line switch. In some cases, you must also provide additional information in the form of text called an *argument*. It's sort of the same as calling a method in an application—you provide the method name, followed by arguments required by the method to execute. In this case, you're using the /? or help command-line switch to obtain help about the command-line utility. Press Enter to see the remainder of the help information and you return to the command prompt.

Try typing **Dir** and pressing Enter. You'll see a list of the contents of the current directory, which is going to be your user folder. Now, type **Dir /A** and press Enter. Suddenly you see a lot of additional information called *attributes* that define each of the directory entries. Type **Dir /OD** and press Enter. Now the entries are listed by date, rather than by name. Look through the list of command-line switches for the Dir utility and try other combinations to see what happens. The Dir utility is completely safe—you won't damage anything on your computer by using it, and working with it for a while will give you a much better idea of how the command line works.

Some of you might want your command prompt to look like the one in the book. Unlike many other applications, the system menu does have a distinct purpose with the command prompt. Click it and you'll see a Properties option on the menu. Click Properties and you see a "Command Prompt" Properties dialog box. The Colors tab looks like the one shown in Figure 9-4.

Select Screen Background and set the background color using the color bar. Select Screen Text and set the foreground color using the color bar. Click OK and your command prompt will use the colors you selected. You can find a simple, straightforward command prompt configuration guide at *http://commandwindows.com/configure.htm* that provides additional information about these features.

The command line is a powerful feature of Windows. Windows 7 significantly limits what you can do at the command line through the User Account Control (UAC). However, you may find that you need to execute some of the more powerful commands at some point. In this case, choose Start | All Programs | Accessories, right-click Command Prompt, and choose Run As Administrator. You'll see a UAC dialog box. Click Yes and—if you have Administrator privileges—you'll see an Administrator command prompt like the one shown in Figure 9-5.

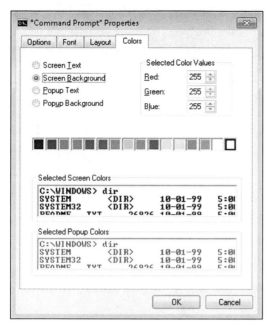

FIGURE 9-4 Change the command prompt colors to make the text easier to see.

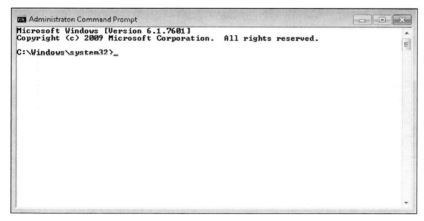

FIGURE 9-5 Use an administrator command prompt to execute commands that require additional privileges.

 Note Closing the Administrator command prompt always removes the rights you've gained. To execute administrator-level commands, you must always open an Administrator command prompt using the instructions in this section.

This window provides several indicators that you're using a different mode from before. The title bar now says Administrator: Command Prompt. In addition, this command prompt opens to the C:\Windows\system32 directory instead of your user folder. This command prompt provides full access to all the available utilities and all their features.

Warning Now that you have full access to all of the utilities, you must exercise the required caution. The command prompt is extremely unforgiving and there's no "undo" command (another reason that people often see command-line applications as something they'd rather not work with unless absolutely necessary). After you execute a command, the result is permanent. If you're working with data, it's always a good idea to have a backup of that data before you change it in any way. Try working with a test system whenever possible to learn how to use new features of a command-line utility.

Understanding Utility Application Uses

Command-line utilities are extremely useful. You can use command-line utilities to modify hardware functionality, the operating system, applications, associated data, the network, and even perform tests with the Internet. Most administrators rely heavily on the command line because it provides fast access to all kinds of information. For example, try typing **IPConfig** and press Enter. What you see is a basic overview of the network setup for the current machine, as shown in Figure 9-6. (Your computer will have different information.)

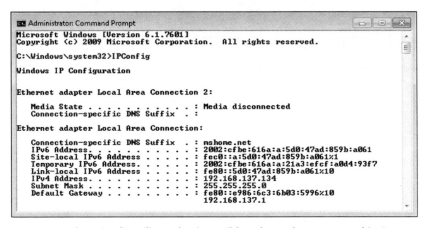

FIGURE 9-6 The IPConfig utility makes it possible to learn about your machine's network connections.

There are so many commands—with such a range of command-line arguments—that entire books have been written on the topic. Even these books hardly exhaust all of the functionality available at the command line. Command-line utilities are commonly used to provide these sorts of services.

- **Information** Many command-line utilities provide information of some sort. The information varies greatly—everything from who's logged onto the system to the network resources that a system uses. In fact, if you want to know something about the computer system, a command-line utility probably exists to provide it. Sometimes there are even multiple utilities that provide the same information, but in different formats to meet users' specific needs.

- **Configuration**   After someone discovers information about a resource, it often becomes necessary to configure it. For example, an incorrect hardware configuration can cause problems for the system that vary from data access to actual system crashes. The configuration tasks that a utility can perform vary, but most are centered on hardware, operating system, user account, application, or network tasks.

- **Data access**   You won't perform word processing or correct a spreadsheet at the command line. However, you can obtain information about applications installed on the system, the user account and network information, and even change the registry. The utilities that you access at the command line can perform all sorts of tasks that are designed to make working with data faster—not necessarily easier. Think about the steps required to change even a single entry in the registry using the RegEdit GUI. The same task commonly requires just one command at the command line. Databases such as SQL Server also provide extensive command-line utilities. Enterprise applications such as Exchange Server also use the command prompts extensively.

- **Automation**   One of the biggest reasons to use the command line is automation. You can create batch files (groups of commands that the operating system executes together as a kind of script) to automate command-line utility execution. Adding this batch file to the Task Scheduler causes it to execute automatically at a certain time. Automation makes life easier for the administrator and user alike, and makes it possible to ensure that tasks get done by having the computer perform it, rather than rely on human memory.

- **Remote access**   Administrators sometimes have hundreds of computers to maintain. An administrator who had to physically go to each of these to perform maintenance would never be able to keep up. Using remote access utilities lets the administrator access the command prompt on a remote system, perform required maintenance tasks, and then move on to the next computer without ever leaving the administrator's office.

- **Background tasking**   Some tasks execute better in the background—outside the user's vision. All services fall into this category. A service is an application that executes in the background. To see just how many services are executing on your system, type **SC Query** and press Enter. Ah, well, that's too many to see. Try typing **SC Query | More** and press Enter. The | is called the *pipe* symbol and it sends the output of the Service Control (SC) manager utility to the More utility, which displays the output one screen at a time. The point is that many services work in the background, and you can query, configure, and control them using command-line utilities.

Many applications have undocumented command-line functionality. For example, you can use Notepad at the command line. Simply type **Notepad <Name of File>** and press Enter to see the file automatically loaded in Notepad. If you want to print the file instead of seeing it, type **Notepad <Name of File> /P** and press Enter instead. The file will go immediately to your printer. This functionality is used to create entries in the registry that allow Notepad to respond to user requests, but you can also use it for your own needs.

Creating the Console Application

Before you can do anything with a console application, you need to create a project for it. This doesn't require anything exotic in most cases. In fact, many developers actually start learning to write code using console applications because they don't require the GUI and other confusing elements that tend to get in the way of learning. It's especially important to choose a descriptive name for your command-line utility because people will have to remember what to type at the command line to use it. Because this application displays the date in various formats, the example uses *DisplayDate* as a name. The following steps describe the method used to create the console application for this chapter.

Creating a Console Application

1. Click New Project. The New Project dialog box appears.

2. Select Visual C# in the left pane and select Console Application in the middle pane. You'll see a description of the template in the right pane.

3. Type **DisplayDate** in the Name field and click OK. The IDE creates a new project for you consisting of a single C# file without any graphical interface, as shown here.

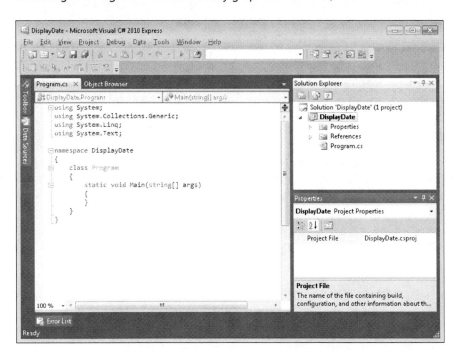

4. Right-click the Program.cs entry in Solution Explorer and choose Rename. The name field changes into a text box.

5. Type **DisplayDate.cs** and press Enter. You see a dialog box asking whether you want to rename all instances of Program in your application.

6. Click Yes. The IDE changes the class name to *DisplayDate*. You're ready to begin working with the example.

Defining Command-Line Parameters

All of the previous examples of command-line utilities in this chapter rely on command-line switches and associated data to perform tasks. The combination of switches and data are parameters. You can divide parameters into three types:

- **Help**   The switch offers some level of help with the command-line utility. Most utilities offer just one level of help, but it's not unusual to encounter several levels of help. To see this for yourself, try typing **Net /?** and pressing Enter. You see a list of subtopics. Now, type **Net Accounts /?** and press Enter. The utility displays a second level of help. Try the WMIC utility as well. It has three levels of help for most topics. For example, type **WMIC TimeZone Get /?** and press Enter to see a help topic about getting time zone information.

- **Required**   Many, but not all, utilities require some information to do anything at all. For example, for the Rename utility to work you must provide the name of something to rename and what to rename it. These parameters are required—you must enter them or the utility displays an error message. Utilities such as Dir have default parameters and don't require any input at all.

- **Optional**   Almost all utilities have some optional parameters that modify their behavior. For example, the Dir utility has a large number of optional parameters that affect the output it presents and where it obtains the directory information.

The vast majority of command-line utilities accept parameters of some sort, even if all they offer is help. It's rare to find a command-line utility where all you can do is type the command to perform a task. A few command-line utilities offer parameters, but don't document them in any way—you must rely on online or other sources to discover the parameters for these utilities. In many cases, the parameters are secret to help ensure that no one misuses the utility. Sometimes, however, the utility is simply poorly designed and the developer didn't include support for the requisite help parameter. The following sections help you create the parameters section of the DisplayDate utility.

Creating the *Main()* Method

The only method that your console application starts with is *Main()*. This method receives a list of command-line arguments, *args*, as a *String[]* array from the application. In most cases, you'll use *Main()* to create a script of sorts for your console application. It will contain the procedure for processing input provided from the command line, as shown in Listing 9-1.

LISTING 9-1 Defining a script of things to do

```
static void Main(string[] args)
{
    // Create a blank variable to hold the date.
    DateTime TheDate = new DateTime();

    // Check for a lack of command line arguments.
    if (args.Count() == 0)
        DisplayQuickHelp();

    // Check for a request for help.
    if (args.Contains("/?"))
        DisplayHelp();

    // Set the date to display.
    TheDate = SetDate(args);

    // Configure the optional formatting.
    String Output = ConfigureDate(TheDate, args);

    // Display the result.
    Console.WriteLine("The current date is: " + Output);
}
```

The goal of this application is to create a date and display it on-screen based on the inputs that the user provides, so the application begins by creating a new *DateTime* object, *TheDate*. It then instantiates *TheDate* with a blank date set to *1/1/0001*. If the application completely fails for some reason, the user will see this date, rather than have to deal with a crashing application.

Because this application requires that the user provide at least one input argument, even if it's to obtain help, the application checks *args.Count()* next. This method returns the number of input arguments. When the number of arguments is 0, the application displays a short, informative help message telling the user how to access help. This technique of dealing with incomplete or incorrect input has several advantages:

- The quick help message is useful for getting the user started with a complex application.

- Unlike regular help, the quick help method can return an error code so that batch files know that an error has occurred.

- Using quick help makes it easier for an administrator or developer to debug the application and the batch files that interact with it.

Note Many command-line utilities provide an error code that you can check within a batch file using the *ErrorLevel* variable. The *ErrorLevel* is actually a return code because it doesn't always indicate an error, but shows how the application ended. The *ErrorLevel* can be an error or one of several expected outcomes. Creating batch files is outside the scope of this book, but you can learn more about the *ErrorLevel* variable at *http://www.robvanderwoude .com/errorlevel.php* or *http://blog.johnmuellerbooks.com/2011/08/11/understanding-the-connection-between-application-output-and-errorlevel.aspx*.

The next step is to determine whether the user has requested help by checking *args* for the */?* string. It doesn't matter where in the command-line arguments that */?* appears—the application will always process help before anything else. The idea here is that the presence of */?*, even if it's a mistake, indicates that the user isn't quite sure what to do. Consequently, the application always gives the */?* command-line switch priority over any other input.

When the application has command-line arguments and none of them is the */?* command-line switch, the application assumes that the user has supplied a required parameter as a minimum and possibly an optional parameter as well. The data parameter is required and the application processes it first because in the event of an error here, the application needs to exit. The optional parameter processing comes next.

Finally, the application outputs the specified date in the requested format. Notice that the application uses the *Console* object, which provides access to the console window. The *WriteLine()* method outputs information to the console and then moves the cursor to the next line (as if you had pressed Enter). In short, *Main()* has acted as a sort of script that outlines the process the application follows in servicing the user requests. Every utility works in a similar fashion, although most utilities are far more complex than this one.

Offering Help at the Command Line

Help is probably the most important feature of a command-line utility, because most people won't be able to use your utility if you don't provide help. The help feature doesn't have to be the length of a novel. All most people need is a short description of what task the utility performs, the command-line syntax, and a description of each parameter. Adding examples is always a good idea, because people often rely on these examples when they experiment to see what the command-line utility does.

If your utility has required parameters, as this one does, you must decide how to handle help when the user doesn't type anything other than the utility name. Many utilities provide a short help screen that tells the user to type the command name plus the */?* command-line switch. This short help emphasizes the point that the user must type some required parameters to make the utility work. Other utilities display the full help screen if the user types just the command name or uses the */?* command-line switch. The choice is up to you.

The command-line syntax is also important. Most command-line help relies on certain conventions to convey information. If your utility requires data as part of the parameters, the data (variable name) appears within angle brackets or curly braces. The Net utility uses curly braces, whereas the WMIC utility relies on angle brackets.

It's also important to provide a method to indication optional parameters. Almost every utility uses brackets ([]) to perform this task. Everything within the bracket is optional. Some utilities also nest the brackets to show that some parameters are actually optional parts of a main parameter. For example, when you look at the help for the Dir utility, you see that the /A command-line switch has nested parameters: [/A[[:]attributes]]. The /A command-line switch is optional. If you use the /A command-line switch, you can include attributes with it (attributes is a variable). When you use attributes, you can separate them from the /A command-line switch using a colon (:). So if you wanted to find only directory entries that have the read-only (R) attribute set, you could use /AR or /A:R.

A utility can accept certain keywords as input. That's the situation for this utility—the user must provide specific keywords as input. When the user has a choice of keywords, such as Yesterday, Today, or Tomorrow in this case, the help screen shows the choices separated by the pipe symbol (|). Utilities such as IPConfig use this particular convention extensively.

With all these requirements in mind, the example application provides both quick help through the DisplayQuickHelp() method and full help through the DisplayHelp() method. The full help uses the conventions described in the previous paragraphs. Listing 9-2 shows the code used for this part of the example.

LISTING 9-2 Creating the help display

```csharp
static void DisplayQuickHelp()
{
    // Display a short help message.
    Console.WriteLine("This utility requires input arguments!");
    Console.WriteLine("Use DisplayDate /? to obtain help information.");

    // Exit the utility after displaying a short help message.
    Environment.Exit(1);
}

static void DisplayHelp()
{
    // Display a description.
    Console.WriteLine("DisplayDate:");
    Console.WriteLine("\tDisplays the selected date in the specified format.");
    Console.WriteLine();

    // Display the command line syntax.
    Console.WriteLine("DisplayDate /Yesterday | /Today | /Tomorrow [/?] " +
                      "[/Long | /Short]");
    Console.WriteLine();
```

```
// Display the individual command line switches.
Console.WriteLine("\t/Yesterday\tShows yesterday's date.");
Console.WriteLine("\t/Today\t\tShows today's date.");
Console.WriteLine("\t/Tomorrow\tShows tomorrow's date.");
Console.WriteLine("\t/?\t\tDisplays this help message.");
Console.WriteLine("\t/Long\t\tShows the date in long format.");
Console.WriteLine("\t/Short\t\tShows the date in short format.");
Console.WriteLine();

// Provide an example.
Console.WriteLine("Example (shows today's date in long format):");
Console.WriteLine("\tDisplayDate /Today /Long");

// Exit the utility after displaying help.
Environment.Exit(0);
}
```

It's important to document the various parts of the help, as shown in the example. Notice that each component of the help screen has its own section in the method to make apparent what purpose that part of the help screen serves.

Each of the help lines relies on the *Console.WriteLine()* method to output information. As before, the *WriteLine()* method outputs information to the console screen so that the user can see it. The *Console* object includes a number of other useful methods you should examine and try in your own applications. For example, you can read data from the console—you can ask the user questions and obtain a typed response using the *ReadLine()* method.

Remember that \t is a special character called a *tab*. Tabs are the primary way to align content in the console window. Because some of the entries are longer than others, some parts of the help screen require multiple tabs to obtain the desired presentation.

Checking for Required Arguments

Whether your utility has required arguments or not depends on what you can assume about the task that the utility is supposed to perform. Some utilities have required arguments because there's no way to provide a good default argument when the user doesn't provide a value. In deciding whether to require arguments, you must determine whether it's reasonable to provide a default value. In this case, because the utility provides a specific date as output, you can't really assume a default. (It's possible to make a weak argument for setting the default as today, but the example ignores that argument to show a required argument.) Listing 9-3 shows the required argument processing for this application.

LISTING 9-3 Processing the required arguments

```
static DateTime SetDate(String[] Arguments)
{
    // Create a blank date.
    DateTime ReturnDate = new DateTime();
```

```
    // Determine which mandatory date the user requested.
    if (Arguments.Contains("/Yesterday"))
        ReturnDate = DateTime.Now.AddDays(-1);
    else if (Arguments.Contains("/Today"))
        ReturnDate = DateTime.Now;
    else if (Arguments.Contains("/Tomorrow"))
        ReturnDate = DateTime.Now.AddDays(1);
    else
        DisplayQuickHelp();

    // Return the result.
    return ReturnDate;
}
```

The *SetTime()* method begins by creating a blank date, *ReturnDate*. It then checks for each of the required parameter options one at a time. If the application finds a particular required parameter, it sets *ReturnDate* to the appropriate value. The *DateTime.Now* property is exceptionally helpful in this case because it returns today's date. The *AddDays()* method can actually add or remove days (depending on whether you use a positive or negative number), so it's easy to obtain yesterday and tomorrow as well. After the code determines which date to display, it returns this value to the caller in *ReturnDate* as a *DateTime* object for easier formatting later.

> **Tip** The *AddDays()* method points out something about method names. In this case, creative use of the input number makes it possible to remove days; consequently, the term *Add* in *AddDays()* isn't necessarily true. Creating a perfect method name isn't always easy (or even possible), but you should consider the ways in which another developer could use the methods you create. A better name for *AddDays()* might be *ChangeDays()*, but there's also room for confusion with this name because changing doesn't necessarily imply simple addition or subtraction. Of course, the developer could have used *AddOrRemoveDays()*, but now the method name is getting a bit long. The point is that you do need to consider the alternatives before settling on a method name.

Notice that the code checks one alternative at a time until it runs out of alternatives. This is a required parameter. When the user doesn't supply a required parameter, an error has occurred. Of course, you could simply display an unhelpful error message. The example takes a different path— it displays the short help message to help the user understand that the utility doesn't have a required parameter and where to obtain help to fix the problem.

Checking for Optional Arguments

Most command-line utilities support some number of optional arguments. Using optional arguments makes the utility flexible and improves the ability of the utility to meet a wide variety of requests. Creating a flexible utility makes the utility more attractive to the user (especially those power users who love gadgets) and improves the chances of the user actually using the utility regularly to perform useful work. The DisplayDate utility supports one optional argument that accepts one of two choices for formatting the date, as shown in Listing 9-4.

LISTING 9-4 Processing the optional arguments

```
static String ConfigureDate(DateTime Date, String[] Arguments)
{
    // Create a default date string.
    String ReturnString = Date.ToLongDateString();

    // Change the date if the user has selected the short date format.
    if (Arguments.Contains("/Short"))
        ReturnString = Date.ToShortDateString();

    // Return the result.
    return ReturnString;
}
```

This is an optional argument, so the user doesn't have to supply it. Because the user might not supply the input, you need to define a default value, which is */Long* in this case. If the user doesn't supply either */Long* or */Short*, the utility will output a long date, as provided by the *ToLongDateString()* method.

> **Note** The *DateTime* object provides a number of formatting options. This example shows only two of the options. You can even create formats of your own to meet specific needs. It's important to realize that the default methods return output based on the biases of a particular language. You can see the biases for your system in the Region and Language applet of the control panel. Using this applet, it's possible for the user to create a custom output format as well, so unless you define a format in code, you can't assume much about the output formatting of these calls except that they default to the regional bias of whatever language the user has selected for the host computer.

If the user supplies the */Short* command-line switch, the *ConfigureDate()* method changes the string in *ReturnString* to the short date version by calling the *ToShortDateString()* method. Notice that the */Long* command-line switch requires no special handling. That's because */Long* is the default, so no special handing is necessary. One of the additions you can make to your help file is to document the default settings so that the user knows what they are.

Testing the DisplayDate Application

Command-line utilities can be hard to test. Depending on the list of required and optional arguments, you may need to test many permutations of the utility before you can assume that it works as expected. Different command-line switch combinations could result in incorrect or corrupted output, so you have to test as many of them as possible. (Testing all of the combinations is best.) One of the best ways to perform this task is to create a batch file that defines each of the possible combinations. You could also use automated testing software. Both of these testing options are outside the scope of this book.

In this case, you really do want to test the example manually. Not only are the number of potential permutations quite limited, but you'll also want to see how the application works for yourself. Part of the testing process is to open a command prompt so that you can see the application at work. The debugger requires special setup in this case (as described in the "Tracing the DisplayDate Application with the Debugger" section of the chapter). The following sections provide some basic testing scenarios for this utility.

Opening the Command Line

Before you can test anything, you need to open a command-line window. This application doesn't do anything special that would require a UAC permission, so you can open a regular command-line window. Use the following steps to set up the command line for testing this example.

Configuring the Command-line Window

1. Choose Start | All Programs | Accessories | Command Prompt and you'll see the expected window.

2. Type **CD <*Book Folder*>** and press Enter (where <*Book Folder*> is the location you've used to store the source code for this book). In many cases, this location will be the \Users\John\ Documents\Visual Studio 2010\Projects folder, but there isn't any guarantee that this is the location. You'll need to know where you're storing the code for this book. If nothing else, you can use these steps to find the precise location of this example:

   a. Type **CD ** and press Enter to move to the root directory of your machine.

   b. Type **Dir DisplayDate /S** and press Enter to locate the precise location of the example on your hard drive.

3. Type **CD Chapter 09\DisplayDate\bin\Release** to access the specific folder for the output of this example.

4. Type **Dir DisplayDate.exe** and press Enter. You should see one entry, as shown here. (The presence of this entry tells you that you're in the right directory.)

Checking the Help Functionality

The first thing you should check is the help functionality of the utility. Because of the way help is designed, you need to perform several checks, which are listed here:

- Accessing the utility without any command-line options to test short help

- Using the */?* command-line switch to check main help

- Accessing the utility using incorrect command-line switches, which should display the short help screen

- Using the correct command-line switches but adding the */?* command-line switch, which should display main help instead of the anticipated output

You can perform these tests in any order. However, to ensure that you do them all, it's probably best to perform them in order the first time. Start by typing **CLS** and pressing Enter to clear the display. Then type **DisplayDate** and press Enter. You should see the short help screen shown in Figure 9-7. (Your directory information will differ from mine, so the screenshot won't look precisely the same as your display.)

FIGURE 9-7 The DisplayDate utility detects that lack of command-line arguments and displays help.

To perform the next test, type **DisplayDate /?** and press Enter. You'll see the full help screen added to the short help as shown in Figure 9-8.

Notice that the tabs you added to the output format the output so that it's easier to read. Even though the command line doesn't rely on a GUI, you still need to consider formatting to ensure that your application is as easy to use as possible. The full help screen provides enough information so that someone who's completely unfamiliar with your command-line utility could use it. A complex utility will probably require additional detailed help information, but simple utilities often provide enough information just using this type of help screen.

To perform the next test, you must supply some incorrect information. Type **DisplayDate /Hello** and press Enter. You should see the short help screen again.

```
C:\Windows\system32\cmd.exe                                    [-][ ][x]

C:\0264 - Source Code\Chapter 09\DisplayDate\bin\Release>DisplayDate
This utility requires input arguments!
Use DisplayDate /? to obtain help information.

C:\0264 - Source Code\Chapter 09\DisplayDate\bin\Release>DisplayDate /?
DisplayDate:
        Displays the selected date in the specified format.

DisplayDate /Yesterday | /Today | /Tomorrow [/?] [/Long | /Short]

        /Yesterday      Shows yesterday's date.
        /Today          Shows today's date.
        /Tomorrow       Shows tomorrow's date.
        /?              Displays this help message.
        /Long           Shows the date in long format.
        /Short          Shows the date in short format.

Example (shows today's date in long format):
        DisplayDate /Today /Long

C:\0264 - Source Code\Chapter 09\DisplayDate\bin\Release>_
```

FIGURE 9-8 Use the */?* command-line switch to see full help information.

The final test ensures that the user receives help no matter what else might appear on the command line. To perform this test, type **DisplayDate /Today /?** and press Enter. You'll see the full help screen. Even though the */Today* command-line switch is perfectly legal, the */?* command-line switch must take precedence. If there's any chance that the user is confused about something, make sure that you present help, rather than execute a potentially damaging command.

Displaying a Date

At this point, you know that the help option works. However, you haven't tested the actual functionality of the utility yet. You must perform three tasks to ensure that the utility works for the following:

- Dates using the default formatting

- Dates using the short formatting

- Dates using the long formatting

In addition, you must ensure that the correct date is displayed given a particular command-line switch. The utility should display yesterday's, today's, and tomorrow's dates when requested. Use the following procedure to perform the tests.

Testing the DisplayDate Utility Functionality

1. Type **CLS** and press Enter. The display will clear to ensure that you can see the utility output with ease.

2. Type **DisplayDate /Yesterday** and press Enter. (It doesn't matter if part of the command appears on the next line—the command will execute as expected.) You'll see yesterday's date in long format as shown on the next page. (Your date will reflect yesterday's date on your system, which will definitely be different from mine.)

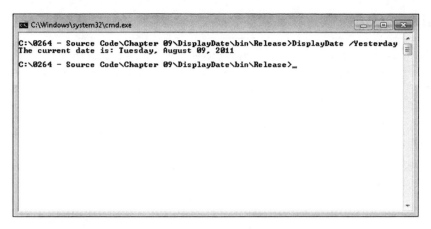

3. Type **DisplayDate /Yesterday /Short** and press Enter. You'll see yesterday's date in short format, as shown here.

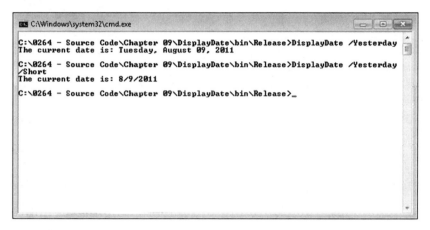

4. Type **DisplayDate /Yesterday /Long** and press Enter. You'll see yesterday's date in long format. Of course, the long format is the default, which is why you see it twice during the testing process.

5. Repeat steps 1 through 4 for the */Today* and */Tomorrow* command-line switches. Simply replace */Yesterday* with the appropriate switch, such as *DisplayDate /Today*.

Now you know that your utility works at the command line. It isn't always possible to test every permutation of command-line switch—especially when creating a complex utility. However, you should try to test as many combinations as possible and focus attention on the combinations that you expect users to rely on heaviest.

Tip It's possible to use batch files to perform testing on your utility. Simply create a text file using Notepad that contains each of the instructions found in the previous two sections (excluding the CLS commands) and give it a .bat extension. The batch file will test each of the combinations far faster than you can.

Tracing the DisplayDate Application with the Debugger

As with any application, DisplayDate is interesting to view in the debugger to see how it works. In fact, viewing other utilities in the debugger can give you considerable insight into creating better utilities of your own. Using the debugger can also help you ensure that the code is working the way you think it will. For example, when testing the help resources for this utility, two different scenarios might produce the same output. Logic dictates that the paths used to achieve those results must be different, but you won't know for sure until you actually trace through the application to check.

Tracing a console application with the debugger is different from a GUI application in one important aspect: You must configure the IDE to pass command-line arguments to the application. Otherwise, the application will always see a blank command line and you'll never be able to test it properly. The first section that follows shows how to configure the command-line arguments in Visual C# 2010 Express. After you learn how to configure the environment, you can follow through the tracing exercises in the section that follows.

Setting the Command-Line Arguments

Command-line utilities require the use of command-line parameters in most cases. This means that you must also apply those parameters when tracing through the application and debugging it or you won't be able to duplicate the command-line utility environment. Fortunately, configuring the command-line arguments isn't too cumbersome. The following steps show you how to perform this task.

Configure the Command-line Arguments

1. Choose Project | *<Project Name>* Properties. In this case, *<Project Name>* is DisplayDate, so you choose Project | DisplayDate Properties. However, the *<Project Name>* will vary with the actual name of the project, so the menu options are always a bit different with each project. The Project Properties window appears.

2. Click the Debug tab. You'll see a list of debugging options like the ones shown here.

3. Type the command-line parameters you want to use in the Command Line Arguments field. Don't include the application name. For example, if you want to emulate *DisplayDate /Today*, you only type **/Today** in the Command Line Arguments field.

4. Click Save or Save All. This step ensures that you see the command-line arguments you want during the tracing process. For some reason, the IDE doesn't automatically save the changes you make to the Command Line Arguments field (even though the changes seem to appear correctly during tracing).

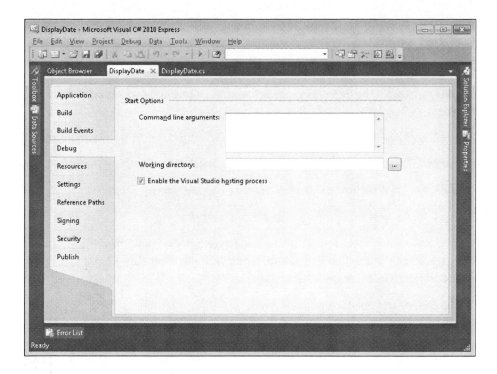

Performing the Trace

It's important to trace through the application to see how it performs. Before you can perform a trace, you must configure the command-line parameters using the technique described in the "Setting the Command Line Arguments" section of the chapter. To start this section, use a simple scenario that will succeed, such as adding the */Today* command-line switch to the Command Line Arguments field. Use the following procedure to perform some simple tests and then play with the utility on your own to see how various command-line switch changes work.

Tracing Through the DisplayDate Utility

1. Place a breakpoint at the line that reads: *DateTime TheDate = new DateTime();* and click Start Debugging. You'll see the debugger stop at the correct instruction.

2. Open the Locals window. You'll see a number of variables including *args*, which is a *String[]* array. Click the plus sign next to *args* and you'll see that it contains one argument, */Today*, as shown here.

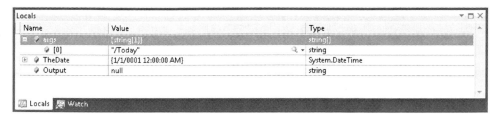

3. Click Step Over three times. The instruction pointer passes over the initial checks to ensure that the input is correct.

4. Click Step Into. You end up in the *SetDate()* method.

5. Click Step Over twice. The instruction pointer is on the *if (Arguments.Contains("/Yesterday"))* statement.

6. Click Step Over twice. Notice that the application sets *ReturnDate* to *DateTime.Now*.

7. Click Step Out. The call returns. However, notice that *TheDate* doesn't have the correct value yet.

8. Click Step Over. *TheDate* now has the correct date—today's date.

9. Click Step Into. You end up in the *ConfigureDate()* method.

10. Click Step Over three times. Notice that the code bypasses the contents of the *if* statement. In short, the output will be in the long date format, not the short date format, because you didn't include the */Short* command-line switch.

11. Click Step Out. At this point, *Output* is still *null*.

12. Click Step Over. Now *Output* has the long date format of *TheDate* as a *String* value.

13. Click Step Over. At this point, the output should appear in a command-prompt window, just as it did when you worked with the application at the command prompt. However, the Taskbar doesn't show a command prompt (unless you failed to close one of the windows earlier).

14. Minimize the IDE. Behind the IDE you'll find a command-prompt window, like the one shown here, where you can see the output of the application.

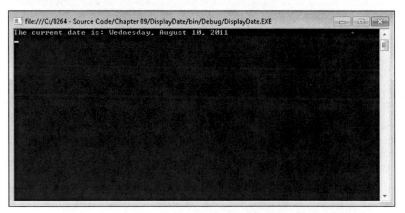

It's interesting to note that you can't access this window without minimizing the IDE because it doesn't appear on the Taskbar for whatever reason. You also won't find it listed on any of the menus, so keep this little trick in mind as you work with utility programs.

15. Click Continue. The application ends. Unlike a GUI application, this utility doesn't have a processing loop where you can continue to interact with it in the debugger until you do something like click Quit.

Get Going with C#

This chapter has provided a quick overview of the command line and its utilities. The command line has been around for a long time and few desktop computer operating systems don't provide some sort of command line. Because the command-line utility sports a text-based interface, it has no fancy requirements to run it, requires fewer hardware resources, allows execution of more commands with fewer actions, and offers a benefit in speed. Balanced with this is the fact that command-line utilities tend to be harder to use and the user must memorize command-line argument sequences to make command-line utilities efficient to use in many cases. In short, it's a balance of speed against ease of use from the perspective of most users.

Before you embark on your own command-line utility challenge, you should discover the kinds of command-line utilities that Windows provides by default. The site at *http://technet.microsoft. com/library/cc754340.aspx* provides a listing of commands that apply to Windows Vista, Windows Server 2008, and Windows 7. If you have an older version of Windows, such as Windows XP, you can find a list at *http://www.microsoft.com/resources/documentation/windows/xp/all/proddocs/en-us/ ntcmds.mspx*. The vendors that create various pieces of hardware and software on your system may also provide command-line utilities. Remember that it's easy to detect a command-line utility by typing **<Command Name> /?** and pressing Enter. You'll see at least a modicum of help in most cases. Many other developers have also contributed command-line utilities you should check out. For example, you can find some useful freeware utilities at *http://www.jfitz.com/dos/index.html*. My blog also has a category devoted to the command line at *http://blog.johnmuellerbooks.com/categories/ Windows%20Command-Line%20Administration%20Instant%20Reference.aspx*.

After you have some idea of what the command line has to offer, try using a few of these commands. You'll discover through use just how efficient the command line makes you. In addition, using other utilities helps you understand how to create better utilities of your own. The two best commands to start with are *Dir* and *FindStr*. If you have Windows 7, try typing **WhoAmI /All** and pressing Enter to see who you are. Research each of the bits of information to determine precisely what the utility is telling you.

Chapter 10, "Using LINQ in Web Applications," moves back to the GUI environment. However, this chapter focuses on web applications. You'll use Language INtegrated Query (LINQ) to create some interesting web applications that perform tasks similar to the desktop counterparts you created in previous chapters. The purpose of this chapter is to demonstrate that you can create many of the same sorts of applications in the web environment that you currently create directly on the desktop. The applications will help you compare and contrast the two environments so that you have a better idea of which application type, web or desktop, works best in a particular situation.

Chapter 10

Using LINQ in Web Applications

After completing this chapter, you'll be able to:

- Develop a LINQ-based web application that relies on a simple list

- Develop a LINQ-based web application that relies on an array

- Develop a LINQ-based web application that relies on a data structure

YOU'VE SEEN IN PREVIOUS CHAPTERS that Language INtegrated Query (LINQ) makes working with some types of programming constructs significantly easier. Not only do you write less code, but using a query also results in less code and that code is automatically optimized for you by the Common Language Runtime (CLR)—the underlying engine that helps you run .NET applications. However, all of those previous examples relied on desktop applications, and you might wonder whether LINQ is also the option of choice for web applications. This chapter demonstrates that LINQ provides the same power for web developers as it does for desktop application developers.

This chapter gets right to the point by examining three different example application types. You've seen similar desktop applications in previous chapters so it's possible to compare the examples in this chapter to those examples to see how desktop and web application development differs. A comparison of one application to another really does help you learn faster. You take what you know now and add to it by viewing another application that uses the same technology in a different way. Web applications are different from desktop applications but the common element in this case is the use of LINQ to help perform the underlying tasks.

Note You must have Visual Web Developer 2010 Express installed to use the examples in this chapter. If you haven't already installed it, the "Installing Visual Web Developer 2010 Express" section of Chapter 1 tells you how to perform this task. In most respects, the IDE for Visual Web Developer 2010 Express works precisely the same as the Visual C# Express IDE that you've used for previous projects so you'll feel right at home. Check out the starter examples in Chapter 2 if you need a refresher on how Visual Web Developer 2010 Express works.

Creating the WebList Project

The WebList project is the web companion to the desktop list project, ListProject1, described in Chapter 3, "Basic Data Manipulation Techniques." Both projects use a similar control set, although a web application has no use whatsoever for a Cancel button. The LINQ query used for both projects is similar. In fact, this project makes every effort to be the same as the project in Chapter 3 to make it easier for you to perform comparisons between the two, especially when you start tracing through this application. The point is to help you better understand web application use of LINQ by making use of the knowledge you've already gained about LINQ on the desktop. The following sections show how to configure, code, test, and trace the WebList project.

Starting the WebList Project

You must create the WebList project before you can do anything else. This project relies on the ASP.NET Web Application template. The following steps help you create a project using this template type and you can use them for projects of your own when you want to use this template as a starting point.

Create an ASP.NET Web Application Project

1. Choose Start | All Programs | Microsoft Visual Studio 2010 Express | Microsoft Visual Web Developer 2010 Express. You'll see the IDE start up.

2. Click New Project. The New Project dialog box appears, as shown on the next page.

 Note Visual Web Developer 2010 Express supports both Visual Basic .NET and Visual C#. Make sure you always select the Visual C# folder to work with the C# templates. Otherwise, you'll create a Visual Basic .NET application.

3. Select Visual C# in the left pane and select ASP.NET Web Application in the middle pane. You'll see a description of the template in the right pane.

4. Type the project name, **WebList**, in the Name field.

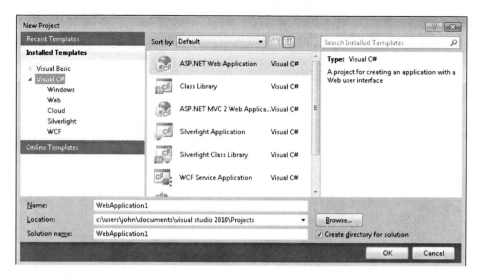

5. Choose a location where you want to store the project files. (Click Browse to display the Project Location dialog box to choose the folder you want to use.) The default location is c:\users\<User Name>\documents\visual studio 2010\Projects; however, you can choose any location on your hard drive to store the project. Unlike the desktop applications created in Chapter 1, "Getting to Know C#," the simple act of creating a project stores files on disk, which is why you must choose a storage location in the New Project dialog box.

6. Clear the Create Directory For Solution option.

7. Click OK. The IDE creates the new project for you, as shown here.

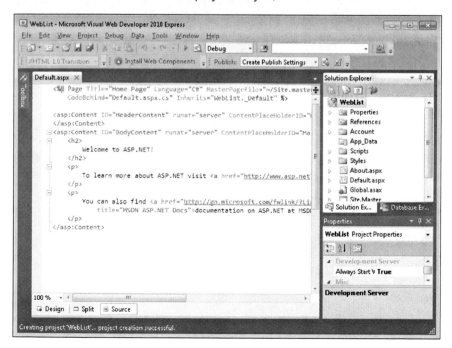

Adding and Configuring the WebList Project Controls

As with desktop applications, you can add controls to a web application by double-clicking the controls in the Toolbox. You can also use the drag-and-drop technique. The controls are different but the functionality is the same. The Visual Web Developer IDE doesn't bring anything new into the picture from a controls perspective.

Because this example is using ListProject1 as a starting point, it would probably be helpful to see that application again. Remember that clicking Test capitalizes each of the entries in the list box. Figure 10-1 shows what the application looks like after you click Test.

FIGURE 10-1 The example in this chapter is a web version of the List Project Version One.

Before you do anything else, highlight the content in the MainContent area on the Design tab and press Delete. This will remove the current custom content for this first page. When you're finished, you can look at the Source tab and see that the second *<asp:Content>* tag is empty like this:

```
<asp:Content ID="BodyContent" runat="server" ContentPlaceHolderID="MainContent">
</asp:Content>
```

The web version of the example doesn't require the Cancel button because you don't actually close web applications. You close the browser that hosts the web application and that code is the responsibility of the browser vendor. Consequently, this example requires a *Button* (for Test) and two *Label* and *Textbox* pairs, just like the desktop example. Add the controls using the following procedure:

Adding the WebList Controls

1. Double-click a *Label* control and then a *TextBox* control in the Toolbox.

2. Press End to move to the end of the controls. Press Enter to create a new line.

3. Perform steps 1 and 2 for the second *Label/TextBox* control pair.

4. Double-click a *Button* control in the Toolbox. Your Design tab should look like the one shown here.

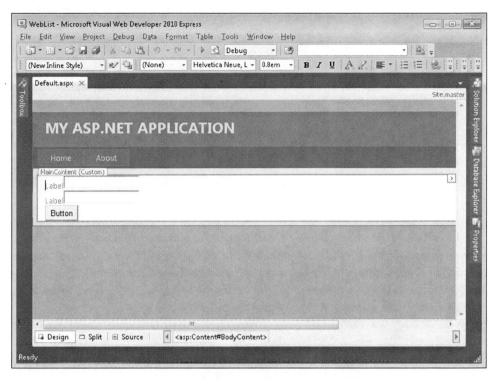

Order is important when working with web applications because the controls flow from left to right, top to bottom. Of course, you can always get fancy and start placing the controls in tables or use other tricks to gain more control over the layout. These sorts of topics are best left to a book on web page design so I won't discuss them here, but you can check out Faithe Wempen's book *HTML5 Step by Step* (Microsoft Press, 2011) to learn more. Now that you have the controls in place it's time to configure them, as shown in Table 10-1.

TABLE 10-1 WebList Control Configuration

Control Name	Property Name	Value
Label1	*(ID)*	*lblSelections*
	AccessKey	*S*
	AssociatedControlID	*txtSelections*
	Text	*Selections*
TextBox1	*(ID)*	*txtSelections*
	TextMode	*MultiLine*
	Height	*95*
Label2	*(ID)*	*lblOutput*

Control Name	Property Name	Value
	AccessKey	O
	AssociatedControlID	txtOutput
	Text	Output
TextBox2	(Name)	txtOutput
	Height	95
	ReadOnly	True
	TextMode	MultiLine
Button1	(ID)	btnTest
	AccessKey	T
	Text	Test

Many of the same changes occur in this application as they do in a desktop application but under a different name. For example, the *(Name)* property is now the *(ID)* property. However, the value is the same as before, such as *txtSelections*. As with WPF applications, you must associate *Label* controls with their *TextBox* counterparts. A few properties are different. For example, when creating a desktop application, you use an ampersand (&) to indicate the access key (or hotkey). When working with a web application, you use an actual *AccessKey* property.

Note Even though web applications support access keys, they don't automatically underline the character in the text that the user can use for quick access. One way to deal with this problem is to establish and publish a convention where the first letter is always used as the access key. You could also use two labels in place of one. The first label would have the *Font.Underline* property set to *True* while the second label would use standard characters. For example, the Selections label would be split in two with the first label containing *S* and the second containing *elections* so that you could underline the as a visual access key hint for the user. This problem doesn't have a perfect solution, but you do need to come up with a consistent method of handling it so that users with special needs or those who prefer a keyboard interface will know how to interact with your application.

You also need to add text to *txtSelections* just as with the ListProject1 example in Chapter 3. The technique for performing this task is somewhat different with a web application. Click in the *Text* property for *txtSelections* and you'll see a downward-pointing arrow control. Click this control and you'll see a window where you can type the values needed for this example. Add a new line by pressing Enter. Press Ctrl+Enter to accept the text you've entered. Your window should look like the one shown in Figure 10-2 after you've entered the values.

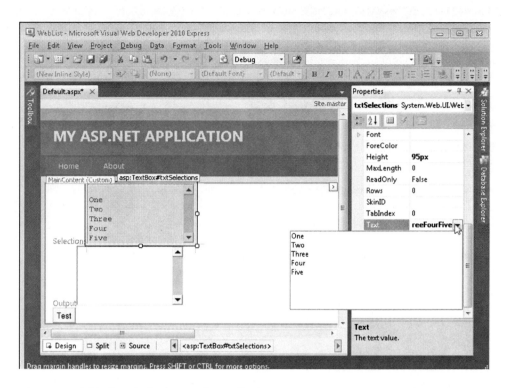

FIGURE 10-2 Add a list of selections to the application.

> **Note** The *AccessKey* setting can produce unpredictable results. In fact, the *AccessKey*
> setting works reliably only with Internet Explorer. For example, if you try this example with
> Firefox, you'll find that pressing Alt+S doesn't place the cursor in the Selections field but it
> does when working with Internet Explorer. Pressing Alt+Shift+S does place the cursor in the
> Selections field when using either browser. The same holds true for the Output field and
> the Test button. Pressing Alt+Shift+O places the cursor in the Output field and pressing
> Alt+Shift+T presses the Test button in both browsers. Make sure you test the *AccessKey*
> setting with the browsers you intend to support and ensure that users know how to use the
> access keys you provide.

Defining the *using* Statement

This example uses a new *using* statement that you haven't seen in the past. Add this *using* statement
to the beginning of your code:

```
using System.Text;
```

The *System.Text* namespace contains some amazing classes you can use to manipulate text in various ways. One of the more powerful classes is *StringBuilder*, which the example in this section uses to quickly overcome a problem you'll encounter when working with web applications and LINQ. You'll read more about this solution in the "Adding the WebList Project Code" section of the chapter.

Adding the WebList Project Code

It's time to add some code to the *btnTest*. Start by double-clicking the Test button. The IDE creates the *btnTest_Click()* event handler for you. Listing 10-1 shows the code you need to add to make the example work.

LISTING 10-1 Creating a LINQ query against a list

```
protected void btnTest_Click(object sender, EventArgs e)
{
    // Obtain the data from the Text property of txtSelections
    // and place it in Output using TheEntry as a temporary variable.
    var Output = from TheEntry
                 in txtSelections.Text.Split(new Char[] {'\n', '\r'})
                 where TheEntry != ""
                 select TheEntry.ToUpper();

    // Convert Output to a String.
    StringBuilder OutputAsString = new StringBuilder();
    foreach (String Item in Output)
    {
        OutputAsString.Append(Item);
        OutputAsString.Append("\r\n");
    }

    // Place the contents of OutputAsString into the Text property of
    // txtOutput.
    txtOutput.Text = OutputAsString.ToString();
}
```

One of the first things you'll notice when working with the *TextBox* control is that, unlike the desktop version, it doesn't provide a *Lines* property. The *Lines* property makes things easy with LINQ because you can simply feed it into a query and everything just works. Unfortunately, now you have a *Text* property to deal with that delivers simple text and not the array you had wanted.

Fortunately, you can use the *Split()* method to fix the problem. It's important to understand how the string appears to the *Split()* method. Every time you press Enter when creating an entry the IDE actually inserts two characters—a line feed *(\n)* and a carriage return *(\r)*. So what *Split()* sees is *One\r\nTwo*, not *One* and *Two* on separate lines. These control characters—line feed and carriage return—create the separation, but *Split()* isn't concerned about that. The first argument tells *Split()* to create a string array with entries that remove the *\n* and *\r* control characters so that all that remains is the text.

Unfortunately, *Split()* creates a new problem. There's one entry for each \n and a second entry for each \r character, which results in empty strings—array entries that don't contain any information. To fix this problem, you must tell the LINQ query that you don't want these empty strings in the output. Consequently, this LINQ query, unlike the one shown in Listing 3-1, contains a *where* clause. The *where* clause states that you want every entry that's not equal to an empty string.

After the LINQ query does its work, you have *Output*, which contains the separate strings from *txtSelections.Text* in uppercase, just as they were in Listing 3-1. Later, in the "Tracing Through the WebList Project Example" section, you'll see that this *Output* matches the *Output* in Listing 3-1. However, *txtOutput* doesn't provide a *Lines* property either, so now you need a specially formatted string to supply to the *Text* property. The *StringBuilder* class is designed to overcome this sort of problem.

The code uses a *foreach* loop to obtain each of the entries in *Output* as a *String, Item*. It then adds this value to *OutputAsString* using the *Append()* method. The *Append()* method is quite powerful because it can mix and match data types, such as *Boolean* and *Int32*, to create a string. Notice the next step. If you want the entries to appear on separate lines in the output, you must now add the carriage return and linefeed back into the string. The code ends by placing the string in *OutputAsString* into *txtOutput.Text*.

To test this application, click Start Debugging. You'll see the ASP.NET Development Server start (as it will for any application you want to debug) and then the test page will appear in your default browser. Figure 10-3 shows how the application output looks when you use the default entries and click Test.

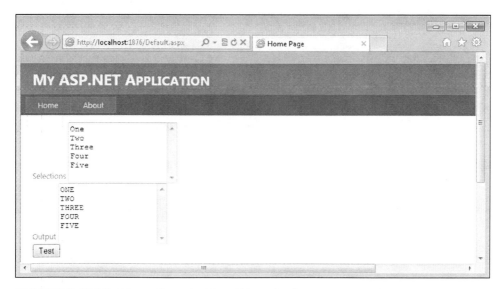

FIGURE 10-3 Click Test to see the output from this application.

It's important to understand that this example is designed to keep individual lines in *txtSelections* together. For example, place the cursor after the last line in Selections and press Enter. Now, type **Hello There**—two words separated by a space. Click Test. You'll see that Hello There remains together, as shown in Figure 10-4, because of the way the *btnTest_Click()* event handler is coded.

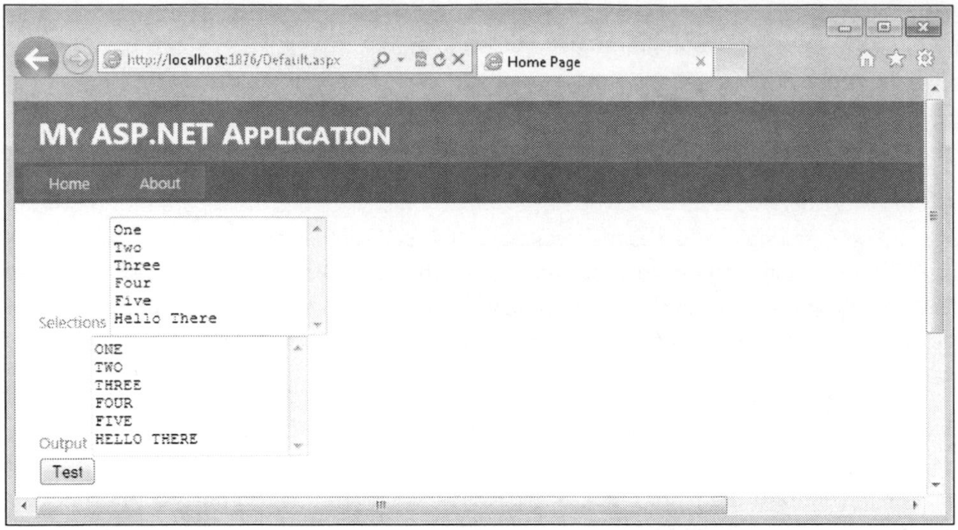

FIGURE 10-4 Adding a new entry and clicking Test displays a result in the Output field.

Tracing Through the WebList Project Example

Create a breakpoint for this application at the *var Output = from TheEntry* line in the *btnTest_Click()* event handler. If you haven't already started the application, click Start Debugging. This tracing session relies on the default entries so remove any entries that you might have added before. Click Test. The debugger will stop at the line where you placed the breakpoint.

At this point, *Output* doesn't contain anything. Click Step Over and you'll see that *Output* now contains some data. Open its entry in the Locals window. Expand the Results View to see the results. If you compare this Results View with the one from the example in Chapter 3 at this point, you'll find that they're precisely the same. Both examples will produce the same results when using the default entries, as shown in Figure 10-5. (Of course, they use slightly different methods to obtain the result.)

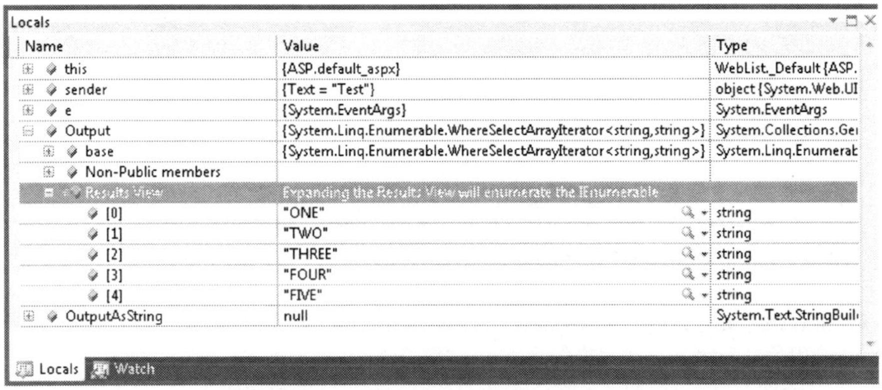

FIGURE 10-5 Click Test to see the output from this application.

Let's examine the LINQ query functionality in detail. The following procedure will help you get through the various steps in the LINQ query.

Tracing the LINQ query

1. Click Step Over. You'll see that the code creates the *StringBuilder, OutputAsString*.

2. Click Step Into three times. You'll end up at the *where TheEntry != ""* line in the code. The Locals window will tell you that *TheEntry* currently contains One.

3. Click Step Into again. Now the instruction pointer moves to the *select TheEntry.ToUpper()* line.

4. Click Step Into five times and you'll see that the value *ONE* has been added to *OutputAsString*.

5. Click Step Over twice and then click Step Into. Now you'll see that *TheEntry* contains an empty string.

6. Click Step Into. Instead of moving to the *TheEntry.ToUpper()* line, the instruction pointer remains at the *TheEntry != ""* line in the code. However, this time *TheEntry* contains Two. Now the process will follow steps 3 through 5.

The important thing to remember is that a *where* clause in a LINQ statement can help you filter data so that the output contains only the elements you need. In this case, the *where* clause removes all of the empty strings. Trace the LINQ process several more times until you're sure you understand it and then click Continue to see the results in your browser. Now add an entry with a space as before and trace through the LINQ query to see how it works with a space. Because the *Split()* method doesn't produce separate entries for a space, the *where* clause doesn't see an empty string and the entry with a space remains whole.

> **Note** Remember that you can stop the ASP.NET Development Server by right-clicking its icon in the Notification Area and choosing Stop. The system won't free the resources used by the development server until you stop the server. Consequently, if you're working on several projects between system reboots, you could end up with a number of these servers eating up system resources. Always stop the development server when you're finished using it.

Creating the WebArray Project

The WebArray project is similar to the Array project in Chapter 4. Of course, this is a web version of the desktop application. It does ask the same questions such as how to use LINQ with an array and demonstrating other techniques for working with the same array. Again, you should compare the two examples as you proceed so that you can continue to build your knowledge based on what you've already learned.

Starting the WebArray Project

Sometimes you'll want to create a simple web application—one that doesn't come with all of the baggage of master pages and predefined features such as login. A simple web application is useful for testing purposes. Of course, you'll have to do a little more work to create a simple web application at the outset but the use of a simple web application pays dividends in simplicity later. You don't have to trace through all of the predefined code that comes with the ASP.NET Web Application template. The following steps show how to perform this task.

Create an ASP.NET Empty Web Application Project

1. Choose Start | All Programs | Microsoft Visual Studio 2010 Express | Microsoft Visual Web Developer 2010 Express. You'll see the IDE start up.

2. Click New Project. The New Project dialog box appears.

3. Select Visual C#\Web in the left pane. Notice that some new templates become available, as shown here.

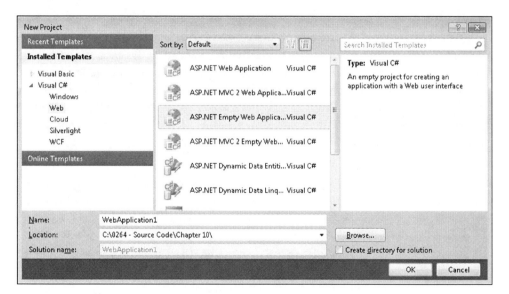

4. Select the ASP.NET Empty Web Application template in the middle pane. You'll see a description of the template in the right pane.

5. Type the project name, **WebArray**, in the Name field.

6. Choose a location where you want to store the project files. (Click Browse to display the Project Location dialog box to choose the folder you want to use.)

7. Clear the Create Directory For Solution option.

8. Click OK. The IDE will create the new project for you as shown here. (Notice that the project has no files at all so you need to add at least one.)

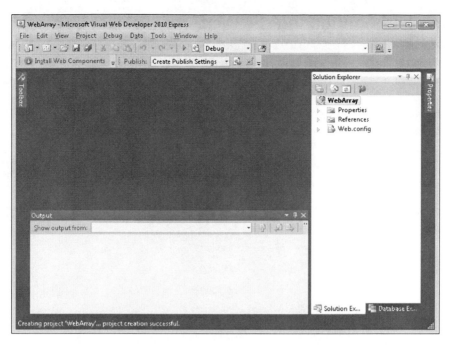

9. Right-click WebArray in Solution Explorer and choose Add | New Item. The Add New Item dialog box appears, as shown here.

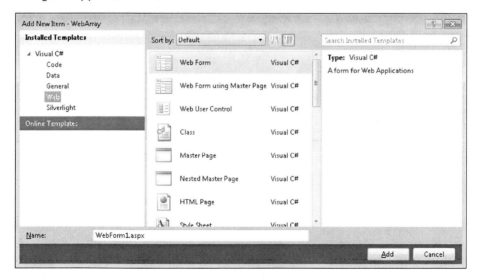

10. Highlight the Web Form entry. You see a description of this item in the right pane.

11. Type **Default.aspx** in the Name field. The first, or default, web page for every site is named Default.aspx. If you don't name it Default.aspx, the web server won't be able to find it unless you provide a specific name in the Address field of the browser.

12. Click Add. The IDE adds a new Web Form to the project. Unlike the WebList project, there isn't much to see with this Web Form—it truly is blank.

Adding and Configuring the WebArray Project Controls

As with the previous example, you'll want to remove the default content before you begin adding any new controls to your project. You'll see some differences between this example and its desktop counterpart. For one thing, you don't need a Quit button because that's handled by the browser. This example could display a dialog box for output just like its desktop counterpart, but it's easier to use a *Label* and *TextBox* pair. Add the *Label* and *TextBox* controls, press Enter, and then add the three *Button* controls. Table 10-2 describes how to configure the controls for this example.

TABLE 10-2 WebArray Control Configuration

Control Name	Property Name	Value
Label1	(ID)	lblOutput
	AccessKey	O
	AssociatedControlID	txtOutput
	Text	Output
TextBox1	(Name)	txtOutput
	Height	95
	ReadOnly	True
	TextMode	MultiLine
Button1	(ID)	btnLINQ
	AccessKey	Q
	Text	LINQ
Button2	(ID)	btnLoop
	AccessKey	L
	Text	Loop
Button3	(ID)	btnConditional
	AccessKey	C
	Text	Conditional
DOCUMENT	Title	Using an Array

The *DOCUMENT* entry is normally associated with the header information for a standard web page. For example, it contains the *<title>* tag, which is used to create a title for the entire document that's displayed in the titlebar of your browser. You access the *DOCUMENT* entry using the drop-down list box in the Properties window. Figure 10-6 shows what your application should look like at this point.

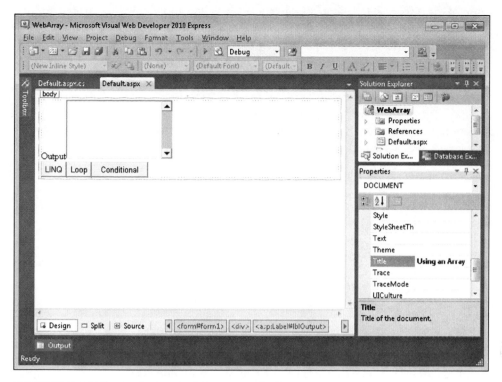

FIGURE 10-6 Add the required controls to your application.

Adding the WebArray Code

It's time to create the code for this application. If you haven't done so already, make sure you read the "Using Alternative Coding Methods" sidebar in Chapter 4, "Using Collections to Store Data." The purpose of these side-by-side illustrations of working with an array is to demonstrate that you always have options when working with C#. You have more than one way to create code and obtain a desired result. In fact, except in the most extreme cases, you'll usually find the opposite is true— many equally valid ways are available for achieving a desired result.

Creating the Array

Before you can do anything, you need to create an array for this example. This means adding a global array and initializing it. To see the code editor for this project, right-click the Default.aspx entry in Solution Explorer and choose View Code. You'll see the code editor with one event handler, *Page_Load()*, defined in it.

The *Page_Load()* event handler is exceptionally important to web applications. A desktop application is always in contact with its code but a web application isn't. When a web application loads, it calls the code on the server to perform a setup for the client and then send a response. Now the response is on the client system as a web page but there isn't any connection to the server—the connection is severed. When a user clicks a button on the form, the client system makes an entirely new request and sends it to the server, which starts the application and creates a response to the request.

Because of the disconnected nature of web applications, the application must store information about the current application status (state in programming terms) on the client system as part of the web page and within cookies. Every time the client makes a request, the server reloads the application for that request. The *Page_Load()* is called for every one of these requests and performs any required setup. One of the most important pieces of setup is initializing the array used for the example. The array doesn't exist between calls—it only exists when *Page_Load()* creates it. Don't worry too much about the complexities of all this just yet. The main thing to get out of this discussion is that the application must re-create the array, *TestArray*, for every client request. The code required to perform this task appears in Listing 10-2.

LISTING 10-2 Defining an array for test purposes

```
// Create an array.
String[] TestArray;

protected void Page_Load(object sender, EventArgs e)
{
    // Initialize the array.
    TestArray = new String[] { "One", "Two", "Three", "Four", "Five" };
}
```

As you can see, the process for creating an array isn't any different in a web application as it is for a desktop application. This example creates TestArray to hold five strings: One, Two, Three, Four, and Five.

Developing the LINQ Version

The LINQ version of the array query code will obtain a list of the first three letters of each array entry and then display a single entry from this list. Listing 10-3 shows the code you need for this example.

LISTING 10-3 Performing a LINQ query against the array

```
protected void btnLINQ_Click(object sender, EventArgs e)
{
    // Create the query.
    var Output = from String TheEntry
                 in TestArray
                 select TheEntry.Substring(0, 3);

    // Display one of the results.
    txtOutput.Text = Output.ToArray<String>()[2];
}
```

The query selects each of the array entries in turn and returns just the first three letters using the *Substring()* method. This part of the example doesn't differ from the desktop counterpart at all.

Because web pages don't support the *MessageBox* class, you need to output the result to *txtOutput.Text*. The technique is the same as the desktop application, using *Output.ToArray()* to access the third element found in *Output*. The output is of type *String* just like the desktop counterpart.

However, as you'll discover in the "Tracing Through the WebArray Example" section of the chapter, this example works somewhat differently than its desktop counterpart. Figure 10-7 shows the output from this version of the example.

FIGURE 10-7 The web version of the application works the same as the desktop counterpart.

Displaying a Dialog Box with ASP.NET

You may decide that you really do want to display a dialog box with the response to this query (or any other query). Remember that the server sends a response to the client and then closes the connection. So no actual interactivity is going on, despite the fact that it may look like it when you're using your browser. Every action you see in your browser is the result of a request followed by a response. (Under certain conditions a server can push content to the client, but a discussion of this topic is well outside the realm of this book so we'll ignore it for the moment.) Normally, interactive elements such as dialog boxes are created using JavaScript on the client end. Fortunately, you can inject—send JavaScript—as part of the response. The following code shows one technique for accomplishing this task:

```
// Display an alert instead.
HttpContext.Current.Response.Write(
    "<SCRIPT LANGUAGE='JavaScript'>alert('" +
    Output.ToArray<String>()[2] +
    "')</SCRIPT>");
```

This code tells the server to send a response to the client—to write that response using the *Write()* method. The text could be anything, but in this case you're supplying a JavaScript script using the *<SCRIPT>* tag. The script consists of one line of code, a call to the *alert()* function. This function accepts a string as input and displays it on-screen in a dialog box.

This technique suffers from a number of problems. First, it displays the dialog box immediately without waiting for the rest of the page to download. Second, it lacks some of the nice features of the *MessageBox* class. For example, you don't have a choice of icons to use and you don't have a way to trap a response from the user using the dialog box. In short, this is a very limited way to work around the *MessageBox* problem unless you want to start delving into complex web page download techniques.

Developing the Loop Version

LINQ queries save considerable programming time and effort in most cases, plus they're easier to read in most cases than their procedural counterparts. However, it's useful to know how loops work in web pages as well because at times you need to use them. Listing 10-4 shows the code required to create a loop version of the example.

LISTING 10-4 Defining a simple loop

```csharp
protected void btnLoop_Click(object sender, EventArgs e)
{
    // Create a variable to hold the result.
    String Output = "";

    // Perform the array processing.
    for (Int32 Counter = 0; Counter < TestArray.Length; Counter++)
    {
        Output = Output + TestArray[Counter] + "\r\n";
    }

    // Display the result on screen.
    txtOutput.Text = Output;
}
```

In this case, the output shows all of the elements contained in *TestArray*. The *for* loop uses Counter to keep track of the current element and add it to *Output*. As with the desktop version of the example, each entry is separated by a carriage return and linefeed. Figure 10-8 shows the output from this example.

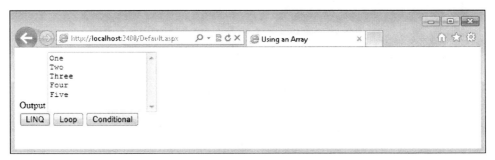

FIGURE 10-8 Click Loop to see the output shown in this figure.

You might wonder whether the server actually sends the carriage return/linefeed pairs. Normally, when you look at HTML tags, you see the *
* or *<p />* tags used to create new lines. It's educational to view the output that the server produces in response to the code you create: The HTML that you get from the C# code you write often contains surprises that you might not have considered. To see whether the server makes a modification in this case, right-click Internet Explorer and choose View Source. (Other browsers, such as Firefox, also support this feature using slightly different wording.) You'll see a customized copy of Notepad open with the generated HTML for this page, as shown in Figure 10-9.

```
  http://localhost:2400/Default.aspx - Original Source

  File   Edit   Format

  1
  2
  3   <!DOCTYPE html PUBLIC "-//W3C//DTD XHTML 1.0 Transitional//EN" "http://www.w3.org/TR/xhtml1/DTD/xhtml1-
      transitional.dtd">
  4
  5   <html xmlns="http://www.w3.org/1999/xhtml">
  6   <head><title>
  7        Using an Array
  8   </title></head>
  9   <body>
 10      <form method="post" action="Default.aspx" id="form1">
 11   <div class="aspNetHidden">
 12   <input type="hidden" name="__VIEWSTATE" id="__VIEWSTATE"
      value="/wEPDwUFLTk0MzQxNTU2MA9kFgICAw9FgICAw8PFgIeBFRleHQFHQFHU9uZQ0KVHdvDQpUaHJlZQ0KRm01cg0KRml2ZQ0KZGRkp
      X2agErMBdVR/SUTP2GVLEG2rukvcZqnn366qW8/Zxo=" />
 13   </div>
 14
 15   <div class="aspNetHidden">
 16
 17       <input type="hidden" name="__EVENTVALIDATION" id="__EVENTVALIDATION"
      value="/wEWBQLusNP1AgK7w5ypDwkYzMT1DwK/vPA5AoOPnoAHLzSVHndhEEwYZVS1YN4dX7D4cAsWN7hJU1+tzkZADg0=" />
 18   </div>
 19      <div>
 20
 21          <label for="txtOutput" id="lblOutput" accesskey="O">Output</label>
 22          <textarea name="txtOutput" rows="2" cols="20" readonly="readonly" id="txtOutput"
      style="height:95px;">
 23   One
 24   Two
 25   Three
 26   Four
 27   Five
 28   </textarea>
 29          <br />
 30          <input type="submit" name="btnLINQ" value="LINQ" id="btnLINQ" accesskey="Q" />
 31          <input type="submit" name="btnLoop" value="Loop" id="btnLoop" accesskey="L" />
 32          <input type="submit" name="btnConditional" value="Conditional" id="btnConditional"
      accesskey="C" />
 33
 34      </div>
 35      </form>
 36   </body>
 37   </html>
```

FIGURE 10-9 Viewing the HTML for an application can help you understand what the server does with the code you write.

The server does send the carriage return/linefeed pairs. However, it pays to see how things work because the server could just as easily make substitutions that you might not have thought about that could cause some browser users problems or not display as expected in certain environments. You can sometimes overcome these problems through careful programming.

Developing the Conditional Loop Version

The previous version (Listing 10-4) of the loop example shows all of the entries in *TestArray*. You'll probably want to duplicate the results of the LINQ example (Listing 10-3). The code shown in Listing 10-5 shows how to obtain the same result by using an *if* statement.

LISTING 10-5 Creating the LINQ query output using a loop

```
protected void btnConditional_Click(object sender, EventArgs e)
{
    // Create a variable to hold the result.
    String Output = "";
```

```
    // Perform the array processing.
    for (Int32 Counter = 0; Counter < TestArray.Length; Counter++)
    {
        // Place a condition on the task. Perform the task only for the
        // third array element.
        if (Counter == 2)
        {
            Output = Output + TestArray[Counter].Substring(0, 3) + "\r\n";
        }
    }

    // Display the result on screen.
    txtOutput.Text = Output;
}
```

The example code uses a *for* loop as before. *Counter* still tracks the index of the current array element. The difference is that an *if* statement keeps the code from doing anything until *Counter* is equal to 2, which is actually the third array element. (Remember that the numbering begins with 0.) When *Counter* is equal to 2, the code calls on *Substring()* to place the first three letters of the current array entry in *Output*. As before, the result is placed in *txtOutput.Text*. Figure 10-10 shows the output from this example.

FIGURE 10-10 Clicking Conditional shows the output in this figure.

Tracing Through the WebArray Example

Tracing through the WebArray example is much like its desktop counterpart in Chapter 4, except for one incredibly important point. Place a breakpoint at the following line of the *Page_Load()* event handler:

```
TestArray = new String[] { "One", "Two", "Three", "Four", "Five" };
```

Click Start Debugging. The debugger will stop at the selected line of code, which is before the web page actually displays. This line of code initializes *TestArray*. In the Immediate window, type **? Page. IsPostback** and press Enter. Because this is the first time that the page has loaded, you see a response of *false*.

Click Continue. You'll see the web page appear. Now click any of the three buttons on the web page. (It doesn't matter which one.) The debugger stops again. It stops because this is an entirely new request. However, the server knows that the client has seen the web page before. Type **? Page. IsPostback** and press Enter. This time you receive a response of *true*. That's because you clicked a button to make another request and the browser sent status information with the request to reflect this fact.

This information is hidden directly on the web page. View the source for the web page and you'll see several *<input type="hidden">* tags in the web page. These tags track state information for the web page so that when the user clicks a button, the server knows which button is clicked and how the web page is currently configured. Of course, part of this information also says that the request is a *postback*—a request from a page that's already displayed in the browser.

It's helpful to trace through each of the event handlers as well. You'll find that the debugger treats them essentially the same as it did with the desktop version but the operation is different. For example, if you had changed the content of *TestArray* during a previous call, you wouldn't see it now. The server absolutely doesn't track state information between calls, so web applications are susceptible to some odd bugs that you'd never encounter in a desktop application. Try playing around with the code to see how this all works for yourself.

Creating the WebStructure Project

The WebStructure project examines the techniques you use to work with structured data from a web application. Structures begin adding complexity to your application. Complexity can cause a number of problems for web applications, including figuring out how to display the information in a way that the viewer will understand and keeping response times to a minimum. The following sections discuss a web version of an application based on the Structure example in Chapter 4. (See the "Creating the Structure Project" section of Chapter 4 for details.)

Starting the WebStructure Project

The example begins with a blank ASP.NET project. You'll need to add a Web Form to it before you move onto the next section. Follow the directions found in the "Starting the WebArray Project" section of this chapter to get started. However, instead of naming your project WebArray, name it WebStructure.

Adding and Configuring the WebStructure Project Controls

You'll find that as your web projects become more complex, the controls and settings you use begin to diverge from a desktop counterpart even more. The Structure project in Chapter 4 defines the same *Label* and *Textbox* pairs as this application does, so no surprises there. It also isn't a surprise that the web version lacks a Quit button.

The web version does require two additional controls that the desktop version doesn't. One control is a hidden *Label* that displays status information as needed. It replaces the message box used by the desktop version. A *Hidden* control is also used to store state. In fact, this control will provide you with the greatest insights into a major difference between desktop and web applications. The need to store state information that affects the actual functioning of the application as it runs is something you find quite often in web applications. Table 10-3 shows the controls you need for this application and their configuration.

TABLE 10-3 WebStructure Control Configuration

Control Name	Property Name	Value
Label1	*(ID)*	*lblName*
	AccessKey	*M*
	AssociatedControlID	*txtName*
	Text	*Name*
TextBox1	*(Name)*	*txtName*
	ReadOnly	*True*
	Width	*180*
Label2	*(ID)*	*lblAddress*
	AccessKey	*A*
	AssociatedControlID	*txtAddress*
	Text	*Address*
TextBox2	*(Name)*	*txtAddress*
	ReadOnly	*True*
	Width	*180*
Label3	*(ID)*	*lblCity*
	AccessKey	*C*
	AssociatedControlID	*txtCity*
	Text	*City*
TextBox3	*(Name)*	*txtCity*
	ReadOnly	*True*
	Width	*180*
Label4	*(ID)*	*lblState*
	AccessKey	*S*
	AssociatedControlID	*txtState*
	Text	*State*
TextBox4	*(Name)*	*txtState*

Control Name	Property Name	Value
	ReadOnly	True
	Width	180
Label5	(ID)	lblZIPCode
	AccessKey	Z
	AssociatedControlID	txtZIPCode
	Text	ZIP Code
TextBox5	(Name)	txtZIPCode
	ReadOnly	True
	Width	180
Button1	(ID)	btnNext
	AccessKey	N
	Text	Next
Button2	(ID)	btnPrevious
	AccessKey	P
	Text	Previous
Label6	(ID)	lblStatus
	AccessKey	T
	ForeColor	Red
	Text	Blank (nothing)
	Visible	False
HiddenField1	(ID)	CurrentRecord
	Value	0
DOCUMENT	Title	Using a Structure

This is a little more configuration than you performed with the desktop version but you'll discover that it's all necessary. When you finish configuring the controls, your page should look like the one shown in Figure 10-11.

Adding the WebStructure Code

It's time to add the code required to make the example work. Some of this code is precisely the same as the code you used for the desktop version (and it's noted so that you know where the code is the same). Most of the differences are due either to differences between desktop and web controls or additional code needed to track state information.

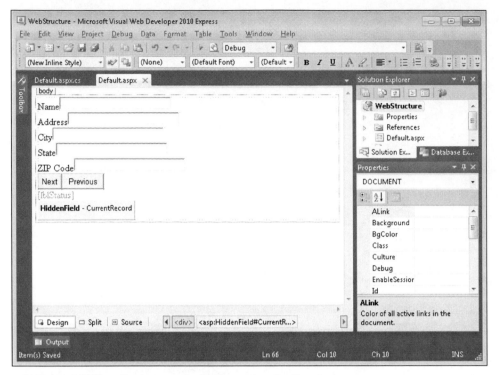

FIGURE 10-11 This application contains hidden and optional controls.

Defining the Data Structure

This example uses the same data structure as the example in Chapter 4. Use the instructions in the "Creating a Structure" section of Chapter 4 to create the data structure.

Loading the Page

In the "Tracing Through the WebArray Example" section of this chapter, you're exposed to the concept of a postback—a request for a web page based on a page that's already displayed on the client system. The code shown in Listing 10-7 shows the importance of the *Page.IsPostBack* property.

LISTING 10-6 Defining a new page

```
protected void Page_Load(object sender, EventArgs e)
{
    // Initialize the array.
    MyAddresses = new List<Addresses>();

    // Add entries to the array.
    MyAddresses.Add(
        new Addresses(
            "Mark Hanson", "123 Anywhere Street", "Somewhere", "UT", "99999"));
```

```
    MyAddresses.Add(
        new Addresses(
            "Kim Abercrombie", "456 5th Avenue", "Outback", "AK", "99998"));
    MyAddresses.Add(
        new Addresses(
            "Armando Pinto", "9925 Galaxy Drive", "Nowhere", "IN", "99997"));

    // Set the initial entry.
    if (Page.IsPostBack)
        CurrentEntry = Int32.Parse(CurrentRecord.Value);
    else
        CurrentEntry = 0;

    // Display the first element on screen.
    ShowEntry();
}
```

The code begins by defining the three records used for this example. They're precisely the same records as the desktop version so that you can compare the two without any interpretation. However, you can no longer set *CurrentEntry* to 0 every time the client requests a new page as you would in the desktop version. The current entry is whatever the client has used last. Only when the client is requesting an entirely new page can you assume that *CurrentEntry* is 0. So, if *Page.IsPostBack* is *false* (this isn't a request from an existing page), the code sets *CurrentEntry* to 0.

This leaves a problem of how to set *CurrentEntry* when *Page.IsPostBack* is *true*. The server could be working with hundreds of clients and has no idea of which record the caller is looking at now. In fact, the server may not even be able to differentiate between callers. The best way to handle this is to have the client tell the server which record is current. In other words, the client must report the state of the page to the server as part of the request. ASP.NET provides a wealth of ways to store state information and you can read about them at *http://msdn.microsoft.com/library/75x4ha6s.aspx*. However, the easiest method when you have just a few state items to store is using a hidden control.

When *Page.IsPostBack* is *true*, the application obtains the *String* stored in the *Value* property of the *CurrentRecord* hidden control and converts it to an *Int32* using the *Int32.Parse()* method. The code then places this value in *CurrentEntry*. At this point, your thoughts should be going back to the discussion of why *ShowEntry()* is created the way it is in Chapter 4. By making it possible for *ShowEntry()* to use a dynamic value, you also make it possible to move that code directly to this example without having to worry about any additional tinkering.

Showing an Entry

Both the desktop and web versions of the application use a *ShowEntry()* method. In fact, it's the same code in both examples. The *ShowEntry()* method appears in the "Adding the Structure Example Code" section of Chapter 4.

Moving Between Records

This application doesn't do much unless it allows the user to move between records. The *btnNext_Click()* and *btnPrevious_Click()* event handlers serve three purposes:

- Display status information The desktop application displays a message box for the first and last records. A web application can't use a message box easily so this application uses a special label for the task.

- Update *CurrentEntry* so that it reflects the correct record number.

- Enable or disable the two buttons as needed to reflect a first or last record condition.

The web version of the example requires some changes because of control differences (displaying the status information) and because of the need to store state on the user's system. Listing 10-7 shows the code for this part of the example.

LISTING 10-7 Changing the record

```
protected void btnNext_Click(object sender, EventArgs e)
{
    // Turn off the status message.
    lblStatus.Visible = false;

    // Determine if this is the last entry.
    if (CurrentEntry + 1 == MyAddresses.Count)
    {

        // If so, disable the Next button.
        btnNext.Enabled = false;

        // Tell the user that this is the last entry.
        lblStatus.Text = "Last Entry!";
        lblStatus.Visible = true;
    }

    else
    {

        // Update the current entry.
        CurrentEntry++;

        // Store the value for future use.
        CurrentRecord.Value = CurrentEntry.ToString();
    }
```

```
        // Determine if it's acceptable to enable the Previous button.
        if (MyAddresses.Count > 1)

            btnPrevious.Enabled = true;

        // Display the current entry.
        ShowEntry();
    }

    protected void btnPrevious_Click(object sender, EventArgs e)
    {
        // Turn off the status message.
        lblStatus.Visible = false;

        // Determine if this is the first entry.
        if (CurrentEntry == 0)
        {

            // If so, disable the Previous button.
            btnPrevious.Enabled = false;

            // Tell the user that this is the last entry.
            lblStatus.Text = "First Entry!";
            lblStatus.Visible = true;
        }

        else
        {
            // Update the current entry.
            CurrentEntry--;

            // Store the value for future use.
            CurrentRecord.Value = CurrentEntry.ToString();
        }

        // Determine if it's acceptable to enable the Next button.
        if (CurrentEntry + +1 < MyAddresses.Count)

            btnNext.Enabled = true;

        // Display the current entry.
        ShowEntry();
    }
```

If you compare this listing to Listing 4-14 in Chapter 4, you'll see that the basic principles between the two listings are the same. However, when the user reaches the first record, the application displays the message shown in Figure 10-12 in red type.

FIGURE 10-12 Using bold colors to display messages can make it easier for users to see when something has gone wrong.

The application displays a similar message when the user reaches the last record. The idea is to provide status information. In addition, notice that the Previous button is disabled—the Next button is disabled when the application reaches the last record.

Both event handlers also support the *CurrentRecord* hidden control. Of course, you can't see this control on the form—it's hidden. To see this control, right-click the browser client area and choose View Source. You'll see a customized version of Notepad open. Scroll through the controls and you'll run across the *CurrentRecord* hidden control shown in Figure 10-13 (with a current record value of 1).

```
http://localhost:1357/Default.aspx - Original Source

File  Edit  Format
36          <input type="submit" name="btnNext" value="Next" id="btnNext" />
37          <input type="submit" name="btnPrevious" value="Previous" id="btnPrevious" />
38          <br />
39
40          <input type="hidden" name="currentRecord" id="CurrentRecord" value="1" />
41
42      </div>
43      </form>
44  </body>
45  </html>
46
```

FIGURE 10-13 Many web applications rely on hidden controls to store state information.

The *CurrentRecord* control appears near the bottom of the source code. Notice that *lblStatus* doesn't even appear in this case. That's because the system isn't displaying a message so the server doesn't even send the control to the client. This is another instance where the server has modified your original design to better suit a particular situation.

Tracing Through the Structure Example

It's important to trace through this example to learn precisely how the calling sequence works. In addition, you want to know how the hidden control, *CurrentRecord*, works. To begin, make sure you place a breakpoint at the *if (Page.IsPostBack)* line of code in the *Page_Load()* event handler. You'll also want to place breakpoints at the *if (CurrentEntry + 1 == MyAddresses.Count)* line of code in the *btnNext_Click()* event handler and the *if (CurrentEntry == 0)* line of code in the *btnPrevious_Click()* event handler.

Click Start Debugging to open a new browser session. The instruction pointer should stop at the breakpoint in the *Page_Load()* event handler. Click Step Over. Notice that the instruction pointer moves to the *CurrentEntry = 0;* line of code. Click Continue in the debugger and the page displays in your browser.

Now let's see what happens when you use one of the buttons in the browser. Click Next in the browser and you'll return to the breakpoint in the *Page_Load()* event handler. Every time the client performs a task, it generates a request to the server. This time the instruction pointer moves to the *CurrentEntry = Int32.Parse(CurrentRecord.Value);* line of code when you click Step Over. The value of *CurrentEntry* hasn't actually changed but this is a new request and the code must process it as a new request.

Click Continue. You'll end up in the *btnNext_Click()* event handler. Trace through this code and you'll find that the *CurrentRecord.Value* property is updated to record 1 this time. Click Continue and you'll see the next page displayed on-screen. Try clicking the two buttons to move back and forth between records to see how things work.

Now, keep the original browser window open and open an entirely new browser window. Copy the address from the original browser into the new browser window. When the new browser window requests a page, you end up in the *Page_Load()* event handler. Because the *Page.IsPostBack* property is *false*, the code sets *CurrentEntry* to 0. Try working with several browser windows and you'll find that the application can easily handle them all and keep track of the current record in each one because of the hidden *CurrentRecord* control.

Get Going with C#

This chapter has demonstrated techniques for using LINQ with web applications. The most important piece of information you should take with you from this chapter is that LINQ works equally well in both environments. Despite major differences between web and desktop applications, the underlying technology provided by LINQ can make the business part of your application almost the same. The differences are there, of course, but using LINQ makes those differences significantly smaller and could make it possible to easily move your desktop application to the web environment when needed.

If you haven't done so already, compare the desktop LINQ examples in this book with the web LINQ examples in this chapter. Besides the similarity of the LINQ queries, discover the similarities between the two environments. Take time to consider the differences as well. Try moving one of the desktop LINQ applications to the web environment so that you can see what changes you actually need to make to the business logic. Of course, you'll want to reduce the amount of work required by using similar control structures whenever possible so that you have a one-to-one correlation between the desktop and web application control setup. (A text box in the desktop application should also appear as a text box in the web application.)

The applications in this chapter are straightforward imitations of desktop applications in a web environment. From a business perspective, these applications work great, and because they're similar to their desktop counterparts, they require far less training than many web applications on the market today. However, most people want a bit more pizzazz than the web applications in this chapter provide. Chapter 11, "Working with Silverlight Applications," looks at one way of adding pizzazz to your next application by employing Silverlight. Using Silverlight makes it easier to add special functionality to your application that only appears in the web environment. This special functionality gives your application an appeal that the web applications in this chapter don't have. Consider the applications in Chapter 11 the next step up when it comes to user interface from the applications in this chapter.

Working with Silverlight Applications

After completing this chapter, you'll be able to:

- Discuss how Silverlight development differs from standard web development

- Create a simple Silverlight application

- Configure Silverlight application debugging

- Create a Silverlight application and that works with XML data

SILVERLIGHT IS A CROSS-BROWSER, CROSS-PLATFORM environment that makes it easier for a developer to create robust web applications. The environment is supported by a small download that plugs into the host browser and makes it possible for the browser to use Silverlight applications. These applications can support advanced graphics, video, and audio. It performs all these tasks and also increases performance by limiting updates to areas of change, rather than updating the entire web page as you discovered standard web applications do in Chapter 10, "Using LINQ in Web Applications." The Silverlight technology is quite complex in some regards, so it's easy to become bogged down in detail. However, you can find a good overview of the technology at *http://msdn.microsoft.com/en-us/library/bb404700.aspx*.

> **Note** You've already learned quite a few of the technologies that you need to work with Silverlight. For example, Silverlight relies on Windows Presentation Foundation (WPF) and the eXtensible Application Markup Language (XAML).

This chapter begins by discussing how Silverlight can help you create great applications quickly. It isn't always a perfect solution, but you'll find that Silverlight does make the development process go much faster.

The highlight of this chapter is the two example applications that you can use to build on the knowledge you've gained from previous chapters, so you can learn about Silverlight quickly. You'll begin by creating a basic (simple) Silverlight application. After that, you'll create a basic XML application equivalent of the applications found in Chapter 5, "Working with XML," and Chapter 7, "Using the Windows Presentation Foundation."

A section after the first example also discusses some Silverlight debugging issues that you need to know about. It's always important to know how to get your application set up for debugging. You'll use this information when you trace through the example applications.

Understanding the Silverlight Development Difference

Most web technologies focus on the server. When you create a standard ASP.NET application, every client change creates a request that is sent to the server. The server makes required changes and sends a new page (or at least part of one) back to the client. The server is in charge. The same is true for just about every other web technology. Yes, you can use JavaScript to perform tasks on the client, but ultimately, to accomplish the overriding application goal, the server is typically in charge. Silverlight is different. It focuses on the client, not the server. In fact, Silverlight runs as a browser plugin on the client. There is a server connection, and you can certainly add server support in to your Silverlight application setup, but the focus is still on the client.

Warning Silverlight is currently not compatible with 64-bit browsers. Consequently, you'll always receive a notice telling you that the Silverlight plugin isn't installed when you open a Silverlight page using the 64-bit version of Internet Explorer. Attempting to install Silverlight in this environment won't work. The best-case scenario is that the Silverlight application will simply crash and users will need to close Internet Explorer.

From a developer perspective, Silverlight feels similar to working with a Windows Presentation Foundation (WPF) desktop application, but in a web environment. You do have contact with the server, so performing tasks such as streaming audio and video is relatively easy, but you also have a strong contact with the client. For example, in Chapter 10 you discovered that it's not possible to use the *MessageBox. Show()* method with an ASP.NET application. You instead have to resort to creating JavaScript code that uses the *alert()* function. Silverlight does provide access to the *MessageBox.Show()* method.

Note The remainder of the chapter will point out some differences between WPF and Silverlight. For example, you'll discover that Silverlight doesn't support hotkeys.

One of the most important advantages of using Silverlight for your development efforts is that users can work with it offline. When the Silverlight application is downloaded onto the client computer, a loss of contact with the server isn't a problem unless the client actually requires server resources. With careful programming practices, it's possible to make a Silverlight application almost stand alone. In fact, even though this book doesn't cover it, you can create a Silverlight Out of Browser application that works from the desktop and not the web. (Visual Web Developer 2010 Express doesn't support this kind of development.) You can also move your Silverlight application to a Windows Phone environment.

Developing a Basic Silverlight Application

This first application is going to perform some simple tasks. The intent of this application is to get you started with Silverlight in a basic way. Later examples in this chapter will build on what you learn with this example, but for now, the task is to get something up and running so that you can see what Silverlight has to offer. With this in mind, the following sections show how to create a basic Silverlight application, add and configure some controls, add a bit of code to do something interesting, and then trace through the result.

Starting the BasicSilverlight Application

Before you can do anything, you need to create the Silverlight project. It isn't very different from the sorts of projects you've created in the past. The following steps get you started.

Create a Silverlight Application Project

1. Choose Start | All Programs | Microsoft Visual Studio 2010 Express | Microsoft Visual Web Developer 2010 Express. You'll see the IDE start up.

2. Click New Project. The New Project dialog box appears.

3. Select Visual C# in the left pane, and then open the Silverlight folder. You'll see the list of Silverlight application types shown here.

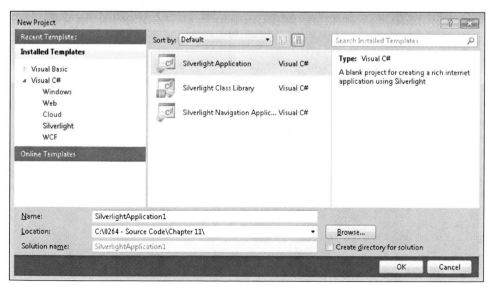

Select Silverlight Application in the middle pane. You'll see a description of the template in the right pane.

4. Type the project name, **BasicSilverlight**, in the Name field.

5. Choose a location where you want to store the project files. (Click Browse to display the Project Location dialog box to choose the folder you want to use.) The default location is c:\users\<User Name>\documents\visual studio 2010\Projects; however, you can choose any location on your hard drive to store the project. Unlike the desktop applications created in Chapter 1, "Getting to Know C#," the simple act of creating a project stores files on disk, which is why you must choose a storage location in the New Project dialog box.

6. Select the Create Directory For Solution option. The solution will actually contain two projects and you want them to appear as subfolders within the same solution folder.

7. Click OK. You'll see the New Silverlight Application dialog box shown here.

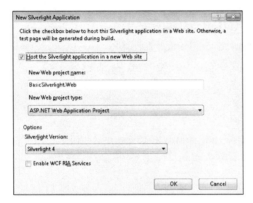

As you can see, this dialog box contains a number of options:

- The Host The Silverlight Application In A New Web Site option creates a new web site, rather than adding a project to an existing site. The examples in this chapter will always create a new site because it makes it easier to see how Silverlight works.

- The New Web Project Type drop-down list box lets you choose from three different project types. Normally, you'll accept the default option, which is the project type used in Chapter 10.

- The Silverlight Version automatically selects Silverlight 4. You should only use Silverlight 3 for compatibility purposes.

- The Enable WCF RIA Services option is only useful if you have the Windows Communication Foundation (WCF) Rich Internet Applications (RIA) services installed on your system. You can read more about WCF RIA at *http://msdn.microsoft.com/library/ee707344.aspx*.

8. Click OK to accept the default options. The IDE will create the new project for you, as shown here.

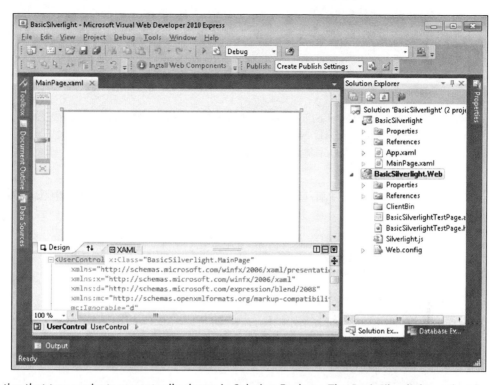

Notice that two projects are actually shown in Solution Explorer. The BasicSilverlight project is the client-side Silverlight portion of the example. The BasicSilverlight.Web project is the server-side ASP.NET portion of the example. When a client makes a request for the page from the server, the server sends the Silverlight client portion of the example with the web page. What the client sees is a combination of the ASP.NET page and the Silverlight application. To create this combination, you work with the two projects shown.

Note When you compile the application later, Visual Studio compiles the Silverlight application first. It then copies the compiled Silverlight application to the ASP.NET application. You don't have to do anything special to create the combination of the Silverlight application and the ASP.NET application—everything is automatically done for you.

Look through the list of files in this project and you'll find an .ASPX file (the ASP.NET application) and an .HTML file (an HTML version of the test page). The names of these two pages are BasicSilverlightTestPage.aspx and BasicSilverlightTestPage.html. You usually won't modify these two pages and will work with the Silverlight application instead. However, if you look at either page, you'll find that they contain some error-handling code and a placeholder for the Silverlight application.

Notice that the BasicSilverlight project contains a number of files, including two files of special interest. You'll modify these two files at different times:

- **MainPage.xaml**   This is the main page for the application. It's the first page the application loads. You'll put the user interface on this page.

- **App.xaml**   This is an application-level page. You put any resources that the entire application will use on this page. Application-wide resources could include pictures or brushes. Normally, you only use this page when you have multiple subpages in your application.

Of course, each of the pages included with the BasicSilverlight project includes code-behind files. These code-behind files let you handle events, perform configuration tasks, and use C# to do other things at either the page level or the application level.

Adding and Configuring the BasicSilverlight Project Controls

In general, you'll focus your attention on the Silverlight control and not on the ASP.NET application. However, some developers use a combination of both applications to create the desired result. To keep things simple, this application (and all the others in the chapter) modifies the *MainPage.xaml* file exclusively. Table 11-1 shows how to configure the controls for this example.

TABLE 11-1 BasicSilverlight Control Configuration

Control Name	Property Name	Value
LayoutRoot. ColumnDefinitions	ColumnDefinition	330*
	ColumnDefinition	270*
label1	Content	Select an Image:
	Margin	0,12,0,0
radioButton1	Name	rbAPOD1
	Content	Sun Pillar Over Ontario
	GridColumn	1
	GroupName	ImageSelect
	IsChecked	True
	IsEnabled	Cleared (False)
	Margin	0,46,0,0
	TabIndex	0
radioButton2	Name	rbAPOD2
	Content	Annular Planetary Nebula
	GridColumn	1
	GroupName	ImageSelect
	IsEnabled	Cleared (False)
	Margin	0,68,0,0

Control Name	Property Name	Value
	TabIndex	1
radioButton3	Name	rbAPOD3
	Content	Castle and Meteor by Moonlight
	GridColumn	1
	GroupName	ImageSelect
	IsEnabled	Cleared (False)
	Margin	0,90,0,0
	TabIndex	2
radioButton4	Name	rbAPOD4
	Content	NGC 7331 and Beyond
	GridColumn	1
	GroupName	ImageSelect
	IsEnabled	Cleared (False)
	Margin	0,112,0,0
	TabIndex	3
radioButton5	Name	rbAPOD5
	Content	Summer Triangle Over Catalonia
	GridColumn	1
	GroupName	ImageSelect
	IsEnabled	Cleared (False)
	Margin	0,134,0,0
	TabIndex	4
image1	Name	APOD_Image
	GridColumn	0
	Height	200
	Margin	10,10,0,0
	Source	http://apod.nasa.gov/apod/ image/1108/sunpillar_ stankiewicz_3888.jpg
	Stretch	Fill
	Width	300
UserControl	DesignHeight	300
	DesignWidth	600

This project uses a new feature of the designer—columns. You add a column to the *Grid* control, *LayoutRoot*, by selecting the grid in the designer. Move the mouse cursor along the top or side of the grid, as shown in Figure 11-1.

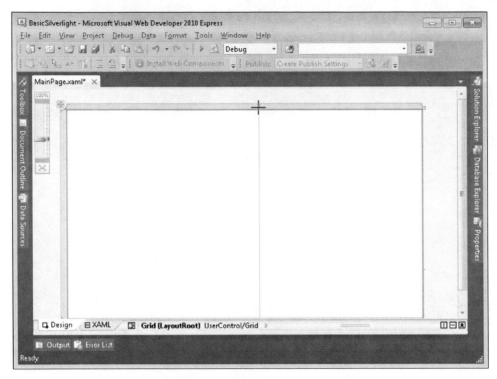

FIGURE 11-1 Create columns to help in control placement.

Click to create a division in the grid. The division will contain two *<ColumnDefinition>* tags. Each column is separately configurable and helps to create an eye-pleasing layout for your web application.

The *Margin* property makes it easy to precisely place a control on-screen. This property actually has four numbers (left, top, right, and bottom) separated by commas as a value. In most cases, you'll focus on using the left and top values. For example, to precisely set the position of *label1*, you set the left property to 0 and the top property to 12, as shown in Figure 11-2.

As soon as you provide a *Source* property value for *APOD_Image*, the IDE will download the image for you. Figure 11-3 shows what your finished window should look like.

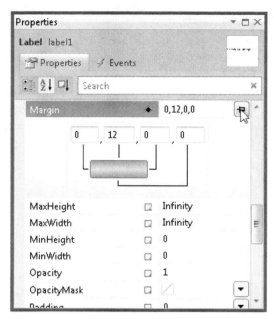

FIGURE 11-2 This Properties window aid helps provide precise control placement.

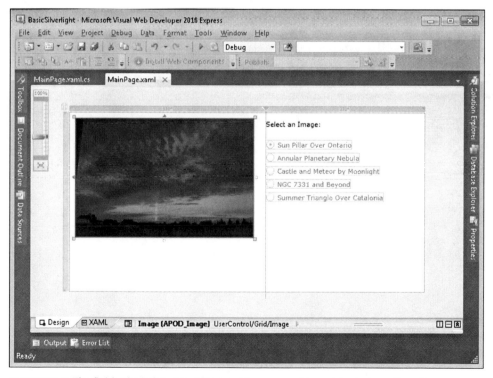

FIGURE 11-3 The finished window provides graphics on one side and controls on the other.

Adding the BasicSilverlight Project Code

The example application must perform a number of tasks. Each of the radio buttons will display a different image in *APOD_Image*. However, it doesn't make sense to create a *Click* event handler for each radio button because that could lead to errors later. For example, you might remember to make a needed change in all but one of the radio button *Click* event handlers, leading to problems with that one radio button that could be difficult to troubleshoot later. This example shows a different technique for handling the clicks. The following sections detail each of the code changes you must make to run this example.

Adding the Required Using Statement

By default, your Silverlight application doesn't include any support for handling images. Because this example uses an image, you must add the following *using* statement to your code:

```
using System.Windows.Media.Imaging;
```

Initializing the Global Variable

Even with a high-speed connection, it takes a little while for the application to download the image from the host website. Because of the way this application is coded (for ease of understanding), it can only do one thing at a time. If it's downloading the image, it can't also be servicing user requests. Consequently, the application must keep track of whether it's downloading an image or servicing a user request using a global variable, *ImageOpened*. Listing 11-1 shows the code needed to initialize *ImageOpened*.

LISTING 11-1 Using a global variable to track image status

```
// Track whether the image is loaded.
Boolean ImageOpened;

public MainPage()
{
    InitializeComponent();

    // The image can't be loaded yet.
    ImageOpened = false;
}
```

Handling Images in Real-World Applications

You've used enough real-world applications to know that the image normally downloads in the background while users continue to interact with the application in the foreground. The background and the foreground represent two different tasks. Each of these tasks require a *thread*, which is simply a term denoting one path of execution. You may have even heard the term *multithreaded*, which simply means that an application can perform more than one task at a time.

Creating an application that can keep track of multiple tasks at the same time is quite a bit harder than performing one task at a time. This book doesn't discuss multithreading techniques, but it's important for you to realize that they do exist. At some point, you'll want to create an application that can download an image and respond to user requests at the same time. In fact, your application could perform a number of tasks at once, such as printing and looking up data in the background while the image is being downloaded.

Enabling the Buttons After an Image Loads

The application begins with one of the images, Sun Pillar over Ontario, loading. Consequently, the application also begins with the radio buttons disabled so that users can't try to click one of them while the image is still downloading. As soon as the image is downloaded, the user interface can become active again.

Select *APOD_Image*, choose Events in the Properties window, and then double-click *ImageOpened* to create the event handler for this section of the example. Listing 11-2 shows the code required to perform this task.

LISTING 11-2 Performing tasks after the image loads

```
private void APOD_Image_ImageOpened(object sender, RoutedEventArgs e)
{
    // When the image has finished loading, then set ImageLoaded true.
    ImageOpened = true;

    // Enable each of the buttons.
    rbAPOD1.IsEnabled = true;
    rbAPOD2.IsEnabled = true;
    rbAPOD3.IsEnabled = true;
    rbAPOD4.IsEnabled = true;
    rbAPOD5.IsEnabled = true;
}
```

This event handler responds to the *ImageOpened* event of *APOD_Image*. Another event, *Loaded*, fires when the image is loaded into the control, but before the control has completely displayed it. You might initially be tempted to create an event handler for the *Loaded* event, but the *ImageOpened* event is the appropriate event in this case because you want the image visible before enabling the radio buttons.

The code performs two tasks. First, it sets *ImageOpened* to *true* to indicate that the image has finished loading. Second, it enables each of the five radio buttons so that users can choose a different image.

Handling Radio Button Clicks

The point of this example is to let users select an image by clicking a radio button. The example has five radio buttons, but you could create as many radio buttons as desired for the task. In fact, you wouldn't even need to use radio buttons. The example would work just as well with a *ListBox* control. If you were to add another five images, a *ListBox* control would be a better choice because 10 radio buttons would look cluttered. However, because none of the other examples in the book uses radio buttons, this one does.

One of the issues with using the *RadioButton* control is that each *RadioButton* is separate. It has its own properties, events, and methods. Writing event-handler code for each of the *Click* events for the five radio buttons is error-prone. Creating a single event handler works better. Begin by creating the event handler shown in Listing 11-3.

LISTING 11-3 Letting a user make a new image selection

```
private void APOD_Select(object sender, RoutedEventArgs e)
{
    if (ImageOpened)
    {
        // Set ImageOpened to false.
        ImageOpened = false;

        // Disable the buttons.
        rbAPOD1.IsEnabled = false;
        rbAPOD2.IsEnabled = false;
        rbAPOD3.IsEnabled = false;
        rbAPOD4.IsEnabled = false;
        rbAPOD5.IsEnabled = false;

        // Create a string to hold the base URL.
        String BaseURL = "http://apod.nasa.gov/apod/image/1108/";

        // Obtain access to the selected radio button.
        RadioButton SelectedButton = (RadioButton)e.OriginalSource;
```

```
        // Use the radio button name to choose an image.
        switch (SelectedButton.Name)
        {
            case "rbAPOD1":
                APOD_Image.Source = new BitmapImage(
                    new Uri(BaseURL + "sunpillar_stankiewicz_3888.jpg"));
                break;
            case "rbAPOD2":
                APOD_Image.Source = new BitmapImage(
                    new Uri(BaseURL + "shapley1_eso_900.jpg"));
                break;
            case "rbAPOD3":
                APOD_Image.Source = new BitmapImage(
                    new Uri(BaseURL + "per_110812_ladanyi_1000c.jpg"));
                break;
            case "rbAPOD4":
                APOD_Image.Source = new BitmapImage(
                    new Uri(BaseURL + "NGC7331_crawford900c.jpg"));
                break;
            case "rbAPOD5":
                APOD_Image.Source = new BitmapImage(
                    new Uri(BaseURL + "stpan_casado_900.jpg"));
                break;
        }
    }
}
```

This event handler begins by setting *ImageOpened* to false because part of the task of this event handler is to specify a new image to download. The code also disables the five radio button controls for the duration of the image download.

A *Click* event handler usually receives information about the control that called it. However, the data type used to receive this information isn't the same data type as the control. The next step is to create a copy of the control so that you can access its properties. *SelectedButton* is a *RadioButton* control that obtains its information from *e.OriginalSource*. To make *e.OriginalSource* compatible with *SelectedButton*, you must coerce the data type, as shown by placing *(RadioButton)* in front of *e.OriginalSource*.

The code uses *SelectedButton.Name* to discover which control the user clicked. The *switch* statement detects this information and selects a *case* based on it. The *case* statement then changes the *APOD. Image.Source* property to match the URL of the radio button that the user clicked. When the *Source* property changes, the application automatically downloads the new image and displays it on-screen.

Now that you have an event handler that can handle all five radio buttons, you need to create a connection between the radio buttons and the event handler. In this case, you can't double-click the *RadioButton* control or even double-click an event entry in the Properties window. You must select the *APOD_Select* event handler from the drop-down list box for the *Checked* event for each of the radio buttons, as shown in Figure 11-4.

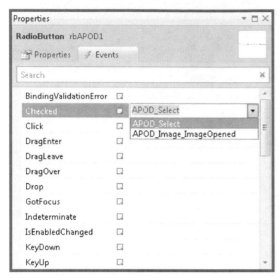

FIGURE 11-4 Use a common event handler for each of the radio buttons.

Tracing Through the BasicSilverlight Project Example

This example doesn't rely on any sort of postback strategy like a standard ASP.NET application would use. All the logic for this application appears in the client-side Silverlight control. With this in mind, you should create a breakpoint at these two places:

- The *if (ImageOpened)* line of code in the *APOD_Select()* event handler

- The *ImageOpened = true;* line of code in the *APOD_Image_ImageOpened()* event handler

Many of your users won't have Silverlight installed on their systems or may require an update to their existing Silverlight installation, but the code takes care of this need for you automatically. Users who start the application and do not have Silverlight installed on their systems will see the browser display shown in Figure 11-5.

When the application initially starts, the code goes immediately to the *APOD_Select()* event handler because the first radio button is selected. The *Checked* event handler fires if a radio button is selected when the application loads. If you don't have some sort of control in place, the event handler could try to handle an event before the rest of the application is ready to handle it. Consequently, make sure you look for this particular problem if you see that your Silverlight application appears to constantly load without ever completing the loading process. In many cases, a freeze is due to an event handler that tries to do useful work before the application is ready. At this point, *ImageOpened* is false, so the application skips all the event handler code.

Click Continue. The page will continue to load. Eventually, the image will download and you'll end up in the *APOD_Image_ImageOpened()* event handler. Click Continue again, and you'll see the initial page. Every time the user clicks a different radio button, the code will call the *APOD_Select()* event handler first, and then the *APOD_Image_ImageOpened()* event handler after the image loads.

FIGURE 11-5 Silverlight tells the user when an installation is needed.

Configuring Your Silverlight Application for Debugging

Silverlight is a more complex environment than other sorts of applications in this book because it has both a client and a server component. Consequently, you may encounter a few problems debugging your applications. The following sections help you create an environment for debugging your applications with a lot less effort so that you can get to work more quickly.

Setting the Browser Configuration

Most developers today use multiple browsers to check their web applications. At the very least, most developers will check operation in both Internet Explorer (because it has the largest market share) and Firefox (because it is also very popular). Sites such as *http://www.netmarketshare.com/browser-market-share.aspx?qprid=1* provide you with the current statistics, but the combination of Internet Explorer and Firefox covers more than 70 percent of the market.

When you debug a standard web application, you can simply copy the URL for the ASP.NET Development Server into whatever browser you want to test. You could attempt the same technique when working with Silverlight. The browser will still display the application without problem, but you may encounter issues getting the debugger to cooperate. In general, set the browser you want to use for debugging as the default browser for the system. Here's where you find the appropriate setting for each browser:

- **Internet Explorer** Click Make Default on the Programs tab of the Internet Options dialog box to make Internet Explorer the default browser.

- **Firefox** Click Check Now on the General Tab of the Advanced settings found in the Options dialog box.

Debugging with Firefox

The default Firefox configuration has caused problems for people working with Visual Web Developer 2010 Express. You can start up the application and it runs just fine, but apparently the debugger will ignore any breakpoints you set. It turns out that Firefox works well with standard web applications, but chokes on the combination of client-side Silverlight application and server-side ASP.NET application. Fortunately, you can change this behavior using the following steps.

Configuring Firefox to Debug Silverlight Applications

1. Type **about:config** in the Address field and press Enter. You see a warning message about changing the settings.

2. Click I'll Be Careful, I Promise! You see a list of preferences.

3. Locate the dom.ipc.plugins.enabled entry in the list. (The items are in alphabetical order.)

4. Verify that this setting is set to *false*. If not, double-click it to set it to *false*.

5. Close and then reopen the browser. The breakpoints will work as they should at this point.

Adding XML Data Support to a Silverlight Application

The BasicSilverlight example helps you understand some of the more interesting aspects of working with Silverlight. However, it's also important to discover how Silverlight compares and contrasts to the desktop applications you worked with in the past. Chapters 5 and 7 discuss how to work with XML from a desktop application. The example in this section creates a Silverlight version of the XMLSetting project found in the "Using XML to Store Application Settings" section of Chapter 5 and the WPF_XML project found in the "Developing the WPF Data Store Application" section of Chapter 7 so that you can see how Silverlight compares to other techniques you've worked with in the book.

Starting the SilverlightXML Application

You'll need to create a new solution to start this example. Use the procedure found in the "Starting the BasicSilverlight Application" section of this chapter to get started. However, instead of typing BasicSilverlight in the Name field in step 4, type **SilverlightXML** instead. You'll end up with a solution consisting of two projects as you did before. The IDE will also automatically open MainPage.xaml for you.

Adding and Configuring the SilverlightXML Project Controls

The SilverlightXML project has the same basic control setup as the desktop versions. However, it doesn't require a Quit button because that task is handled by the browser. Table 11-2 shows the controls for this example.

TABLE 11-2 SilverlightXML Control Configuration

Control Name	Property Name	Value
label1	Name	lblMessage
	Content	Type Something
	Margin	12,12,0,0
	TabIndex	0
textBox1	Name	txtMessage
	Margin	12,46,0,0
	TabIndex	1
checkBox1	Name	chkChecked
	Content	Check Me
	Margin	12,75,0,0
	TabIndex	2

Note Notice that there isn't any sort of hotkey provided with this example. It turns out that Silverlight doesn't directly support hotkeys, so it isn't as friendly to keyboard users as it is for those who like the mouse. Unlike a WPF application, you can't even directly assign a *Target* property value to *lblMessage*, but must instead type **Target="{Binding ElementName=txtMessage}"** into the XAML to create the connection to *txtMessage*. There's a workaround for this problem, but it requires some heavier coding and is well outside the scope of this book. You can find a great answer to this problem at *http://www.rajneeshnoonia.com/blog/2010/05/silverlight-hot-keys/*.

Adding the SilverlightXML Project Code

The code for this project is interesting because it differs from the WPF example. You'd expect quite a few similarities between the two and you won't be disappointed, but the differences are also quite interesting. The following sections describe the code used for this example.

Adding the Required References and Using Statements

This example requires XML support because you're reading and writing an XML file on the local hard drive. The ability to perform this task is a significant advantage of using Silverlight. Use the following procedure to add the required reference to the SilverlightXML project.

Adding a Reference to a Silverlight Project

1. Right-click the References folder for the SilverlightXML project in Solution Explorer. Make certain that you right-click the correct folder—the SilverlightXML.Web project also contains this folder.

2. Choose Add Reference. The Add Reference dialog box appears as shown here.

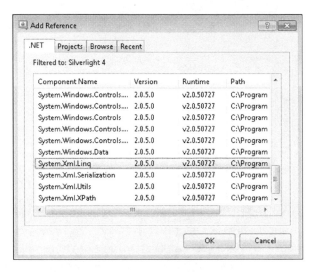

3. Click the .NET tab if it isn't already selected.

4. Highlight the System.Xml.Linq entry and click OK. The IDE will add a reference to this assembly to the SilverlightXML project.

After you add the required reference, you must also add a number of *using* statements to the top of the Mainpage.xaml.cs file. These statements provide access to XML data manipulation, information about the application used to create a directory for storing the data, and something new—isolated storage, which is explained in the "Creating the Global Variables" section of the chapter.

```
using System.Xml.Linq;
using System.IO;
using System.Reflection;
using System.IO.IsolatedStorage;
```

Creating the Global Variables

Like many applications in the book, this example requires a number of global variables to work correctly. Listing 11-4 shows the global variables used for this example.

LISTING 11-4 Storing the data

```
// Define an isolated storage location for this application.
IsolatedStorageFile ISO;
```

```
// Create a global variable used to hold the directory
// for the settings file.
String SettingsDirectory;

// Create a global variable containing the name and
// location of the settings file.
String SettingsFile;
```

Web applications have a major difference—you can't trust them completely. You don't want a web application to have complete access to your hard drive. However, it's convenient to allow limited access to the hard drive to store information between sessions and perform other tasks. In fact, that's the reason that cookies are commonly used—to store small pieces of information on the hard drive for the web page in question.

Silverlight provides an extension to this policy of keeping web applications at bay by providing something called *isolated storage*. As the name implies, this storage is isolated from everything else on the hard drive. It provides greater flexibility than cookies or other means of storing data, but the web application still has a quota placed on it so that it can't consume all the hard drive space. In short, isolated storage is a secure method of providing greater access to system resources that most web applications enjoy.

This application uses the *IsolatedStorageFile* object, *ISO*, to access isolated storage on the hard drive. The application doesn't actually know where this storage is located and can garner nothing from the information it provides to the system for creating the isolated storage. As far as Silverlight is concerned, this storage is located somewhere in limbo. The application can interact with the storage just as it can any other hard drive, but only using the *ISO* object and only a secure manner. You'll see how this difference affects the code as the example progresses.

The *SettingsDirectory* and *SettingsFile* variables are used for precisely the same purposes as they are for the WPF example. In both cases, the *String* objects store information used to access the application's data on disk.

Saving the Settings

As with the other versions of this example, this one begins by saving the settings to disk. (After all, you can't load what isn't there.) Listing 11-5 contains the code needed to save the settings to isolated storage.

LISTING 11-5 Storing the data

```
private void SaveSettings()
{
    // Create a document to hold the settings.
    XDocument SettingData = new XDocument(
        new XDeclaration("1.0", "utf-8", "yes"),
        new XElement("Settings",
```

```csharp
            new XElement("txtMessage", txtMessage.Text),
            new XElement("chkChecked", chkChecked.IsChecked)));

    // Create the folder used to store the data if necessary.
    if (!ISO.DirectoryExists(SettingsDirectory))
        ISO.CreateDirectory(SettingsDirectory);

    // Try this procedure out and simply fail if it isn't permitted.
    try
    {

        // Create the required file stream.
        IsolatedStorageFileStream Output =
            new IsolatedStorageFileStream(
                SettingsFile, FileMode.OpenOrCreate, ISO);

        // Save the settings to disk.
        SettingData.Save(Output);

        // Close the output.
        Output.Close();
    }
    catch
    {
        // Display an error message.
        MessageBox.Show("Unable to save settings!");
    }
}

private void txtMessage_LostFocus(object sender, RoutedEventArgs e)
{
    // Save the settings.
    SaveSettings();
}

private void chkChecked_LostFocus(object sender, RoutedEventArgs e)
{
    // Save the settings.
    SaveSettings();
}

private void chkChecked_Checked(object sender, RoutedEventArgs e)
{
    // Save the settings.
    SaveSettings();
}
```

The *SaveSettings()* method begins by creating an *XDocument, SettingData*, that contains a complete XML document that the application can save to disk. This document contains the text in *txtMessage.Text* and the checked status of *chkChecked.IsChecked*.

As with the WPF example, you must verify that the directory used to store the data exists. Remember that this directory is in isolated storage, so you must use *ISO* to access it. However, the essential process is precisely the same as the WPF example where you check for the existence of the directory first and then create it if necessary.

> **Note** Silverlight applications seem far more prone to exceptions than other kinds of programming you've worked with in the book so far, so you'll find that you need to use *try...catch* blocks more often. In addition, because this is a web application, you must try to create the exception handling to require minimal interaction on the part of the user. Sometimes this means taking a straightforward approach such as simply not saving settings when the client system won't allow it, rather than trying to get the user to cooperate in fixing the problem.

The next section of code creates an *IsolatedStorageFileStream, Output*, to transfer the data from the application to isolated storage. The *IsolatedStorageFileStream()* constructor requires that you provide the path and filename information for the file, what you want to do with the file, and the isolated storage object, *ISO*. The code then calls *SettingData.Save()* with a *Stream* object rather than a *String*, as was done with previous examples. The point is that you don't actually know where the file is kept on the hard drive—all you know is the relative path within the storage location for the file. It's absolutely essential that you always close the *IsolatedStorageFileStream* object when you're finished using it. Otherwise, the data in the file has a tendency to become corrupted or simply incomplete.

This application also differs from the previous examples in that it has no Quit button and no way to detect that a form is closing. In fact, the user can close the browser without alerting the Silverlight application at all. Consequently, this example saves the data in *txtMessage* and *chkChecked* every time there's a change. Normally, you detect these changes using the *LostFocus* event, which fires whenever the user moves to a different control. However, when working with a check box, it's also a good idea to add a *Checked* event handler, just in case the user doesn't move to a different control before closing the window.

Restoring the Settings

As with both the Windows Forms example in Chapter 5 and the WPF example in Chapter 7, this example restores any settings in the application's constructor. The process is more akin to the technique used for the WPF example because Silverlight relies heavily on WPF for the user interface. Listing 11-6 shows the code required for this part of the example.

LISTING 11-6 Restoring the data

```
public MainPage()
{
    InitializeComponent();
```

```csharp
// Obtain the configuration information for this application.
Object[] Configuration =
    Assembly.GetExecutingAssembly().GetCustomAttributes(false);

// Obtain the company name.
String CompanyName = "Company";
foreach (var Value in Configuration)
    if (Value.GetType() == typeof(AssemblyCompanyAttribute))
    {
        CompanyName = ((AssemblyCompanyAttribute)Value).Company;
        break;
    }

// Obtain the executable name.
String Title = "Title";
foreach (var Value in Configuration)
    if (Value.GetType() == typeof(AssemblyTitleAttribute))
    {
        Title = ((AssemblyTitleAttribute)Value).Title;
        break;
    }

// Obtain the version number.
String Version = "0.0.0.0";
foreach (var Value in Configuration)
    if (Value.GetType() == typeof(AssemblyFileVersionAttribute))
    {
        Version = ((AssemblyFileVersionAttribute)Value).Version;
        break;
    }

// Create an isolated storage instance for the application data.
ISO = IsolatedStorageFile.GetUserStoreForApplication();

// Store the location of the settings directory.
SettingsDirectory =
    System.IO.Path.Combine(CompanyName, Title, Version);

// Store the location of the settings file.
SettingsFile = SettingsDirectory + "\\Settings.XML";

// Check for a settings file.
if (ISO.FileExists(SettingsFile))
{
    // Obtain access to the file.
```

```
IsolatedStorageFileStream Input =
    new IsolatedStorageFileStream(
        SettingsFile, FileMode.Open, ISO);

// Try to perform this task. If it fails, use the default settings.
try
{

    // Load the file containing the settings.
    XDocument SettingData = XDocument.Load(Input);

    // Change the control settings to match the file settings.
    txtMessage.Text = SettingData.Root.Element("txtMessage").Value;
    chkChecked.IsChecked =
        Boolean.Parse(SettingData.Root.Element("chkChecked").Value);

    // Close the input.
    Input.Close();

}
catch
{
    // Close the damaged file.
    Input.Close();

    // Delete the damaged file.
    ISO.DeleteFile(SettingsFile);
    }
    }
}
```

The basic technique for obtaining a directory location for the file is precisely the same as the WPF application, except for an important difference. Desktop applications have rights that web applications don't. The Windows Forms and WPF versions of this example both find a way to store the data in the user's local application data path. The technique is different, but the results are the same. The Windows Forms version of the code looks like this:

```
SettingsFile = Application.LocalUserAppDataPath + "\\Settings.XML";
```

whereas the WPF version looks like this:

```
// Store the location of the settings directory.
SettingsDirectory =
    Environment.GetFolderPath(Environment.SpecialFolder.InternetCache) +
    "\\" + CompanyName + "\\" + Title + "\\" + Version;
```

This Silverlight application must use isolated storage because it doesn't have the right to access a specific location on the hard drive directly. Consequently, the path created by the initial code in this part of the example is a relative path—a path that starts at an unknown location. The kind of path created by both the Windows Forms and the WPF applications is an absolute path—you know precisely where the data is stored.

Because you don't know where the file actually appears on the hard drive, it's important that the code relies on *ISO* to find the data. The example uses *ISO.FileExists()* to determine whether the file exists on the hard drive. If the file exists, the code creates an *IsolatedStorageFileStream*, *Input*, using the filename and path, the required access, and *ISO* as inputs.

Loading the document comes next. This code must always appear in a *try...catch* block. Even if the file exists, the system may not allow access to it. In addition, unlike the controlled environment of a desktop application, it's hard to know whether the file is even complete or usable. Perhaps a glitch caused damage to the file during the save process earlier. As with saving the file, you call *XDocument. Load()* using a *Stream* object, rather than a *String* that contains an absolute path. When the file is loaded, the code uses precisely the same technique as with the two desktop examples to restore the settings. It's absolutely essential that the code calls *Input.Close()* to close the data file when loading is complete.

The *catch* portion of this code takes a straightforward approach to the problem of a corrupted file. First, it closes *Input*. If you don't close *Input*, you can't do anything else with the file. The code then calls *ISO.DeleteFile()* to remove the corrupted file from the hard drive. Yes, this means that the settings (any that are still accessible) are lost and that the user is going to be irritated, but this is probably the best way to deal with the problem when you don't have good control over the computing environment. The user can change the default settings as needed and the application will automatically save them for the next session.

Tracing Through the SilverlightXML Project Example

This example has a few interesting points that you'll definitely want to trace through. The first place to put a breakpoint is the *ISO = IsolatedStorageFile.GetUserStoreForApplication();* line in the constructor. Use the following procedure to step through this part of the application.

Tracing Through Isolated Storage Usage

1. Click Start Debugging. The ASP.NET Development Server starts. The instruction pointer will stop at the line with the breakpoint.

2. Click Step Over.

3. Open the Watch window. Type **ISO** in the Name field and press Enter. You'll see information about *ISO* appear in the window as shown here. (The screenshot is expanded to show additional detail.)

   Notice that none of the public information—the information you can access in an application—tells you the location of the isolated storage. However, you can find out how much space the application is allowed to use (1 MB is the default), the amount of space left, and the amount of space used by files.

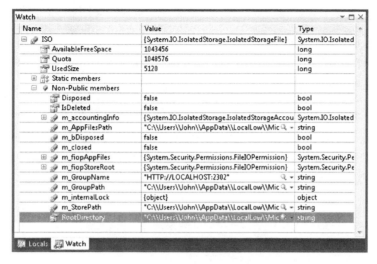

4. Drill down into the Non-Public Members list and locate the *RootDirectory* entry. This entry contains the isolated storage location on the hard drive. However, it's only accessible while you work with the debugger. See the "Finding the XML File on Your Hard Drive" sidebar for a technique for locating the physical location when the debugger isn't running or when you need to locate the file on a user's computer.

5. Click the little magnifying glass in the *RootDirectory* entry. The Text Visualizer dialog box appears, as shown here.

6. Highlight the entire content of the Value field. Press **Ctrl+C**. This action copies the content of the Value field to the clipboard.

7. Open a copy of Windows Explorer. Highlight the content of the Address field and press **Ctrl+V**. Press Enter. Windows Explorer will take you directly to the root of isolated storage.

8. Double-click Microsoft, then double-click SilverlightXML, and then double-click 1.0.0.0. You see the *Settings.XML* file that holds the application information. Even though this location is supposedly secret (and it is to the application) it's important to realize you can find it when necessary. However, you can never access it directly in your code without seeing an exception.

9. Click Close to close the Text Visualizer in the debugger.

10. Click Step Over twice. The code creates *SettingsDirectory* and *SettingsFile*.

11. Type **SettingsDirectory** in the Name field of the Watch window and press Enter. Type **SettingsFile** and press Enter. You'll see two new entries, as shown here.

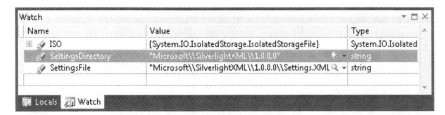

Relative paths normally appear this way in the debugger. Notice the lack of a drive letter and the fact that the entry begins with a directory name. These paths are relative to the location specified in *ISO*.

12. Click Step Over three times. The code creates *Input*, which is an object that streams data from the *Settings.XML* file to the application. Open the Locals window and drill down into the Non-Public Members folder, as shown here.

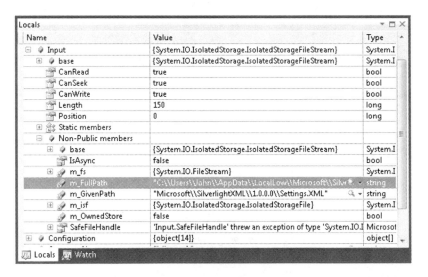

The public members tell you how you can interact with the file. In addition, you can discover the file length (150 bytes) and the current read position within the file. As you read data from the file, the *Position* property changes to show the new read position. Looking at the private members, the *m_FullPath* property contains the full path to the file. Again, you can use the Text Visualizer to obtain the full path and locate it in Windows Explorer, but this information isn't available to the application.

13. Click Continue. You see the page appear on-screen. If you've configured the settings in the past, you'll see them reappear, as shown here.

Another interesting way to interact with this application is to set breakpoints in each of the event handlers so that you can see when the application calls them. You may be surprised to find that the event handlers are actually called multiple times when it seems as if a single call will do the job. For example, click the *Checkbox* as you'll find that the application calls both the *txtMessage_LostFocus()* and *chkChecked_LostFocus()* event handlers. In actual operation, only the *txtMessage_LostFocus()* event handler is called. The reason that the *chkChecked_LostFocus()* event handler is also called is because the browser loses focus to the debugger.

To see what is actually happening, you need to use a different tracing technique. Stop debugging the application. Make sure you close the page in your browser and also stop the ASP.NET Development Server. Change the three event handlers so that they each include a call to *System. Diagnostics.Debug.WriteLine()*, like this:

```
private void txtMessage_LostFocus(object sender, RoutedEventArgs e)
{
    // Save the settings.
    SaveSettings();
    System.Diagnostics.Debug.WriteLine("In txtMessage_LostFocus");
}

private void chkChecked_LostFocus(object sender, RoutedEventArgs e)
{
    // Save the settings.
    SaveSettings();
    System.Diagnostics.Debug.WriteLine("In chkChecked_LostFocus");
}
```

```csharp
private void chkChecked_Checked(object sender, RoutedEventArgs e)
{
    // Save the settings.
    SaveSettings();
    System.Diagnostics.Debug.WriteLine("In chkChecked_Checked");
}
```

These calls place information in the Output window so you can see what's happening without debugger interference. Use the following steps to perform a quick test.

Testing the *Debug.WriteLine()* Method

1. Start the debugger again.

2. Type something new in Type Something.

3. Press Tab.

4. Press Space to change the Checked field.

5. Press Tab again. The Output window will contain entries like the ones shown here.

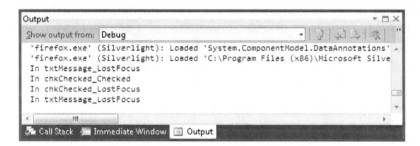

This particular issue points out a problem with debuggers. When you're dealing with certain events, you can get false information from the debugger. In this case, the real-world operation of the application is to call only the *txtMessage_LostFocus()* event handler. Chapter 12, "Debugging Applications," discusses issues such as this one in greater detail.

Finding the XML File on Your Hard Drive

When you worked with XML files in the other chapters, it was relatively easy to find the file because it had a specific location. Isolated storage doesn't have a precise location on your drive—at least, it's not a location that you can ask the application about using the debugger. Finding the XML may seem impossible. Fortunately, you can find the file using the command line. Here's how you'd locate the file used for this example.

1. Open a command prompt using the techniques found in Chapter 9.

2. If you're using Windows XP, type **CD \Documents and Settings** and press Enter. If you're using Windows Vista or later, type **CD \Users** and press Enter.

3. Type **Dir SilverlightXML /S** and press Enter. The *Dir* command obtains a directory listing, *SilverlightXML* is one of the directories used for the example, and */S* tells the *Dir* command to look in all the subdirectories for the required information. You'll see a strange directory name such as C:\Users\John\AppData\LocalLow\Microsoft\Silverlight\is\avd3jqsd.j0a\gnogfzl0.tzi\1\s\yhlpiz1vxuuikv3dluvceu1shnoa1tu22qiyklgf ouke1ivim5aaaada\f\Microsoft.

4. Use the directory information to locate the directory with Windows Explorer. You'll see the *Settings.XML* file after you drill down into the 1.0.0.0 folder.

Using a unique name for the isolated storage directory will help you find the physical location of the directory on your hard drive using the *Dir* command. Otherwise, trying to find the XML files you create will truly be like looking for a needle in a haystack.

Get Going with C#

Browser environments, such as Silverlight, help make web development easier. All the user needs is a small download to get started. In fact, the Silverlight application automatically prompts the user to perform the download. You'll discover that Silverlight can perform a vast array of complex tasks. It's still important for you to know how to write code to describe the process to perform the task, but Silverlight reduces the amount of code you have to write to gain really nice effects for your application. Presentation is everything on the web—another site is always just one click away, so your site has to shine if you want others to remain long enough to get the message you want to present. If you don't take anything else from this chapter, remember that Silverlight provides the means to creating great-looking websites quickly.

The examples in this chapter provide a good starting point, but the more you work with Silverlight, the better you'll get at using it. Try converting a few of the other examples in this book to a form that you can use with Silverlight. For example, try converting the WebStructure example found in the

"Creating the WebStructure Project" section of Chapter 10 to a Silverlight form. Ask yourself what the advantages are of using Silverlight for this application. Of course, equally important is to ask yourself if there are any disadvantages. Never blind yourself to the fact that every programming technique and technology comes at some cost—knowing the cost can help you make better decisions regarding which tool to use in a particular instance.

You've spent a lot of time tracing through applications throughout the book. Tracing is an essential skill—one that developers should learn early and use often. However, tracing isn't quite the same as debugging. Yes, you're using the same tools, but you're using them in different ways. Chapter 12 moves on to the task of debugging an application—looking for errors in it. Like tracing, debugging is an essential skill and you already have a significant advantage over anyone who's trying to learn debugging without learning tracing first. You already have a good idea of where to look and what to look for in applications that are working correctly. Now you need to learn how to use those skills to find the error in code.

Chapter 12

Debugging Applications

After completing this chapter, you'll be able to:

- Define how debugging fits within the application development cycle

- Create special breakpoints that respond to particular events

- Step through the code, looking for errors

- Create watches to look at global variables

- Work with visualizers to see data in new ways

- Locate special data in your application

- Interact with the call stack

- Use the Immediate window to execute commands

- Understand how exceptions work

A BUG IS AN ERROR in your application. Bugs happen in many different ways and you may not even know that your application has a bug until someone else brings it to your attention. The best-tested code on the planet will likely have a bug in it. So it's often a third party who brings the bug to your attention and then you must remove the bug in a process called debugging.

Finding bugs can be hard. In fact, in some situations, it can be downright impossible. However, you can normally find the problem by using careful analysis and the techniques described in this chapter. You've already performed many of the tasks required for debugging by simply tracing your applications throughout the book. In many situations, debugging simply becomes an advanced form of tracing in which you need to play around with the code a bit more than you do during tracing.

Debugging usually requires some advanced techniques and this chapter discusses the common methods you'll employ. For example, instead of using a breakpoint to stop your code and monitor it, you might rely instead on the *Debug* or *Trace* class methods to provide information as the application runs. You'll also have to dig deeper into variables using watches and see what the data actually means using visualizers. Drilling down into the data and understanding what it truly means is important as well.

This chapter also shows you how to verify the location of a particular call and determine precisely how an application is executing the procedures you create. You'll use the Immediate window more often to ask the application questions and rely on detailed exception information to help you understand a particular bug. All of these debugging elements appear in the sections that follow.

 Note Most of the example screenshots in this chapter come from the XMLSetting example found in Chapter 5, "Working with XML." The techniques work with any application, though, so feel free to try the examples with your favorite application.

Understanding the Debugging Basics

Understanding the nature of bugs is important. Not every bug happens because you type the wrong code. In fact, the compiler will often help you locate these sorts of bugs before anyone else even sees the code. Many developers break bugs down into five categories (in order of increasing complexity and difficulty):

- **Syntax** An error where you've mistyped something. In many situations, the IDE will tell you about the error. When you type *if* as *iff*, the IDE will tell you about the mistake. However, you could also make subtle typing mistakes. When two variables have similar names, you could type the name of one when you meant the other (such as typing *Point* for *Points*). Sometimes the IDE will tell you about these errors, other times the compiler will catch the error, but often you need to check the variable names yourself to ensure that you used the correct variable.

- **Compile** Code that's unacceptable to the compiler for some reason. This is the only sort of bug that the end user never sees because if the code won't compile, there isn't an executable for the user to try. A compile bug can be hard to find. For example, you might leave out an ending brace for an *if* statement. The compiler may point out an area that isn't even near the end of the *if* statement because the compiler can't detect the end of the *if* statement without that ending brace. In other cases, the compiler can be unnervingly correct about the location of the error. For example, you might not supply a variable of the correct type as input to a method, but may not recognize the fact until after you look at the method's documentation in Help.

- **Runtime** The application compiles, but won't run properly. The IDE almost never finds this sort of error. The compiler could find it in some situations, but often it's not until you see an exception that you know there's a bug. For example, you might create the right type of variable, initialize it correctly, and even use it correctly for a method call. However, because some property for the variable is wrong, the method can't accept it as input.

- **Semantic (logic)** The application compiles and runs, but doesn't produce the desired output. None of the automated features of the IDE or the compiler will help you locate this sort of bug. Everything is typed correctly, the variables are initialized, and as far as the application is concerned, everything is working correctly. For example, you might create a *for* loop where the ending condition is off by one. The *for* loop will comply with your request to perform a task once too often, but the output will still be wrong. An application's logic can go wrong in all kinds of ways, which is why you need to spend time tracing through the application to ensure that you understand how it actually works.

- **Environmental** The application generally produces the correct result, but something displays an exception or the incorrect output because of an external problem. For example, a web service may not be online when you need it or it might not produce the result you anticipated at all times. The issue need not be producible. Line noise can cause data errors, which can cause a glitch in your application. An issue could even be user-induced. Maintenance performed at a certain time of day can cause an application to fail. To locate the problem, you'd have to debug the application at that specific time of day.

It's obviously better when you find bugs yourself. Any application that you intend to give to someone else should be thoroughly tested. Companies often go to great lengths to test applications as thoroughly as possible using both human input and automated techniques, but bugs still get through. When that happens, you generally get an error report from a user that states the application doesn't work. Users have no idea of what sort of information you need to find a bug, so it's always a good idea to ask the user specific questions:

- Which version of the application are you using?

- Does your equipment meet all of the requirements for running the application?

- How severe is the problem—did it result in data loss?

- What did you see when the error occurred?

- Did you see specific error information? If so, what was it?

- Does the error always occur or is there any pattern to when it occurs?

- Can you provide a list of steps to reproduce the error? Double-check any procedure you provide to ensure that it's complete.

Get as much information as you can because every bit of information, even seemingly unrelated details, often helps locate and fix the error. Try to obtain contact information for the user so that you can get additional information when you need it. If you still find yourself at a loss to reproduce the error, try to go to the user's computer to see the error on the user's computer. (Operator error is a significant problem that you can often reduce or eliminate with a redesign of the user interface or additional error checking.) When a direct visit is out of the question, try remotely accessing the user's system, recording logs of debugging information, or trying other approaches to get the information you need.

When you finally think you have enough information, don't focus on just one part of the application. Many developers fail to find bugs because they become fixated on a particular application element. Look in these areas for potential sources of problems:

- **Variables**   Ensure that every variable is defined with precisely the correct type, initialized correctly, and contains the right information. Structures and complex objects are often the source of hard-to-find bugs in applications.

- **Nomenclature**   Typos are evil. One variable can end up posing for another because of a typo. It's also possible to call the wrong method, supply the wrong arguments, and do all kinds of other strange things with typos.

- **Code**   Trace through the logic of your code. The tracing techniques in this book are invaluable to understanding a problem. It's better to spend an hour tracing through the code until you understand the scope of the problem than waste several days fruitlessly viewing the source code without ever discovering the problem.

- **Exception handling**   Exceptions register extraordinary events. When something happens outside the code's normal resources to handle, the application raises an exception. If the exception handling isn't specific or it simply covers over the error, you'll find it difficult to fix anything.

- **User interface**   When the user doesn't understand an application, it won't work properly. Many developers deride the user for being the source of user error, but the truth is that most user errors are preventable with a good interface. The secret is to make choices and controls as obvious as possible, check the user selections, and verify choices when necessary. However, it's impossible to eliminate every possible user error, so robust error handling is also a requirement. Applications that lack complete error handling are always candidates for bugs.

Tip It never hurts to have someone else look at your code. You've looked at the code for some amount of time and could easily disregard an error. It isn't a problem of vigilance or inadequacy. When humans become familiar with something, they tend to disregard it. Fresh eyes can often find the glaring bug that tired eyes miss.

Debugging is a process of finding bugs in code and removing them. You've already been using tracing, an invaluable technique for learning how to code, so you already know how to use one of the most important debugging tools. The rest of this chapter focuses on the tools in the book that you've used less often or not at all.

More Info It's important to understand that the Express edition products don't come with every debugging feature. For example, when working with the full edition of Visual Studio, you can create complete breakpoints that don't always stop application execution. A breakpoint can stop execution when the application reaches a certain point in the application code, based on a condition, when the application reaches the breakpoint a certain number of times, or when the breakpoint appears as part of the code for a certain process or thread. You can read more about conditional breakpoints at *http://msdn.microsoft.com/library/7sye83ce.aspx* and *http://geekswithblogs.net/sdorman/ archive/2009/02/14/visual-studio-2008-debugging-tricks-ndash-advanced-breakpoints.aspx*.

Working with the breakpoints is also more flexible in the full product. For example, you can configure the breakpoint not to stop the application. The breakpoint can instead print a message or you can even tell the IDE to run a macro that performs a number of tasks automatically.

To make it easier to see where the application has stopped, the full product also lets you apply a label to the breakpoint. The label makes the breakpoint less generic and easier to identify. Otherwise, you always have to look through the code to see just where you stopped. You can read more about breakpoint labels at *http://msdn.microsoft.com/library/ dd293674.aspx*.

Stepping Through the Code

It isn't always possible to set a breakpoint in your code, stop the action, and see precisely how the application is functioning. In fact, the SilverlightXML example in Chapter 11, "Working with Silverlight Applications," demonstrates quite the opposite. When you trace through that example, you find that the debugger creates false event triggers when you use breakpoints. Often, stepping through the code means setting breakpoints carefully and then relying on other means of observation to see how the code works. That's where the *System.Diagnostics* namespace comes into play. It contains a number of useful classes that help you interact with your application in other ways. From a debugging perspective, the *Trace* and *Debug* classes are most useful, but you'll see other classes from this namespace as the chapter progresses.

Note The *Debug* and *Trace* classes share most of the same methods, so it might seem a bit odd that Microsoft provides both of them. The major difference is that the *Debug* class methods are only active in the debug version of an application, whereas the *Trace* class methods are active in both the debug and release versions of an application.

Working with the *Debug* Class

The *Debug* class helps you step through your code by seeing how values change and which methods are called as you interact with the application. You don't create an instance of the *Debug* class to use it. The *Debug* class comes with static methods—those that are available directly from the class whenever you need them. Two methods (and many permutations) are normally used to send messages: *WriteLine+* and *Print()*. You can use these two methods in various ways, but the *WriteLine()* method provides more options for displaying information. For example, you can use it to output the value of an object. You can also use a *Write()* method when you don't want the cursor to move to the next line before displaying the next message.

You may not want to display a message all of the time, but only when certain conditions exist. In this case, you can use the *WriteIf()* or *WriteLineIf()* methods to check for a *Boolean* condition first and then display the information on screen when the *Boolean* condition is *true*. For example, you may want to check on the value of a variable and output a message when the variable contains that value or something different than expected.

It's often helpful to indent the output of these messages. The indentation provides a sort of formatting that makes the output easier to understand. Just how you use the indentation is up to you, but many people indent according to the level of information within the method. As you enter various structures, you indent more. You'll see how this works later in the section. The *Indent* property value begins at 0 and you can increase or decrease it as needed (but it can't become a negative number). Instead of working with the *Indent* property directly, you can also rely on the *Indent()* and *Unindent()* methods to perform the task.

> **Tip** You can change the amount that the IDE indents items by changing the *IndentSize* property value. Using a smaller indent allows you to display more information on a line and is especially helpful when you have a lot of indent levels. However, the smaller indent size also makes it harder to see the indents and you could possibly miss an indent when looking at the output.

Sometimes you need to know whether the application has met some requirement. When you can express this requirement as a *Boolean* value, you can use the *Assert()* method to check it. Asserting whether something is *true* or *false* gives you a way of stopping the action when a potential error occurs so that you can view what is happening in the application. Using an *Assert()* can be especially effective when an error is intermittent or requires a special set of steps to reproduce.

> **Note** The *Debug* class contains a few methods that aren't included in this chapter because they're of limited use. For example, the *Fail()* method displays an error message whenever the application encounters it. You could possibly use this method inside an error handler. This chapter also doesn't discuss the topic of listeners because they're outside the scope of the book. You can read more about listeners at *http://support.microsoft.com/kb/815788.*

Adding Debug Statements to the Example

This section shows how you might add some debugging statements to an existing application. The code shown in Listing 12-1 is a combination of the code found in Listings 5-5 and 5-6 in Chapter 5 with debugging statements added. The debugging statements you add to an application depend on what you need to find and your particular debugging style. These additions show application flow and help you better understand the methods in the *Debug* class.

LISTING 12-1 Adding debugging information to an application

```
public Form1()
{
    // Output a status message.
    System.Diagnostics.Debug.WriteLine("Entering the Constructor");

    InitializeComponent();

    // Store the location of the settings file.
    SettingsFile = Application.LocalUserAppDataPath + "\\Settings.XML";

    // Check for a settings file.
    if (File.Exists(SettingsFile))
    {
        // Indent the output.
        System.Diagnostics.Debug.IndentLevel++;

        // Output a status message.
        System.Diagnostics.Debug.WriteLine(File.Exists(SettingsFile),
            "The File Exists");
        System.Diagnostics.Debug.Print("The File Exists");

        // Load the file containing the settings.
        XDocument SettingData = XDocument.Load(SettingsFile);

        // Make sure the document actually contains some data.
        System.Diagnostics.Debug.Assert(
            SettingData.Document != null, "The document is empty.");

        // Output the SettingData content.
        System.Diagnostics.Debug.WriteLine(
            "\r\n" + SettingData.Document, "SettingData.Document");

        // Change the control settings to match the file settings.
        txtMessage.Text = SettingData.Root.Element("txtMessage").Value;
        chkChecked.Checked = Boolean.Parse
            (SettingData.Root.Element("chkChecked").Value);
    }
```

```csharp
    // Outdent the output.
    System.Diagnostics.Debug.IndentLevel--;

    // Output a status message.
    System.Diagnostics.Debug.WriteLine("Leaving the Constructor");
}

private void btnQuit_Click(object sender, EventArgs e)
{
    // Display a status message.
    System.Diagnostics.Debug.WriteLine("The User Clicked Quit");

    // End the program.
    Close();
}

private void Form1_FormClosing(object sender, FormClosingEventArgs e)
{
    // Display a status message.
    System.Diagnostics.Debug.WriteLine("Starting to Save the Settings");

    // Display a supplementary message.
    System.Diagnostics.Debug.IndentLevel++;
    System.Diagnostics.Debug.WriteLineIf(
        chkChecked.Checked, "Detected that chkChecked is Checked.");
    System.Diagnostics.Debug.IndentLevel--;

    // Create a document to hold the settings.
    XDocument SettingData = new XDocument(
        new XDeclaration("1.0", "utf-8", "yes"),
        new XElement("Settings",
            new XElement("txtMessage", txtMessage.Text),
            new XElement("chkChecked", chkChecked.Checked)));

    // Save the settings to disk.
    SettingData.Save(SettingsFile);

    // Display a status message.
    System.Diagnostics.Debug.WriteLine("Settings Are Saved");
}
```

The code begins by adding status messages to the output. You'll find messages for entering the constructor and checking the existence of the file. Notice that when the code enters the *if (File Exists(SettingsFile))* statement, the application increases the indent level so that you can tell from the output that you're looking inside a structure (an *if* statement in this case).

Look at the code for outputting "The File Exists" status message. This code shows both a *WriteLine()* and a *Print()* version of the output. The *WriteLine()* version can output more information because it can get the *String* value of *File.Exists(SettingsFile)*. In many cases the simple message output by *Print()* is fine, but don't discount the flexibility offered by *WriteLine()* when debugging your application.

The next debugging statement to look at is the *Assert()* method call. When *SettingData.Document != null* is *false*, the document is empty. At this point, you'll see an error message and the application will stop at this point so that you can see what's happening. The output will also contain the information so that you can record it later.

Look at the next *WriteLine()* statement. This statement combines a carriage return and a line feed with the content, which is the content of the XML document in *SettingData*. You can create combinations of data this way to format the output. In this case, the document will appear on a separate line so that it's formatted properly in the output.

Leaving the *if* statement comes next. The first thing the debugging statements do is reduce the code indent. You could also do this by calling *Unindent()* if desired. The constructor ends with a message to the output that says, "Leaving the Constructor." The code for the other two methods is more of the same kinds of statements you've seen in the constructor. Follow these steps to test the code.

Running the Debugging Statements

1. Click Start Debugging. The application starts.

2. Change both settings in some way. Make sure that Check Me is selected so that you receive the output of the *WriteLineIf()* method in the *Form1_FormClosing()* event handler.

3. Click Quit. The application ends. Now it's time to see whether you received any output.

4. Choose Debug | Windows | Output. The Output window appears.

5. Choose Debug in the Show Output From field. When you scroll down a little, you'll see all of the debugging messages, as shown here.

All of the expected entries are there. Notice that the use of indentation makes it easier to see when you're in the *if* statement. The contents of the *SettingData.Document* property are also formatted so that you can easily see the XML. Look at how the *WriteLineIf()* method worked. Because you selected Check Me, you can see the output from this statement of "Detected that chkChecked is Checked."

6. Perform steps 1 through 5 again, except this time ensure that Check Me isn't selected. Take time to view the output and make sure that the changes you made the last time are there and that the *WriteLineIf()* method works as expected.

So far you haven't see the *Assert()* method in the constructor work. Change the condition for that statement to read *SettingData.Document == null*. Making this change will cause the assertion to occur. The following procedure will help you test the *Assert()* method.

Testing the *Assert()* Method

1. Run the application again and this Assertion Failed dialog box appears.

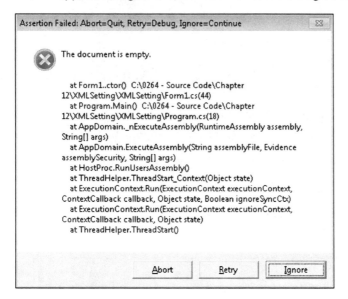

2. Click Retry. The application stops at the line containing the *Assert()* method, just as if there were a breakpoint there.

3. Click Continue. You'll see the application dialog box as normal.

4. Click Quit. The application will end. Now look in the Output window and you'll see the information from the *Assert()* method, as shown on the following page.

```
Output                                                                    ▾ □ ×
Show output from: Debug                              ▾ | ⟳ | ⤵ ⤴ | ⇥ | ☑
Entering the Constructor
    The File Exists: True
    The File Exists
    ---- DEBUG ASSERTION FAILED ----
---- Assert Short Message ----
The document is empty.
---- Assert Long Message ----


    at Form1..ctor()  C:\0264 - Source Code\Chapter 12\XMLSetting\XMLSetting\Form1.cs(44)
    at Program.Main()  C:\0264 - Source Code\Chapter 12\XMLSetting\XMLSetting\Program.cs(18)
    at AppDomain._nExecuteAssembly(RuntimeAssembly assembly, String[] args)
    at AppDomain.ExecuteAssembly(String assemblyFile, Evidence assemblySecurity, String[] args)
    at HostProc.RunUsersAssembly()
    at ThreadHelper.ThreadStart_Context(Object state)
    at ExecutionContext.Run(ExecutionContext executionContext, ContextCallback callback, Object state, Boolea
    at ExecutionContext.Run(ExecutionContext executionContext, ContextCallback callback, Object state)
    at ThreadHelper.ThreadStart()

The thread '<No Name>' (0xed4) has exited with code 0 (0x0).
    SettingData.Document:
<Settings>
  <txtMessage>Yellow</txtMessage>
  <chkChecked>true</chkChecked>
</Settings>
Leaving the Constructor
The thread '<No Name>' (0x1268) has exited with code 0 (0x0).
The User Clicked Quit
Starting to Save the Settings
    Detected that chkChecked is Checked.
Settings Are Saved
⊨ Error List   ▣ Output
```

The Assert Long Message section probably looks really confusing, but that's called a *stack trace*. You'll learn more about stack traces in the "Understanding the Call Stack" section of the chapter. For now, look at the first line. It tells you that you're currently in the *Form1* constructor. Below that you see that the constructor was called by a method called *Main()* in *Program*. The lines after this leave the application and get into the .NET Framework.

5. Perform steps 1 through 4 again. However, this time click Ignore in step 2. This time the application doesn't stop—it immediately displays the application's dialog box. The *Assert()* method output still appears in the Output window, but the application didn't stop as before. You can still review the *Assert()* information later.

6. Perform steps 1 through 4 again. However, this time click Abort in step 2. The application simply stops at this point—you never see the application's dialog box. But the *Assert()* method information still appears in the Output window.

7. Change the *Assert()* method condition back to *SettingData.Document != null*. Otherwise, the application will continue stopping at that point even though nothing is wrong.

Note It's important to remember that the full version of Visual Studio comes with the ability to create both release and debug builds. Visual C# 2010 Express can only create debug builds, so the debugging information you insert into your application will always be accessible. If you were to create a release build of this example with a full version of Visual Studio you'd find that none of the debugging statements is available. The debugging statements only appear in debug builds.

Working with the *Trace* Class

The *Debug* and *Trace* classes are similar. You use them precisely the same way, but at different times. The *Debug* class members are designed for debugging situations. The *Trace* class members are designed for tracking application usage and functionality. As a result, *Debug* class members are only available in debug builds, whereas *Trace* class members are available for both debug and release builds.

There are a number of other differences between the two classes. For example, the *Trace* class lacks the *Print()* method. However, the *Trace* class replaces *Print()* with a number of equally useful *TraceError()*, *TraceInformation()*, and *TraceWarning()* methods. The purpose of these alternative methods is to write output data to the trace listeners. You can also provide a specific message level—akin to the levels provided in the event log.

Note The *Trace* class also includes a *Refresh()* method that's used with .config files. The *Refresh()* method makes it possible to update the *Trace* configuration information while the application is running. Normally, you won't even use the .config file to configure trace unless you're using advanced troubleshooting techniques that include custom listeners. If you'd like to learn more, read the Knowledge Base article at *http://msdn.microsoft.com/ library/ms733025.aspx* and the information about the *AutoFlush* property at *http://msdn .microsoft.com/library/system.diagnostics.trace.autoflush.aspx*.

Working with Watches

The Watch window is one of the most flexible ways of tracking variables that the debugger provides. You've used the Watch window in a few of the chapters in the book. For example, it is highlighted in the "Tracing Through the SilverlightXML Project Example" section of Chapter 11. However, the Watch window is far more flexible than the book has shown you so far. You can use the Watch window to perform tasks such as the following. (All of these tasks are performed when you've paused the code in some way during a debugging session.)

- Add a variable by typing its name, right-clicking the variable in the Code Editor, and choosing Add Watch, or by dragging it from the Code Editor and dropping it onto the Watch window.

- Add a variable property, such as *SettingData.Document*, by typing it in the Watch window or by highlighting the entire entry, right-clicking the entry, and choosing Add Watch. You can also drag it from the Code Editor and drop it onto the Watch window.

Note IntelliSense will help you with hints about what to type next in the Watch window. Sometimes it's a good idea to try typing something in the Watch window to see what options are available. You could get an idea of how to fix something by checking out the available options.

- Execute a variable method, such as *SettingData.Root.Element("txtMessage")*, by typing it in the Watch window or by highlighting the entire entry, right-clicking the entry, and choosing Add Watch. You can also drag it from the Code Editor and drop it onto the Watch window.

- Create a conditional statement, such as *SettingData.Document == null*, by typing it in the Watch window.

- Ask for data that doesn't even exist in the current application, such as *System.Environment.GetEnvironmentVariable("UserName")*, by typing it in the Watch window.

In fact, you have many ways to display information in the Watch window—limited only by your ability to create an expression that defines what you want to see. Figure 12-1 shows examples of the tasks described at the beginning of this section.

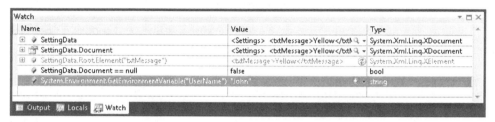

FIGURE 12-1 The Watch window provides a significant amount of flexibility in debugging applications.

Note The Watch window offers a few odd ways of displaying information. For example, you can type a class such as *System.Xml.Linq.XDocument* in the Watch window. You'll see the *ToString()* output of the class, which is *System.Xml.Linq.XDocument*. It's possible to drill down into the class entry to see the classes that it comes from. Overall, this isn't a very useful way to work with the Watch window. You really don't gain much insight into your application using this particular entry, even if the Watch window will accommodate your request.

The Watch window contains three columns that contain the expression you want to view, the value of that expression, and the expression type. Using Name for the title of the first column is a misnomer—it's better to replace it with Expression because you can type almost any valid expression and obtain instant feedback about it. Here are some of the specific tasks that you can perform using the window:

- Change an expression by double-clicking its entry and then modifying the content of the resulting edit box.

- Remove an entry by highlighting it and press Delete.

- Drill down into an entry or obtain additional information about it by clicking the plus sign next to it, such as *SettingData.Document*.

- Change an entry value by double-clicking its entry in the Value column and typing a new value in the edit box. For example, you could change "Yellow" to "Blue", as shown here.

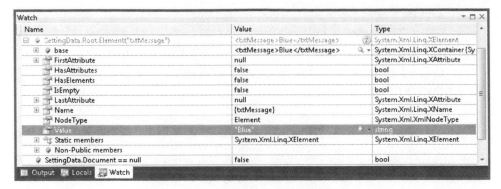

The change normally appears in red so that you know what has changed. This feature makes it possible to perform "what if" scenarios when an application fails.

■ Copy the information to the clipboard by right-clicking the entry and choosing Copy. You can then paste the information anywhere you need it.

■ Select a range of entries by highlighting the first entry in the range and then Shift+Clicking the last entry in the range. (You can use this technique to copy and paste multiple entries.)

Using Visualizers

A visualizer makes it possible to see the data in a formatted manner. Some data is already quite readable in the Locals and Watch windows. For example, you can see most *String* values quite easily. However, if the string contains special escape characters, such as a carriage return or line feed, you won't see it precisely as the user sees it. Still, you can make sense of the information in the window. The same can't be said for HTML or XML data. For example, when you see *SettingData* in the Locals window, most of the information appears off-screen and the information you can see isn't all that readable, as shown in Figure 12-2.

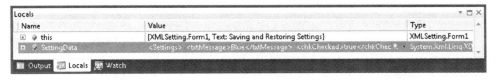

FIGURE 12-2 The Locals and Watch windows will display a magnifying glass icon when a visualizer is available.

Look carefully at the right side of the Value column. You see a magnifying glass icon and a down arrow. Clicking the magnifying glass displays the *SettingData* content using the default visualizer (which is the text visualizer), like the one shown in Figure 12-3.

FIGURE 12-3 The Text Visualizer displays content using plain text.

You may not always want to use the default visualizer. In this case, you can choose a new visualizer by clicking the down arrow to display the list of choices, as shown in Figure 12-4.

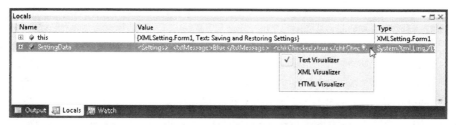

FIGURE 12-4 Clicking the down arrow shows a list of available visualizers.

Because *SettingData* contains XML data, you might want to choose the XML Visualizer option. Doing so displays the XML Visualizer, as shown in Figure 12-5.

FIGURE 12-5 The XML Visualizer window displays XML in a formatted way, complete with color coding.

The difference is that you can now collapse subnodes when desired and the text is also color-coded. These features make the XML far easier to view and can help you hide unneeded complexity from the view. What this should also demonstrate is that you can use more than one visualizer for any given object in many cases. While you're at it, try the HTML Visualizer option. What you'll see is that the tags are completely hidden and all you see is the data. Even this view could be helpful at times.

> **Note** It's possible to create customize visualizers as needed. You may need to create a visualizer to view data from objects that you create correctly, or you may simply want to see standard data in a new way. The article at *http://www.devsource.com/c/a/Using-VS/Write-Your-Own-Visualizer-for-VS-Debugging/* tells one way to create a custom visualizer. Another useful article that shows how to create a custom visualizer appears at *http://geekswithblogs.net/technetbytes/archive/2008/06/11/122792.aspx*. Some custom visualizers are available for free download, such as the Cache Visualizer discussed at *http://msdn.microsoft.com/magazine/cc300778.aspx*.

Drilling Down into Data

Debugging an application often requires an understanding of how something is constructed, which means drilling down into objects. Sometimes a problem doesn't even exist in the current object—it exists in a base object—the object that's used as a starting point for creating the current object.

When you create a class, you can derive that class from other classes to save time. Chapter 8, "Working with Libraries," gives you a good starting point for understanding classes. When you view *TheClass* in the Watch window (see Listing 8-7), you don't see a base class because *TestClass* (see the "Adding the TestLibrary Code" section of Chapter 8) is a freestanding class that isn't based on any other class, as shown in Figure 12-6.

Watch			
Name	Value		Type
TheClass	{TestLibrary.TestClass}		TestLibra
_AllowAdditions	true		bool
_AllowDeletions	true		bool
_BallList	Count = 0		System.(
AllowAdditions	true		bool
AllowDeletions	true		bool
BallCount	0		int
BallList	Count = 0		System.(
OnBallAdded	null		TestLibra
OnBallDeleted	null		TestLibra
OnEndOfBalls	null		TestLibra
Output Locals Watch			

FIGURE 12-6 The Watch window provides a significant amount of flexibility in debugging applications.

Now look at the *SettingData* object in XMLSetting. When you click the plus sign next to this entry in the Locals window, you see a base entry. The base entry signifies that *SettingData* relies on another class for some features. Click the plus sign next to the base and you'll see that it, too, contains a base entry. In fact, there are a number of base entries, as shown in Figure 12-7.

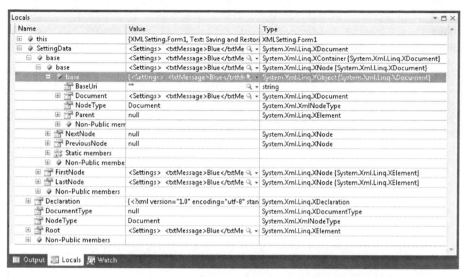

FIGURE 12-7 Exploring base class entries is essential to understanding the classes you use.

Drilling down tells you quite a bit about *SettingData*. You discover that:

- *SettingData* is an *XDocument* type.

- The *XDocument* class relies on the *XContainer* base class.

- The *XContainer* class relies on the *XNode* base class.

- The *XNode* class relies on the *XObject* base class.

It doesn't happen often, but the problem you need to fix could be because of something you don't understand with the *XNode* class, not the *XDocument* class. Of course, you always start at the beginning—the object, which is *SettingData*. Then you trace your way downward through the base classes as needed. Some problems truly are buried.

Tip Many developers become overwhelmed when they begin to understand the complexity of some of the classes they're using. It's essential to take each element on its own—not to become buried by everything that's going on, but to look at just one aspect of the object at a time. You eventually begin to see patterns in how objects are put together and come to understand that things aren't as complex as you initially thought. Always work entirely through a level before you move to the next level and take things one item at a time—work methodically to avoid missing the problem and to keep the issues surrounding the problem in focus.

When you drill down into an object, you'll discover some properties are actually structures. You discovered how structures work in the "Understanding Structures" section of Chapter 4, "Using Collections to Store Data," and saw an example of structure use in the "Creating the Structure Project" section of that same chapter. Structures are incredibly useful for collecting data into a container. The *Declaration* property of *SettingData* is actually a structure consisting of *Encoding*, *Standalone*, and *Version*, as shown in Figure 12-8.

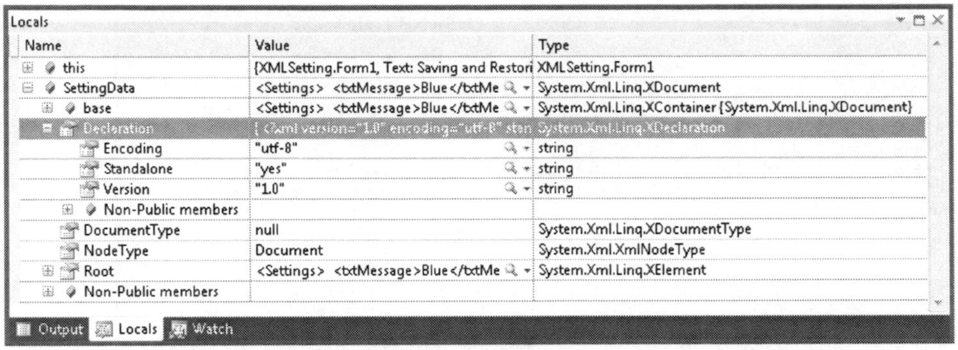

FIGURE 12-8 Make sure you understand the content of any structures.

Before you can fully understand *Declaration*, you must consider the use of *Encoding*, *Standalone*, and *Version* in the application. Drilling down into these elements gives you a good idea of how they're used and you can always verify your assumptions by reading about them in help. For example, *Version* defines which version of XML the document uses.

It's also important to realize that a structure can contain other structures. For example, look at the *Root* property. It contains a property called *Name*, which contains a property called *Namespace*, which contains a property called *NamespaceName*. These levels create a hierarchy of information that you must consider as you work through issues with your application during debugging.

Many objects contain a special category called Non-Public Members. These variables are protected in some way, so your application can't normally access them. However, knowing what these variables contain can help you during the debugging process by providing clues as to the internal workings of the object.

You'll also see a special category called Static Members. These variables may or may not be protected, but they aren't associated with a particular object. You can create as many versions of a particular class as needed, but the static data is always the same. Previous examples in the book have used static methods to perform a task without creating an instance of the class, such as the *Environment.GetFolderPath()* method used in Listing 5-2. Static data is the same concept applied to data. The *XNamespace* class has three such properties: *None*, *Xml*, and *Xmlns*. The values of these properties are always defined, even if you haven't created an instance of the class. Use the following procedure to see static data in action.

Seeing static data in action

1. Choose Debug | Windows | Immediate. The Immediate window opens.

2. Type **? XNamespace.Xml** and press Enter. You'll see the value of this static property, as shown here.

This command tells the IDE to display the value of *XNamespace.Xml*. No matter how you access this value, the output remains constant. In fact, you can also try it with an instance of the *XNamespace* class.

3. Drill down into *Root | Name | Namespace* | Static Members. You'll see the same information you received when you requested the static data directly, as shown here. However, you can't access this data using the object because the data is static.

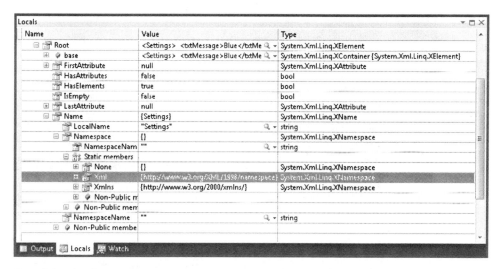

4. Type **? SettingData.Root.Name.Namespace.Xml** in the Immediate window and press Enter. The Immediate window will either not display anything at all or you'll see an error message, like the one shown here that says you need to access the property directly using the type.

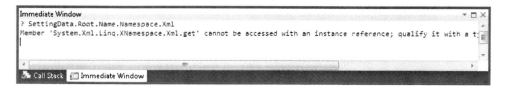

Understanding the Call Stack

An application begins the call stack the moment it starts. Every time your application calls a method, it creates a new entry on the call stack. When the method returns, the entry is removed from the call stack. Consequently, the call stack answers two important questions:

- Where's the code executing now?

- How did it get to this point?

You may have seen the call stack already because it appears as part of the output of an exception or an assert message. However, you can see the call stack at any time during the debugging process by choosing Debug | Windows | Call Stack. The call stack is helpful in a number of situations:

- It can help you determine when a method is called too early—before the data the method requires to function is ready.

- It also helps you determine when a method is called too late—after the event is over.

- The call stack can also help you locate the source of an exception when the exception has been passed up from an underlying class. (See the "Working with Exceptions" section of the chapter for details.)

- You can also see how the method is called when the method could be called from multiple locations.

Every application begins by calling some external code for configuration and setup purposes. It then calls the *Main()* method in your Program file, as shown in Figure 12-9.

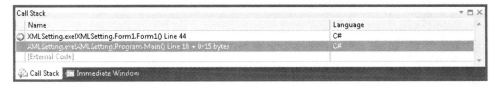

FIGURE 12-9 The call stack helps you understand the exact sequence of events that starts your application.

Of course, now you're wondering what this *Main()* method is all about. Double-click its entry in the Call Stack window and you'll see the IDE open up the appropriate file. The Call Stack window places a green arrow next to the entry you clicked so that you know which entry you're looking at in the Code Editor window. You'll also see a special green highlight that shows where the call was made in the file, as shown in Figure 12-10.

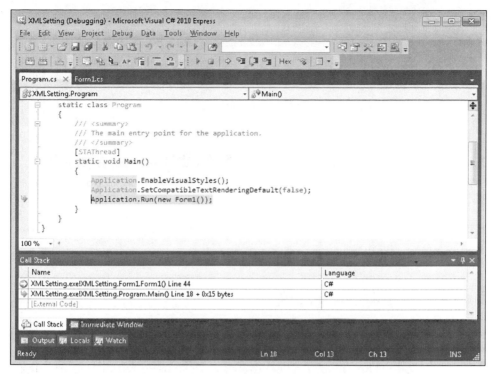

FIGURE 12-10 You can use the Call Stack window entries to locate code in other files.

When you finish looking at the entry, you can double-click the top line (the one with the yellow, right-pointing arrow in a red circle) in the Call Stack window to return to your original location. The Name column shows the following information about every call:

■ Module names (the file in which the call appears)

■ Parameter types (the kind of parameters used for each call)

■ Parameter names (the names of the parameters used for each call)

■ Line numbers (the number of the line for the call within the host file)

■ Byte offsets (the position of the code within the compiled file)

You can change this information by right-clicking the Call Stack window and choosing different entries. For example, many developers find it helpful to add parameter values to the Call Stack window to make it easier to see how a call is made. The byte offsets take up space that could be used for other purposes, so many developers remove this information from view.

All of the external code used to start the application appears in a simple bracket, [*External Code*]. If you really want to know what this code is, you can right-click the Call Stack window and choose Show External Code. Figure 12-11 shows a typical example of the external code used for an application.

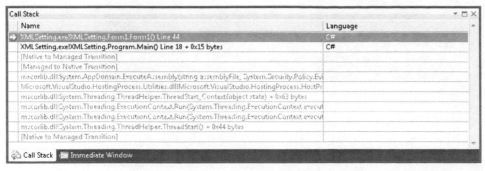

FIGURE 12-11 The external code for your application can consist of a number of calls and prove confusing to review.

It looks pretty confusing, and for the most part you can't access it, either. In most cases, you really don't need to know about the external code.

Using the Immediate Window

The Immediate window has a strange name, but it has a practical purpose. During the debugging process, you can ask questions using the Immediate window. You can ask all sorts of questions, and whenever possible the Immediate window provides you with useful results. Here are some of the question types you might ask:

- What is the value of a variable?

- What is the output of a method?

- Does an expression produce the intended result?

You've used the Immediate window quite a bit throughout the book to ask questions about the application you're working with. In fact, you've used the Immediate window several times in this chapter alone.

Most people begin an Immediate window query with a question mark (?). However, you don't absolutely have to include the question mark—the IDE assumes that you supplied it. The question mark merely reminds you that you're asking a question and not necessarily changing anything at all in the code or the variables it uses. For example, whether you type **Environment.GetEnvironment Variable("ComputerName")** or **? Environment.GetEnvironmentVariable("ComputerName")**, you still get the name of the system running the application.

The Immediate window does make it possible to make changes to the application environment though. For example, if you type **txtMessage.Text = "Yellow"** and press Enter, the value of the *txtMessage.Text* property changes. You can verify the change by typing **? txtMessage.Text == "Yellow"** and pressing Enter. The Immediate window will display an output value of *true*, unless it isn't possible to change property value (in which case, you would have received an error when you initially tried to change it).

You could make a mistake when typing a command. The Immediate window doesn't force you to reenter the command from scratch. Press the up arrow and you see the previous command. Now use standard editing methods to change the command so that it executes correctly this time. Press End to place the cursor at the end of the line, and then press Enter to execute the modified command.

The Immediate window also comes with all of the usual clipboard features. Here's how you perform the standard tasks:

- Highlight the target text and press Ctrl+C, or right-click the window and choose Copy to copy information to the clipboard.

- Highlight the target text and press Ctrl+X, or right-click the window and choose Cut to cut the information from the Immediate window and place it on the clipboard.

- Place the cursor where you want to insert information and press Ctrl+V, or right-click the window and choose Paste to paste information on the clipboard into the Immediate window.

Sometimes the Immediate window becomes cluttered with too many messages. In this case, right-click the window and choose Clear All. The IDE will clear all of the current content from the Immediate window.

Working with Exceptions

An exception occurs whenever the application code attempts to do something incorrect or the resources required to perform a lawful task aren't available. For example, you'll see an exception if your code tries to divide a number by zero because the output is undefined. Likewise, if you request data from a web service and the web service isn't online, you'll see an exception telling you that the data isn't available. The book has provided many examples of using *try...catch* blocks to handle exceptions, but it's useful to know how to work with exceptions when they do occur. The following sections help you in two ways. First, you discover what that exception dialog box is trying to tell you. Second, you learn how you can communicate exception information to an administrator in a way that the administrator will understand.

Understanding an Exception Dialog Box

Exceptions can occur anywhere in the IDE. The assumption is that the exceptions will occur in your code, and normally they do, but exceptions can occur in other places, too. For example, type **File.Open("C:\\DoesNotExit.txt", FileMode.Open)** and press Enter in the Immediate window. You'll see the FileNotFoundException Was Unhandled dialog box shown in Figure 12-12.

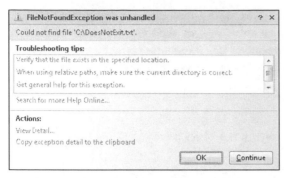

FIGURE 12-12 The IDE relies on exceptions to tell you about coding issues, even when those issues occur in the Immediate window.

This technique is actually quite handy because you can see what exceptions might occur when you perform certain tasks. It makes it easier to add exception handling to the application based on tasks your code could actually perform.

The Troubleshooting Tips field of the FileNotFoundException Was Unhandled dialog box contains standard methods for handling the exception. Click any of the links to see help on that particular solution. For example, when you click the Verify That The File Exists In The Specified Location link, you see a suggestion to use the *File.FileExists()* method to determine whether the file exists before you open it.

The Actions section contains a list of things you can do now. For example, when you click View Detail, you see additional information about the exception. As with many other debugging features, you can drill down into the data, as shown Figure 12-13.

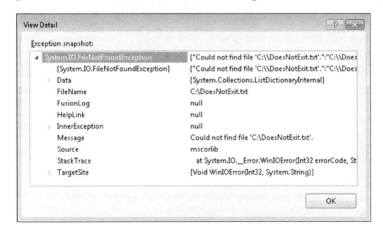

FIGURE 12-13 The Exception dialog boxes provide full access to all of the data associated with the exception.

You can also click Copy Exception Detail To The Clipboard. This feature makes it possible for you to ask others about the exception. For example, you could send a colleague an e-mail with the exception information. Here's the information you'd see for this particular exception:

```
System.IO.FileNotFoundException was unhandled
  Message=Could not find file 'C:\DoesNotExit.txt'.
  Source=mscorlib
  FileName=C:\DoesNotExit.txt
  StackTrace:
       at System.IO.__Error.WinIOError(Int32 errorCode, String maybeFullPath)
       at System.IO.FileStream.Init(String path, FileMode mode, FileAccess access,
Int32
         rights, Boolean useRights, FileShare share, Int32 bufferSize, FileOptions
options,
         SECURITY_ATTRIBUTES secAttrs, String msgPath, Boolean bFromProxy, Boolean
         useLongPath)
       at System.IO.FileStream..ctor(String path, FileMode mode, FileAccess access,
         FileShare share)
       at System.IO.File.Open(String path, FileMode mode)
  InnerException:
```

After you're done with the Exception dialog box, click OK or Continue. Clicking OK simply clears the dialog box without doing anything else. When you click Continue, you see a short version of the exception information in the Immediate window.

Communicating with the Administrator Using the Event Log

It's generally a bad idea to display Exception dialog boxes in a production application. The user has no idea what to do with the information. Because the user isn't trained to do anything with the information, it's unlikely that you'll see the output from the exception. For that matter, even the administrator may not become aware of a significant problem until it's too late to do something about it. Unhandled events can also cause data loss and all sorts of other problems. Exception dialog boxes are a useful debugging aid, but they don't belong in well-designed, properly tested production applications.

You still need some way of getting the information about the error. One approach is to create a log file and fill it with information using the *Trace* class methods. However, this means getting onto the user's computer to collect the information in some way. This approach does have its advantages and you'll use it sometimes, but you have another way to obtain the exception information—the event log. Using the event log provides a standardized entry that an administrator can view and forward to the developer as needed. If you create a complete event log entry, you'll have a good idea of what's going wrong with the application, or at least a good place to look.

The .NET Framework makes it possible to create event log entries. However, to create event log entries that make sense, you need to create an event log source. The following steps show you the process for creating an event log source and then writing events to the event log using the Immediate window.

Creating an Event Log Entry

1. Close all copies of Visual C# 2010 Express.

2. Choose Start | All Programs | Microsoft Visual Studio 2010 Express. Right-click Visual C# 2010 Express and choose Run As Administrator. A User Account Control dialog box appears.

3. Click Yes. You'll see the IDE displayed as normal. However, notice that the title bar tells you that you're in administrator mode.

4. Click XMLSetting in the Recent Projects list. The XMLSetting application loads.

5. Set a breakpoint in the constructor (if you don't already have one set there) and click Start Debugging. The instruction pointer stops where you placed the breakpoint.

6. Choose Debug | Windows | Immediate. The Immediate window is displayed. At this point, you're ready to begin creating an event log entry. To create such an entry, you need an event source. However, creating an event source requires administrator privileges. Normally, you'll create an event source for your application as part of the installation program. For the sake of simplicity, this procedure is creating an event source directly in the Immediate window.

7. Type **System.Diagnostics.EventLog.CreateEventSource(Application.ProductName, "Application")** and press Enter. You see, "Expression has been evaluated and has no value" as output. This code creates an event source for you. You only need to perform this task once—when you install the application. Now you can use the event source for creating event log entries.

8. Open the Event Viewer console found in the Administrative Tools folder of the Control Panel.

9. Select the Windows Logs\Application folder.

10. Type **System.Diagnostics.EventLog.WriteEntry(Application.ProductName, "This is a Test!", System.Diagnostics.EventLogEntryType.Information, 20, 2000)** in the Immediate window and press Enter. You see, "Expression has been evaluated and has no value" as output. This code creates the actual event entry. Here are the event arguments in order:

    - Event source

    - Message you want to record

    - The kind of event entry, such as information, warning, or error

    - The event identifier

    - The event category

11. Choose Actions | Refresh in the Event Viewer. You see a new event log entry like the one shown on the following page.

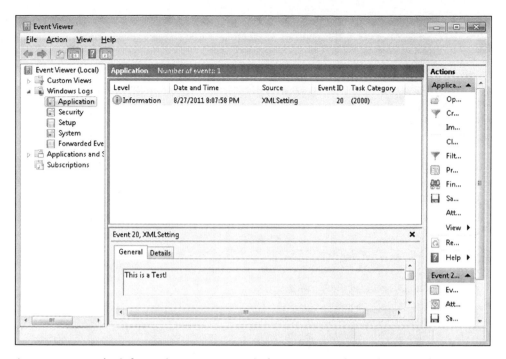

As you can see, the information appears precisely as you typed it in the Immediate window. This is what the administrator will see, even if the user sees nothing at all.

12. Type **System.Diagnostics.EventLog.DeleteEventSource(Application.ProductName)** in the Immediate window and press Enter. This action removes the event source because you won't be using it anymore. Always clean up old event sources to keep the host system clean. Normally you'd include this call in the uninstall application.

13. Close the Event Viewer.

14. Stop the debug session and close Visual C# 2010 Express. You don't want to leave an administrator mode version of the application running to prevent potential damage to your system.

The code you've just typed in the Immediate window will normally appear in three different parts of your application. Now you know another purpose for the Immediate window—testing sequences that you can't normally test (at least not easily) as a unit.

Get Going with C#

This chapter has helped you understand the nature of debugging in C#. The important thing to remember is that bugs happen to everyone and no one finds every bug in his or her code. Most of the code in the world today has some type of bug in it that a third party will eventually point out, to the chagrin of the developer who created it. When someone does discover a bug, it's more important to focus on fixing the problem than on affixing blame.

Take time to work through the examples in the book again. Introduce errors and then work through the techniques in this chapter to locate and understand the problem. Practice really does make perfect in this situation. As you work through more problems where you already know the source of the bug, you can start to see patterns that will become useful when you don't know the source of the error. Try making changes to see what sorts of things happen with each specific change. The examples in this book are meant for discovery—use them to discover the debugging techniques you need for real-world applications.

You've reached the end of the book! By now you've tried a considerable number of example types and have a firm basis for learning more about C#. To continue with your C# language-learning process, you should read the book *Microsoft Visual C# 2010 Step by Step*. The most important thing you should have learned from this book is that there's a lot of code out there that you can use to discover new techniques. In addition, employing the tracing methods you've been using in this book will help you see how code of nearly any complexity works with enough time and patience. If you do have questions about the content of this book or about any of the examples, please feel free to contact me at *John@JohnMuellerBooks.com*. Make sure to follow me on my blog at *http://blog.johnmuellerbooks.com/*.

Index

A

AcceptButton property, 92
access keys, 270
AccessKey setting, 271
Active Server Page (ASP).NET forums, 29
AddBall() method, 225
AddDays() method, 254
Add() method, 105
AddRange() method, 105, 231
alert() function, 296
anchoring, 114
APOD_Image_ImageOpened() event handler, 308
APOD_Select() event handler, 308
Append() method, 273
application data, viewing, 73–75
Application.GetResourceStream() method, 204
application projects, adding, to solutions, 226
applications, configuring, 230–232
App.xaml, 300
arguments
    checking for optional, 254–255
    checking for required, 253–254
    setting command-line, 260–261
array projects
    Array project
        adding code in, 93–95
        adding controls to, 91
        configuring controls for, 92–93
        starting, 91
        testing conditional theories in, 100–101
        testing loop theories in, 97–100
        tracing, 96–97
    WebArray project, 276–285
        adding code, 279–284
        adding/configuring controls, 278–279
        starting, 276–277
        tracing, 284–285

array queries
    conditional loop version of, 283–284
    LINQ version code for, 280–281
    loop version of, 282–283
arrays
    about, 90
    creating, in WebArray project, 279–280
ASP.NET
    Development Server, 275
    displaying dialog box with, 281
    Silverlight vs., 296–297
    WebList project, 266–267
Assembly.GetEntryAssembly() method, 192
Assert() method, 330, 333, 334, 335
atom syndication format, 153
automation services, 247

B

background tasking services, 247
balls (TestApplication project)
    adding/removing, 233–236
    displaying a list of, 237
    displaying ball data, 232–233
    moving between, 236
BasicSilverlight project, 297–309
    adding code, 304–308
        enabling buttons, 305–306
        handling radio button clicks, 306–308
        images in real-world applications, 305
        initializing global variable, 304–305
        using statement, 304
    adding/configuring controls, 300–303
    adding XML data support to, 310–323
    configuring, for debugging, 309–310
    creating, 297–300
    debugging with Firefox, 310
    setting browser configuration, 309
    tracing, 308–309

D

About the Author

JOHN PAUL MUELLER is a freelance author and technical editor. He has writing in his blood, having produced 88 books and over 300 articles to date. The topics range from networking to artificial intelligence and from database management to heads-down programming. Some of his current books include a Windows command-line reference, books on VBA and Visio 2007, a C# design and development manual, and an IronPython programmer's guide. His technical editing skills have helped more than 60 authors refine the content of their manuscripts. John has provided technical editing services to both *Data Based Advisor* and *Coast Compute* magazines. He's also contributed articles to magazines such as *Software Quality Connection, DevSource, InformIT, SQL Server Professional, Visual C++ Developer, Hard Core Visual Basic, asp. netPRO, Software Test and Performance*, and *Visual Basic Developer*. Be sure to read John's blog at *http://blog.johnmuellerbooks.com/*.

When John isn't working at the computer, you can find him outside in the garden, cutting wood, or generally enjoying nature. John also likes making wine and knitting. When not occupied with anything else, he makes glycerin soap and candles, which come in handy for gift baskets. You can reach John on the Internet at *John@JohnMuellerBooks.com*. John is also setting up a website at *http://www.johnmuellerbooks.com/*. Feel free to take a look and make suggestions on how he can improve it.

Your Free eBook Reference

Microsoft

Start Here!™

FUNDAMENTALS OF
Microsoft
.NET Programming

Rod Stephens

When you purchase this title, you also get the companion volume, *Start Here!™ Fundamentals of Microsoft® .NET Programming*, for free.

To download your eBook, go to
http://go.microsoft.com/FWLink/?Linkid=230718
and follow the instructions.

Need help? Please contact:
mspbooksupport@oreilly.com
or call 800-889-8969.

What do you think of this book?

We want to hear from you!

To participate in a brief online survey, please visit:

microsoft.com/learning/booksurvey

Tell us how well this book meets your needs—what works effectively, and what we can do better. Your feedback will help us continually improve our books and learning resources for you.

Thank you in advance for your input!

CPSIA information can be obtained at www.ICGtesting.com
Printed in the USA
LVOW051623100112

263229LV00014B/1/P